THE WORLD'S GREATEST AIRCRAFT

An illustrated history of the most famous
civil and military planes

Exeter Books

NEW YORK

Series Editor: Peter Allez-Fernandez
Book Editor: Len Cacutt

This edition published in the USA by
Exeter Books
Distributed by Bookthrift
Exeter is a trademark of Bookthrift
Marketing, Inc.
Bookthrift is a registered trademark of
Bookthrift Marketing, Inc.
New York, New York

ISBN 0–7917–0011–9

Typeset by J&L Composition Ltd, Filey,
North Yorkshire, England
Printed and bound in Spain

Contents

Contents

Introduction

Deciding on a choice of the world's most famous aircraft is no easy matter. There is no objective yardstick that can be used to decide on how famous an aircraft is. But there are some criteria which help make the choice easier. Manfred von Richthofen with his triplane was a legend even in his own lifetime. The Messerschmitt Bf 109 worked its way into the history books through the sheer numbers in which it was built, and in Britain the Spitfire became a symbol of an entire nation's war effort. The indestructible DC-3 survived not only the war, but is still being used all over the world today, more than half a century after its maiden flight. In contrast, there are virtually no working Junkers Ju 52s left, but they were known to a generation of Germans as the 'Tante Ju'. Nor is being famous necessarily the same as being successful. The tragic series of crashes involving Comets and Starfighters has made more headlines than the technical innovations they embodied, and Concorde's record-breaking performances rapidly eclipsed the financial disaster this ambitious project represented. But more successful from an economic point of view have been two of the undisputed stars of the world of modern aviation, the Airbus and the Tornado, both of which reflect the upturn experienced by the European aircraft industry during the past few decades. All the aircraft described here represent an epoch, a country, a design team and outstanding technical performance. All of them have become celebrities of the air.

Peter Alles-Fernandez

Fokker Dr.I Triplane

Conceived as a counter to the Sopwith Triplane, the Fokker Dr.I was one of the most agile combat aircraft in history. Flown by such men as Manfred von Richthofen, the small number built shot down many times their own number of enemy aircraft on the Western Front. It was in one of these aircraft that von Richthofen, the legendary Red Baron, met his death.

Manfred von Richthofen and his scarlet Fokker Dr.I triplane have become a legend in their own right. This is despite the fact that Leutnant Werner Voss shot down many more aircraft from his Fokker triplane, and von Richthofen's kills were mostly achieved with other aircraft. What is more, the number of these aircraft flying in World War 1 was comparatively small, and it was only designed as an answer to, and built along the same lines as, the British Sopwith Triplane. But the renown of the Fokker Dr.I still eclipses that of any other aircraft which flew in this war.

Released by the Sopwith Experimental Department on 28 May 1916, the first Triplane was a very neat fighting scout with a fuselage and tail almost identical to those of the Sopwith Pup, perhaps the most agile and well-loved aircraft of its day. Sopwith designed the Triplane for several reasons. Its three wings were much narrower (smaller chord) than the biplane wings of the Pup, so that though span remained unchanged the wing area actually was reduced. The more powerful (130-hp/97-kW) instead of 80- or 100-hp/60- or 75-kW) engine made the Triplane significantly faster. The narrower wings gave the pilot a better view, especially as the

middle wing was on the same level as his eyes. The narrow chord also meant that the centre of pressure (the point through which the resultant lift force acts) did not move so far from front to rear, or vice versa, as in a normal broad-winged machine during violent manoeuvres, and as this meant the fuselage could be short it enhanced manoeuvrability. Manoeuvrability was also assisted by keeping the span short, which with three wings was simple.

Frightening example

All the Triplanes went to the Royal Naval Air Service and, in no small measure because of the tremendous aggressiveness and skill of the pilots, soon struck a chill into the hearts of German flyers. The Triplanes really got into action during the Battle of Arras in April 1917. So great was their success that an official historian wrote: 'The sight of a Triplane

A replica of the Fokker Dr.I painted to represent von Richthofen's famous aircraft, though the face painted upon the engine cowling simulates that of the aircraft flown by Werner Voss.

Fokker Dr.I

Specification

Type: single-seat fighting scout
Powerplant: one 110-hp (82-kW) Oberursel Ur.II nine-cylinder rotary piston engine
Peformance: maximum speed 115 mph (185 km/h) at sea level, and 103 mph (165 km/h) at 13,125 ft (4000 m); climb to 3,280 ft (1000 m) in 2 minutes 55 seconds; service ceiling 20,015 ft (6100 m); range 186 miles (300 km); endurance 1 hour 30 minutes
Weights: empty 894 lb (406 kg); maximum take-off 1,291 lb (586 kg)
Dimensions: span, upper 23 ft 7 in (7.19 m), centre 20 ft 5¼ in (6.23 m) and lower 18 ft 8½ in (5.70 m); length 18 ft 11 in (5.77 m); height 9 ft 8 in (2.95 m); wing area, including axle fairing 200.85 sq ft (18.66 m²)
Armament: two 7.92-mm (0.31-in) LMG 08/15 machine-guns with 500 rounds per gun

The Fokker Dr.I serialled 152/17 (construction no. 1864) was one of a batch of 30 from early in the type's production run. Allocated to Jasta 11, this aircraft was on occasion flown by Manfred von Richthofen, and survived the war to go on display in a Berlin museum in an all-red scheme.

Fokker Dr.I

This all-black Dr.I had unusual white crosses on its fuselage and wings (it is believed other black German machines had white-outlined black crosses). It was the aircraft of Leutnant Josef Jacobs of Jasta 7, who finally gained 41 confirmed victories. This put him level with Hauptmann Bruno Loerzer in eighth place in Germany.

Perhaps the most famous fighter of all time, the triplane number 425/17 was the last mount of the 'Red Baron', Rittmeister Manfred, Freiherr von Richthofen, the top-scoring ace of World War 1 with 80 confirmed kills. He was shot down on 21 April 1918. Here the old cross can just be seen under the new one.

formation induced the enemy pilots to dive out of range.' The moment a Triplane crashed behind the German lines the wreckage was studied in the finest detail. Even the commander of the Imperial German Air Service, General von Höppner, publicly eulogized the British fighter. By the spring of 1917 almost every important aircraft company in the Central Powers – at least 14 – had a design team furiously trying to produce a triplane fighter. But it was the wily Dutchman, Anthony Fokker, who achieved success. So eager was he to beat his rivals that, as well as studying the Sopwith Triplanes at first hand, flying at the front, he completely illegally had the wreckage from the first crashed specimen sent to his own factory at Schwerin!

The latest fighter prototype at the Schwerin works at that time was the D.VI (a company designation unrelated to the later production D.VI), intended for the Luftfahrttruppe (air force) of Austro-Hungary. In June 1917 chief designer Reinold Platz quickly re-drew the drawings and the D.VI emerged round 1 July 1917 as the first triplane to fly in Germany. It was immediately tested by Lt Werner Voss, already a famed ace. Platz had already designed extremely advanced biplane fighters with completely cantilever wings, and he made the D.VI the same way, unbraced wings being easier on a short-span triplane. The two lower wings were attached to the top and bottom of the fuselage, and the only struts were long steel-tube inverted-Vee cabane struts carrying the top wing high above the fuselage. This wing was the only one with ailerons, whereas the Sopwith Triplane had had ailerons on all three wings, linked by light rods. Powered by a 110-hp (82-kW) Oberursel Ur.II rotary engine, the D.VI flew excellently, though before being sent to Hungary in August the upper wing, with its ailerons, was increased in span. To eliminate slight wing vibration, light wooden streamline I-type struts were added linking the wings near their tips. Armament was two synchronized 0.31-in (7.29-mm) LMG 08/15 guns.

Further developments

The D.VI, often incorrectly called the V 3, was succeeded by the first of the Fokkers to have a *Versuchs* (experimental) number, the V 4. Two V 4 triplanes, with balanced ailerons squared-off at the wingtips, were ordered on 11 July 1917. In August a number of V 7 triplanes were ordered with more powerful engines, such as the 160-hp (119-kW) Siemens-Halske Sh.III, 160-hp (119-kW) Ur.III, 145-hp (108-kW) Steyr-built Le Rhône and 170-hp (127-kW) Goebel Goe.III. These introduced modified wings with span increasing in equal steps from bottom to top. They retained the I-strut linking the wings, and all had horn balances on the ailerons and elevators, those on the ailerons projecting beyond the tips of the wings. No data survive, but because of their power the V fighter prototypes were probably more formidable than the eventual production fighter triplane.

Action at the Front

Lt Voss spent over 20 hours testing the two V 4 prototype triplanes in August 1917, and by the end of that month had them to his satisfaction. Both had by that time seen action at the front, and Fokker himself had also done a lot of active flying in them (previously he had had to don the uniform of a German officer and fly on active operational missions to test his synchronizing gear, despite the fact he was a Dutch civilian!).

Voss made the first operational flight in Fok.103/17 (Fokker No.103 for year 1917), the second V 4 prototype, on 30 August 1917. He claimed a victory on this mission. Two days later, on 1 September, von Richthofen flew the original V 4 (102/17) and scored his 60th victory. Flying with von Richthofen's *Jagdgeschwader* 1 (JG1) the two prototypes scored success after success. Voss monopolized the second Dr.I (103/17) scoring a remarkable 20 confirmed victories in it in 24 days before being killed in a classic fight on 23 September with no fewer than six S.E.5a fighters.

Structurally it was typical Fokker and Platz, with very strong mixed construction. The wings were almost wholly wood, with steel at the main joints and the attachments of bracing wires. Each wing had a single built-up box spar with main longerons of spindled (machined away for lightness on a router) hardwood, carrying built-up plywood ribs. Trailing edges were wire, resulting in the characteristic scalloped appearance when the fabric covering was doped and tightened.

Fokker Dr.I cutaway drawing key

1 Starboard upper wing tip
2 Wing panel fabric covering
3 Starboard upper interplane strut
4 Aileron cable run
5 Two-blade wooden propeller
6 Starboard centre wing
7 Lower interplane strut
8 Propeller hub fixing bolts
9 Ventilated engine cowling
10 Oberursel Ur.II (le Rhône) nine-cylinder rotary engine
11 Engine compartment fireproof bulkhead
12 Engine bearer struts
13 Reduction gearbox
14 Plywood side fairing panel
15 Carburettor
16 Rudder pedal bar
17 Pilot's footboards
18 Compass mounting
19 Control column
20 Control column-mounted secondary throttle control
21 Gun firing cables
22 Ammunition boxes
23 Fuel tank (20-Imp gal/91-litre capacity)
24 Wing spar box construction
25 Centre wing/fuselage attachments
26 Fuel filler cap
27 Twin 7.92-mm (0.31-in) LMG 08/15 machine guns
28 Ring-and-bead gunsight
29 Diagonal wire bracing
30 Centre section V-struts
31 Aileron cables
32 V-strut attachment
33 Plywood covered leading edge
34 Upper wing spar box
35 Wing ribs
36 Port upper interplane strut
37 Wing tip construction
38 Rib bracing tapes
39 Aileron horn balance
40 Welded steel tube aileron construction
41 Aileron control horn
42 Wire trailing edge
43 Port centre wing construction
44 Interplane strut attachment
45 Wing root cut-out, forward and downward visibility
46 Machine gun breeches
47 Padded cockpit coaming
48 Engine instruments
49 Engine throttle and fuel cock controls
50 Pilot's seat
51 Sliding seat adjustment
52 Welded steel-tube fuselage construction
53 Aft end of plywood side fairing panel
54 Plywood top decking
55 Port lower interplane strut
56 Fuselage top longeron
57 Horizontal spacers
58 Port lower wing tip
59 Wing tip skid
60 Tailplane centre section mounting
61 Welded steel tube tailplane construction
62 Rudder horn balance
63 Steel tube leading edge
64 Elevator horn balance
65 Steel tube elevator construction
66 Rudder fabric covering
67 Sternpost
68 Rudder control horn
69 Elevator control horn
70 Tailskid hinge mounting
71 Steel-shod tailskid
72 Elastic cord shock absorbers
73 Fuselage vertical spacers
74 Lifting handles
75 Fuselage fabric covering
76 Diagonal wire bracing (double wires)
77 Tailplane control cables
78 Fuselage bottom longeron
79 Control cable guides
80 Mounting step
81 Seat support frame
82 Dust proof fabric bulkhead
83 Pilot's floor
84 Control column mounting shaft
85 Lower wing centre section spar box
86 Undercarriage strut attachments
87 Main undercarriage V-struts
88 Port mainwheel
89 Wheel disc fabric covering
90 Wheel spokes
91 Pivoted half-axle
92 Axle fairing construction
93 Axle spar box
94 Elastic cord shock absorbers
95 Starboard mainwheel
96 Tyre valve access
97 Starboard lower wing tip skid

First of the Fokker triplanes, this neat prototype is commonly (but incorrectly) known as the V 3. Its true designation was D.VI, in an early-1917 series of D designations unrelated to the official series which included the famed D.VII. Powered by a 110-hp (82-kW) Ur.II rotary, it was flown by Leutnant Werner Voss in mid-1917.

One of the best surviving photographs of a genuine Dr.I. This aircraft provided the basis for the restored triplane N864DR which, after a busy flying career, was donated to the Australian War Memorial at Canberra. Numerous replicas of this famous fighter have been built in recent years, powered by non-rotary engines.

The small fuselage and tail were accurately welded in jigs from pre-shaped steel tubes, the fuselage then having light wooden fairings added prior to being covered in fabric. The traditional rubber-sprung main landing gears had an axle faired by a small wing, a feature of many Fokker fighters. Again a common feature of the day was the absence of a fin, the only vertical tail surface being the simple rounded rudder pivoted to the fuselage sternpost. The small riveted fuel tank was immediately behind the spinning engine, and beneath the guns; the usual armament, seldom altered in practice, comprised two LMG 08/15 (commonly called 'Spandau') machine-guns with belt magazines inside the fuselage behind the tank and the breeches immediately in front of the pilot inside the cockpit.

It added up to a simple, relatively cheap and fairly agile fighter, which with the standard 110-hp (82-kW) engine could climb faster than many more powerful aircraft and also turn inside them, a factor which in a dogfight was vital. But the speed was unimpressive by late 1917 standards and the range and endurance were exceptionally poor – only a skilled pilot could keep a Dr.I airborne longer than 80 minutes whereas 2 (if not 3) hours was easily within the grasp of all Allied fighter pilots.

Richthofen's Flying Circus

But for the brief period from October 1917 the 318 Fokker Dr.I triplanes, plus the two prototypes, were to carve out a niche in the hall of fame of military aviation. As with the Sopwith which inspired it, this was to some extent because of the brilliant flyers who went to war in it. No more famous flying unit has ever existed than von Richthofen's JG1, often called 'Richthofen's Flying Circus' because of the large number of fighters under one command, their carefully planned and organized combat techniques and, not least, their brilliant and often highly personal colour schemes. Of

course, the 318 production Dr.Is equipped not just the four *Jagdstaffeln* (fighter squadrons) of JG1 but several other *Jagdgeschwäder*, notably JG2 and JG3.

The successful service career of the Dr.I was briefly marred by a spate of crashes in the first two weeks of combat duty by production aircraft. The cause was eventually traced to shockingly bad workmanship at the Schwerin factory, and all Dr.Is were at once grounded until their wings had been stripped of fabric and inspected. In many cases properly made wing spars had to be produced, and the factory spent almost the whole of November 1917 urgently repairing or rebuilding the wings of Dr.Is. Thus it was not really until late November that the Dr.I became effective in numbers on the Western Front, and it is remarkable that such a relatively small number of a basically outdated design should have acquired so great a reputation.

This reputation is, of course, inextricably interwoven with the great Red Baron himself, Rittmeister Manfred, Freiherr von Richthofen, a German aristocrat who was the top-scoring ace of World War 1 and perhaps the most famous fighter pilot of all time. Though most of his victories had been gained on other types, such as the Albatros D.III, he favoured the Dr.I over faster biplanes and continued to fly one almost exclusively on combat missions in 1918. It was in one of two Dr.Is regularly flown by him that he met his death on 21 April 1918 – probably at the hands of Roy Brown, a Canadian captain with No. 209 Squadron, RAF (the RAF was then just 20 days old). The Freiherr (not actually a baron) died from a single bullet that went diagonally through his body, penetrating the heart.

The last Dr.I was delivered in May 1918, at a time when this type was rapidly being taken out of service in favour of the considerably superior Fokker D.VII. At no time were there more than 171 Dr.Is in active service – the maximum was reached in May 1918 – and by the middle of June this had fallen to 125. During the summer, most of them had been transferred back to Germany to defend their home territory. Other famous Dr.I pilots apart from Richthofen were Kurt Wolff, with 33 aircraft shot down, Voss with 48, Erich Löwenhardt with 53, and Ernst Udet with 62. Richthofen himself had 80 kills to his credit.

This Dr.I was on the strength of Jasta 18 in the final year of the war. After the Armistice it was acquired by France and preserved. The interplane strut linked the single spars of the three wings. Not all Dr.Is were fitted with the ash skid attached under the tips of the lowest wing to prevent damage.

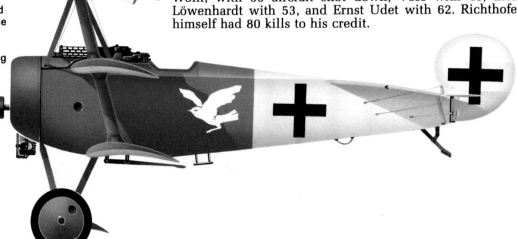

Dornier Flying-boats

In April 1983 Dornier flew the Do 24TT, a big turboprop amphibian derived from the pre-war Do 24. No company is better fitted to test the market for marine aircraft than this famous German firm, with a heritage of all-metal flying-boats no other company can match.

Professor Dr Claude Dornier was probably the best builder of flying boats anywhere in the world in the years before 1930, as well as being one of the great exponents of the modern all-metal aircraft. His very first design, the RS I in 1915, was not only made almost entirely of steel and aluminium alloys, but was also the largest aircraft in existence, with a wingspan of 142 ft 8 in (43.5 m). This was the first in the RS series (RS stood for *Riesenflugzeug See*, or Extra Large Seaplane) which was used after the war ended in 1918.

As well as the RS series Dornier's company, Zeppelin-Werke Lindau GmbH, had almost completed the prototype of a smaller but still very capable flying-boat, the Gs I. Powered by two 270-hp (201-kW) Maybach Mb.IV water-cooled engines arranged in tandem at the centre of a rectangular monoplane wing, the Gs I had a slim and very efficient hull, stabilizing sponsons of the kind favoured by Dornier, and a twin-finned biplane tail. The four-seat enclosed cockpit in the bows gave an appearance like the head of a serpent, but as a tough transport flying-boat it had no equal when it flew on 31 July 1919. It was later flown from Lindau to the Netherlands, but the fact remained that the machine contravened the rules imposed by the Allies and the Allied Control Commission had it sunk off Kiel on 25 April 1920.

Dornier went ahead with small aircraft, such as the Delfin, Libelle and Komet, but he never gave up his work on big and powerful flying-boats. His wartime design for the Gs II, rather larger than the Gs I with 1,033.4 sq ft (96 m²) of wing instead of 861.1 sq ft (80 m²), and a laden weight raised from 9,513 lb (4315 kg) to 12,566 lb (5700 kg) appeared to be just what the infant airlines and air forces needed. Under the noses of the hated Control Commission, Dornier set up an Italian subsidiary, Societá di Costruzioni Meccaniche di Pisa, at Marina di Pisa. He carried on designing at Lindau, the works there being renamed Dornier Metallbauen GmbH in 1922, and licensed the big Gs II machines to the Italian subsidiary, even buying two 300-hp (224-kW) Hispano-Suiza engines from Paris for the prototype of the improved Gs II. Dornier redesignated it as the Type J, and named it Wal (whale). The prototype flew on 6 November 1922.

Dornier was correct in his assessment of the market. The Wal was ideally suited to both commercial and military operations for the next 15 years, having very satisfactory performance and payload, a robust all-metal structure and

This Wal was one of the later examples of the 17,637-lb (8000-kg) gross weight civil family, in this case with BMW VI engines. These later variants had the same 1,033-sq ft (96-m²) wing area, but rounded tips and span increased from 74 ft (22.5 m) to 76 ft (23.2 m). D-2069 *Monsun* (monsoon) served with Deutsche Lufthansa. Note the giant D/F loop aerial.

Dornier Superwal

Specification

Dornier Superwal (four engines)

Type: transport flying-boat

Powerplant: (this example) four 460/485-hp (343/362-kW) Napier Lion VIII W-12 water-cooled piston engines

Performance: maximum speed 130 mph (210 km/h); cruising speed (typical) 100 mph (161 km/h); normal operating ceiling 6,500 ft (2000 m); range with maximum payload 620 miles (1000 km)

Weights: empty 21,781 lb (9880 kg); maximum loaded 30,865 lb (14000 kg)

Dimensions: span 93 ft 10 in (28.6 m); length 80 ft 8.5 in (24.6 m); height 19 ft 8.2 in (6 m); wing area 1,475 sq ft (137 m²)

Accommodation: normal operating crew of four and up to 19 passengers; maximum payload 8,375 lb (3800 kg)

Dornier built three of the twin-engined Superwals, with 650-hp (485-kW) Condor engines, followed by 16 of the four-engined version. The first of the four-engined machines was this example, one of seven (together with all three twin-Condor Superwals) delivered to the German airline Deutsche Lufthansa. D-1337 was the only one powered by 485-hp (362-kW) Napier Lion engines, the other Lufthansa machines having the 525-hp (391-kW) Siemens-built Bristol Jupiter air-cooled radial. The radiators for the Lions can be seen mounted athwartships above the push-pull nacelles, and the side-by-side cockpit offset to port was enclosed in this version.

D-1337

Dornier Flying-boats

This regular Military Wal was one of a substantial number operated by the Spanish navy. Many earlier Spanish Wals had been built by CMASA, but the example shown was a Dornier-built Do J IId, with BMW VI engines. It is shown during the Civil War while serving with I-G 70 Grupo at Puerto de Pollensa, in Majorca.

The Luftwaffe Do 18D reached the peak of its brief career in 1939–40, when the type equipped four *Staffeln* (squadrons) of the *Küstenfliegergruppen* (coastal groups). This example served at Kamp, on the Pomeranian coast, with 2/KüFlGr 906. By 1941 the Do 18Ds were being converted as Do 18H crew trainers, the more powerful Do 18Gs then becoming Do 18Ns.

The 22,046-lb (10000-kg) gross weight Wal was the last and largest version, dating from 1933. Span was increased to 89 ft 2.9 in (27.2 m) and wing area to 1,206 sq ft (112 m²). This example was one of those that made 328 scheduled crossings of the South Atlantic, operating from the ships *Westfalen* and *Schwabenland*. Note the length of the hydraulic catapult.

of the hull from which bombs and other stores could be hung, and there were various schemes for defensive guns.

Of course, with the benefit of hindsight the Wal can be criticized. Tandem engines are inefficient, can lead to cooling problems and can cause severe stresses in the rear propeller. The Wal's very broad wingtips were aerodynamically poor, and the high induced drag inevitably reduced the attainable range. The large 'park bench' balancing surfaces attached to the ailerons were a scheme outmoded by 1930, and the open cockpit of most Wals would have been disliked by the softer pilots of later times. But in overall terms no other marine aircraft came near it. Altogether at least 300 and possibly more than 320 Wals were built, including between 157 and 177 in Italy (156 by SCMP and its successor CMASA of 1929, a Fiat subsidiary), at least 56 by Dornier at Friedrichshafen from 1932, 40 by CASA in Spain, about 40 by Aviolanda in the Netherlands and three by

excellent reliability. Airline Wals set new standards in interior appointments, and with glass portholes resembled staterooms in luxury yachts. The many military versions were fitted with four small stub wings along the upper part

One of the three Wals built under licence by Kawasaki. Dornier Wals were also built under licence in Italy, Spain and Holland with the result that the variations of this model were in many ways very different from one another.

Kawasaki in Japan. It is doubtful if any aircraft has left the original factory in so many different variations. There were four major and nine minor variations in span, six quite different designs of nose and cockpit, eight different designs of tail, at least 17 different basic types of engine, and a host of gross weights from 8,818 lb (4000 kg) to more than 22,046 lb (10000 kg).

Though some early customers continued to specify the Hispano, many of the pre-1925 Wals were powered by the 360-hp (268-kW) Rolls-Royce Eagle IX, and this rather outdated V-12 was fitted to a Wal that set 20 world records for speed/height/range with payloads up to 4,409 lb (2000 kg) on 4, 9, 10 and 11 February 1925. Other Wals, with three different types of engine, made crossings of the North and South Atlantic, flew from Europe to near the North Pole and to various places in the Far East, and also flew round the world. Airline Wals often had an enclosed cockpit (always from 1931) and began as six- to nine-seaters, with space for loose cargo. In 1931 Dornier began production of the '8-tonne Wal' first flown the previous year with 690-hp (515-kW) BMW VI engines and a 1,033.4-sq ft (96-m²) wing. This became the standard model, though again with many variations, and it led to the 8.5-tonner in 1933, and the corresponding Militär-Wal 33 which was produced for the Luftwaffe as the Do 15. In the same year appeared the biggest version, the 10-tonne Wal, with 1,205.6 sq ft (112 m²) of wing, which was operated by Deutsche Lufthansa from the

The original Do X 12-engined monster is seen here after its refit with Curtiss Conqueror water-cooled engines. It is shown after its long trip to the Americas in brief service with Lufthansa. It then went to the DVL research organization before becoming the biggest exhibit in the Berlin air museum, where it was destroyed by bombs.

depot ships *Westfalen* and *Schwabenland* and made 328 crossings of the South Atlantic in regular mail service. Among export customers were Argentina, Chile, Colombia, Italy, Japan, the Netherlands, Portugal, the Soviet Union, Spain, the UK and Yugoslavia.

Different enough to have a different name, Superwal, the Type R enlarged version first flew on 30 September 1926. This was constructed at another Dornier factory, at Manzell on the Swiss shore of the Bodensee (Lake Constance). The prototype of this much bigger boat had two Rolls-Royce Condors of 650 hp (485 kW) each, and another had two 800-hp (597-kW) Packard A-2500s, but most other Superwals had two push/pull pairs, the most common engines being the Siemens-built Bristol Jupiter, Pratt & Whitney Hornet, and, for the CASA-built military Superwals, the 500-hp (373-kW) Hispano-Suiza.

Model X monster

Just as the RS I had been the biggest aeroplane of its day, so did Dornier's liking for size manifest itself in an extreme

D-AEAV was one of a small batch of Fokker-built Do 24T-1 flying-boats completed as unarmed civil aeromedical transports operated by the *Reichsluftdienst* (air service). They operated mainly within and around Germany in 1941–4, carrying seven stretchers or a larger number of sitting patients or war casualties.

This Do 24T-2 was one of the later (1943) production series from the Dutch assembly line, the main external difference being the tall HDL 151 dorsal turret fitted with a Mauser MG 151/20 cannon instead of the French HS 404 cannon of the Do 24T-1. This boat served with 7 *Seenotstaffel* SBK XI in the Aegean Sea, chiefly on rescue duties.

form in 1926 when work began at Manzell on the Model X. This monster flyingboat was the ultimate scaled-up Wal, with no fewer than six push/pull pairs of engines, still the largest number ever used to propel a single aircraft. The Do X first flew in the hands of Richard Wagner on 12 (often reported as 25) July 1929, powered by Siemens Jupiters. Planned as a long-range passenger machine with 66 to 72 seats, it took off on 31 October 1929 with 10 crew, 150 passengers and nine stowaways, a total not exceeded for 20 years. On 4 August 1930 the Do X emerged after a rebuild with water-cooled Curtiss Conqueror engines with plain struts instead of auxiliary wings between the nacelles, the US engines giving extra power (640 instead of 525 hp/477 instead of 391 kW) and avoiding customs problems on a visit to the USA in 1930–1. The Italian air force used two of these monsters with 580-hp (433-kW) Fiat A 22R engines.

On 26 September 1939 a Blackburn Skua flown by Lieutenant B. S. McEwan scrambled from HMS *Ark Royal* and shot down a shadowing Do 18D, the first aircraft shot down by British forces in World War 2. The Do 18 was the natural successor to the Wal, designed in early 1934 to meet both a requirement for an updated Militär-Wal and a more modern South Atlantic boat for Lufthansa. The prototype Do 18a flew on 15 March 1935, powered by tandem 540-hp (403-kW) Junkers Jumo 5 diesel engines giving great range and endurance. Similar to the 8-tonne Wal in size and weight, the Do 18 was naturally much improved aerodynamically, with a tapered wing with rounded tips and 'double wing' flaps and ailerons, a central wing pylon incorporating the cooling radiators, and a well-streamlined hull of graceful form. Small numbers of several versions were produced for civil applications, and in summer 1936 deliveries began from the Weser company of the military Do 18D series, most of which had 600-hp (447-kW) Jumo 205C diesels and were used for armed reconnaissance with coastal units. Delay in development of the Blohm und Voss Bv 138 led to continued

D-ABYM *Aeolus* was the Do 18 V3 (third prototype). Powered by tandem 600-hp (447-kW) Jumo 205C diesel engines, all three were later designated as Do 18E transports and used from 1936 on Lufthansa's routes on the North, and later South, Atlantic. Just before joining the airline, on 10–11 July 1936, *Aeolus* made a 30-hour 21-minute test flight over the Baltic.

Dornier Do 24T cutaway drawing key

1 Bow navigation light
2 Towing/mooring ring
3 Fore hull structure
4 Retractable mast
5 Ammunition magazine racks
6 Spent cartridge chute
7 Bow compartment (see equipment stowage)
8 Turret mechanism
9 Bow 7.92-mm MG 15 machine-gun
10 Bow turret
11 Removable turret dome
12 Nose decking
13 Nose mooring lug
14 Mooring rope stowage
15 Bulkhead
16 Crawlway
17 Rudder pedal assembly
18 Bulkhead door frame
19 Instrument panel shroud
20 Co-pilot's control column
21 Compass
22 Windscreen panels
23 Cockpit roof glazing
24 Sliding entry panels
25 Hatch runners
26 Flight deck windows
27 Navigator's station
28 Co-pilot seat
29 Pilot's seat
30 Seat adjustment lever
31 Side-mounted control column
32 Floors support frame
33 Radio-operator's position
34 'Vee' bottom hull structure
35 Fuselage/sponson fairing
36 Access panels
37 Sponson nose ribs
38 Sponson main fuel cells (four, approx 77 Imp gal/350 litre capacity each)
39 Sponson abbreviated fuel cell (36.6 Imp gal/180 litre capacity)
40 Port sponson mooring lug
41 Rib reinforcement
42 Sponson main spar/fuselage frame
43 Sponson/forward wing strut lower attachment

44 Fuel collector tank (46 Imp gal/210 litres)
45 Access panels
46 Fuselage hull step
47 Sponson rear spar/fuselage frame
48 Sponson/aft wing strut lower attachment
49 Mooring lug
50 Non-slip sponson walkway
51 Forward midships bay (two-stretcher accommodation; 28 oxygen bottles stowed along centre-line walkway)
52 Forward bay hinged entry hatch
53 Sponson/forward wing strut
54 Fuselage main frame bulkhead

Dornier Wal variants

Gs I: wartime flying-boat design, first flown in 1919 and sunk by Allied authorities

Wal: initial military version of 1922 built by Marina di Pisa and licensees; Rolls-Royce Eagle, Hispano, Lorraine, Napier, Bristol, Packard, Liberty, Wright, BMW, Junkers, Piaggio and other makes of engine; 1,033.4-sq ft (96-m²) wing, gross weight 5.7 tonnes

Wal Type J: initial commercial model from early 1923, generally as for military, a few with enclosed cockpit

8.0-to Wal: strengthened and more powerful 1931 model, usually with 690-hp (515-kW) BMW VI engines, still 1,033.4 sq ft (96 m²) but span increased from 73 ft 9.8 in to 76 ft 1.4 in (22.5 to 23.2 m); passenger seating increased from nine to 14

8.5-to Wal: further uprated version generally as 8.0-to but cleared to 18,739 lb (8500 kg) in 1933

10-to Wal: further enlarged 1933 model with span of 89 ft 2.9 in (27.2 m), 1,205.6-sq ft (112-m²) wing area, usually 690-hp (515-kW) BMW VI engines

Do-15: Luftwaffe designation for uprated military version of 1933; 18,739-lb (8500-kg) weight, 1,033.4-sq ft (96-m²) wing, usually BMW VI engines in German service

Superwal/2m: various twin-engine Type R Superwals usually with two 650-hp (485-kW) Condor or 800-hp (597-kW) Packard engines, 93 ft 10 in (28.6 m) span, 1,539.3-sq ft (143-m²) wing, 19 passenger seats, gross weight 10.5 tonnes

Superwal/4m: four-engine Superwal series, with 480-hp (358 kW) Jupiter VI, 525-hp (391-kW) Siemens Jupiter, 550-hp (410-kW) Hornet or 460-hp (343-kW) Napier Lion; same span but wing reduced to 1,474.7 sq ft (137 m²) area and gross weight increased to 14 tonnes

A49-4 was the fourth of five of the oldest Do 24K-1s flown from the Dutch East Indies to Australia on 19 February 1942. Many later escapees reached Broome, Northern Territory, a fortnight later, only to be destroyed there by Japanese fighters. A49-4 served with RAAF No. 41 Sqn on transport duties to the New Guinea theatre.

production of the Do 18 into World War 2 the total of all versions being in the region of 160 including 75 Do 18Ds. The main wartime version was the Do 18G and the unarmed Do 18H crew trainer, both powered by the 880-hp (656-kW) Jumo 205D. By 1941 most surviving Do 18s of all types were converted as Do 18N air/sea rescue aircraft.

The last aircraft that can be said to have descended from the Wal was the Do 24, a considerably larger boat that at last abandoned tandem engines, though it adhered to the use of sponsons for stability on the water. It had its origins in the requirement of the MLD, the Dutch naval air force, for a successor to its mainstay, the trusty Wal. In 1934 the MLD

55 Medical attendant: station
56 Fuselage/wing strut attachment fairing
57 Port engine nacelle intake
58 Fuselage porthole
59 Starboard crew entry door
60 Bulkhead
61 Radio equipment installation
62 Roof external strakes
63 Three-blade VDM metal propellers
64 Spinners
65 Starboard sponson
66 Roof (starboard) entry hatch
67 Centre engine nacelle intake
68 Engine exhausts
69 Engine upper air intakes
70 1,000-hp (746-kW) Bramo 323R-2 radial engine
71 Cowling ring
72 Hinged engine inspection/ maintenance panels

73 Cooling louvre
74 Oil tank cover
75 Servicing handgrip
76 Engine bearers
77 Firewall/bulkhead
78 Centre engine oil tank
79 Centre nacelle frames
80 Centre nacelle pick-up/ hoist bar
81 Starboard wing fuel tank
82 Starboard engine nacelle fairing
83 Starboard aerial mast
84 Wing front spar
85 Aerial
86 Wing ribs
87 Wing metal skinning
88 Starboard navigation light
89 Starboard formation/ identification light
90 Starboard aileron

91 Aileron hinge fairings
92 Wing rear spar
93 Aileron control runs
94 Aileron trim tab
95 Wing centre/outer-section join
96 Aileron inboard profile
97 Centre-section underwing flap
98 Flap actuating hinges
99 Antenna
100 D/F loop
101 Rear spar structure
102 Wing rib/flap cut-out
103 Flap control runs
104 Port engine nacelle fairing
105 Port wing fuel tank
106 Port aerial mast

113 Sponson/forward wing strut upper attachment
114 Twin landing lights
115 Sponson/wing strut diagonal bracing
116 Fuselage/wing aft inverted 'Vee' struts (housing fuel lines from sponsons)

133 Wing rear spar
134 Port navigation light
135 Port formation/ identification light
136 Port aileron
137 Hull aft step

160 Tailplane rear spar/tailfin attachment
161 Starboard tailfin structure
162 Aerial attachment
163 Rudder balance
164 Rudder frame
165 Rudder upper trim tab
166 Starboard rudder post
167 Rudder lower trim tab
168 Trim tab actuating linkage
169 Starboard elevator tab
170 Port rudder balance
171 Starboard elevator structure
172 Elevator control linkage

173 Rudder linkage
174 Port aerial attachment
175 Tailplane inboard end rib structure
176 Tailplane front spar/ fuselage frame attachment
177 Fuselage aft main frame
178 Control linkage
179 Stern mooring rope stowage
180 Tailplane brace struts
181 Port tailfin
182 Tailplane/fin attachment
183 Port elevator hinge
184 Rear turret ammunition stowage
185 Port rudder post
186 Rear turret
187 Turret ring
188 Tail gunner's armour plating
189 Port rudder
190 Rudder lower trim tab hinge fairing
191 Port rudder lower trim tab
192 Tail navigation light
193 Tail mooring ring
194 7.92-mm MG 15 stern machine-gun

107 Oil tank cover
108 Front spar
109 Hinged leading-edge (inspection/servicing access)
110 Fuselage/wing centre-line diagonal brace strut
111 Fuselage/wing forward inverted 'Vee' struts (housing control runs)
112 Wing centre/outer section front spar join

117 Wing centre/outer section join rib
118 Sponson/aft wing strut upper attachment
119 Midships dorsal decking
120 Sponson/aft wing strut
121 Fuselage air ventilation plant
122 Fuselage main frame bulkhead
123 Centre-line walkway
124 Aft bay hinged entry hatch
125 Aft midships bay (four × stretcher accommodation)
126 Hull 'Vee' bottom structure
127 Galley/hot plate (port)
128 Blanket/survival clothing cupboard (starboard)
129 Fuselage midships mooring lug
130 Aileron underwing fairings
131 Bulkhead door
132 Aileron underwing mass balances

138 'Vee' bottom sternpost frame
139 Reinforced fuselage frame
140 Turret support
141 Compressed air bottles
142 Turret ring
143 Dorsal turret
144 20-mm MG 151 cannon
145 Toilet
146 Peat bag (toilet sanitary refill)
147 Porthole
148 Master compass
149 Aft fuselage centre-line catwalk
150 Tail surface control rod linkage
151 Fuselage aft frames
152 Fuselage skinning
153 Ventral stringers
154 Control rods
155 Fuselage/tailplane fairing
156 Tailplane front spar
157 Elevator control rod
158 Elevator hinges
159 Tailplane ribs

Dornier Flying-boats

The last military flying-boats in service in Europe, the Spanish Ejercito del Aire's Do 24T-2s survived on coastal patrol and rescue duties from Puerto de Pollensa until 1970, serving with the 58th Escuadrilla de Salvamento. Their superb rough-water seaworthiness has never been equalled by any other aircraft of any size.

refined its ideas and opened talks with Dornier, soon deciding that the Do 18 was not quite big enough. The MLD wanted not only long range and more than two engines but also the ability to operate safely at great distances from land and, if necessary, alight on quite rough seas. During 1935 Dornier went ahead with the design of the three-engine Do 24 purely for the MLD, charging the Dutch government a fee for the design process as well as selling a licence to Aviolanda, which had finished building Wals in 1931. Four prototypes were put in hand, the Do 24 V3 being the first to fly and being powered, like the Do 24 V4, with the engine specified by the customer for commonality with its Martin 139WH-1 bombers, the Wright Cyclone F52. Dornier fitted the first two prototypes with the heavier and less powerful Jumo 205 diesel for possible use by the Luftwaffe, but not much was done with them before the war.

Successful trials

A wholly modern stressed-skin boat, the Do 24 hung its shapely hull under the rectangular centre section on two pairs of inverted-V struts, with a fifth diagonal strut to react to the pull of the engines (in contrast to the big streamlined pylon of the Do 18). The tail had twin fins on the ends of the wide-span tailplane, and there was provision for a gun turret in the bow, amidships and at the extreme tail. The MLD also specified wing bomb racks for up to 12 stores of 220 lb (100 kg) each, and a heavy load of mission equipment. Flight trials, including operations from very heavy seas, showed that the Do 24 possessed exceptional strength and good performance. In autumn 1937 the MLD signed for 60, to be licence-built in the Netherlands, but in the event Dornier built 12 (including the Do 24 V3 and V4 prototypes), with the designation Do 24K-1, using the 875-hp (652-kW) F52 engine, while Aviolanda, De Schelde and other Dutch companies undertook to build the other 48, designated Do 24K-2, powered by the 1,000-hp (746-kW) Cyclone G102.

Continuing the story of the Do 24 into the 1980s, this ex-Do 24T-2 has acquired a new wing and triple turboprop powerplants while retaining the original hull and tail units. Currently undergoing flight testing and research into composite materials and corrosion problems, a commercial future for the Do 24TT remains to be realized.

This Do 24MS minesweeper was one of a small number (possibly only two) converted for the task from regular Luftwaffe Do 24T-1 rescue/reconnaissance machines. An auxiliary motor/generator set in the hull fed the heavy current pulses through the duralumin ring conductor; the magnetic field exploded mines below the aircraft.

All the Do 24K-1s had been delivered by the outbreak of war, but when Germany invaded the Netherlands on 10 May 1940 only 25 of the Do 24K-2s had been despatched. Three were captured intact, and when these were tested at Travemünde the Luftwaffe discovered they were superb boats, and Dutch production was quickly restarted. Under the control of the Weser company the Do 24K-2s were modified without bomb gear but with MG15 nose and tail guns and captured Hispano 20-mm cannon in the amidships turret, as well as large hatches and comprehensive internal furnishings for the air/sea rescue mission. Designated Do 24N-1, the production boats entered Luftwaffe service from August 1941, 11 being delivered by November when the stock of engines was exhausted. Production then continued with the Do 24T-1 with the 1,000-hp (746-kW) BMW Bramo Fafnir 323, a total of 170 in all being supplied. Such was the demand for this fine boat that a second source was organized at the former Potez-CAMS factory at Sartrouville, France, where 48 additional Do 24s were built.

From early 1943 most were of the Do 24T-2 sub-type with extra radio and sometimes radar, as well as an MG 151 replacing the Hispano cannon amidships. Very similar boats designated Do 24T-3 were prepared for Spain, 12 being flown to the Spanish seaplane base at Puerto Pollensa, Majorca, in 1944.

Every Do 24 was heavily involved in the events of the war. The MLD boats in the Dutch East Indies had almost all been destroyed by the end of March 1942. Towards the end of the war, the Luftwaffe's losses of flying boats were very high, but the Spanish Do 24T-3s were still in use long after the war. As late as 1972, holidaymakers in Majorca were able to see a number of Do 24T-3s. The last of these was flown to the Dornier factory in Friedrichshafen to be preserved for posterity. A number of squadrons of the French Aéronavale were using about 40 Do 24T-2s between them, and one machine which a Luftwaffe flight engineer flew to Sweden in 1945 was used by the Flygvapen as a Tp 24 for a total of seven years.

de Havilland Moths

A product of the 1920s, the classic Moths represented a successful venture to enable the public to enjoy the sport of flying, and sowed the seeds of private aircraft ownership that were to blossom throughout the inter-war years.

The de Havilland Moth was much more than simply a series of light aircraft. With this plane, de Havilland proved their theory that the British middle classes loved recreational flying and represented a previously untapped market. For the same reasons, in 1923 the Daily Mail sponsored a competition for light aircraft – we would call them ultra-lights today – at Lympne. There was a demand for the production of an aircraft that a small flying club or even the man in the street could afford and would be correspondingly easy to fly. A number of interesting small aircraft were entered for the competition, but de Havilland realised that a machine with a capacity of less than 1.1 litre was too under-powered for an inexperienced pilot and would be dangerous.

Accordingly the works at Stag Lane set about producing a scaled-down version of the D.H.51 three-seater, the new aircraft being a two-seat single-bay biplane, tough enough to withstand the rigours of instructional work and not so cramped as to be uncomfortable during cross-country flying. Powered by a four-cylinder 60-hp (45-kW) engine specially designed by Major F.B. Halford and named the A.D.C. Cirrus I, the new D.H.60 was a model of robust simplicity, its fuselage being in effect a plywood box built round spruce longerons and stiffened by vertical and horizontal members screwed to the plywood.

Named Moth in recognition of Geoffrey de Havilland's renown as a lepidopterist, the first D.H.60 (G-EBKT) was flown at Stag Lane by 'DH' himself on 22 February 1925. On that day was set a pattern for private flying that was to be emulated the world over until World War 2. Efforts to canvass support from government sources were successful when Sir Sefton Brancker, Director of Civil Aviation, announced the founding of five Air Ministry-subsidized Moth-equipped flying clubs, the Lancashire Aero Club, the London Aeroplane Club, the Newcastle Aero Club, the Midland Aero Club and the Yorkshire Aeroplane Club. By the end of 1925 20 Cirrus Moths had been completed, of which 16 had been delivered to the clubs and two to private owners. 1926 brought forth 35 more Moths, of which 14 were exported, nine of them to Australia; Major Halford produced an 85-hp (63-kW) Cirrus II engine which was fitted in a Moth to be piloted by Geoffrey de Havilland in the King's Cup Race, but a broken oil pipe let through Hubert Broad into first place in a Cirrus I Moth. Another famous British sporting pilot, Neville Stack, flew the second Moth proto-type (G-EBKU), powered by the first production Cirrus II, from Croydon to India where it attracted much interest as it embarked on six months joyriding in the sub-continent.

G-ATBL was a D.H.60G Gipsy Moth which was exported to Switzerland. It returned to England where it continued to fly, and is seen here at the Shuttleworth Trust at Old Warden, a perfect setting for the aircraft that established light aeroplane flying as a purely enjoyable pastime.

de Havilland D.H.82A Tiger Moth

Specification

D.H.82A Tiger Moth Mk II
Type: two-seat ab initio trainer biplane
Powerplant: one 130-hp (97-kW) de Havilland Gipsy Major 1 four-cylinder air-cooled inverted inline piston engine
Performance: maximum speed 104 mph (167 km/h) at sea level; initial climb rate 635 ft (194 m) per minute; service ceiling 13,600 ft (4145 m); range 300 miles (483 km)
Weights: empty 1,115 lb (506 kg); maximum take-off 1,825 lb (828 kg)
Dimensions: span 29 ft 4 in (8.94 m); length 23 ft 11 in (7.29 m); height 8 ft 9½ in (2.68 m); wing area 239 sq ft (22.20 m²)
Armament: none

A de Havilland D.H.82A Tiger Moth of the University of London Air Squadron based at RAF Fairoaks in 1950. The University Air Squadrons received Tiger Moths to replace Avro Tutors in 1939, retaining them until they received de Havilland Chipmunks in the early 1950s. The RUL code prefix on this aircraft signifies Reserve Command, University of London Air Squadron, and it carries standard post-war yellow training bands on its fuselage and wings. This aircraft is fitted with a blind flying hood for instrument flying training; in use this would unfold on a metal framework to cover the rear cockpit.

Moth variants

D.H.60 Moth (Cirrus I): 1925–26 model; two prototypes (G-EBKT and G-EBKU); eight pre-production; 31 production aircraft
D.H.60 Moth (Cirrus II): 1926–27 model; 32 built
D.H.60 Genet Moth: six aircraft (J8816–J8821) for Air Ministry; Genet engines
D.H.60X Moth (Cirrus III): 1928 model; 338 built by de Havilland at Stag Lane
D.H.60G Gipsy Moth: introduced 1928; 595 built by de Havilland at Stag Lane; 40 aircraft built by Morane-Saulnier in France; 18 built by Moth Aircraft Corp, in USA; 32 built by Larkin Aircraft Supply, Melbourne, for Australian government
D.H.60M Moth (Metal Moth): introduced 1928; four pre-production aircraft; 536 built by DH at Stag Lane; 40 built by DH Canada; 161 built by Moth Aircraft Corp, in USA; 10 built by Norwegian Army Aircraft Factory in 1931
D.H.60GIII Moth: Gipsy III in wooden Moth; introduced in 1932; 47 built by de Havilland at Stag Lane
D.H.60GIII Moth Major: Gipsy Major III or IIIA; introduced in 1934; one prototype (G-ACNP) and 96 production aircraft
D.H.60T Moth Trainer: Gipsy II; military trainer; introduced 1931; two prototypes (G-ABKS and G-ABKU) and initial production of 47 aircraft
D.H.61 Giant Moth: six/eight-passenger cabin biplane; Jupiter VI or XI, Jaguar VIC or Pratt & Whitney Hornet engines; introduced in 1928
D.H.71 Tiger Moth: two experimental monoplanes G-EBQU (Gipsy) and G-EBRV (Cirrus II) produced in 1927
D.H.75 Hawk Moth: first high-wing Moth; one D.H.75 prototype (de Havilland Ghost engine), five **D.H.75A** (Lynx, Whirlwind or Cheetah engine), and one **D.H.75B** (Whirlwind)
D.H.80A Puss Moth: high-wing cabin monoplane; Gipsy III, Gipsy Major or Gipsy (high compression) engines; introduced 1930; one **D.H.80** prototype (G-AAHZ) and 259 production aircraft built at Stag Lane; 25 built by DH Canada
D.H.81 Swallow Moth: two-seat low-wing monoplane; only one built
D.H.82T Tiger Moth: eight similar to D.H.60T but with Gipsy III; service trials led to D.H.82 and D.H.82A
D.H.82 Tiger Moth: 114 initial military training biplanes built by de Havilland at Stag Lane
D.H.82A Tiger Moth: in RAF, **Tiger Moth MkII**; basic ab initio trainer; total of about 7,290 produced between 1934 and 1945; 795 built by de Havilland at Hatfield, 3,216 by Morris at Cowley, remainder by DH Canada, DH Australia, DH New Zealand, and in Portugal (91), Norway (37) and Sweden (23); Gipsy III and Gipsy Major (various versions); total includes 786 **D.H.82C** with Menasco Pirate D4 engine built by DH Canada (200 sold to USA as **PT-24** in 1942); at least 17 converted to **Thruxton Jackaroo** (four-seat cabin conversion), 1957–9
D.H.82B Queen Bee: radio-controlled gunnery target; RAF 380, Royal Navy 420
D.H.83 Fox Moth: four-passenger cabin biplane; introduced in 1932; Gipsy Major or Gipsy Major IC
D.H.85A Leopard Moth: three seat high-wing cabin monoplane; introduced in 1933; Gipsy Major (**D.H.85**) and Gipsy Six R (D.H.85A); one prototype (G-ACHD) and 131 production aircraft
D.H.87 Hornet Moth: two-seat cabin biplane; introduced in 1934; Gipsy Major I; prototype D.H.87 (G-ACTA), **D.H.87A** with elliptical wings and tips
D.H.87B with squared wings and tips; 163 made
D.H.94 Moth Minor: two-seat low-wing monoplane; introduced in 1937

The prototype D.H.60 Moth G-EBKT, which was first flown by Captain Geoffrey de Havilland on Sunday 22 February 1925 at Stag Lane. It differed from subsequent production aircraft in having an unbalanced rudder and exhaust pipe on the starboard side. Moving the pipe to the port side allowed access to an aft baggage locker.

The so-called 1927-model Moths, of which 150 were produced, were all powered by the Cirrus II, and one of these (G-EBPP) was shipped to Australia where Major Hereward de Havilland set up an agency in Melbourne to assemble imported Moths. Numerous outstanding lightplane flights were made by enthusiastic private owners, typical being Lady Bailey's altitude record for light aircraft of 17,283 ft (5268 m) on 5 July of that year, and Lieutenant R. R. Bentley's two extraordinary return flights between the UK and Cape Town totalling 51,652 miles (83125 km) in G-EBSO. Six aircraft, powered by 75-hp (56-kW) Armstrong Siddeley Genet radials, were bought by the Air Ministry for use at the Central Flying School.

1928 introduced the 90-hp (67-kW) Cirrus III engine and a split-axle landing gear which, on account of the new cross-braces between the landing gear, resulted in this model being termed the D.H.60X Moth. By the end of the year 403 Moths of all types had been produced and production was running at 16 per week; moreover, licences to build Moths had been negotiated with the Finnish Government Aircraft Factory and Veljekset Karhumäki O/Y (also of Finland) and the General Aircraft Co. of Sydney, Australia.

Meanwhile stocks of war-surplus Renault engine components, employed in the Cirrus engines, had been exhausted and in 1926 'DH' asked Major Halford to design a new replacement engine; the first example of this, the legendary Gipsy, was completed in July 1927 and within 16 weeks a production shop at Stag Lane was built. After trials in an early Moth (G-EBOH), the new engine gained its certificate and appeared in the production D.H.60G Gipsy Moth. One of

these, flown by W. L. Hope, won the 1928 King's Cup Race at 105 mph (169 km/h). Records tumbled, and many memorable flights followed; 'DH' himself in his own Gipsy Moth (G-AAAA) established a new lightplane height record at 19,980 ft (6090 m) on 25 July 1928, and Hubert Broad remained aloft for 24 hours (using extra fuel tanks in the fuselage); DH's son Geoffrey flew a Gipsy Moth for 600 hours in nine months during 1929; covering 51,000 miles (82075 km) with only routine inspections; when tested afterwards

de Havilland D.H.82A Tiger Moth cutaway drawing key

1 Starboard navigation light
2 Automatic leading edge slat, open
3 Slat hinges
4 Starboard upper and wing panel
5 Wing fabric covering
6 Starboard interplane struts
7 Pitot static tubes
8 Starboard lower wing panel
9 Diagonal wire bracing
10 Leading-edge stiffening ribs
11 Lattice rib construction
12 Fuel tank, capacity 22.8 Imp gal (104 litres)
13 Fuel contents gauge
14 Filler cap
15 Main spar attachment joint
16 Centre section 'N' struts
17 Cowling step
18 Detachable engine cowlings
19 de Havilland Gipsy Major four-cylinder inline engine
20 Fixed nose cowling
21 de Havilland two-bladed fixed-pitch wooden propeller
22 Spinner
23 Splined propeller shaft
24 Cooling air intake
25 Internal air duct
26 Engine mounting points
27 Engine bearer struts
28 Accessory equipment
29 Sloping engine bay bulkhead
30 Oil filler cap
31 Forward rudder pedals
32 Oil tank, capacity 2.5 Imp gal (11.4 litres)
33 Control column
34 Instrument venturi
35 Front pilot's (instructor's) seat
36 Tailplane trim control lever
37 Rear rudder pedals
38 Seat safety harness
39 Engine throttle lever
40 Instructor's instrument panel
41 Slat locking lever
42 Rear view mirror
43 Fuel tank sump and gravity feed pipe
44 Centre section root rib
45 Rear spar attachment joint
46 Cockpit side hatches
47 Cockpit bulkhead
48 Windscreen panel
49 Ignition switches
50 Student pilot's instrument panel
51 Throttle lever
52 Fire extinguisher bottle
53 Rear pilot's (student or solo flight) seat
54 Gosport speaking tube
55 Padded facia panel
56 Outline of blind flying hood closed position
57 Seat harness attachment
58 Blind flying hood, folded down
59 Starboard side locker door
60 Stowage locker
61 First aid kit
62 Plywood covered turtle decking
63 Anti-spin strakes
64 Control cable runs
65 Starboard tailplane
66 Starboard fabric covered elevator
67 Tailfin construction
68 Rudder horn balance

The Thruxton Jackaroo was a post-war four-seat cabin conversion of the Tiger Moth undertaken by Jackaroo Aircraft Ltd, starting in 1957, G-AOIR (shown here), being the fourth produced that year. Most were powered by the 145-hp (108-kW) Gipsy Major 1C in place of the more usual 130-hp (97-kW) Gipsy Major I of the Tiger.

the cost of replacement parts was only just over £7! (The cost of a Gipsy Moth, ex-works, was a mere £475.)

The introduction of the inverted Gipsy III in 1931 led to the D.H.60GIII Moth, whose prototype (G-ABUI) first flew in March 1932. This was followed by orders from all over the world. The third production aircraft was fitted with a special high-compression Gipsy IIIA which developed 133 hp (99 kW); flown by Hubert Broad, it finished fifth in the 1932 King's Cup Race at 131.34 mph (211.5 km/h). One long-distance flight by a D.H.60GIII is worthy of mention, that by the Portuguese pilot Carlos Bleck, who flew from Lisbon to Goa (Portuguese India), averaging 105 mph (169 km/h) over the 6,000 miles (9655 km) in February 1934. From the 58th airframe onwards the designation was changed to Moth Major to mark a change to the standard 130-hp (97-kW) Gipsy Major, although externally the aircraft was indistinguishable from the earlier type (the cooling fins of the Major's cylinders tapered inwards towards the crankcase, while those of the Gipsy III did not). Among British sporting owners of Moth Majors was the Duchess of Bedford; at the age of 72 the old lady took off for a solo flight in the G-ACUR over the North Sea on 23 March 1937, but was never seen again.

Last of the classic D.H.60s, and a link between them and the famous Tiger Moth ab initio trainer, was the D.H.60T Moth Trainer of which 63, including two prototypes, were produced, prompted by an order for 10 aircraft for the Swedish air force in 1931. Light training armament (such as camera gun, light reconnaissance camera and practice bombs, etc) were specified, and subsequent batches were supplied to the Egyptian air force, the Brazilian air arms, and Iraq.

Also in 1927 were produced in great secrecy two small monoplanes, designated D.H.71 and intended for high-speed lightplane research. Given the name Tiger Moth (in no way to be confused with the later D.H.82), G-EBQU and G-EBRV were each powered initially by 85-hp (63-kW) A.D.C. Cirrus II engines, but the former was soon re-engined with Major Halford's new 135-hp (101-kW) Gipsy engine. Both were entered for the 1927 King's Cup Race, but one was scratched and the other withdrew from the race having averaged 166 mph (267 km/h). Shortly afterwards, with wings reduced in span from 22 ft 6 in (6.86 m) to 19 ft 0 in (5.79 m), the first aircraft was flown by Broad to establish a world Light-plane Class III speed record over a 62.1-mile (100 km)

69 Fabric covered rudder construction
70 Tail navigation light
71 Rudder operating lever
72 Sternpost
73 Elevator operating lever
74 Elevator construction
75 Tailplane rib construction, fabric covered
76 Sprung tailskid, linked to rudder
77 Tailplane bracing strut
78 Fuselage lower longeron
79 Elevator cables
80 Fuselage fabric covering
81 Primary fuselage structure, square-section tube
82 Rudder cables
83 Port upper wing panel rear spar
84 Inter-spar bracing strut
85 Front spar
86 Wing internal wire bracing
87 Fixed trailing-edge construction
88 Wing tip construction
89 Port navigation light

90 Port automatic leading-edge slat, closed
91 Interplane struts
92 Early type air pressure airspeed indicator
93 Diagonal wire bracing
94 Aileron pulley and operating lever
95 Port aileron construction
96 Rear spar
97 Wing tip construction
98 Main spar
99 Interplane strut attachment joint
100 Leading-edge stiffening ribs
101 Inter-spar bracing strut
102 Lattice rib construction
103 Wing walkway
104 Main undercarriage shock
105 Port mainwheel
106 Pivoted axle strut
107 Drag strut
108 Starboard mainwheel

The light aeroplane that made the greatest impact on sporting aviation throughout the world in the 1920s was the D.H.60 Gipsy Moth, and it was flown in almost every country that supported flying facilities. Shown here with Australian registration, the Gipsy Moth was used by flying clubs at Adelaide, Brisbane, Longreach, Melbourne, Perth and Sydney.

The classic Tiger Moth was licence-built in Canada, New Zealand, Australia, Portugal, Norway and Sweden. The example depicted here was one of 20 D.H.82As produced by AB Svenska Järnvagsverkstaderna, Lindingö, as the Sk 11A for the Flygvapen.

closed circuit at 186.47 mph (300 km/h) on 24 August 1927.

Much closer to the true Moth tradition was the D.H.75 Hawk Moth, a four-seat cabin high-wing monoplane for which a new engine had been developed by Major Halford by inclining two Cirrus Is to mate on a common crankshaft as a V-8. The new engine, the Ghost, provided power of only 198-hp (148 kW), and after the prototype Hawk Moth had flown on 7 December 1928 the first two D.H.75A production aircraft were powered by 240-hp (179-kW) Armstrong Siddeley Lynx geared radials. Only five other aircraft were believed to have been built, of which one, designated D.H.75B, was fitted with a 300-hp (224-kW) Wright Whirlwind R-975 radial.

The next Moth, the D.H.80 Puss Moth, was also a high-wing cabin monoplane, this time a 'club three-seater' with the pilot seated forward of a two-place bench seat. This attractive little aeroplane remained in production for three years from mid-1930 until a total of 350 had been built, of which roughly half were exported. A spate of early accidents (in one of which the famous sporting pilot Bert Hinkler was killed on 7 January 1933) was diagnosed as the result of wing failure following control flutter, cured by mass-balanced ailerons and strengthened wing struts. Jim and Amy Mollison (the latter was Amy Johnson before her marriage) were the outstanding Puss Moth pilots; the former in G-ABXY *The Heart's Content* made the first solo east–west crossing of the North Atlantic on 18–19 August 1932; he also became the first to fly from England to South America, the first to make a solo east–west crossing of the South Atlantic and the first to make crossings of both North and South Atlantic.

Next in line, however, the D.H.82, was to eclipse even the magnificent D.H.60. The D.H.60T Moth Trainer had been in use by the RAF for some years when Air Ministry Specification 15/31 was issued calling for an improved version. Eight pre-production aircraft, using D.H.60 fuselages, were produced, but with the top wing centre-section moved forward and the outer sections swept back 19 in (48.26 cm) at the tips, thereby avoiding large changes in the centre of gravity position; this change in effect created the basis of the famous D.H.82 Tiger Moth. The first 35 production aircraft to Specification T.23/31 for the RAF were designated Tiger Moth Mk Is and entered service with the CFS and FTS, followed by two float-equipped aircraft to Specification T.6/33, but large-scale production started at Stag Lane early in 1934 with the issue of T.26/33, only to be switched to de

Havilland's new factory at Hatfield later in that year. Known in the RAF as the Tiger Moth Mk II, the new version departed from the Moth's traditional use of fabric and stringers behind the cockpits in favour of plywood decking, as well as provision for a blind-flying hood over the rear cockpit. Further contracts as well as Specification T.7/35 were received in 1935, so that pre-war production amounted to 1,150 at Hatfield, 227 by the de Havilland factory at Toronto, one by de Havilland at Wellington, New Zealand, and three by the DH Technical School. The vast majority had entered RAF service, but many had also gone to foreign owners and air forces as well as British flying clubs. On the outbreak of war most of the civil aircraft in the UK were impressed, the civilian schools providing the aircraft for the service's Elementary Flying Training Schools. In 1941 production of the de Havilland Mosquito at Hatfield forced the company to move Tiger Moth production to Morris Motors at Cowley, Oxford, where a total of 3,216 examples was produced before manufacture ended on 15 August 1945. Many of these Tiger Moths were shipped overseas where they provided the ab initio flying equipment of the schools that constituted the great Empire and Commonwealth Air Training Plan. Indeed, there were precious few wartime RAF pilots whose first experience of flight was not in the cockpit of a 'Tiger'.

After the war surplus Tiger Moths flooded into the civil market, while others continued to serve in the RAF for a number of years until replaced by the Percival Prentice and de Havilland Chipmunk.

Exuding nostalgia for RAF pilots of a former generation, this photo shows a de Havilland-built Tiger Moth being flown solo in 1941. So sensitive was the little trainer that it was possible to induce yaw simply by putting one's hand out into the slipstream as if to signal one's intention to turn!

Junkers Ju 52

For all its seemingly archaic appearance, with fixed landing gear, angular lines and corrugated skin, the classic Junkers Ju 52/3m represented the common denominator of every land operation by Germany's Wehrmacht, whether in advance or retreat. 'Tante Ju' was indeed the German counterpart of America's Douglas C-46 Skytrain.

Towards the end of the 1920s, the German Lufthansa was widely regarded as the most efficient airline in the world, while other aviation companies were having problems keeping their heads above water in the major economic crisis that was occurring at the time. The company offered convenient flights throughout Europe with its large fleet of aircraft, mostly consisting of developments of the all-metal monoplane built by Professor Hugo Junkers in 1915, the J 1.

The great majority of these early aircraft (the J 10, F 13, A 20, F 24, W 33, W 34, Ju 46 and Ju 52) were single-engined low-wing monoplanes, but in 1924 there appeared a three-engine airliner, the G 23, powered by a 195-hp (145-kW) Junkers L 2 and two 100-hp (75-kW) Mercedes engines. It is thought that, as a result of Versailles Treaty restrictions imposed on German aircraft manufacture, this prototype was produced at Junkers' Fili factory near Moscow; production of about nine aircraft (as well as that of the much more numerous G 24) was subsequently undertaken in Sweden. The G 24, usually powered by three 280/310-hp (209/231-kW) Junkers L 5 inline engines, served in numerous con-

This Ju52, designated C-352-L, was built by CASA in Spain with BMW 132 radial engines produced under licence.

figurations and with a number of airlines, including Lufthansa which retained them in service until 1933–4.

The year 1926 was busy for the Junkers concern, two new designs (the G 31 tri-motor transport and the W 33/34) being the most important to fly. The former was a beefier version of the successful G 24, and the latter an excellent single-engine transport which was built in large numbers. Almost at once the Junkers designers embarked on a new, but considerably enlarged single-engine transport, the Ju 52, which embodied the cumulative experience of earlier designs and was primarily intended for freight carrying. Like its predecessors it was of standard Junkers all-metal construction with corrugated, load-sustaining duralumin skinning, and featured the patented Junkers full-span double wing. Five aircraft were built, of which four underwent development with various powerplants in Germany and one (CF-ARM) went to Canada. The first aircraft flew on 13 October 1930.

Despite its single engine (usually of around 780-825 hp/582–615 kW) the Ju 52 was able to carry 15–17 passengers when required. However the following year the Junkers design team, under Dipl. Ing. Ernst Zindel, undertook work to adapt the Ju 52 to feature three 525-hp (392-kW) Pratt & Whitney Hornet nine-cylinder radials, and the prototype of

The 18-seat Ju 52/3mg7e, shown here, was a major production variant and featured automatic pilot and wide cabin doors. Subsequent versions had the wheel fairings removed, as sand and mud tended to clog the wheels.

Three Junkers Ju 52/3mg6e mine clearance aircraft of the Minensuchgruppe, probably over the Mediterranean; the rudder markings are said to have denoted the number of minesweeping sorties flown – a somewhat hazardous task.

this version, the Ju 52/3m (*Dreimotoren*, or three-motor), made its maiden flight in April 1932. Subsequent deliveries were made to Finland, Sweden and Brazil, as well as to Deutsche Lufthansa. Ultimately Ju 52/3ms flew with airlines in Argentina, Austria, Australia, Belgium, Bolivia, China, Colombia, Czechoslovakia, Denmark, Ecuador, Estonia, France, Great Britain, Greece, Hungary, Italy, Lebanon, Mozambique, Norway, Peru, Poland, Portugal, Romania, South Africa, Spain, Switzerland, Turkey and Uruguay. Powerplants included Hispano-Suiza, BMW, Junkers Jumo, Bristol Pegasus, Pratt & Whitney Hornet and Wasp engines. Commercial Ju 52/3ms delivered to Bolivia were employed as military transports towards the end of the Gran Chaco war of 1932–5.

Starting late in 1932, Ju 52/3ms were delivered to Lufthansa, with D-2201 *Boelcke* and D-2202 *Richthofen* inaugurating the airline's Berlin–London and Berlin–Rome services before the end of that year. In due course no fewer than 230 Ju 52/3ms were registered with Deutsche Lufthansa, continuing to fly commercial services to Spain, Portugal, Sweden, Switzerland and Turkey almost to the end of World War 2.

Despite the stringencies of treaty restrictions imposed on Germany since 1919, clandestine adventures had continued by which potential military personnel had undergone training in foreign lands, particularly the USSR. Thus when, following her walk-out from the disarmament talks in 1932, Germany set about the covert establishment of a military air force, it fell to such aircraft as the Ju 52/3m to provide the basis of its flying equipment, and in 1934 the first military version, the Ju 52/3mg3e, appeared.

The Ju 52/3mg3e was an attempt to produce a bomber version quickly and without unduly interrupting the highly profitable commercial production line. Powered by three 525-hp (392-kW) BMW 132A-3 radials, this version normally carried a bomb load of 600 kg (1,321 lb), comprising six 100-kg (220-lb) bombs, and featured a dorsal gun position and a ventral 'dustbin', each mounting a single 7.92-mm (0.31-in) MG 15 machine-gun. Deliveries of the Ju 52/3mg3e to the new Luftwaffe totalled 450 in 1934–5, the first unit thus equipped being Kampfgeschwader 152 'Hindenburg'. In 1937 this Geschwader's IV Gruppe was re-designated KGrzbV1; this designation (*Kampfgruppe zur besonderen Verwendung*, or bomber group for special operations) was roughly comparable to the RAF's 'bomber transport' category, and was intended to reflect a dual role, bombing and military transport duties. It thereby perpetuated the originally intended function of the Ju 52/3m. In the event Ju 52/3m-equipped KGrzbV seldom if ever during World War 2 engaged in bombing operations.

When, on 18 July 1936, the Spanish Civil War broke out and Germany quickly aligned herself with the right-wing Nationalists, 20 Ju 52/3ms and six Heinkel He 51s were sent

to Spain, being assembled into the Legion Cóndor under General Hugo Sperrle during the following November. And it was as transports that the Junkers were initially employed, bringing 10,000 Moorish troops to Spain from Morocco. Thereafter they were developed in three bomber *Staffeln* of Kampfgruppe 88, and were flown in raids on the Republican-held Mediterranean ports and in support of the land battle for Madrid. By mid-1937 they were deemed to be poor bombers and were largely replaced by such aircraft as the Dornier Do 17 and Heinkel He 111. Nevertheless the Ju 52/3m3ge continued to serve both as a bomber and a tran-

Junkers Ju 52/3mge cutaway drawing key

1 Starboard navigation light
2 Drooping aileron section of Junkers 'double wing'
3 Aileron hinge fairings
4 Control linkage
5 Underwing inspection panels
6 Corrugated wing skin
7 Aerial mast
8 Wing strut diagonal bracing
9 Starboard oil filler cap
10 House-flag mast
11 Starboard engine cowling (NACA cowling)
12 Junkers metal two-blade propeller
13 Centre BMW 132A radial engine (in Townend ring)
14 Exhaust
15 Filter intakes
16 Engine bearers
17 Bulkhead
18 Centre oil tank
19 Oil filler cap
20 Flat windscreen panels
21 Co-pilot's seat
22 Radio-operator's jump-seat
23 Pilot's seat
24 Control column
25 Rudder pedals
26 Raised cockpit floor level

Equipped with large dural hoops below the fuselage, Ju 52/3mg6e aircraft of the Minensuchgruppe were flown over coastal waters round Europe in attempts to render Allied minelaying harmless. The aircraft shown, 3K+IB, belonged to the Gruppenstab and operated from Malmi over the Gulf of Finland during the winter of 1943–4.

A Ju 52/3mg7e (1Z+NA) of Stab IV/TG 1 (previously KGzbV 1) on the Courland Front during the last winter of the war; by then the Luftwaffe's transports were mainly engaged in parachuting supplies to beleaguered Wehrmacht units.

27 Control linkage
28 Control lines
29 Port BMW 132A radial engine (in NACA cowling)
30 Bulkhead
31 Engine bearers
32 Engine oil tank
33 Oil filler cap
34 Fuel filler cap
35 Mainwheel support strut
36 Mainwheel spat
37 Exhaust
38 Port mainwheel
39 Corrugated wing skin
40 Multi-spar wing structure
41 Diagonal cross-brace members
42 Pitot head
43 Port navigation light
44 Drooping aileron section of Junkers 'double wing'
45 Aileron hinge fairings
46 Trim tab
47 Tab control
48 Control runs
49 Inner section trailing-edge flap
50 Control linkage
51 Port wing fuel tanks
52 Fuselage/wing ball-and-socket attachment points
53 Centre aisle
54 Single-seat cabin arrangement (17 maximum)
55 Upper fuselage longeron
56 Luggage rack
57 Ceiling lights
58 Aerial
59 Two-seat rear bench
60 Passenger entry door
61 Underfloor control lines
62 Entry vestibule
63 Entry steps attachment
64 Toilet compartment
65 Rear cabin bulkhead
66 Cabin ventilation
67 Cargo compartment
68 Luggage loading hatch
69 Baggage shelves
70 Aft fuselage frames
71 Inspection walkway
72 Lower fuselage longeron
73 Fuselage construction
74 Control lines
75 Rear fuselage frame
76 Fin/fuselage attachment
77 Tailskid spring
78 Tailskid
79 Port tailplane structure
80 Port elevator
81 Lower rudder hinge
82 Control linkage
83 Multi-spar tailplane construction
84 Elevator corrugated skin
85 Fin construction
86 Rudder control linkage
87 Rudder post
88 Rudder structure
89 Corrugated skin
90 Rear navigation light

Junkers Ju 52

Specification

Junkers Ju 52/3mg7e
Type: 18-seat military transport
Powerplant: three 830-hp (619-kW) BMW
132T-2 nine-cylinder air-cooled radial
engines
Performance: 183 mph (295 km/h) at sea
level; initial climb rate 680 ft (208 m) per
minute; service ceiling 18,045 ft (5500 m);
range 802 miles (1290 km)
Weights: empty 14,462 lb (6560 kg);
maximum take-off 23,180 lb (10515 kg)
Dimensions: span 95 ft 11½ in (29.25 m);
length 62 ft 0 in (18.90 m); height 14 ft 9 in
(4.50 m); wing area 1,189.45 sq ft (110.50 m²)
Armament: (typical) one 7.92-mm (0.31-in)
MG 15 machine-gun in dorsal position
and two 7.92-mm (0.31-in) machine-guns
mounted to fire abeam through side windows

A Junkers Ju 52/3mg7e of 2.Staffel, KGzbV 1, based at Milos, Greece, in May 1941 prior to the invasion of Crete. Under the command of Generalmajor Gerhard a fleet of 493 Ju 52/3ms was assembled for the landings, known as Operation 'Mercury', but owing to confusion over the island during the initial assault subsequent waves of transports were delayed and the element of concentration was lost; of every four paratroopers dropped, one was killed or wounded. By the end of the operation more than 170 Ju 52/3ms had been lost or seriously damaged.

33

One of the first tasks of the German air force contingent in Spain was to lift 10,000 Moroccan troops from North Africa to the war zone. The aircraft shown, a Ju 52/3mg3e, is depicted in the markings of the Legion Cóndor's Kampfgruppe 88 late in 1936.

sport with German and Spanish Nationalist forces until the end of the Civil War.

To war in earnest

Operations from Germany's poorly surfaced military airfields had resulted in 1935 in the introduction of the Ju 52/3mg4e with tailwheel in place of tailskid, and by 1938 this version was being standardized among the KGrzbV. In March that year, at the time of the Austrian *Anschluss*, German troops were carried forward by KGrzbV 1 and 2 in a massive show of strength, the former based at Fürstenwalde with 54 aircraft, and the latter at Brandenburg-Briest.

By the time Germany was ready to crush Poland the Luftwaffe's *Transportverband* possessed an inventory of 552 aircraft, of which 547 were Ju 52/3mg3e and Ju 52/3mg4e aircraft (the balance being two obsolete He 111 transports, a Junkers G 38, a Ju 90 and a Focke-Wolf Fw 200). Losses in the month-long campaign of September amounted to 59 Junkers Ju 52/3ms, all but two to ground fire or flying accidents. In the course of 2,460 flights the aircraft carried 19,700 troops and 1,600 tons of supplies.

In the relatively swift and clinically organized invasion of Norway in the following year, the number of Ju 52/3ms available had risen to 573, equipping all four *Gruppen* of KGzbV 1, and KGrzbV 101, 102, 103, 104, 105, 106 and 107, an average of 52 aircraft in each *Gruppe*. A small number of twin float-equipped Ju 52/3m Wasser aircraft was also employed in the Norwegian campaign, alighting in the fjords to disembark troops, engineers and supplies. A new version, the Ju 52mg5e, with provision for alternative wheel, float or ski landing gear had been introduced, powered by three 830-hp (619-kW) BMW 132T-2 engines.

Among the important operations undertaken by the Junkers in Norway were the capture by airborne forces of Stavanger-Sola airport and of the Vordingborg bridge. A total of 29,000

First Junkers Ju 52/3mge to serve with Deutsche Lufthansa was this aircraft, D–2201 (c/n 4013), in May 1932, named *Boelcke* after the World War 1 fighter pilot. Early aircraft flew the Berlin–London and Berlin–Rome services.

men, 259,300 Imp gal (1,180,000 litres) of aviation fuel and 2,376 tons of supplies were airlifted during the campaign, for the significant loss of 150 aircraft.

However, before the conclusion of the Norwegian campaign, the majority of Ju 52/3ms were being withdrawn back to Germany in preparation for Operation 'Yellow', the great assault in the West. As a result of losses in Norway the number of Junkers available was only 475, to which was now added 45 DFS 230 assault gliders, the whole transport force being commanded by General Putzier. Because of the need to conserve the Ju 52/3ms for a likely air assault on the UK, the Luftwaffe's transports were largely confined to airborne attacks in the initial stage, and it was against the Netherlands and Belgium that most of these were launched, in particular on the Moerdijk bridges and on Rotterdam's Waalhaven airport. Large numbers of Ju 52/3ms were employed in each attack and losses, mainly from anti-aircraft gunfire, were extremely heavy; in the five days that it took the Wehrmacht to crush the Netherlands, no fewer than 167 Junkers were totally destroyed, and a similar number badly damaged.

By the end of 1940 a total of 1,275 Ju 52/3ms had been delivered to the Luftwaffe, of which some 700 aircraft had already been struck off charge for one reason or another. After the collapse of France no further major operations involving the use of Ju 52/3ms were launched until the advance by German forces through the Balkans in April 1941. By then a number of new versions had appeared, namely the Ju 52/3mg6e, which was similar to the Ju 52/3mg5e but equipped with improved radio and the Ju 52/3mg7e with automatic pilot, accommodation for up to 18 troops and wider cabin doors; it also featured provision for two 7.92-mm (0.31-in) machine-guns to fire through the cabin windows. Operations in the Balkans and Aegean also saw the first operations by the *Minensuchgruppe* (minesweeping group), equipped with the Ju 52/3mg6e fitted with large dural hoops energized by an auxiliary motor to explode Allied mines sown in abandoned harbours.

Despite its ultimate capture, Crete proved a disaster for the *Transportverband*. Assigned to the task of an airborne invasion of the island, the 493 Ju 52/3ms and about 80 DFS 230 gliders were intended to attack in three waves. However, as a result of confusion on the ground caused by dense clouds of

South African Airways flew a total of 15 Ju 52/3ms, of which the first, ZS-AFA *Jan Van Riebeeck* is seen here. Nine aircraft were handed on to the South African Air Force, these being employed on a transport shuttle between South Africa, Egypt and Italy.

Since April 1986, this Junkers Ju-52 has been flying for Lufthansa again, exactly 50 years after it was first brought into service by the same airline with the registration D-AQUI. Later it was used in Norway and the USA before returning to Germany to be restored. (Photo: Lufthansa, with the consent of Senat. Bremen, No. MBB 86-0402/32)

Junkers Ju 52

As well as serving with the German Legion Cóndor, Ju 52/3ms were supplied to the Spanish Nationalist forces, this 3mg4e bearing the markings of the Grupo de Bombardeo Nocturno 1-G-22 early in 1938. In Spanish service the Ju 52/3m was nicknamed *Pava* (turkey), its last bombing sortie being against Belmez on 26 March 1939.

dust, there were numerous collisions and delays, so that what had been planned as an attack concentrated in time and area degenerated into widespread confusion and dissipated effort. German causualties were more than 7,000 men (of whom about 2,000 were paratroops) and 174 Ju 52/3ms, representing more than a third of the Luftwaffe's available transport force.

It has often been averred that the Balkan campaign was a lost cause for the Allies, yet the heavy losses inflicted on this vital enemy assault arm proved of immense importance when Germany launched Operation 'Barbarossa' less than two months later, and henceforth (apart from isolated instances of commando-type operations) the use of air transport was confined within the Luftwaffe to logistic supply and evacuation. Indeed, on the opening day of 'Barbarossa' the Luftwaffe could field no more than 238 serviceable Ju 52/3ms, a far cry from the numbers available in 1939 and 1940.

The nature of warfare on the Eastern Front quickly determined the role to be played by the Ju 52/3m, with scorched earth tactics employed by the retreating Russians demanding considerable dependence by the Wehrmacht on air supplies. Production of the Ju 52/3m increased to 502 in 1941, 503 in 1942 and 887 in 1943. New versions continued to appear; the Ju 52/3mg8e dispensed with the wheel spats (found to be a hindrance in the quagmire conditions on the Eastern Front), but included a 0.51-in (13-mm) MG 131 gun in the dorsal position, while some aircraft had 850-hp (634-kW) BMW 132Z engines; the Ju 52/3mg9e, which appeared in 1942, featured strengthened landing gear to permit a take-off weight of 25,353 lb (11500 kg) and was equipped to tow the Gotha Go 242 glider; the Ju 52/3mg10e was a naval version with provision for floats, and the Ju 52/3mg12e had 800-hp (597-kW) BMW 132L engines. Only one other version reached the Luftwaffe (late in 1943), namely the Ju 52/3mg14e with an MG 15 machine-gun mounted in a streamlined position over the pilot's cabin.

It may be said of the Ju 52/3m that its star shone brightest in adversity from 1942 onwards. When in February that year six German divisions were trapped at Demyansk, the Luftwaffe performed the prodigious task of sustaining 100,000 troops, and in three months delivered 24,300 tons of material, airlifted 15,446 men into the pocket and evacuated 20,093 casualties: the cost of this effort was a loss of 385 flying personnel (including Major Walter Hammer, commanding KGrzbV 172) and 262 aircraft. Far greater disasters befell the German armies at Stalingrad and in North Africa, and in a single raid on Sverevo in the dreadful winter of 1942–3 52 Junkers were destroyed by Russian bombers. In the final attempts to succour (and eventually to evacuate) the Axis armies in Tunisia in April 1943 the Luftwaffe lost 432 transport aircraft, almost all of them JU 52/3ms, in less than three weeks.

The story of 'Tante Ju' did not end on VE-Day, when fewer than 50 such aircraft remained airworthy of the 4,835 said to have been built in Germany. The principal post-war operator of the aircraft was France where Ateliers Aéronautiques de Colombes produced more than 400 examples of a version known as the AAC1 Toucan; apart from 85 which flew post-war services for Air France, others were operated by Aéro-

A ground view of a Ju 52/3mg4e showing the ventral gun position retracted; this version differed from the Ju 52/3mg3e in having a tailwheel in place of a skid. The photo emphasizes the characteristic corrugated skinning, a feature that, although ridiculed, bestowed considerable strength with lightness on the airframe.

Cargo, Air Atlas, Aigle Azur, Air Nolis, Air Ocean, TAI and many other airlines. The Toucan served with the Armée de l'Air and Aéronavale, and was used in fairly large numbers in the Algerian and Indo-China wars. In Spain CASA produced 170 aircraft, known as the C-352-L, with licence-built BMW 132 radials. Ten aircraft were reconditioned by Short Bros and Harland at Belfast, and entered service with British European Airways as G-AHOC to G-AHOL on 18 November 1946 on the Croydon–Liverpool–Belfast service. In Switzerland three Ju 52/3mg4e transports which were originally delivered to the Swiss Fliegertruppe on 4 October 1939 were still flying in the early 1980s.

In common with most of Germany's successful wartime aircraft, the Ju 52/3m underwent extensive development, resulting in the appearance of the Ju 252 and Ju 352. The former, whose prototype first flew in October 1941, was a larger aircraft than the Ju 52/3m, powered by three 1,340-hp (1000-kW) Junkers Jumo 211F liquid-cooled engines in annular cowlings, and had accommodation for 21 passengers in a pressurized cabin; the corrugated skinning was dispensed with. Originally it was intended to produce 25 aircraft for Lufthansa, but in view of the deteriorating war situation the order was reduced to 15, and all were delivered to the Luftwaffe. Some Ju 252As served with Lufttransportstaffel 290 (later redesignated Transportstaffel 5).

A quartet of early Ju 52/3mg3es bearing pre-war Luftwaffe markings; note the extended and awesomely situated ventral 'dustbin' gun positions and tailskids. The ventral gunner was protected from the slipstream by a fairing in which very exposed steps were incorporated to allow entry to the fuselage while the aircraft was airborne.

Douglas DC-3/C-47/Dakota: world workhorses

The Douglas C-47 and its numerous derivatives has for nearly half a century remained the most versatile workhorse aviation has known. Born in the brassy years of the American mid-1930s as the Douglas DC-3, it became the standard pre-war airliner, went to war in uniform the world over, and returned to civilian clothes afterwards.

In the middle of 1935 C. R. Smith, then President of American Airlines, ordered a larger and more luxurious version of the DC-2 from Douglas, so as to gain the upper hand over competing companies with their Boeing 247s and DC-2s.

The project leader at Douglas, Fred Stineman, had his team design a new type of aircraft known as the Douglas Sleeper Transport, with 14 sleeping berths. Soon, however, it was realised that if 21 seats were installed instead, and a pair of

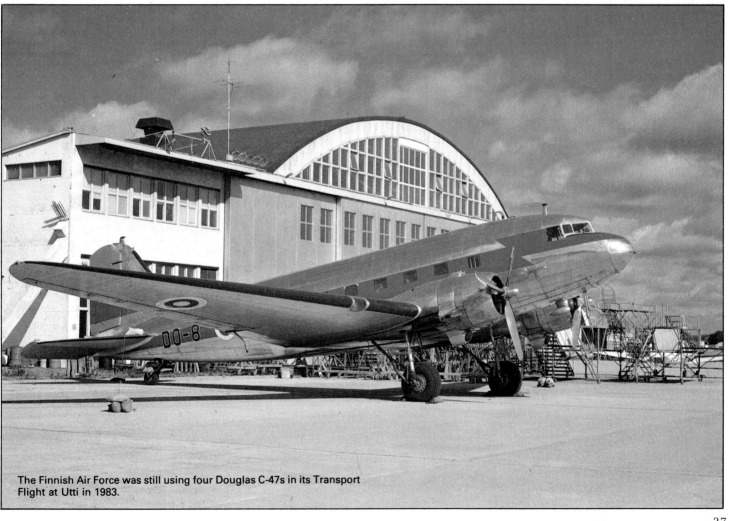

The Finnish Air Force was still using four Douglas C-47s in its Transport Flight at Utti in 1983.

Douglas C-47 Skytrain

Specification

Douglas C-47 Skytrain

Type: cargo, supply or 21/28-seat troop transport, 14-litter ambulance, or glider tug

Powerplant: two 1,200-hp (895-kW) Pratt & Whitney R-1830-92 radial piston engines

Performance: maximum speed 227 mph (365 km/h) at 7,500 ft (2285 m); initial climb rate 940 ft (287 m) per minute; service ceiling 24,000 ft (7315 m); range 1,600 miles (2575 km)

Weights: empty 18,200 lb (8256 kg); maximum take-off 26,000 lb (11794 kg)

Dimensions: span 95 ft 6 in (29.11 m); length 63 ft 9 in (19.43 m); height 17 ft 0 in (5.18 m); wing area 987 sq ft (91.69 m²)

Payload: 8,000 lb (3629 kg) to 10,000 lb (4536 kg) of military cargo (depending on aircraft variant)

General Eisenhower is on record as having stated that the C-47 was one of the four principal instruments of Allied victory in World War 2 (the others being the bazooka, Jeep and atom bomb). Typical example of the Skytrain was this C-47A-65-DL of the 81st Troop Carrier Squadron, 436th Troop Carrier Group, based at Membury in England between 3 March 1944 and February 1945 (it also took part in the airborne assault on Southern France, based at Voltone, Italy, during July and August 1944). The mission tally on 'Buzz Buggy', together with invasion stripes, suggest participation in the Normandy, South France, Nijmegen and Bastogne operations, both as a paratrooper and glider tug.

One of the 98 US Navy R4D-8s, modified to 'Super DC-3' standard with swept wings, lengthened fuselage, enlarged tail and fully enclosed undercarriage. Redesignated the C-117D, this version had a top speed of 270 mph (435 km/h).

The RCAF contributed three Article VI transport squadrons with Dakotas (Nos 435, 436 and 437) to the RAF during World War 2, the first two in the Far East and No. 437 in Europe. Shown here is an RCAF Dakota used for training pilots in airborne forces duties.

Wright Cyclone 900 hp (671 kW) engines installed, the increased payload could increase their income by 50% more than the DC-2, with fuel costs rising by only 3%. At 3 p.m. on 17 December 1935, the 32nd anniversary of the Wright Brothers' first flight, the prototype, X14988, set off on its maiden flight from Clover Field (now Santa Monica). It was piloted by Carl A. Cover and still designated DST (Douglas Sleeper Transport).

The prototype entered service as American Airlines' flagship on 11 July 1936 as orders poured in to Douglas. By the end of 1939 the DC-3 (third Douglas Commercial) had joined Braniff, Eastern, Northwest, Pennsylvania-Central, Transcontinental & Western, and United, as well as American in the United States, while overseas KLM was the first to take deliveries, followed by Panagra, Panair do Brasil, LAV, CMA, Australian National, Sweden's ABA, Czechoslovakia's CLS, Swissair, Air France, Sabena, LOT, LARES, and MALERT. Licences to build were negotiated with Nakajima in Japan (the first aircraft being completed on 30 September 1938), and with the Soviet Union, which purchased 18 DC-3s before World War 2 and went on to produce huge numbers which served with Aeroflot and the military, first as the PS-84 and later as the Lisunov Li-2.

When war broke out in Europe most of the commercial airlines reduced their operations and in due course many of the DC-3s of subjugated nations found themselves serving with Lufthansa, while others were seized by the Italians.

The single Douglas XC-47C (42-5671) of 1943 had Edo amphibious floats, each incorporating two retractable landing wheels and a 300-US gal (1136-litre) fuel tank.

Douglas C-47 Dakota IV cutaway drawing key

1 Hinged nose cone access to instruments and controls
2 Rudder pedals
3 Instrument panel
4 Windscreen de-icing fluid spray nozzle
5 Starboard propeller
6 Windscreen panels
7 Co-pilot's seat
8 Engine throttles
9 Control column
10 Cockpit floor level
11 Access panels to control cable runs
12 Pitot static tubes
13 Aerial cables
14 Propeller de-icing fluid tank
15 Pilot's seat
16 Cockpit bulkhead
17 Cockpit roof escape hatch
18 Whip aerial
19 Starboard landing/taxiing lamp
20 Windscreen de-icing fluid tank
21 Starboard baggage compartment
22 Electrical fuse panel
23 Crew entry door
24 ADF loop aerial housing
25 Life raft stowage
26 Port baggage compartment
27 Main cabin bulkhead
28 Radio operator's seat
29 Air scoop
30 Heating and ventilating system heat exchanges
31 Astrodome observation hatch

The Argentine air force and navy operate helicopters and fixed wing aircraft in support of that nation's bases in Antarctica, and ski-equipped C-47 of the 1st Escuadron Antartico, Fuerza Aerea Argentina, based at Marambio.

Pending the arrival in service of the two-seat TF-104G Starfighter trainers, the Force Aérienne Belge flew the C-47 with a specially modified nose to accommodate the NASRR radar of the F-104G single-seater to provide an air experience vehicle.

32 Starboard outer wing panel
33 Pneumatic leading-edge de-icing boot
34 Starboard navigation light
35 Starboard aileron
36 Aileron cable controls
37 Trim tab
38 Trim tab control gear
39 Flap control shaft
40 Starboard outer flap
41 Fuselage frame and stringer construction
42 Centre fuselage main frames
43 Centre wing section corrugated inner skin
44 Port main fuel tank, capacity 201 US gal (794 litres)
45 Port auxiliary fuel tank, capacity 210 US gal (760 litres)

46 Wing spar attachments
47 Flap hydraulic jack
48 Centre section flap
49 Floor beam construction
50 Cabin window panels
51 Window panel grommets for small arms attachments
52 Paratroop seating, 28-paratroops
53 Starboard emergency exit window
54 Port emergency exit window
55 Cabin lining panels

56 Overhead heating and ventilating duct
57 Rear cabin frames
58 Fuselage skin plating
59 Rear cabin bulkhead
60 First aid kit
61 Access door to tail controls
62 Fin root fillet
63 Starboard tailplane

64 Starboard elevator
65 Fin leading-edge pneumatic de-icing boot
66 Fin construction
67 Aerial cables
68 Rudder aerodynamic balance
69 Hinge post
70 Rudder construction
71 Fabric covering
72 Rudder trim tab

73 Trim tab control gear
74 Rudder and elevator control horns
75 Fuselage tail fairing
76 Elevator trim tab
77 Port elevator construction
78 Fabric covered elevator
79 Leading-edge pneumatic de-icing boot
80 Tailplane construction
81 Tailplane attachment joint
82 Rudder stop cables
83 Tailplane centre section
84 Tailwheel
85 Shock absorber leg strut
86 Tailwheel mounting plate
87 Tailwheel strut
88 Rudder and elevator control cables
89 Tail fuselage joint frame
90 Toilet

91 Rear freight door
92 Forward freight door
93 Paratroop/passenger door
94 Fuselage stringer construction
95 Freight floor
96 Wing root trailing-edge fillet
97 Inboard split trailing-edge flap
98 Flap shroud construction
99 Fuel filler caps
100 Outer wing panel bolted joint
101 Wing panel joint capping strip
102 Outer split trailing-edge flap
103 Port aileron
104 Aileron fabric covering
105 Detachable wing tip joint rib
106 Port navigation light
107 Leading-edge pneumatic de-icing boot
108 Wing stringer construction
109 Rear spar
110 Centre spar
111 Wing rib construction
112 Front spar
113 Leading-edge nose ribs

114 Leading-edge stringers
115 Port landing/taxiing lamp
116 Port mainwheel
117 Main undercarriage rear strut
118 Shock absorber leg strugs
119 Undercarriage knee joints
120 Exhaust pipe
121 Undercarriage bungee cables
122 Engine nacelle fairing
123 Oil tank capacity 29¼ US gal (109 litres)
124 Undercarriage retraction jack
125 Mainwheel well
126 Engine fireproof bulkhead
127 Engine bearer struts
128 Oil cooler
129 Cooling air exit flaps
130 Exhaust collector pipe
131 Engine air intake
132 Engine cowlings
133 Pratt & Whitney R-1830-90C air-cooled 14-cylinder two-row radial engine
134 Propeller hub pitch change mechanism
135 Hamilton Standard constant speed three-bladed propeller

41

Douglas DC-3, C-47

A Douglas Dakota III of No. 24 Squadron, RAF. The squadron was strictly speaking a communications unit, based at Hendon during World War 2, and flew Dakotas on mail and VIP services to Malta from 1943 onwards.

Douglas C-47 of the small Arkia Israel Inland Airlines Ltd, shown carrying military recognition markings at the time of the Israeli-Egyptian conflict of 1956 (the Suez Crisis).

In the USA, however, Air Transport Command had, between the wars, grown into a sizeable military carrier, albeit to a great extent employing aircraft leased from commercial operators. Indeed it was not until September 1940 that transport aircraft featured significantly in the procurement programme. At this time an order was placed for 545 DC-3s, to be designated C-47 Skytrain. None of these had been delivered at the time of Pearl Harbor when the total transport inventory consisted of about 50 Douglas C-32s, Douglas C-33s and Douglas C-39s – all military versions of the DC-2. By the end of 1941 military orders had been increased by 70 C-47s and nearly 100 C-53s – the US Army's passenger version. In the meantime the USAAC had established the 50th Transport Wing (on 8 January 1941) to administer all transport duties, this being followed by the 51st, 52nd and 53rd in 1942, the 54th, 60th and 61st in 1943, and the 322nd in 1944. Together these Wings comprised a peak total of 32 Groups, in turn comprising over 190 transport squadrons during the war.

The military C-47 differed from the DC-3 principally in its stronger cabin floor and rear fuselage, large loading doors and 1,200-hp (895-kW) Pratt & Whitney R-1830-92 engines. Utility bucket seats along the cabin walls replaced the airline type, window grommets were inserted to permit the use of small-arms in combat, and the all-up weight increased from 25,000 lb (11340 kg) to 29,300 lb (13290 kg).

Production of the C-47 was undertaken at a new plant at Long Beach, California, a total of 953 being completed before production switched to the C-47A, which differed principally in having a 24-volt electrical system in place of the previous 12-volt system. Long Beach could not cope with the quickly increasing military orders, however, and in 1942 a Douglas-operated plant at Tulsa, Oklahoma, joined the programme, producing 2,099 C-47s while Long Beach completed 2,832. The third major production version was the C-47B, characterized by R-1830-90 or Dash-90B engines with superchargers and extra fuel (originally intended specifically for flight over the 'Hump' in the China-Burma-India theatre); of this variant Long Beach built 300 and Tulsa, 2,808, plus 133 TC-47B trainers with Dash-90C engines. Almost all the 600-odd US Navy R4D Skytrain and Skytrooper transports procured during the war were diverted from US Army contracts, and acquired sub-designations under the overall designation R4D.

In service the C-47 went wherever Allied troops served, being among the first to cross to the UK after the USA's entry to the war. In 1942 Troop Carrier Command was formed to provide mobility for airborne forces, and as a result the C-47

assumed the roles of paratroop transport and glider tug. In the first major Allied airborne assault, the invasion of Sicily in July 1943, C-47s (with a handful of other aircraft types) dropped 4,381 paratroops; in the massive assault on Normandy in June the following year C-47s carried more than 50,000 airborne troops in the first 50 hours.

In the RAF the C-47 and its derivatives were named Dakota (the choice of name being alliterative rather than geographically significant), the Dakota I corresponding to the C-47, the Dakota II to the C-53, the Dakota III to the C-47A and the Dakota IV to the C-47B. Some 1,895 aircraft served with 25 RAF squadrons, first joining No. 31 Squadron on the Burma front in June 1942. It remained with that service until 1950, when it was replaced by the Vickers Valetta.

As transport demands increased, so variations of the basic C-47 proliferated. A float-equipped amphibian, the XC-47C (42-5671) was produced with twin Edo floats each accommodating two retractable wheels and a 300-US gal (1136-litre) fuel tank. The impressed DC-3s were all accorded distinct US Army designations to distinguish between those equipped as 21-seat or 14-berth aircraft, variations in sub-type of Twin Wasp or Cyclone engines, entry and loading door configuration (some had doors on the starboard side of the fuselage), and all-up weight limitations. Most of these ex-airliners were retained for staff transport purposes so as to avoid maintenance and operating complications on the operational squadrons. The ex-DC-3s were designated C-48 to C-52 (with many sub-variants), while the C-53 Skytrooper included not only 193 impressed DC-3s but also many new-built aircraft to airliner standard. The two C-68s were late model DC-3s impressed in 1942, but the four C-84s were early 28-seat DC-3Bs with Wright R-1820-71 engines. The C-117 was a Tulsa-built VIP transport version with 28 seats in an airliner-style cabin; only 17 were completed of a contract for 131 (the remainder being cancelled after VJ-day), some of them having their superchargers removed and being given the designation C-117B. Eleven VC-47 staff transports were restyled C-117Cs, and as late as 1962 were serving as VC-117As and VC-117Bs. Finally there was a strange experiment involving the conversion of a C-47 (41-18496) to a glider, the XCG-17, in an attempt to produce a suitable vehicle for towing behind a C-54 Skymaster.

After the war many Skytrains and Skytroopers were declared surplus and sold to civil operators at home and abroad. The superchargers were removed from the C-47Bs, these aircraft becoming C-47Ds, service staff transports being designated VC-47As and VC-47Ds. When the Military Air Transport Service (MATS) was formed on 1 June 1948, 248

This Douglas C-47 Dakota is still in use, over 50 years after the first flight by this sturdy aircraft type, flying between Antigua and neighbouring islands for Seagreen Air Transport.

Douglas DC-3, C-47

Douglas DC-3 of SMB Stage Lines, USA. The DC-3 played an important part in developing a network of national air routes in America during the pre-war period from 1936–41 when air transport increased by 600 per cent, much of it carried in the ubiquitous DC-3s that then dominated airline fleets.

One of the most recent developments in the DC-3 story is the re-engineering of existing airframes with three Pratt & Whitney PT6A-45 turboprops giving improved performance in high altitude/high temperature conditions. But despite these enhancements few significant sales have been made. It is known as the Conroy Tri-Turbo 3.

C-47s were taken on charge, including a batch of SC-47Bs and SC-47Ds equipped to carry a lifeboat for sea rescue. A total of 105 C-47s operated with MATS during the Berlin Airlift of 1948.

During the Korean War Combat Cargo Command of the USAF employed C-47s to drop and supply parachute forces, while RC-47Ds, were used for flare dropping during night bombing raids. In 1953 26 aircraft were modified as AC-47Ds for use by MATS to check air-ways navigation aids.

Service with the US Navy ...

As mentioned above, the C-47 and its derivatives served with the US Navy as the R4D. The R4D-1 with R-1830-82 engines corresponded to the early C-47; two R4D-2s (equivalent to the C-49) were staff transports, later styled R4D-2F and R4D-2Z, and were the only R4Ds with Wright R-1820 engines. The R4D-3 and R4D-4 matched the US Army's C-53 and C-53C Skytrooper, while the US Navy's principal cargo variant was the R4D-5 with Dash-92 engines and 24-volt system, corresponding to the C-47A. The R4D-6 was equivalent to the C-47B with Dash-90B engines, and the R4D-7 to the TC-47B trainer.

Immediately after Pearl Harbor the Naval Air Transport Service came into being, almost exclusively equipped with R4Ds, and Squadrons VR-1, VR-2 and VR-3 were soon flying naval and marine personnel on quasi-airline schedules throughout the Pacific theatre. US Marine Corps paratroops were flown on combat missions in R4D-3s and R4D-5s.

All manner of technical duties demanded special US Navy variations, radio and radar countermeasures being undertaken by the R4D-4Q, R4D-5Q and R4D-6Q, electronic warfare by the R4D-5E and R4D-6E, Antarctic operation by the ski-equipped R4D-5L and R4D-6L, and navigation training by the R4D-5T and R4D-6T. Other versions of this remarkable aircraft included the R4D-5S and R4D-6S air-sea warfare trainers and the R4D-5Z and R4D-6Z (and R3D-2Z already mentioned) staff transports.

The other major US Navy variant was the R4D-8 which materialized from Douglas' venture to modernize the DC-3 as the Super DC-3 after the war, with swept-back, angular wings, lengthened and strengthened fuselage, enlarged tail, uprated R-1820-80 engines and deepened engine nacelles. Some 98 conversions from earlier R4Ds were authorized, and these appeared in R4D-8L (winterized), R4D-8T (trainer) and R4D-8Z (staff transport) versions, while in Korea the US Marine Corps night fighter squadron VMF(N)-513 flew R4D-8s as flare droppers on close support missions.

... and other forces

Dakotas (to use their RAF name) served with the British Commonwealth air forces during World War 2, being flown by Nos 33, 34, 36 and 38 Squadrons of the Royal Australian Air Force in the Far East; Nos 435, 436 and 437 Squadrons of the Royal Canadian Air Force; and Nos 40 and 41 Squadrons of the Royal New Zealand Air Force. Many of their aircraft continued to serve in the post-war services, No. 38 Squadron of the RAAF flying operational sorties in Malaya, and No. 91 Wing, RAAF, in Korea. Ex-USAAF C-47s and derivatives were supplied to the air forces of Argentina, Belgium, Bolivia, Brazil, Burma, Cambodia, Chile, Nationalist China, Colombia, Cuba, Denmark, Ecuador, Egypt, Ethiopia, France, West Germany, Greece, Guatemala, Haiti, Honduras,

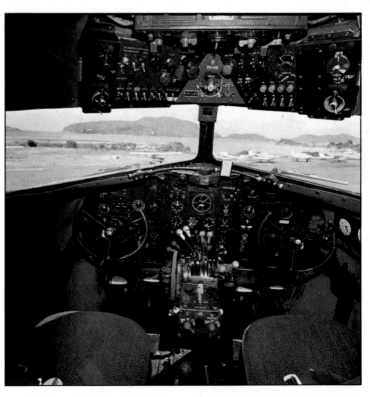

The cockpit of one of the oldest DC-3s still in use, built in 1937. It has 85,000 hours on the clock and belongs to Air BVI (British Virgin Islands) and still looks in good condition.

Brainchild of Captain Ronald Terry at the USAF Aeronautical Systems Division, the AC-47 gunships of the 1st Special Operations Wing carried a number of laterally-firing multi-barrel guns with which to saturate jungle targets in Vietnam as the aircraft circled slowly overhead.

India, Indonesia, Iran, Israel, Italy, South Korea, Laos, Mexico, Netherlands, Norway, Nicaragua, Paraguay, Peru, Philippines, Portugal, Rhodesia, Salvador, Saudi Arabia, South Africa, Spain, Sweden, Syria, Thailand, Turkey, Uruguay, Venezuela, Vietnam, Yemen and Yugoslavia. Russian-built Li-2s were also provided for the air forces of Bulgaria, Communist China, Czechoslovakia, Hungary, North Korea, Mongolia, Poland and Romania. To these should be added aircraft supplied during the past 30 years, either by the USA or from surplus stocks held by the above

nations, to the air forces of Chad, Congo, Benin, Finland, Gabon, Ivory Coast, Kampuchea, Libya, Malagasy, Malawi, Mali, Mauretania, Morocco, Niger, Nigeria, Oman, Pakistan, Panama, Papua/New Guinea, Rwanda, Senegal, Somalia, Sri Lanka, Togo, Uganda, Zaire and Zambia. At the last count it was estimated that more than 2,200 C-47s (etc) were still performing quasi-military duties outside the United States, not to mention the many commercial DC-3s still giving useful service among the smaller airlines of the world.

Vietnam

It is perhaps also worth mentioning that a handful of ageing C-47s are still being used by the US Air Force, particularly for shuttle flights. The aircraft made a notable comeback in 1972 after the delivery of the military AC-47, nicknamed 'Puff the Magic Dragon', for use at the air support base at Ton Son Nut. This version had three rapid-firing 7.62-mm 'miniguns' on swivel mounts on the port side of the cabin and was used by a special activity group of the US Air Force for overflying jungle targets: the on-board gunners would spray the area concerned with a veritable hail of bullets from their miniguns. This method was also used later on by newer, more heavily-armed aircraft. The EC-47 was used by tactical electronic warfare squadrons for radio monitoring purposes, and the EC-47Q was so laden down with electronic defence equipment that it could only get off the ground using more powerful Pratt & Whitney R-2000 engines. Of the total of nearly 13,000 machines built, there are now, half a century after the DC-3's first flight, nearly 700 still in use for both civil and military purposes. In short-distance transport and as a supply plane, it is still very much holding its own. It has become a legend in its own time.

An example of the vast spectrum of duties undertaken by the ubiquitous DC-3 is afforded by this aircraft operated by the Finnish company Kar-Air for geophysical survey duties featuring sensors in nose, wings and tail.

Douglas DC-3/C-47 variants

DST: prototype plus six aircraft in initial production batch, plus 18 built subsequently; majority for American Airlines; Wright Cyclone engines
DST/DC-3: mix of 14-berth, and 18- or 21-seat aircraft built 1936–7; 13 aircraft for TWA; Cyclone or twin Wasp engines
DC-3: commercial airliner to individual furnishing requirements; 417 aircraft, many subsequently commandeered for military use
C-41(DC-3-253): only one, modified from DC-2(38-502)
C-41A(DC-3-253A): only one, equivalent to luxury DC-3 for 23 passengers (40–70)
C-47: 953 aircraft for War Department built at Long Beach; 12-volt system. Twin Wasp engines (41-7722/ 7866; -18337/18699; -38564/38763; 42-5635/5704; -32768/32923; 49-2612/2641 for Greece post-war; among these were 106 US Navy **R4D-1s** 3131-3143; 4692-4706; 01648-01649; 01977-01990; 05051-68687/89, -1074222, 44-83228/29)
C-49J: 34 R-1820-71 powered ex-DC-3s fitted as troopers with side seating (43-1961/94)
C-49K: 23 R-1820-71 powered ex-DC-3s fitted as troopers with side seating (43-1995/-2017)
C-50: designation applied to ex-DC-3s with minor variations to interiors and engine powers; four R-1820-85-powered aircraft (41-7697/7700)
C-50A: two aircraft similar to above but fitted as troopers (41-7710/11)
C-50B: three R-1820-81 powered ex-DC-3s with starboard door (41-7703/05)
C-50C: one R-1820-79 powered ex-DC-3 (41-7695)
C-50D: four R-1820-79 powered ex-DC-3s fitted as troopers (41-7696, -7709, -7712/13)
C-51: one R-1820-83 powered ex-DC-3 (41-7702)
C-52: one Pratt & Whitney R-1830-51 powered ex-DC-3 with 27,700-lb (12565-kg) all-up weight (41-7708)
C-52A: one R-1830-51 powered ex-DC-3 (41-7714)

C-52B: two R-1830-51 powered ex-DC-3s fitted as troopers (41-7706/07)
C-52C: one R-1830-51 powered ex-DC-3 (41-7701)
C-53: named Skytrooper, 193 impressed aircraft and 16 new-build aircraft, all powered by Pratt & Whitney R-1830-92 engines (41-20045/46, -20051, -20053, -20060, -20136, 42-6455/79, -6481/-6504, -15530/69, -15870/94, -47371/82, 43-14404/05; included 20 **R4D-3** for US Navy 05073-05084, 06992-06999)
SX-53A: one prototype with full span slotted flaps (42-6480) and 15 production **C-53A** examples (42-6455/79)
C-53B: five ex-airline long-range DC-3s (41-20047, -20052, -20057/59)
C-53C: 17 ex-DC-3s fitted as troopers with side seats (43-2018/34; included 10 **R4D-4** for US Navy, 07000-07003, 33815-33820)
C-53D: similar to C-53C; 159 aircraft (42-68693/851)
C-68: two 21-seat ex-DC-3s impressed in 1942 with Wright R-1820-92 engines (42-14297/98)
C-84: four 1937-type DC-3b 28 seat airliners with R-1820-71 engines (42-57157, 42-57511/13)
C-117A: 17 Tulsa-built military airliner-style aircraft completed in 1945 with R-1830-90C supercharged engines; some converted to **C-117B** (45-2545/61); **C-117C** designation covered 11 **VC-47C** staff transport conversions which later became **VC-117As** and **VC-117Bs**)
05072; 12393-12404; 30147; 37660-37685; 91104)
C-47A: 4,931 aircraft built at Long Beach and Tulsa; 24-volt system (42-23300/24419; -32924/32935; -92024/93158; -93160/93823; -100436/101035; -108794/108993; 43-15033/16132; -30640/30761; -47963/48262; among these were 248 US Navy **R4D-5s** 12405-12446; 17092-17248; 39057-39095)
C-47B: 3,241 aircraft built at Long Beach and Tulsa with supercharged R-1830-90 or -90B engines; included 133 TC-47B trainers (42-93159; 43-16133/16432; -48263/

49962; 44-76195/77294; 45-876/1139; among these were 147 **R4D-6s** for US Navy 17249-17291; 39096-39098; 39100; 50740-50752; 50753-50839, and 43 **R4D-7s** 99099, 39101-39108; 99824-99857)
YC-47F: prototype Super DC-3 (51-381/) originally termed **YC-129**; transferred to US Navy as prototype **R4D-8**
C-48: designation applied to 36 DC-3s impressed from US airlines in 1941; all with R-1830-90 engines and maximum all-up weight of 26,850-lb (12179 kg); one C-48 21-seater (41,7681); three **C-48A** 18-seaters (41-7682/4); 16 **C-48B** 14-berth DSTs (42-38324/26, 42-56089/91, 42-56098/102, 42-56609/12, 42-56629); 16 **C-48C** 21 seat DC-3s with R-1830-51 engines (42-38327, 42-38332/38, 42-38358/60, 42-78026/28)
C-49: designation applied to six impressed Wright R-1820-powered DC-3s (41-7685/89, 41-7694; two of these

became US Navy **R4D-2F** and **R4D-2Z** VIP transports)
C-49A: one R-1820-powered ex-DC3 (41-7690)
C-49B: three R-1820-powered ex-DC-3s with seating variation and starboard entry door (41-7691/93)
C-49C: two R-1820-powered ex-DC-3s fitted as troopers with side seats (41-7715 and 41-7721)
C-49D: 12 R-1820-71 powered ex-DC-3s fitted as troopers with side seats (41-7716/20, 42-38256, -43624, -65583/84, -68860, 44-52999)
C-49E: 23 R-1820-79-powered ex-DC-3s (42-43619/23, -56092/97, -56103/07, -56617/18, -56625/27, -56634)
C-49F: nine R-1820-71-powered 14-berth ex-DSTs (42-56613, -56616, -56620/21, -56623, -56628, -56633, -56636/37)
C-49G: eight R-1820-97-powered ex-DC-3s (42-38252, -38255, -56614/15, -56630/32, -56635)
C-49H: 19 R-1820-97-powered ex-DC-3/DSTs (42-38250/51, -38253/54, -38257, -38328/31, -57506, -65580/82)

Quetzalcoatl, the feathered snake-god of the Toltecs, creates a very unusual green and brown livery on the fuselage of this DC-3 belonging to a club in Fort Lauderdale, Florida.

Spitfire: fighter supreme

Comment on the Supermarine Spitfire is almost superfluous: this magnificent thoroughbred fighting machine is perhaps the best-known British aircraft of all time. It remained in production right through World War 2, remaining a fully competitive interceptor while also being developed into a number of other roles such as PR aircraft, tactical fighter-bomber and shipboard fighter.

The Spitfire is perhaps the most famous British aircraft of all time. Though it played a minor role in the Battle of Britain compared with the less glamorous Hawker Hurricane, it was probably the most important single type of aircraft on the Allied side in World War 2. It was built in larger numbers than any Allied type outside the Soviet Union, remained in production throughout the entire war and was developed to a greater extent than any other aircraft in history. Britain was fortunate that, as a purely private venture by the chief designer with the support of his board, the nation possessed a prototype in 1936 of a fighter which was capable of being developed to much more than twice the engine power and much more than twice the laden weight in order to stay in the very forefront of the air-combat battle.

Had Britain relied upon official specifications the only 1936 fighter would have been the Supermarine 224, a clumsy machine with an airframe structurally resembling the Schneider Trophy seaplanes, with a 660-hp (492-kW)

No exponents of the Spitfire deserved a greater reputation than the Free Poles, many of whom had relatives living under the Nazi yoke. This Spitfire IX was the mount of the CO of No. 303 (Polish) Sqn, RAF.

Goshawk engine and armed with four machine-guns, two in the fuselage and two in the fixed 'trousered' landing gears. The designer, Reginald Mitchell, was unimpressed with his creation, went back to his drawing board and created the Type 300. This was much smaller and better streamlined, had retractable landing gear, was of all stressed-skin construction, and was intended to be powered by the new Rolls-Royce PV.12 engine of some 900 hp (671 kW). All the guns were in the wings, firing outside the disc of the propeller; and, thanks to young Squadron Leader Ralph Sorley, the Air Ministry had decided that future fighters might need eight machine-guns. Moreover, the absence of a modern British gun was being made up by a licence to make the American Browning (itself a World War 1 gun), and by late 1935 this

46

gun in British 0.303-in (7.7-mm) calibre was being planned for production at the BSA company. Mitchell schemed the wing of the Type 300 with a distinctive elliptical shape to accommodate all eight guns well outboard, with belt magazines quickly replenished through hatches in the skin.

It so happened that this wing, so characteristic of the Spitfire, was one of the best ever designed for a fighter of this era. The elliptical shape played no part in this, and merely made it difficult to make. But aerodynamically the profile was good for speed over 90 per cent that of sound (over Mach 0.9), and during World War 2 Spitfires were dived to Mach 0.92, much faster than any of the German jets. By this time Supermarine had developed a new wing, and when it was later fitted to the first Supermarine jet fighter many pilots, including the chief test pilot, wished the old Spitfire wing had been used instead!

Flight test and production
Like its lifelong enemy the Messerschmitt Bf 109, the new Supermarine fighter had a narrow landing gear pivoted near the fuselage and retracting out and up into the wings. Again like the Bf 109, the Spitfire used a water/glycol engine cooling liquid which was piped to radiators under the rear

around it and assigned the serial number K5054 (curiously, an earlier number than that of the prototype Hurricane, K5083, which was built six months earlier). The trim new prototype was flown unpainted by chief test pilot 'Mutt' Summers at Eastleigh airfield (now Southampton airport) on 5 March 1936. The aircraft handled like a dream, but such was the difficulty of training workers to make modern stressed-skin aircraft that the planned mass production was slow to get under way. The first Spitfire I reached No. 19 Squadron at Duxford in July 1938, and only five had been delivered at the time of the Munich crisis in September that year. By 1939 the Mk I was being made more effective as the clouds of war gathered. The Merlin engine, into which the PV.12 (used in the prototype) had been developed, was being improved in more powerful versions. The first de Havilland and Rotol constant-speed three-blade propellers were at last becoming available. The cockpit was given a bulged hood providing more room and a better view, and a thick slab of Perspex and glass was added at the front to make the windscreen bulletproof. The seat and engine bulkhead were given armour, and the two rather small fuel tanks (total 85 Imp gal/386 litres) ahead of the cockpit were made self-sealing against bullet holes. Previously the engine

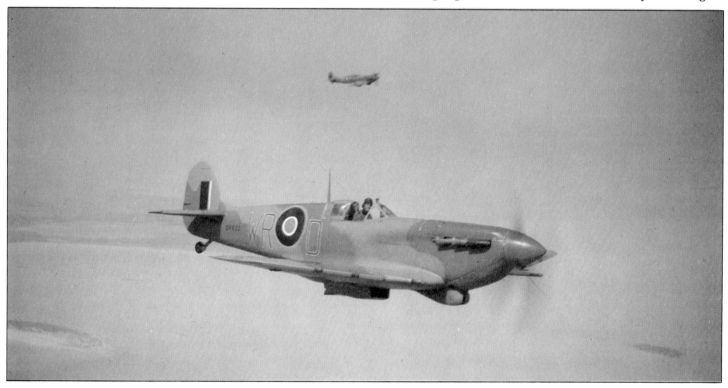

A fine study of a Spitfire VB (EP622) belonging to No. 40 Sqn, South African Air Force, operating in the Taranto area of Italy during late 1943. The clipped wings bestowed greater speed and roll-rate at low altitudes, but the outline is marred by the bulging filter on the carburettor air intake.

part of the inner wing, though in the British aircraft an odd asymmetric arrangement was chosen, with the coolant radiator under the right wing and a slim oil-cooler radiator under the left. Other features included split flaps (worked, like the landing gear, by a hydraulic system with a hand pump in the cockpit), a comfortable cockpit with a Perspex (ICI transparent acrylic plastic) hood that the pilot could slide to the rear on runners, six plain stub exhausts on each side, a fixed tailskid and a hefty but crude two-blade wooden propeller (because none of the new variable-pitch propellers was available in the UK).

Altogether the new fighter was the most beautiful of its era. The Air Ministry had written specification F.37/34

had been fitted with ejector exhaust stacks and a pump to work the hydraulic system, and after the outbreak of war improved radio was fitted together with IFF (identification friend or foe), an automatic radio interrogator which gave positive identification of other aircraft in the vicinity (though this did not stop many tragic mistakes).

In 1938 Joe Smith, who on Mitchell's untimely death had become chief designer, had begun a planned process of development of later marks of Spitfire. One major scheme involved a 'B' series wing with the two inboard guns on each side replaced by a large 20-mm Hispano cannon, with drum feed. In early 1940 a batch of 30 Mk IBs was delivered, but the cannon were not then reliable. The corresponding 'C' type wing removed all the machine-guns and provided the formidable armament of four cannon in close pairs. This remained relatively rare.

By 1941 there had been many experimental or special variants, including the intended speed-record Speed Spit-

Supermarine Spitfire VA

Specification

Type: single-seat interceptor fighter
Powerplant: one 1,478-hp (1103-kW) Rolls-Royce Merlin
45 Vee piston engine
Performance: maximum speed 369 mph (594 km/h) at
19,500 ft (5945 m); initial climb rate 4,740 ft (1445 m)
per minute; service ceiling 36,500 ft (11125 m);
maximum range 1,135 miles (1827 km)
Weights: empty 4,998 lb (2267 kg); maximum take-off
6,417 lb (2911 kg)
Dimensions: span 36 ft 10 in (11.23 m); length 29 ft 11 in
(9.12 m); height 9 ft 11 in (3.02 m); wing area
242 sq ft (22.48 m²)
Armament: eight 0.303-in (7.7-mm) Browning machine-
guns with 350 rounds per gun

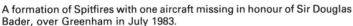

A formation of Spitfires with one aircraft missing in honour of Sir Douglas
Bader, over Greenham in July 1983.

The personal aircraft of Wing Commander Douglas Bader when he
commanded the Tangmere Wing in early 1941, this Mk VA was one of the
last Spitfires built without cannon armament, which was distrusted by
Bader. The aircraft was one of a batch of 450 Mk Is ordered from Vickers-
Armstrongs (Supermarine) on 22 March 1940. The order was
subsequently amended to cover Mk V aircraft: most were Spitfire VBs, but
a small batch of Spitfire VAs was also built. Bader was flying this aircraft,
which unlike others had no provision for bomb armament, when he
collided with a Messerschmitt Bf 109 over France and baled out to
captivity on 7 August 1941.

W3185

Spitfire

fire, two seaplanes, a part-plastic example to conserve scarce materials, a strengthened Mk III and two Mk IVs which introduced the larger Griffon engine and a four-blade propeller. Production, however, had been confined to the Mk I and the almost identical Mk II which was built at a vast shadow factory at Castle Bromwich near Birmingham. And the next major production model, the Mk V, was not greatly different. It had a strengthened fuselage like the Mk III, a more powerful Merlin with wider blades on its three-blade propeller, provision for 'A', 'B' or 'C' wings, attachments under the belly for a 30-Imp gal (136-litre) drop tank (on occasion a much larger tank could be attached here) or a bomb of up to 500 lb (227 kg). The most common model was the Mk VB with two cannon and four machine-guns, but at the end of Mk V production the four-cannon 'C' armament became more common. Aircraft destined for the Mediterranean theatre had a dust and sand filter under the nose which spoilt both the appearance and performance. Aircraft expected to operate mainly at low level had the tips of the wings removed, which was effected by the undoing of two bolts. These so-called 'clipped-wing Spits' needed a slightly longer take-off and landing run and were poorer at high altitude, but at low level they were faster and even more agile. Manoeuvrability in the Mk V was in any case improved by the use of aluminium instead of fabric to skin the ailerons. No fewer than 6,479 Spitfire Vs were built, more than any other mark.

Large numbers of Spitfires were given to the Soviet Union in World War 2, 1,188 of them being Mk IXs. This particular example was the subject of an interesting local modification: its armament was removed and a second cockpit for an instructor added behind the first.

Supermarine Spitfire IX cutaway drawing key:

1 Starboard wingtip
2 Navigation light
3 Starboard aileron
4 Browning 0.303-in (7.7-mm) machine-guns
5 Machine-gun ports (patched)
6 Ammunition boxes (350 rounds per gun)
7 Aileron control rod
8 Bellcrank hinge control
9 Starboard split trailing-edge flap
10 Aileron control cables
11 Cannon ammunition box (120 rounds)
12 Starboard 20-mm Hispano cannon
13 Ammunition feed drum
14 Cannon barrel
15 Rotol four-bladed constant speed propeller
16 Cannon barrel fairing
17 Spinner
18 Propeller hub pitch control mechanism
19 Armoured spinner backplate
20 Coolant system header tank
21 Coolant filler cap
22 Rolls-Royce Merlin 61 liquid-cooled 12-cylinder Vee piston engine
23 Exhaust stubs
24 Forward engine mounting
25 Engine bottom cowling
26 Cowling integral oil tank (5.6-Imp gal/25.5-litre capacity)
27 Extended carburettor air intake duct
28 Engine bearer struts
29 Main engine mounting member
30 Oil filter
31 Two-stage supercharger
32 Engine bearer attachment
33 Suppressor
34 Engine accessories
35 Intercooler
36 Compressor air intake scoop
37 Hydraulic reservoir
38 Hydraulic system filter
39 Armoured firewall/fuel tank bulkhead
40 Fuel filler cap
41 Top main fuel tank (48-Imp gal/218-litre capacity)
42 Back of instrument panel
43 Compass mounting
44 Fuel tank/longeron attachment fitting
45 Bottom main fuel tank (37-Imp gal/168-litre capacity)
46 Rudder pedal bar
47 Sloping fuel tank bulkhead
48 Fuel cock control
49 Chart case
50 Trim control handwheel
51 Engine throttle and propeller controls
52 Control column handgrip
53 Radio controller
54 Bullet-proof windscreen
55 Reflector gunsight
56 Pilot's rear view mirror
57 Canopy framing
58 Windscreen side panels
59 Sliding cockpit canopy cover
60 Headrest
61 Pilot's head armour
62 Safety harness
63 Pilot's seat
64 Side entry hatch
65 Back armour
66 Seat support frame
67 Pneumatic system air bottles
68 Fuselage main longeron
69 Optional long-range auxiliary fuel tank (29-Imp gal/132-litre capacity)
70 Sliding canopy rail
71 Voltage regulator
72 Cockpit aft glazing
73 IFF radio equipment
74 HF aerial mast
75 Aerial cable lead-in
76 Radio transmitter/receiver
77 Radio compartment access hatch
78 Upper identification light
79 Rear fuselage frame construction
80 Fuselage skin plating
81 Oxygen bottle
82 Signal cartridge launcher

Test pilot 'Mutt' Summers taxis the prototype Supermarine Spitfire (K5054) in its immaculate pale blue finish. Note the massive two-blade propeller and flush exhaust stubs, one for each of the six cylinders on the engine's right-hand bank. However, the narrow-track landing gear was always a tactical problem.

Though intended only as a hasty lash-up to get the two-stage (60 Series) Merlin into a Spitfire as soon as possible, the Mk IX continued in production until 5,665 had flown. This F.IX served with No. 402 Sqn, RCAF.

BS428

83 IFF aerial
84 Starboard tailplane
85 Starboard elevator
86 Fin front spar (fuselage frame extension)
87 Fin rib construction
88 HF aerial cable
89 Rudder mass balance
90 Rudder construction
91 Sternpost
92 Rudder trim tab
93 Trim control jack
94 Tail navigation light
95 Elevator tab

96 Port fabric-covered elevator construction
97 Elevator horn balance
98 IFF aerial cable
99 Tailplane rib construction

100 Elevator hinge control
101 Rudder control rod
102 Tailplane spar/fuselage frame attachment
103 Fuselage double frame
104 Non-retracting, castoring tailwheel
105 Tailwheel strut
106 Rudder control lever
107 Sloping tail assembly joint frame
108 Tailwheel shock absorber strut
109 Battery
110 Tail control cable runs
111 Fuselage bottom longeron
112 Wing root trailing edge fillet
113 Radio and electrical system ground socket
114 Trailing edge flap shroud ribs
115 Rear wing spar
116 Radiator shutter jack
117 Aileron cable runs
118 Gun heater air duct
119 Flap hydraulic jack

120 Flap synchronizing jack
121 Port split trailing-edge flap
122 Aileron control bellcrank
123 Aileron hinge control rod
124 Port aileron construction
125 Wing tip construction
126 Port navigation light
127 Wing lattice rib construction
128 Front spar
129 Browning 0.303-in (7.7-mm) machine-guns
130 Ammunition boxes (350 rounds per gun)
131 Machine-gun muzzle blast tubes
132 Machine-gun ports (patched)
133 Leading edge nose ribs
134 Ammunition box armour protection
135 Cannon ammunition box (120 rounds)
136 Port 20-mm Hispano cannon
137 Ammunition feed drum
138 Cannon wing fairing
139 Cannon barrel
140 'C'-wing outboard cannon muzzle fairing (blanked-off)
141 Recoil spring
142 Inboard leading edge lattice ribs
143 Main undercarriage wheel well
144 Oil radiator
145 Coolant radiator
146 Main undercarriage hydraulic jack
147 Retraction link
148 Wing spar/fuselage attachment joint
149 Oil pipe runs to radiator
150 Main undercarriage leg pivot fixing
151 Gun camera
152 Camera port
153 Jettisonable slipper tank, capacity 30, 45 or 90 Imp gal (136, 205 or 409 litres)
154 Mainwheel leg shock absorber
155 Undercarriage torque links
156 Port mainwheel
157 Mainwheel fairing door
158 Starboard mainwheel
159 Starboard wheel fairing door

51

Photo-reconnaissance

A small proportion of the Mk Vs (229) were completed as photo-reconnaissance aircraft, and though this was confusing they were then designated PR.IV (there had already been the quite different Griffon-engined Mk IV). PR versions had the guns replaced by 66½ Imp gal (302 litres) of extra fuel in the leading edge of the wing. Two cameras were fitted in the rear fuselage, in a heated bay, taking photographs on either side of the track with a small overlap in the centre. The pilot had extra oxygen and the engine a larger oil supply.

The Mk VI was the first high-altitude interceptor version, with a pressurized cockpit and pointed wingtips that increased span to 40 ft 2 in (12.24 m). Such aircraft were needed in 1941 to catch ultra-high-flying Junkers Ju 86P and 86R raiders, a problem which posed severe problems with extreme cold that iced up the windscreen and stopped guns working. An even more important advance in the high-altitude regime was being provided by Rolls-Royce with the 60-series of Merlin engines. These had two superchargers in series, with an intercooler to reduce the temperature of the air and thus increase its density still further. At altitudes of about 30,000 ft (9145 m) these engines gave twice the power of earlier Merlins, and when fitted to a Spitfire they were instantly distinguishable by a slightly longer nose, six instead of three exhaust stubs on each side, a four-blade propeller and symmetrical radiators, the oil cooler being joined by an extra cooling radiator on the left side. In combat none of these differences was obvious, so in 1942 the much more formidable Mk IX Spitfire was an unpleasant surprise that removed the previous advantage enjoyed by the Focke-Wulf Fw 190.

The definitive Spitfire VIII

The Mk IX was simply a Mk V with the new engine – in fact a hasty lash-up to get the Merlin 61 (later the 63, 66 or 70) into action quickly. The definitive model was the Mk VIII, a much better aircraft; yet the Mk IX was kept in production to the amazing total of 5,665 and was still being built in 1945! It came with a profusion of variations, including LF (32 ft 7 in/ 9.88 m), F (the regular 36 ft 10 in/11.23 m) and HF (40 ft 2 in/ 12.24 m) wings, the three previous armament schemes plus an 'E' wing with two cannon and two 0.5-in (12.7-mm) guns, and bomb loads up to 1,000 lb (454 kg). Even more remarkably, when Spitfires were built with the American-made Packard V-1650 (Merlin 266) they were not the Mk VIII type but the lash-up Mk IX airframes, the result being designated Mk XVI. Large numbers of LF.XVIE with 'E' armament and clipped wings were used by the 2nd TAF in 1945.

One of the rarest and most interesting Spitfires was this early Mk I, from the second production batch at the Supermarine works ordered in 1937 and delivered just after the outbreak of war. It was converted as a PR Type C, one of the first photo-reconnaissance aircraft assigned to Benson in 1941.

This Spitfire VB was one of more than 600 Spitfires handed to the USAAF as reverse Lend-Lease. In the markings of the 78th Fighter Group as a trainer, it was actually operated in 1942 by the 4th FG, the group formed from the four RAF Eagle Squadrons, based at Debden, Essex.

Operators of the Spitfire throughout World War 2, and the only unit to see action with the Mk 21, RAF No. 91 Sqn used the Mk VC with a tropical filter in the Mediterranean theatre in 1943. This Mk VC was made at Castle Bromwich; with the extra drag of the filter it was on the slow side.

The prototype Spitfire XII shows off its purposeful lines. All Mk XIIs had the clipped wings shown, suiting the type to the low-level interception role, and also introduced into production Spitfires the larger Rolls-Royce Griffon engine, housed in a lengthened nose with 'bumps' over the tops of the cylinder banks.

Only relatively small numbers were produced of the beautiful Mk VIII – in the opinion of most pilots, the nicest of all Spitfires to fly – and the Mk VII. The latter was a marriage of the two-stage Merlin engine with the pressurized cockpit of the Mk VI, with double-layer sealed canopy and a modified 'C' type wing with reduced-span ailerons. Some Mk VII aircraft had a broader rudder with pointed top, later made standard on Merlin 60-series aircraft, and another refinement was a retractable tailwheel. These were also features of the Mk VIII which in addition introduced a neat tropical filter, most of this type going to overseas theatres including the Pacific. The last of the Merlin Spitfires, the Mk XI, or PR.XI, was the most important Allied reconnaissance aircraft in the European theatre, being used by the RAF and USAAF on lone unarmed sorties from England to target areas as distant as Berlin. Most had the pointed rudder, and all a

The Forca Aérea Portuguesa, the air force of the UK's oldest ally, was handed 110 Spitfires in 1943, 92 of them Mk VBs and the other 18 early Mk Is. This Mk I was assigned to Esquadrilha XZ and served with a Grupo de Caca (fighter wing) until 1948. (The Mk VBs served till 1952.)

P7666 was a Spitfire IIA made at the Castle Bromwich shadow factory. It was paid for by members of the Observer Corps (soon to be the Royal Observer Corps) and was the personal aircraft of Squadron Leader Don Finlay, a pre-war Olympic hurdler who was CO of No. 41 Sqn at Hornchurch in 1940.

retractable tailwheel, but the one distinctive feature of this unarmed mark was the deep underside of the engine cowl, as a result of the oversize oil tank necessary on such long missions.

Apart from the original Mk IV, the first Spitfire with a Griffon engine was the Mk XII. The bigger engine resulted in a longer nose with bumps on top to accommodate the fronts of the cylinder blocks. The Mk XII was a hastily contrived low-level interceptor to catch Fw 190 hit-and-run raiders, and it reached almost 350 mph (563 km/h) at sea level, compared with 312 mph (502 km/h) for a Mk IX. A batch of 100, in two versions, was supplied to two RAF home-defence squadrons in 1942. They were totally unlike earlier Spitfires, notably in that on take-off they swung violently to the right instead of gently to the left, because the propeller rotated in the opposite direction. All had clipped wings, and some had retractable tailwheels.

One of the few operational units to use the pointed-wing high-altitude. F.VII, No. 131 Sqn RAF had previously used the Mks I, II, V and IX. The pressurized F.VII was painted in the high-altitude scheme of Medium Sea Grey and PRU (Photo Reconnaissance Unit) Blue, and is seen here with 'invasion stripes'.

Undoubtedly the nicest of all 'Spits' to fly or fight with, the Mk VIII got into the war late because of the prolonged output of the 'interim' Mk IX. This Mk VIII belonged to Wing Commander Glenn Cooper, CO of No. 457 Sqn, RAAF, based at Darwin and, from December 1944, Morotai in the Moluccas.

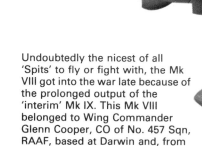

More powerful engines

Predictably, Rolls-Royce fitted two-stage supercharging to the big Griffon and the result, the 65-series engine, was much more than twice as powerful as the original Merlin at all heights. It also made the Spitfire 3 ft (0.91 m) longer and gave it two deep radiators. This great engine was first used in the Mk XIV, which though to some extent a quick lash-up of 1943, was an outstanding aircraft in all respects. On the ground it could be distinguished, apart from the massive nose, by its five-blade propeller. This affected directional stability, so a larger vertical tail was fitted. Directional stability again became marginal in later F (fighter) and FR (fighter-reconnaissance, with rear-fuselage camera) versions which had a cut-down top to the rear fuselage and a beautiful teardrop, or 'bubble', canopy giving uninterrupted fully to the rear.

The Mk XIV was the most important Spitfire in the final year of World War 2. It was joined by a few of the definitive Mk XVIII version, but the Mk VIII/IX saga was repeated and only a few XVIIIs were built. Last of the Spitfires with the original basic wing was the PR.XIX, the two-stage Griffon successor to the PR.XI and the type used on the RAF's last Spitfire sortie in Malaya in 1954. Post-war arabic numerals were used for the surviving aircraft such as the LF.16, FR.18 and PR.19.

After World War 2 three generally similar models of Spitfire entered service with a new airframe which took full advantage of the power of the two-stage Griffon and was markedly heavier. The wing, no longer of simple curving (so-called elliptical) shape, was even stronger than before and carried four cannon, extra fuel and stronger landing gear covered by wing doors when retracted. The large tail had metal-skinned rudder and elevators and the systems were totally re-engineered.

The first model of this new Spitfire family was the F.21, in production from September 1944; some had the Griffon 85 with a six-blade contra-rotating propeller. The F.22 introduced a teardrop canopy and (like the last F.21s) 24-volt electrics; late F.22s had a long-span tailplane and the new vertical tail of the Spiteful, and a rear-fuselage fuel tank whose use was prohibited on grounds of directional instability. The last mark of all, the F.24, had a usable rear tank, and minor changes such as rocket launchers and electrical gun-firing. The last of 20,334 Spitfires, an F.24, was delivered in February 1948.

To meet an urgent Fleet Air Arm need for a modern carrier-based fighter in 1941, Air Service Training produced a navalized Spitfire VB called the Seafire IB. At this time the FAA also had many earlier Seafires, produced by converting Spitfires already built. The chief wartime Seafire, the Mk III, was a navalized Mk VC with a Merlin 32 or 55 giving high power at low level via a four-blade propeller, and with manually folded wings which gave some loss of performance and torsional rigidity; Westland (which made many Spitfires) and Cunliffe-Owen shared production. The single-stage Griffon powered the Seafire XV, a much more deadly machine, and the trim Mk XVII with teardrop canopy. After the war the powerful Mks 45, 46 and 47 brought the Spitfire/Seafire family to a close with aircraft weighing up to 12,750 lb (5783 kg) yet capable of impressive all-round performance fully demonstrated in the Korean war. Seafire production amounted to 2,556 excluding conversions.

Deck handlers 'spot' Seafire IIC fighters at the stern of the flight deck of a Royal Navy fleet carrier in 1943. Right at the stern is a Fairey Albacore with wings folded. The Seafire IIC, the first mark built as such rather than converted from a Seafire, did not have folding wings but was a hooked Spitfire VC.

The prototype of the Spitfire 21 in flight. This last variant entered Royal Air Force service very late in World War 2. The airframe had been totally redesigned and was powered by a Griffon 61 or 64 driving a Rotol five-blade propeller (though some examples had the Griffon 85 driving a six-blade contra-rotating propeller) and had a standard gun armament of four 20-mm Hispano cannon. Records show that 122 mark 21 Spitfires were produced.

Standard unarmed photo-reconnaissance version of the Spitfire for the second half of the war, the Mk XI (No. 541 Sqn, Benson, 1944) could be distinguished by its deeper nose (housing an enlarged oil tank for missions as far as Berlin and back) and windscreen without bullet-proof panel.

Spitfire variants

A Spitfire FXIV at the Greenham Airshow.

Spitfire I: original production model with 1,030-hp (768-kW) Merlin II, eight Browning 0.303-in (7.7-mm) guns (at first four not fitted because of short supply) or (Mk IB) two 20-mm and four 0.303-in (7.7-mm) guns (total 1,566)

Supermarine Spitfire I (early)

Spitfire II: Castle Bromwich aircraft with small changes and 1,175-hp (877-kW) Merlin XII (total 750 IIA and 170 IIB)

Supermarine Spitfire IIA

Spitfire III: experimental prototype (1 only) with 1,280-hp (955-kW) Merlin XX

Supermarine Spitfire III

Spitfire IV: Griffon prototype; same mark number used for 229 PR versions of Mk V

Spitfire V: strengthened fuselage for 1,440-hp (1074-kW) Merlin 45 or 1,470-hp (1097-kW) Merlin 50; drop tank and bomb provisions; F or LF span; 'A', 'B' or 'C' armament (total 94 Mk VA, 3,923 Mk VB and 2,447 Mk VC)

Supermarine Spitfire VB

Spitfire VI: high-altitude interceptor with 1,415-hp (1056-kW) Merlin 47, pressurized cockpit and HF 40 ft 2 in (12.24 m) pointed wings (total 100)

Supermarine Spitfire HF.VI

Spitfire VII: high-altitude interceptor with two-stage Merlin 61, 64 or 71, pressurized cockpit, retractable tailwheel, often broad pointed rudder (total 140)

Supermarine Spitfire HF.VII

Spitfire VIII: definitive fighter with two-stage Merlin 61, 63, 66 or 70; unpressurized; LF, F or HF wings (total 1,658)

Supermarine Spitfire VIII

Spitfire IX: temporary stop-gap marriage of two-stage Merlin 61, 63, 66 or 70 with Mk V airframe; LF, F or HF wings; 'B', 'C' or 'E' armament (total 5,665)

Supermarine Spitfire IXC

Spitfire X: pressurized version of PR.XI; Merlin 77; one example with HF wing (total 16)
Spitfire XI: unarmed reconnaissance aircraft; Merlin 61, 63 or 70 (total 471)

Spitfire XII: low-level interceptor; single-stage Griffon II or IV of 1,735-hp (1294-kW); LF wing; 'B' guns (total 100)

Supermarine Spitfire XII

Spitfire XIII: low-level PR aircraft based on Mk V but with Merlin 32 (three-blade propeller, of DH type unlike other late Spitfires); four 0.303-in (7.7-mm) guns only (total 18)
Spitfire XIV: two-stage Griffon 65 or 66 of 2,050-hp (1529-kW) driving five-blade propeller and redesigned and strengthened airframe with symmetric deep radiators, broad tail and often teardrop canopy; F or LF span; 'C' or 'E' guns (total 957)

Supermarine Spitfire XIVE

Spitfire XVI: Mk IX with Packard Merlin 266; F or LF span; usually 'C' or 'E' guns; many with teardrop canopy (total 1,054)

Supermarine Spitfire LF.XVI

Spitfire XVIII: definitive fighter with two-stage Griffon; F span; 'E' guns; teardrop canopy and extra wing fuel; FR.XVIII (postwar FR.18) with rear-fuselage reconnaissance camera (total 300)

Spitfire XIX: unarmed PR version; two-stage Griffon; most pressurized (total 225)
Spitfire XX: single prototype rebuilt from Mk IV and prototype MK XII

Spitfire 21: redesigned airframe; mainly Griffon 61 or 64 driving five-blade propeller; four 20-mm guns (total 122)

Supermarine Spitfire 21

Spitfire 22: minor changes; some with 2,375-hp (1772-kW) Griffon 85 and contraprop (total 278)

Supermarine Spitfire 22

Spitfire 24: minor changes; Spiteful tail; short-barrel Mk V cannon (total 54)
Seafire IB: navalized Spitfire VB (total 166)
Seafire IIC: catapult hooks and strengthened landing gear; Merlin 32 and four-blade propeller (total 372)
Seafire III: double-folding wing; 1,585-hp (1182-kW) Merlin 55M (total 1,220)
Seafire XV: single-stage 1,850-hp (1380-kW) Griffon VI and asymmetric radiators as Spitfire XII; most with sting hook; late production teardrop canopy (total 390)
Seafire XVII or 17: as Seafire XV with teardrop canopy; often strengthened landing gear; some (FR.17) with camera in place of rear tank (total 232)
Seafire 45: same new airframe as Spitfire 21; non-folding wing; Griffon 61 (five-blade) or 85 (contraprop) (total 50)
Seafire 46: as Seafire 45; teardrop canopy; FR.46 with rear-fuselage camera; late production Spiteful tail (total 24)
Seafire 47: folding wing (most hydraulic); 2,375-hp (1772-kW) Griffon 87 or 88 with contraprop and carburettor air inlet just below spinner; increased fuel; late production all FR type with camera (total 140)

TZ114 was one of the last wartime Spitfires, built as an FR.XIV at the Supermarine works with teardrop hood and cut-down rear fuselage. After the war it was assigned to the Indian Air Force where it served with No. 6 Sqn. The reconnaissance camera (see FR.XVIII) was no longer fitted.

First of the new-generation aircraft with the two-stage Griffon and five-blade propeller, the impressive Mk XIV was one of the few types able to catch 'V-1' flying bombs. This F.XIV was used in 'anti-Diver' duties by S/L R. A. Newbury, CO of No. 610 Sqn at Lympne, Kent.

This Messerschmitt Bf 109E-3/B, built by Erla in Leipzig, fell into British hands in November 1940 when it was captured over the mouth of the Thames. Today it is on show at the RAF Museum in London.

Messerschmitt Bf 109

Longest-serving of all German interceptors, Willy Messerschmitt's classic Bf 109 was the cornerstone of the Luftwaffe's fighter arm throughout World War 2, being built in greater numbers than any other aircraft and credited with more air victories than any other fighter in the history of aerial warfare.

When aircraft designer Willy Messerschmitt began planning the Bf 109 in his Bavarian aircraft factory, he adapted some of the features of his four-seater passenger aircraft, the Bf 108 Taifun, and created a small, angular low-wing monoplane with a retractable undercarriage and an enclosed cockpit. The new Junkers Jumo 210A was to have been the engine, but this was not yet complete. Instead, the 695-hp (518-kW) Rolls Royce Kestrel VI was imported, and the new machine was completed in September 1935.

When flown in competition with the Ar 80 V1, Fw 159 V1 and He 112 V1, at the Travemünde trials, the Bf 109 V1 performed well despite minor problems and, amid general surprise, was rewarded by a contract for 10 prototype development aircraft (although it was not in fact declared the outright winner, 10 Heinkel aircraft also being ordered).

Three further prototypes (the Bf 109 V2 registered D-IUDE, Bf 109 V3 D-IHNY and Bf 109 V4 D-IOQY) were flown in 1936, powered by Jumo 210A engines and with provision for two synchronized Mg 17 machine-guns in the nose decking. However, rumours abounded that the British Hawker Hurricane and Supermarine Spitfire were to be armed with four guns, so that by the time the Bf 109 V4 prototype flew a third Mg 17 was planned to fire through the propeller hub.

The proposed two-gun Bf 109A production version did not therefore materialize, and the first pre-production Bf 109 B-0 examples were flown early in 1937, at the same time as the Bf 109 V5, Bf 109 V6 and Bf 109 V7 prototypes. Considerable operational experience was gained by three Staffeln of Jagdgruppe 88, which were equipped with production examples of the Bf 109B-1, Bf 109B-2 and Bf 109C-1 versions during the Spanish Civil War, experience that not only assisted in the development of the aircraft itself

but of air combat in general; for it was largely through men such as Werner Mölders and Adolf Galland (the former arguably the finest fighter pilot of all time, and the latter to become Germany's General of Fighters during World War 2), who fought in Spain with the Bf 109, that there came to be evolved the basic air fighting tactics which were to last until the end of the era of gun fighting air-combat.

By the beginning of World War 2 in September 1939, the Luftwaffe had standardized its fighter equipment with the Bf 109. The Bf 109D series, although produced in fairly large numbers and still in service, was giving place to the Bf 109E (widely known as the 'Emil'). Ten pre-production Bf 109E-0s appeared late in 1938 with two nose-mounted MG 17 machine-guns and two in the wings, and powered by the 1,100-hp (812-kW) DB 601A engine. Production Bf 109E-1s started leaving the Augsburg factory at the beginning of 1939 with alternative provision for two 20-mm MG FF cannon in place of the wing machine-guns. Maximum speed was 354 mph (570 km/h) at 12,305 ft (3750 m) and service ceiling 36,090 ft (11000 m), performance figures which helped the Bf 109E to eclipse all of its opponents in the first eight months of the war. A sub-variant, the Bf 109E-1/B, introduced soon after, was a fighter-bomber capable of carrying a 551-lb (250-kg) bomb under the fuselage.

Production of the Emil was shifted from Augsburg to Regensburg in 1939 (to make way for the Bf 110 twin-engine fighter) as a massive subcontract programme was undertaken by Ago, Arado, Erla and WNF, no less than 1,540 aircraft being delivered that year. On the eve of the invasion of Poland the Jagdverband comprised 12 Gruppen flying 850 Bf 109E-1s and Bf 109E-1/Bs and one with Ar 68s. Some 235 Bf 109D-1s were still serving with the Zerstörergeschwader.

One of the earliest known air-to-air photographs of a Bf 109, this November 1936 picture shows the Bf 109V4 (no. 4 prototype), with Jumo 210A engine and armament of three MG 17 machine-guns, each with 500 rounds. The similarity to later production Bf 109 versions is strikingly apparent.

To speed production by an as-yet small industry the Bf 109 was licensed in 1937 to Fieseler and in 1938 to Focke-Wulf and Erla. This photograph was taken at Bremen in August 1938 and shows the first 10 Bf 109C-2s completed by Focke-Wulf. The C-2 was the final Jumo-engined version, with five MG 17s.

Introduced into Luftwaffe service midway through the Battle of Britain in August 1940, the Messerschmitt Bf 109E-7 featured a modified fuel system and attachments for a ventral drop tank. Being equipped to carry the extra fuel, the new aircraft were able to provide effective escort for the big daylight raids over London in September 1940. 'Red 2' (no. 2058), depicted here, was being flown by Unteroffizier Klick of 3./LG2 when it was shot down by RAF fighters in the famous raids on London of 15 September.

Messerschmitt Bf 109

Specification

Messerschmitt Bf 109E-7

Type: single-seat interceptor fighter

Powerplant: one 1,200-hp (895-kW) Daimler Benz DB 601N 12-cylinder inverted-vee liquid-cooled inline engine

Performance: maximum speed 359 mph (578 km/h) at 12,300 ft (3749 m);
Initial climb rate 3,300 ft (1006 m) per minute; service ceiling 36,500 ft (11125 m); range 680 miles (1094 km)

Weights: empty 4,440 lb (2014 kg); maximum take-off 6,100 lb (2767 kg)

Dimensions: span 32 ft 4½ in (9.86 m); length 28 ft 8 in (8.74 m); height 11 ft 2 in (3.40 m); wing area 174 sq ft (16.16 m²)

Armament: one hub-firing 20-mm (MG FF/M cannon and four 7.9-mm (0.31-in) MG 17 machine-guns in nose decking and wings

Messerschmitt Bf 109

The first occasion on which Bf 109s fought the RAF was during the daylight raid by 24 unescorted Vickers Wellingtons on Wilhelmshaven on 18 December 1939, 12 of the bombers being destroyed for the loss of two Bf 109Es of JG 77.

Deadly production

In 1940 production of the Emil increased to 1,868 aircraft, the D-series being almost entirely discarded from front-line use. Principal sub-variants produced that year were the Bf 109E-2, Bf 109E-3 (with two MG 17s in the nose and two in the wings, plus an MG FF/M firing through the propeller shaft) and the Bf 109 E (with two nose MG 17s and two wing MG FF cannon). All these versions saw widespread action during the great daylight battles over southern England in the Battle of Britain. When employed in the 'free chase' tactic they proved deadly, being generally superior to the Hurricane and well matched with the Spitfire. However, as is now well known, the capabilities of the Bf 109E were frequently squandered when the aircraft were too often tied to close escort on bomber formations, a role in which the Bf 109Es were deprived of their greatest assets, speed and manoeuvrability. Later in the Battle of Britain they were also employed as fighter-bombers (the Bf 109E-4/B). Other variants, which appeared soon after the Battle of Britain, included the Bf 109E-5 and Bf 109E-6 reconnaissance fighters, the latter with DB 601N engine, the Bf 109 E-7 with provision for belly drop-tank, and the Bf 109E-7/Z with GM-1 nitrous oxide engine boost.

Early in 1941 the Emil was beginning to appear in the Mediterranean theatre, tropicalized versions of the above sub-variant serving with JG 27 in North Africa. However, by the time Germany opened its great attack on the Soviet Union in June 1941, the Bf 109F series was beginning to go in the front-line fighter squadrons although the Emil continued to serve for a long time yet.

Powered by the 1,200-hp (895-kW) DB 601E, the Bf 109F was generally regarded as the most attractive of the entire Bf 109 family introducing extended and rounded wingtips and enlarged spinner while Frise ailerons and plain flaps replaced the Emil's slotted flaps. A fully retractable tailwheel superseded the earlier fixed type, and a cantilever tailplane was introduced. In the matter of gun armament, however, the Bf 109F was widely criticized, for it reverted to the hub cannon and two nose decking MG 17s. While this tended to satisfy the German Experten (aces) as benefitting the aircraft's performance, it was pointed out that the majority of Luftwaffe fighter pilots needed a heavier armament with which to achieve a 'kill'.

Pre-production Bf 109F-0s were evaluated by the Luftwaffe during the second half of 1940, and Bf 109F-1s were delivered early the following year. A number of accidents indicated that removal of the tailplane struts left the entire tail unit vulnerable to sympathetic vibration at certain oscillating frequencies of the engine, and strengthening modifications were quickly put in hand. After the Bf 109F-2 (with 15-mm

J-310 was the first Bf 109 to serve Switzerland's Fliegertruppe, delivered on 17 December 1938. Powered by a 680-hp (507-kW) Jumo 210Da engine (like the German Bf 109B) it had an armament of four MG 17 machine-guns (as fitted to the Bf 109C). The Swiss used Bf 109s until the end of 1949, some being assembled locally.

Messerschmitt Bf 109G-14/U4 cutaway drawing key

1 Starboard navigation light
2 Starboard wingtip
3 Fixed trim tab
4 Starboard Frise-type aileron
5 Flush-riveted stressed wing-skinning
6 Handley Page leading-edge automatic slot
7 Slot control linkage
8 Slot equalizer rod
9 Aileron control linkage
10 Fabric-covered flap section
11 Wheel fairing
12 Port fuselage machine-gun ammunition-feed fairing
13 Port Rheinmetall Borsig 13-mm MG 131 machine-gun
14 Engine accessories
15 Starboard machine-gun trough
16 Daimler Benz DB 605AM 12-cylinder inverted-vee liquid-cooled engine
17 Detachable cowling panel
18 Oil filter access
19 Oil tank
20 Propeller pitch-change mechanism
21 VDM electrically-operated constant-speed propeller
22 Spinner
23 Engine-mounted cannon muzzle
24 Blast tube
25 Propeller hub
26 Spinner back plate
27 Auxiliary cooling intakes
28 Cooling header tank
29 Anti-vibration rubber engine-mounting pads
30 Elektron forged engine bearer
31 Engine bearer support strut attachment
32 Plug leads
33 Exhaust manifold fairing strip
34 Ejector exhausts
35 Cowling fasteners
36 Oil cooler
37 Oil cooler intake
38 Starboard mainwheel
39 Oil cooler outlet flap
40 Wing root fillet
41 Wing/fuselage fairing
42 Firewall/bulkhead
43 Supercharger air intake
44 Supercharger assembly
45 20-mm cannon magazine drum
46 13-mm machine-gun ammunition feed
47 Engine bearer upper attachment

Called 'tripala' by the Spanish (the earlier models had a two-blade propeller) the Bf 109E-1 was by far the best fighter in Spain in early 1939, when this picture was taken at a Légion Kóndor base. Armament was two cannon and two MG 17 machine-guns. The Légion transferred 40 Bf 109s to Spain, which built other models post-war.

Right: The Bf 109 V10 flown by Ernst Udet in July 1937 at the Zurich International Flying Meeting. Despite demonstrating an excellent performance, Udet crashed the aircraft during the Circuit of the Alps race after failure of the DB 600 engine.

Left: Wearing the insignia of the Gruppen-Kommandeur, I Gruppe, of a Jagdgeschwader in 1939, the Bf 109D was powered by the DB 600A and was in effect the production version developed from the V10 prototype. It carried an armament of one hub-firing MG FF cannon and two MG 17s and its performance was in most respects better than a Spitfire I.

48 Ammunition feed fairing
49 13-mm Rheinmetall Borsig MG 131 machine-gun breeches
50 Instrument panel
51 20-mm Mauser MG 151/20 cannon breech
52 Heelrests
53 Rudder pedals
54 Undercarriage emergency retraction cables
55 Fuselage frame
56 Wing/fuselage fairing
57 Undercarriage emergency retraction handwheel (outboard)
58 Tail trim handwheel (inboard)
59 Seat harness
60 Throttle lever
61 Control column
62 Cockpit ventilation inlet

63 Revi 16B reflector gunsight (folding)
64 Armoured windshield frame
65 Anti-glare gunsight screen
66 90-mm armourglass windscreen
67 Galland-type clear-vision hinged canopy
68 Framed armourglass head/back panel

69 Canopy contoured frame
70 Canopy hinges (starboard)
71 Canopy release catch
72 Pilot's bucket-type seat (8-mm back armour)
73 Underfloor contoured fuel tank (88-Imp gal/400 litres of 87 octane B4)
74 Fuselage frame

81 Aerial mast
82 D/F loop
83 Oxygen cylinders (three)
84 Filler pipe

75 Circular access panel
76 Tail trimming cable conduit
77 Wireless leads
78 MW 50 (methanol/water) tank (25 Imp gal/114 litres capacity)
79 Handhold
80 Fuselage decking

85 Wireless equipment packs (FuG 16ZY communications and FuG 25a IFF)
86 Main fuel filler cap
87 Aerial
88 Fuselage top keel (connector stringer)
89 Aerial lead-in
90 Fuselage skin plating sections
91 U-stringers
92 Fuselage frames (monocoque construction)
93 Tail trimming cables
94 Tailfin foot fairing
95 Starboard fixed tailplane
96 Elevator balance
97 Starboard elevator
98 Geared elevator tab
99 All-wooden tailfin construction
100 Aerial attachment
101 Rudder upper hinge bracket
102 Rudder post
103 Fabric-covered wooden rudder structure

104 Geared rudder tab
105 Rear navigation light
106 Port elevator
107 Geared elevator tab
108 Tailplane structure
109 Rudder actuating linkage
110 Elevator control horn
111 Elevator connecting rod
112 Elevator control quadrant
113 Tailwheel leg cuff
114 Castoring non-retractable tailwheel
115 Lengthened tailwheel leg
116 Access panel
117 Tailwheel shock-strut
118 Lifting point
119 Rudder cable
120 Elevator cables
121 First-aid pack
122 Air bottles
123 Fuselage access panel
124 Bottom keel (connector stringer)
125 Ventral IFF aerial
126 Master compass
127 Elevator control linkage
128 Wing root fillet
129 Camber-changing flap
130 Ducted coolant radiator
131 Wing stringers
132 Wing rear pick-up point
133 Spar/fuselage upper pin joint (horizontal)
134 Spar/fuselage lower pin joint (vertical)
135 Flaps equalizer rod
136 Rüstsatz R3 auxiliary fuel tank ventral rack
137 Undercarriage electrical interlock
138 Wing horizontal pin forward pick-up
139 Undercarriage retraction jack mechanism
140 Undercarriage pivot-bevel

141 Auxiliary fuel tank (Rüstsatz R3) of 66 Imp gal. (3000 litre) capacity
142 Mainwheel leg fairing
143 Mainwheel oleo leg
144 Brake liners
145 Mainwheel fairing
146 Port mainwheel
147 Leading-edge skin
148 Port mainwheel well
149 Wing spar
150 Flap actuating linkage
151 Fabric-covered control surfaces
152 Slotted flap structure
153 Leading-edge slot actuating mechanism
154 Slot equalizer rod
155 Handley Page automatic leading-edge slot
156 Wing stringers
157 Spar flange decrease
158 Wing ribs
159 Flush-riveted stressed wing-skinning
160 Metal-framed Frise-type aileron
161 Fixed trim tab
162 Wingtip construction
163 Port navigation light
164 Angled pitot head
165 Rüstsatz R6 optional underwing cannon gondola
166 14-point plug connection
167 Electrical junction box
168 Canon rear mounting bracket
169 20-mm Mauser MG 151/20 cannon
170 Cannon front mounting bracket
171 Ammunition feed chute
172 Ammunition magazine drum
173 Underwing panel
174 Gondola fairing
175 Cannon barrel

61

Aircraft VK + AB was Bf 109 V24 (prototype no. 24), works number 5604. It was built in 1940 alongside V23 (CE + BP) as the third and fourth development aircraft for the Bf 109F, with round wingtips, a better-streamlined engine installation and other changes. The Bf 109F was the nicest of all 109s to fly.

JG 54 Grünherz ('Green Heart') moved from northern France to the Soviet Union in 1941, and this photograph was taken on an airfield near the Leningrad front in summer 1942. These Bf 109-G2s bear the badges of III/JG 54 (left) and II/JG 54 (right). The G-2 was the first 'Gustav' to enter service, in late April 1942.

MG 151 replacing the 20-mm MG FF) came the principal version, the BF 109F-3, early in 1942 with a top speed of 390 mph (628 km/h) at 21,980 ft (6700 m).

Bf 109Fs had joined the Geschwaderstab and III Gruppe of Adolf Galland's JG 26 'Schlageter' early in 1941 on the Channel coast, and during the early stages of Operation 'Barbarossa' in the East this version equipped Major Günther Lützow's JG 3 'Udet', Werner Mölders' JG 51, Major Günther von Maltzahn's JG 53 'Pik As' and Major Johannes Trautloft's JG 54. The superiority of the new fighter (even over the Spitfire Mk V in the West) quickly became apparent as the German fighter pilots' victory tallies soared.

The Bf 109F underwent progressive improvement and development: the BF 109F-4 had an MG 151 rebarrelled to 20-mm, the Bf 109F-4/R1 could be fitted with *Rüstsatz* (field conversion kit) comprising two 20-mm MG 151 guns in underwing packs for the bomber-destroyer role, the Bf 109F-4/B fighter-bomber was capable of carrying up to 1,102 lb (500 kg) of bombs, and the Bf 109F-5 and Bf 109F-6 reconnaissance fighters were introduced later in 1942. It was principally in the tropicalized Bf 109F-4 that the 22-year-old Oberleutnant Hans-Joachim Marseille became the highest-scoring Luftwaffe fighter pilot in the West with 158 air victories, although he died baling out from a BF 109G-2 on 30 September 1942 in North Africa.

The Bf 109G (dubbed the 'Gustav' by German pilots) was introduced into service in the late summer of 1942 and came to be built in larger numbers than any other version. It was powered by the 1,475-hp (1100-kW) DB 605A, although pre-production Bf 109G-0s retained the DB 601E. Basic arm-

ament remained two nose-mounted MG 17s and hub-firing 20-mm MG 151/20 cannon. The Bf 109G-1 with pressure cabin, was powered by the DB 605A-1 with GM-1 power boosting, and the tropical version, the Bf 109G-1/Trop, carried 0.51-in (13-mm) MG 131s in place of the MG 17s, necessitating larger breech blocks and giving rise to the nickname *Beule* (bump) on account of the raised fairings foward of the windscreen. The Bf 109G-2 dispensed with the pressure cabin and the Bf 109G-2/R1 was a fighter-bomber; the Bf 109G-3 was similar to the Bf 109G-1 but with FuG 16Z radio, and the Bf 109G-4 was an unpressurized version of the Bf 109G-3. The Bf 109G-5 introduced the DB 605D engine with MW-50 water-methanol power-boosting (making possible a maximum power of 1,800 hp/1343 kW) for combat bursts), while the Bf 109G-5/R2 featured a taller rudder and lengthened tailwheel leg in an effort to counter the aircraft's swing on take-off.

Improvements and add-ons

Most important of all the Gustavs was the Bf 109G-6 which, in various sub-variants, was powered by AM, AS, ASB, ASD or ASM versions of the DB 605 engine; basic armament was the hub-firing 30-mm MK 108 cannon, two nose MG 131s and two underwing 20-mm MG 151/20 guns. Numerous *Rüstsatz* kits were produced including those to produce the Bf 109G-6/R1 fighter-bomber with a bombload of

The illustration shows a Bf 109E-4N of Jagdgeschwader 27, used in North Africa in 1941. It was equipped with four 7.92-mm machine guns.

'Red 4' of Jagdgeschwader 3 'Udet', a Bf 109E-3 of the Battle of Britain period. This version carried an armament of four MG 17 machine-guns and a hub-firing MG FF/M 20-mm cannon.

Pending the introduction of custom designed night fighters, obsolete Bf 109Cs formed the initial equipment of ad hoc night fighter units, in this case 10.(Nacht)/JG 77, based at Aalborg, Denmark, in July 1940.

Equipped with dust filter on the nose intake, this Bf 109E-7/Trop fighter-bomber was among the first German fighters to operate in the Mediterranean, equipping 7./ JG 26 'Schlageter' at Gela in March 1941 for attacks on Malta.

Displaying the wasp markings of the famous 'Wespen-Geschwader' (Zerstörergeschwader 1) the Bf 109E-4/B fighter-bomber supplement the Bf 110 in the ground-attack role and provided top cover after dropping its bomb.

up to 1,102 lb (500 kg), and the Bf 109G-6/R2 bomber-destroyer with two 21-cm (8.27-in) WGr 210 'Dodel' rockets replacing the underwing cannon. The Bf 109G-6.U4 (with an *Umrüst-Bausatz* or factory conversion set) was armed with two 30-mm MK 108 underwing cannon, and the Bf 109G-6U4N night-fighter carried radar. Tropicalized versions of most of these were also produced. The Bf 109G-7 was not built, but the Bf 109G-8 reconnaissance fighter formed part of the equipment of Nahaufklärungsgruppe 13 late in 1943 on the Channel coast. Fastest of all Gustavs was the Bf 109G-10 with the DB 605D with MW-50 and bulged cockpit canopy (known as the 'Galand hood'); top speed was 429 mph (690 km/h) at 24,280 ft (7400 m); the Bf 109G-10/R2 and R6 possessed the revised tail and tailwheel assembly of the Bf 109G-5/R2 and were equipped with FuG 25a IFF equipment; the Bf 109G-10/U4 had provision for a belly gun pack containing two MK 108 30-mm guns, but this could be replaced by a non-jettisonable fuel tank known as the *Irmer Behalter*. The Bf 109G-12 was a two-seat trainer, field-modified from the Bf 109G-1 to provide conversion training on the Schulejagdgeschwader, notably JG 101, 102, 104, 106, 107 and 108 in 1944. Last operational version was the 'universal' Bf 109G-14 with lightened fixed armament but with provision for external guns, WGr210 rockets or bombs. The Bf 109G-16 heavily armoured ground-attack fighter-bomber entered production before Germany's surrender but did not see operational service.

Development of the Bf 109H high-altitude fighter started in 1943, being a progression from the F-series with increased wing span and the GM-1 boosted DB 601E. Maximum speed was 466 mph (750 km/h) at 33,135 ft (10100 m). Pre-production aircraft were evaluated operationally in France and a few sorties were flown by production Bf 109H-1s, but wing flutter problems caused the H-series to be abandoned, although projects included the Bf 109H-2 with Jumo 213E, and the Bf 109H-5 with DB 605 engines.

Last main operational version of the Bf 109 was the K-series, developed directly from the Gustav; indeed the Bf 109K-0 pre-production aircraft were converted G-series airframes. The Bf 109K-2 and Bf 109K-4 (pressurized) were powered by MW-50 boosted 2,000-hp (1492-kW) DB 605 ASCM/DCM engines and armed with one 30-mm MK 103 or MK 108 cannon and two 15-mm (0.59-in) MG 151 heavy machine-guns, and the Bf 109K-6 had provision for two underwing 30-mm MK 103s. Only two Bf 109K-14s (DB 605L with MW-50 and a top speed of 450 mph/725 km/h) saw action before the end of the war, being delivered to Major Wilhelm Batz's Gruppenstab, II/JG 52, in April 1945.

Trials and experiments

With the Focke-Wulf Fw 190 reaching full operational status only after two years of war, the Bf 109 provided the backbone of the Luftwaffe's fighter arm throughout World War 2: with more than 30,000 examples produced (because of confusion caused by the bombing of factories, an accurate production total could not be arrived at, but only the Russian Ilyushin Il-2 had a higher figure, with 36,163 models built), it was natural that experiments and projects abounded.

For example, among the more bizarre trials were those conducted on Bf 109Es to carry a parachutist in an over-wing 'paracapsule'. Another (in the Starr-Schlepp programme) involving the mounting of a Bf 109E on a DFS 230 troop-carrying glider as a means of delivering airborne forces; this experiment was followed later in the war by the well-known *Beethoven-Gerät* composite weapon system involving the use of Bf 109s and Fw 109s mounted atop unmanned Junkers Ju 88s loaded with explosives. A number of radical operational tactics were pioneered by Bf 109 units, including the aerial bombing of American bomber formations with 551-lb (250-kg)

Wearing the white 'theatre band' on the rear fuselage (denoting service in the Mediterranean), this Bf 109F-4/Trop belonged to 6./JG 53 based at Comiso in May 1942 during the Luftwaffe's assault on Malta.

The Bf 109G-14 with 'Galland' hood was a fighter-bomber version of the G-6, this 'Gustav' bearing the markings of III./JG 53. The 'Spiralschnauze' has no significance in this instance. Note the bulges over the breech blocks of the nose-mounted 13-mm (0.51-in) MG 131 guns.

bombs dropped from Bf 109Gs (pioneered by JG 1 in 1943), and the use by JG 300 of day fighters for freelance night combat against night bombers, known as *wilde Sau* tactics.

A development of the Emil was the Bf 109T carrierborne fighter, intended for deployment abroad the German carrier *Graf Zeppelin*. Featuring folding wings, arrester hook and catapult spools, 10 pre-production Bf 109T-0s and 60 Bf 109T-1s were produced between 1939 and 1941, but when the carrier's construction was abandoned most of these aircraft were delivered to the Luftwaffe for land-based operation.

Perhaps the most ambitious of all projects was the Bf 109Z *Zwilling*, involving the union of two Bf 109F airframes and outer wing panels by means of new wing and tail sections; the pilot was to have been accommodated in the port fuselage and two versions were proposed, a Zerstörer with five 30-mm guns and a fighter-bomber with a 2,205-lb (1000-kg) bombload. A prototype was built but this was never flown.

Bf 109s were supplied to numerous foreign air forces from 1939 onwards, and considerable licence-production of the Gustav was undertaken by Avia at Prague and IAR at Brasov in Romania. The most successful of the foreign air arms with Bf 109s was the Finnish air force, its highest scoring pilot, Lentomestari Eino Juutilainen, achieving 94 victories, of which 59 were scored in Gustavs; he was the highest-scoring non-German/Austrian fighter pilot of all time and his aircraft was never once hit in combat.

Despite the absence of unit markings it is known that this Bf109 was serving in autumn 1943 with II/JG 26, one of the crack fighter units in northern France. It is a G-6/R6, the R6 modification adding the pair of 20-mm MG151 cannon and ammunition in underwing gondolas. The slats are clearly visible here.

Taken in 1944, when many Bf 109s were being used in the anti-bomber role with heavy rocket mortars, this photograph shows a pair of G-6/Rs2 with the most common of these weapons, the Wfr Gr21 which lobbed 21-cm rockets from the tubes under the wings. They were called *Pulk Zerstörer* ('formation destroyer').

Messerschmitt Bf 109 variants

Bf109a (later Bf109V1): D-IABI, first prototype; 695-hp (518-kW) Rolls-Royce Kestrel V engine; first flight in September 1935
Bf109 V2, V3 and V4: three prototypes, (D-IUDE, D-IHNY and D-IOQY); Jumo 210A engines
Bf109B: pre-production **Bf109B-0** with Jumo 210B; **Bf109B-1** with Jumo 210D; **Bf109B-2** with Jumo 210E and later, 210G engines
Bf109 V10 and V13: two prototypes, (D-ISLU and D-IPKY); Daimler-Benz DB 600 engines
Bf109C: developed from **Bf109 V8** prototype; **Bf109C-0** and **Bf109C-1** with four MG17 guns; **Bf109C-2** with five MG17s
Bf109 V13: modified with boosted DB 601 engine; world speed record of 379.38 mph (610.54 km/h) on 11 November 1937
Bf109D: developed from Bf109 V10 and V13 prototypes; **Bf109D-0** with DB 600Aa and armament of one 20-mm and two 7.92-mm (0.31-in) guns; **Bf109D-1** similar; **Bf109D-2** with two wing MG 17s; **Bf109D-3** with two MG FFs in wings
Bf109 V14: prototype (D-IRTT); fuel-injection DB 601A engine; two 20-mm and two 7.92-mm (0.31-in) guns; **Bf109 V15** (D-IPHR) similar but one 20-mm gun
Bf109E: **Bf109E-0** with four 7.92-mm (0.31-in) guns; **Bf109E-1** (and **Bf109E-1/B** bomber) similar; **Bf109E-2** with two 20-mm and two 7.92-mm (0.31-in) guns; **Bf109E-3** with one hub 20-mm and four 7.92-mm (0.31-in) guns; **Bf109E-4** (also **Bf109E-4/B** and **Bf109E-4/Trop**) similar to Bf109E-3 but no hub gun; **Bf109E-4/N** with DB610N engine; **Bf109E-5** and **Bf109E-6** reconnaissance fighters with two 7.92-mm (0.31-in) guns; **Bf109E-7** similar to Bf109E-4/N with provision for belly tank (**Bf109E-7/U2** ground attack sub-variant); **Bf109E-7/Z** with GM-1 boost; **Bf109E-8** with DB601E engine; **Bf109E-9** reconnaissance fighter
Bf109F: **Bf109F-0** from E-airframes with DB 601N engine; **Bf109F-1** wih one 20-mm and two 7.92-mm (0.31-in) guns; **Bf109F-2** with one 15-mm and two 7.92-mm (0.31-in) guns (**Bf109F-2/Z** with GM-1); **Bf109F-3** with DB601E engine; **Bf109F-4** and **Bf109F-4/B)** with one 20-mm and two 7.92-mm (0.31-in) guns and DB 601E; **Bf109F-5** and **Bf109F-6** reconnaissance fighters with two 7.92-mm (0.31-in) guns; trials aircraft included one with BMW 801 radial, one with Jumo 213, one with butterfly tail and one with wing fences
Bf109G: **Bf109G-0** with DB601E engine; **Bf109G-1** with DB 605A-1 and GM-1; **Bf109G-1/Trop** with one

20-mm and two 15-mm guns (*Beule*); **Bf109G-2** was unpressurized version of Bf109G-1 (also **Bf109G-2/R1** fighter-bomber); **Bf109G-3** with FuG 16Z radio; **Bf109G-4** unpressurized version of Bf109G-3; **Bf109G-5** with enlarged rudder had DB605D with MW-50; **Bf109G-6** with variations of DB 605 (see text) and two 13-mm (0.51-in), one 30-mm and two underwing 20-mm guns (also R and U sub-variants, see text); **Bf109G-8** reconnaissance fighter; **Bf109G-10** with DB605G and MW-50; **Bf109G-12** was two-seat trainer; **Bf109G-14** with one 20-mm and two 15-mm guns plus provision for underwing guns or rockets; **Bf109G-16** ground-attack fighter
Bf109H: high-altitude fighter developed from F-series; **Bf109H-0** pre-production; **Bf109H-1** with DB601E, **Bf109H-2** and **Bf109H-3** with Jumo 213; **Bf109H-5** with DB 605L
Bf109J: proposed Spanish licence-built version, not proceeded with
Bf109K: development from Bf109G-10; **Bf109K-0** with DB 605D and GM-1; **Bf109K-2** and **Bf109K-4** (pressurized) with DB 605ASCM/DCM and MW-50, and one 30-mm and two 15-mm guns; **Bf109K-6** with three 30-mm and two 15-mm guns; **Bf109K-14** with DB605L and MW-50
Bf109L: proposed version with Jumo 213E engine; maximum estimated speed 474 mph (763 km/h); not built)
Bf109S: proposed version with blown flaps; not built
Bf109T: carrierborne version of Bf109F for carrier *Graf Zeppelin*; 10 **Bf109T-0** converted by Fieseler; 60 **Bf109T-1** with DB601N; **Bf109T-2** was conversion of T-1 with deck gear removed
Bf109TL: project based on near-standard Bf109 with two underwing Jumo 109-004B turbojets; abandoned in 1943
Bf109Z Zwilling: twin Bf109F airframes with single pilot and five 30-mm guns (**Bf109Z-1**); **Bf109Z-2** with two 30-mm guns and 2,205-lb (1000-kg) bombload; **Bf109Z-3** and **Bf109Z-4** conversion of Bf109Z-1 and Bf109Z-2 respectively with Jumo 213 engines; one prototype built but not flown; led to Me 609 project
Me 209 V1, V2, V3 and V4: D-INJR, D-IWAH, D-IVFP and D-IRND; high-speed prototypes developed for speed records
Me 309 V1, V2, V3 and V4: GE-CU, GE-CV, GE-CW and GE-CX; high-speed, high-altitude fighter prototypes intended to replace Bf109F
Me609: projected development of Bf109Z *Zwilling* twin-Bf109; abandoned

Sunderland: sealane sentinel

Derived from the civil Empire Flying Boat, the Sunderland gained a legendary reputation in World War 2 as the chief patrol flying-boat of the Commonwealth forces. It was tough, reliable and could turn its hand to almost any maritime task including U-boat sinking, air-sea rescue and evacuation. The Germans found it a very prickly customer and nicknamed it 'The Flying Porcupine'.

Just as the Short S.23 C-class 'Empire' flying-boat marked a startling advance on all previous civil transport aircraft in Imperial Airways, so did its military derivative, the Sunderland, mark an equally great advance on marine aircraft in the RAF. Sometimes called 'The Pig' (not unkindly) by its crews, it was dubbed 'The Flying Porcupine' by Luftwaffe pilots who tried to attack it. When the last of these well-loved boats was retired from the RAF on 20 May 1959 it had set a record of 21 years' continuous service in the same oceanic duty. On the side, it had performed many other missions, including remarkable feats as a transport.

The Sunderland had its origins in a 1933 Air Ministry specification, R.2/33, calling for a new maritime reconnais-

This photograph was probably taken in the last year of the war, in Lough Erne, Northern Ireland. It shows a Z-Zebra, Mk V (renamed Mk 5 after the war) of 201 Squadron, which had previously used the code letters ZM.

sance flying-boat to replace the Short Singapore III biplane then just coming off the production line at the Rochester works of Short Brothers. The same company's chief designer Arthur (later Sir Arthur) Gouge immediately began to prepare a tender to the new requirement. He was already well advanced with planning a new civil transport flying-boat. Almost alone among British designers, Gouge realized that the all-metal stressed-skin monoplanes being built in the USA and Germany were a better species of flying machine,

Short S.25 Sunderland III

Specification

Type: long-range reconnaissance and anti-submarine flying-boat

Powerplant: four 1,065-hp (794-kW) Bristol Pegasus XVIII nine-cylinder radial piston engines

Performance: maximum speed 212 mph (341 km/h); initial climb rate 790 ft (241 m) per minute; service ceiling 15,000 ft (4570 m); range 3,000 miles (4828 km) at 145 mph (233 km/h); endurance 20 hours

Weights: empty (typical) 33,000 lb (14969 kg); 58,000 lb (26308 kg)

Dimensions: span 112 ft 9½ in (34.38 m); length 85 ft 4 in (26.01 m); height (on beaching chassis) 32 ft 2 in (9.79 m); wing area 1,487 sq ft (138.14 m²)

Armament: one 0.303-in (7.7-mm) Vickers GO machine-gun in nose turret, two 0.303-in (7.7-mm) Browning machine-guns in mid-upper turret, four similar Brownings in tail turret, optional second nose-turret gun, four fixed Brownings firing ahead and twin 0.5-in (12.7-mm) Brownings fired from waist hatches; assorted ordnance to total weight of 4,960 lb (2250 kg) housed in hull and cranked out under wings prior to attack

This Blackburn-built Mk III, NJ188, is depicted as it was in its first career when it was WH-C of RAF Coastal Command No. 228 Squadron. No. 228 was one of the original 1938 Sunderland units, and scored the first RAF U-boat kill in January 1940. It saw extensive service at Gibraltar, Crete, Malta and other Mediterranean areas before returning to the UK via North Africa. During the Crete evacuation one of its boats airlifted out 82 personnel in addition to its crew of 10. This Mk III was replaced in No. 228 Sqn by a Mk V (No. 228 was first to receive this mark) and was then itself turned into a Mk V by fitting Twin Wasp engines. Then it became a Sandringham 5 of BOAC (G-AHZF) and finally was passed to Qantas in July 1951 as VH-EBY!

NJ188

WH C

Short Sunderland

Another early-war Sunderland was this Mk II of No. 201 Squadron, one of the first to have both ASV radar and the dorsal turret (which was offset to starboard). By this time the mid-upper and tail guns were belt-fed Brownings, though the nose guns were usually Vickers. Propellers had spinners, and the engines flame-damped exhausts.

and he designed the S.23 as a stressed-skin cantilever mono-plane with a smooth skin and the greatest attention to the reduction of drag. It was an ideal basis for the new RAF machine, the S.25.

Military changes

Gouge made his submission in 1934, the specified armament being a 37-mm Coventry Ordnance Works gun in a bow cockpit or turret and a single Lewis machine-gun in the extreme tail. Compared with the civil S.23, the military boat had a completely new hull of much deeper cross-section, and with a long nose projecting ahead of a flight deck quite near the wing. When construction was well advanced it was decided to alter the armament to a nose turret with one machine-gun and a tail turret with four, a complete reversal of original thoughts on firepower. The shift in centre of gravity could only be countered by moving back the wing or altering the planform so that taper was mainly on the leading edge. The first prototype, K4774, now named Sunderland, was completed with the original wing, basically similar to that of the C-class transport, and flown without armament by J. Lankester Parker from the River Medway on 16 October 1937. After preliminary trials it went back into the factory to have the 'swept-back' wing fitted, flying again on 7 March 1938.

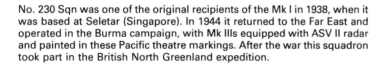

No. 230 Sqn was one of the original recipients of the Mk I in 1938, when it was based at Seletar (Singapore). In 1944 it returned to the Far East and operated in the Burma campaign, with Mk IIIs equipped with ASV II radar and painted in these Pacific theatre markings. After the war this squadron took part in the British North Greenland expedition.

Powered by 1,010-hp (753-kW) Bristol Pegasus XXII engines, more powerful than those of the civil machine, the Sunderland was far more capable than any previous RAF aircraft. Fuel was housed in six vertical drum tanks between the spars with a capacity of 2,025 Imp gal (9206 litres), later increased to 2,552 Imp gal (11602 litres) by four further cells aft of the rear spar. In the original Sunderland I the normal crew was seven, accommodated basically on two decks and with comprehensive provision for prolonged habitation, with six bunks, galley with cooking stove, workshops and stowage for a considerable quantity of equipment including

Short Sunderland III cutaway drawing key

1 Twin Vickers 0.303-in (7.7-mm) machine guns
2 Bomb aiming window, retractable
3 Bomb aimer's station
4 Retractable nose turret
5 Front entry/mooring hatch
6 Mooring cable stowage
7 Hull planing bottom
8 Anchor
9 Parachute stowage
10 Anchor winch
11 Dinghy
12 Front turret rails
13 Cockpit bulkhead
14 Mooring ladder
15 Toilet compartment door, starboard side
16 Nose gun turret hydraulic reservoir
17 Instrument panel
18 Windscreens
19 Cockpit roof glazing
20 Overhead control panels
21 Co-pilot's seat
22 Signal cartridge rack
23 Pilot's seat
24 Control column
25 Raised cockpit floor level
26 Autopilot controllers
27 Stairway between upper and lower decks
28 Front entry door
29 Fuselage chine member
30 Crew luggage locker
31 Rifle rack
32 Wardroom door
33 Planing bottom hull construction
34 Wardroom bunks
35 Window panels
36 Folding table
37 Upper deck floor level
38 Parachute stowage
39 Fire extinguisher

40 Navigator's seat
41 Chart table
42 Forward ASV radar aerial mast
43 Navigator's instrument panel
44 Flight engineer's aft-facing seat
45 Radio operator's station
46 Air intake duct
47 Wing/fuselage attachment main frames
48 Wing root rib cut-outs
49 Air conditioning plant
50 Engineer's control panels
51 Carburettor de-icing fluid tank
52 D/F loop aerial
53 Astrodome observation hatch
54 Auxiliary power unit
55 Forward inner fuel tank, 529-Imp gal (2405-litre) capacity
56 Fold-down, leading-edge maintenance platform
57 Starboard inner engine nacelle
58 Cowling air flaps
59 Detachable engine cowlings
60 Flame suppressor exhaust pipe

61 Forward inner fuel tank 325-Imp gal (1477-litre) capacity
62 Oil coolers
63 Forward outer fuel tank, 132-Imp gal (600-litre) capacity
64 Starboard wing tip float
65 De Havilland three-bladed, constant speed propeller, 12 ft 9 in (3.89 m) diameter
66 Propeller hub pitch change mechanism
67 Engine reduction gearbox
68 Bristol Pegasus XVIII, nine cylinder radial engine, 1065 hp
69 Exhaust collector ring
70 Oil filter
71 Oil tank, 32-Imp gal (145-litre) capacity
72 Flame suppressor exhaust pipe
73 Leading edge de-icing
74 Starboard ASV aerial array

75 Starboard navigation light
76 Aileron hinges
77 Starboard aileron
78 Fixed tab
79 Aileron control horns
80 Control cable runs
81 Starboard 'Gouge-type' trailing-edge flap
82 Flap guide rail
83 Rear outer fuel tank 147-Imp gal (668-litre) capacity
84 Flap jack
85 Rear inner fuel tank 111-Imp gal (505-litre) capacity
86 Pitot tubes
87 Aerial mast
88 Observation window
89 Propeller de-icing fluid tank
90 Windscreen de-icing fluid tank
91 Bomb carriage traversing drive motor
92 Smoke floats and flame floats
93 Tailplane control cable runs

94 Reconnaissance flares
95 Turret fairing
96 Mid-upper gun turret, offset to starboard
97 Twin Browning 0.303-in (7.7-mm) machine guns
98 Fuselage skin plating
99 Spare propeller blade stowage
100 Fire extinguisher
101 Rear entry door
102 Maintenance platform stowage
103 Observation window
104 Fuselage frame and stringer construction
105 ASV Mk II search radar aerial array
106 Leading edge de-icing
107 Starboard tailplane
108 Starboard elevator
109 Fin root attachments

110 Fin construction
111 Leading edge de-icing
112 Fin tip construction
113 Fabric covered rudder construction
114 Rudder tabs
115 Tail gun turret
116 Four Browning 0.303-in (7.7-mm) machine guns
117 Elevator tab
118 Fabric-covered elevator construction
119 Port tailplane construction
120 Leading edge de-icing
121 Tailplane spar fixing fuselage double frames
122 Tail fuselage fabric draught screen
123 Smoke and flame floats

124 Handrail
125 Tail fuselage walkway
126 Reconnaissance flare chute, stowed
127 Mooring shackle
128 Tow bar
129 Rear beaching trolley
130 Camera stowage
131 Dinghy paddles
132 Distress flares
133 Emergency ration container
134 Dinghy stowage
135 Crew luggage locker
136 Tool locker
137 Bilge keel construction
138 Rear fuselage deck level
139 Crew rest bunks
140 Trailing-edge wing root fillet
141 Reconnaissance camera mounting
142 Ditching flare chutes
143 Ladder to upper deck level
144 Rear wardroom
145 Twin bunks
146 Fuselage bomb door, open
147 Retractable bomb carriage
148 Four 100-lb (45.4-kg) bombs
149 Bomb store and loading room: maximum bomb load, 2,000 lb (907 kg)
150 Port flap shroud
151 Port 'Gouge-type' trailing-edge flap
152 Fabric-covered aileron construction
153 Aileron tab, fixed

154 Trailing-edge lattice ribs
155 Wing tip construction
156 Port navigation light
157 Rear spar
158 Wing rib construction
159 Front spar
160 Leading edge de-icing
161 Port ASV radar aerial
162 Wing-tip float construction
163 Float support struts
164 Diagonal wire bracing
165 Wing spar girder construction
166 Landing lamps
167 Leading-edge rib construction
168 Diagonal wire-braced wing ribs
169 Fold-down, leading-edge maintenance platform
170 Engine nacelle construction
171 Engine mounting ring
172 Port outer engine nacelle
173 Oil cooler intakes
174 Oil coolers
175 Exhaust shroud heat exchangers
176 Port inner engine nacelle
177 Emergency escape hatch
178 Ice chest
179 Drogue container
180 Galley compartments, port and starboard
181 Watertight trailing aerial socket
182 Main beaching gear leg strut
183 Twin beaching wheels

When the Sunderland was young four Pegasus XXII engines of 1,050 hp (783 kW) each were ample, but later the portly boats were burdened by tons of extra gear and festooned with radar dipole arrays. This early example of the popular flying-boat was the third production Sunderland, L2160, photographed about June 1938.

four rifles and three spare propeller blades. At the upper level it was possible to walk aft from the two-pilot flight deck past the cubicles of the radio operator (left) and navigator (right) and through the deep front spar into the domain of the flight engineer with extensive instrument panels inside the wing centre section. One could crawl through the rear spar to an aft upper deck filled with reconnaissance flares, smoke and flame floats, marine markers and other pyrotechnics. The main offensive load, comprising up to 2,000 lb (907 kg) of bombs, depth charges, mines or other stores, was hung beneath the centre section on carriers running on lateral tracks. In combat large side hatches were opened beneath the wing and the weapons run out under the wings by a drive motor which cut out when the bomb carriages had reached full travel on each side. Defensive armament was concentrated in a Nash and Thompson FN.13 hydraulic tail turret with four of the new Browning 0.303-in (7.7-mm) guns. In the bows was an FN.11 turret with a single VGO (Vickers gas-operated) machine-gun, with a winching system for retracting the turret aft so that the big anchor could be passed out through a bow hatch.

Despite its great bulk the hull was well shaped, and drag at the nominal 100 ft (30.5 m) per second was actually lower than for the much smaller biplane Singapore III. Wing loading was, of course, in the order of twice that common on RAF aircraft of the mid-1930s, but Gouge's patented flaps (which had broad chord and rotated aft about a part-cylindrical upper surface) provided increased area and added 30 per cent to lift coefficient for landing. Hydrodynamically, a new feature was the bringing of the planing bottom to a vertical knife-edge at the rear (second) step, thereafter sweeping the bottom line smoothly up and back to the tail. Flight-control surfaces were fabric-covered and driven manually, with no servo-tab assistance, but the Sunderland responded admirably to powerful control demands. A twin-wheel beaching chassis could be attached under the main spar and at the rear of the planing bottom.

Into RAF service

RAF service began in June 1938 when the second production Mk I (L2159) was ferried out to No. 230 Sqn at Seletar, Singapore. About 40 were in service at the outbreak of war, and by late 1941 the total output of the Mk I had risen to 90, of which 15 were built by a second-source supplier, a works set up at the Denny shipyard at Dumbarton and run by Blackburn. From late 1939 until 1942 Sunderlands were camouflaged, though in their harsh environments paint flaked off rapidly. Early home-based units, such as Nos 204, 210 and 228 Sqns, plus No. 10 Sqn of the RAAF which arrived to collect its aircraft and stayed in the UK for the next 6½ years, were intensively in action from the first day of the war. Successes against U-boats were at first non-existent, but rescues of torpedoed crews made the headlines, starting on 18 September 1939 when two of No. 228 Sqn's aircraft took the whole crew of 34 from the *Kensington Court* and got them to hospital in Plymouth an hour after their ship sank off the Scillies.

By 1940 Sunderlands were being improved in various ways, notably by the addition of two VGO guns aimed from hatches at the rear of the upper deck on each side, with the front part of each hatch opening into the slipstream to give the gunner a calmer area for aiming. Other changes included the progressive addition of a second gun to the nose turret,

The final production Sunderland was the Mk V, with American Twin Wasp engines giving more power than the old nine-cylinder Pegasus. The Mk V was accepted by 228 Sqn in February 1945. This example was serving at the end of the war with No. 4 OTU (Operational Training Unit); its serial number was SZ568. The Mk V was fitted as standard with ASV Mk VIc radar with scanners faired into underwing blisters.

After the start of World War 2 the patrol flying-boats of RAF Coastal Command were at first painted in this style of marine camouflage, switching to grey/white in 1942. This Sunderland I served with No. 230 Sqn, which in late 1938 had been the first full RAF Sunderland squadron. In 1940 it moved to the Mediterranean, N9029 operating from Crete.

replacement of the bracket-type (Hamilton-licence) de Havilland propellers by 12 ft 6 in (3.81-m) constant-speed propellers with spinners, addition of pulsating rubber-boot de-icers to the wings and tail and, from October 1941, ASV Mk II radar which covered the upper rear of the hull with matched dipole Yagi aerials in groups of four and added long dipole-equipped horizontal poles under the outer wings to give azimuth (homing) guidance. At the 150-mph (241-km/h) speeds which were hardly ever exceeded by Coastal Command Sunderlands on patrol these prominent arrays had little effect on performance.

In any case, though the defensive armament was actually quite light, and contained no gun greater than rifle calibre, the Sunderland soon gained great respect from the enemy. On 3 April 1940 a Sunderland off Norway was attacked by six Ju 88s, shot one down, forced another to land immediately, and drove the rest off. Later another was attacked by eight Ju 88s over the Bay of Biscay and shot down three (confirmed by the grateful skippers of the convoy it was escorting in that notorious area).

Further development

In late 1941 production switched to the Mk II, with Pegasus XVIIIs with two-speed superchargers and, in the last few of this mark, improved armament in a twin-Browning nose turret, two more Brownings in an FN.7 dorsal turret on the right side of the hull at the trailing edge, and four Brownings in an FN.4A tail turret with ammunition doubled to 1,000 rounds per gun. Only 43 of this mark were produced, 15 of them at a third source, the Short & Harland company at Queen's Island, Belfast (later the home of the parent company). This limited production resulted from the fact that in June 1941 a Mk I had begun testing an improved planing bottom, with the Vee-type main step smoothly faired to reduce drag in the air. This hull resulted in the designation Mk III, and it succeeded the Mk II from December 1941. No fewer than 461 were delivered, 35 coming from a fourth

The cockpit of a Sunderland Mk 5, which flew with the RAF until 15 May 1959. Sunderlands landed on the Wannsee during the Berlin Blockade.

Short Sunderland

assembly shop on Lake Windermere. The Mk III was effectively the standard wartime boat, and its exploits were legion
in all theatres.

In the Mediterranean, Sunderlands were called upon to
undertake many dangerous missions, none worse than the
prolonged evacuation from Crete when many trips were
made with as many as 82 armed passengers in addition to
the crew, which by this time had grown to 10. A Sunderland
made the necessary visual reconnaissance of Taranto before
the Fleet Air Arm attack of 11 November 1940. Over the
Atlantic the Sunderland shared with the Consolidated
Catalina the main effort against U-boats, but when the latter
received Metox passive receivers tuned to ASV Mk II they
received ample warning of the presence of British aircraft
and kills dropped sharply. The RAF response was the new
ASV Mk III, operating in the band well below 50 cm and
with the aerials neatly faired into blisters under the outer
wings. When thus fitted the Sunderland became a Mark IIIA.

The U-boat sensors could not pick up this radar, and once
again, in early 1943, kills became frequent. The response of
the U-boats was to fit batteries of deadly Flak, typically one
or two 37-mm and two quadruple 20-mm, and fight it out on
the surface. Now the odds were heavily against the flying-
boat, which needed forward-firing fire-power. Curiously,
though the bow was ideally arranged for it, really heavy
forward-firing armament was never fitted to the Sunderland,
nor was the Leigh light, though many aircraft received four
fixed 0.303-in (7.7-mm) Brownings, firing straight ahead,

Sunderlands were flown by France's Aéronavale up until 1960. Flotilla 7E
received a number of them after World War 2 and in 1951 added another
19 of the RAF's redundant Mk 5s. The RNZAF operated this flying-boat,
still looking spic and span after years of service in and on an inhospitable
sea, right up to 1967.

No. 35 Sqn of the South African Air
Force had a total of 15 of these
Sunderland GR.5s in service, using
them to transport troops home
from the various war fronts. Later
they were used to form a long-
distance patrol unit, stationed in
Congella, Durban. The turrets on
the back of the fuselage were
removed, but the ASV Mk VIc radar
was retained (the radome is under
the wing).

This Mk I, stationed in Mount Batten (Plymouth) with No. 10 Squadron of
the Royal Australian Air Force, was photographed in 1941 when it was
equipped with ASV radar. The censor retouched this top-secret
equipment before the photograph was published. The gunning position
was at the back of the fuselage.

together with a pilot gunsight. The one thing these guns did
sometimes succeed in doing was to knock out the U-boat
gunners as they ran from the conning-tower hatch the few
metres to their guns. In addition, heavier lateral armament
became common, to combat the more numerous and more
heavily armed Luftwaffe long-range fighters. Though the
latter's cannon always gave a considerable edge at stand-off
range, Sunderlands did at least fit locally contrived installations of single VGOs or Brownings from the escape hatches
in the galley compartments (last but one in the main row of
portholes). This became a standard fit in late 1943, at which
time Short also added an installation of one or two of
the much more effective 0.5-in (12.7-mm) Brownings from
upper rear hatches behind the trailing edge. Thus the
number of guns rose in a year from five to 18, believed the
greatest number of guns carried by any regular British
service aircraft.

In late 1942 severe shortage of equipment by BOAC, the
national civil airline, resulted in six Sunderland IIIs being
stripped of all armament (turrets were replaced by bulbous
fairings) and put into joint BOAC-RAF service between
Poole and Lagos (West Africa) and Calcutta (India). BOAC
investigated the engine installation and cruising angle of

A Sunderland Mk V moored opposite the Tower of London and Traitors'
Gate. The flying-boat was taxied through the open Tower Bridge in
London in October 1982.

attack to such effect that mean cruising speed – which had seldom bothered the RAF – was improved by more than 40 per cent. Spartan bench seats for seven passengers, the main payload being mail, gradually gave way in the BOAC Hythe class to an excellent airline interior for 24 passengers (16 with sleeping accommodation), plus 6,500 lb (2948 kg) of mail, and the engines were modified to Pegasus 38 (later 48) standard. By 1944 the number of civil Sunderland IIIs had grown to 24, and after the war the Hythes, eventually totalling 29, were supplemented by a complete civil rebuild, the S.26 Sandringham, which went into production as a basic post-war transport for BOAC (as the Plymouth class) and other airlines.

Meanwhile the increasing demands made on the military Sunderland, especially after the start of warfare in the Pacific, led in 1942 to specification R.8/42 for a more powerful long-range flying-boat, to which Short Brothers responded with the Hercules-engined Sunderland IV. Eventually this grew so different from the Sunderland, with an improved hull, new tail and completely revised arm-ament, that it was renamed the Seaford I. Surprisingly, this saw only brief post-war service, but formed the basis for the civil Solent. The need for more power remained, however, and in early 1944 the decision was taken simply to re-engine

building 47, 48 and 60. This version entered service with No. 228 Sqn in February 1945. A further 33 were produced by conversion from Mk IIIAs. In August 1945 large contracts were cancelled, the last Sunderland coming from Belfast in June 1946, where, as at Dumbarton, some dozens of new boats were packed with new military equipment and deliberately sunk shortly after the end of the war.

Subsequently the Sunderland V was redesignated Sunder-land MR.5, as which it remained the standard RAF ocean flying-boat until retirement (appropriately, from Seletar) on 15 May 1959. In post-war years Sunderlands played a very large role in the Berlin Airlift; they were also the only RAF aircraft to be in action throughout the Korean War, flying 13,380 hours in 1,647 sorties. Aircraft of Nos 201 and 230 Sqns provided the entire heavy transport support for the 1951–4 British North Greenland Expedition. Others served as close-support bombers in Malaya, and one flew a doctor to HMS *Amethyst* in the Yangtse river while under fire from Chinese shore artillery. Sunderlands also formed an important part of the post-war strength of the RAAF, RNZAF, SAAF and France's Aéronavale. The last was stood down by the RNZAF in March 1967, but the surviving boat in the RAF Museum came from the Aéronavale in the Pacific.

This was one of more than 100 Sunderlands from which armament was removed to facilitate operations in the transport role. NZ4103, with individual name *Mataatua*, served in the south-west Pacific theatre with the RNZAF Flying Boat Transport Unit in 1944–6. These Mk IIIs were later replaced by the GR.5 which equipped Nos 5 and 6 Sqns post-war.

a Mk III with Pratt & Whitney R-1830-90B Twin Wasps, almost the same engine as used in the Catalina and Dakota and many other types and already in widespread RAF service. The 14-cylinder engine conferred a substantial improvement in climb, ceiling and engine-out performance, yet had hardly any effect on range, though cruising speed tended to be slightly higher. Operationally the US-engined machine had a big advantage in being able to cruise with two engines out on one side whereas the Sunderland III in this state lost height steadily. (In fairness to Bristol, the Twin Wasp was a larger engine than the 9-cylinder Pegasus, and nothing like as powerful as the 1,800-hp/1343-kW Hercules used in the Seaford.)

After trials in March 1944 the Twin Wasp Sunderland was accepted for production as the Mk V, with de Havilland Hydromatic propellers without spinners. ASV Mk III was fitted as standard, and in the course of 1944 Rochester, Belfast and Dumbarton all switched to the Mk V, respectively

Short Sunderland variants

Short S.25: prototype (K4774), originally flown with wing similar in plan to civil C-class S.23 and 950-hp (709-kW) Pegasus X engines

Sunderland prototype October 1941

Short Sunderland: four 1,010-hp (753-kW) Pegasus XXII, one machine-gun in nose turret and four in tail turret, weapon load 2,000 lb (907 kg) (total 89)

Sunderland 1 production standard

Short Sunderland II: four 1,065-hp (794-kW) Pegasus XVIII, ASV radar and (in course of production) improved armament (total 43)

Late production Sunderland Mk II

Short Sunderland III: improved planing bottom, progressively other changes including much heavier armament installations and (Mk IIIA) ASV III radar (total 461)

Sunderland Mk III

Short Sunderland IV: four 1,700-hp (1268-kW) Hercules XIX, prototype of Seaford with 1,800-hp (1343-kW) Hercules 100

Sunderland IV

Short Sunderland V: four 1,200-hp (895-kW) Pratt & Whitney R-1830-90B (total 155) (total Sunderland production 749)

Sunderland V

Focke-Wulf Fw 190

When the Focke-Wulf Fw 190 appeared in the skies over France in September 1941 RAF Intelligence simply could not credit that this squat, angular fighter really had the measure of the sleek, slender Spitfire V. Yet Kurt Tank's 'Butcher Bird' not only came to dominate those skies for eight months but remained one of the finest fighters in Europe until the end of Hitler's war.

Conceived in 1937 as a contemporary of the Hawker Typhoon and for the same reason, to replace the first generation of monoplane interceptors (the Hawker Hurricane and the Messerschmitt Bf 109), the design of the Focke-Wulf Fw 190 was tendered with two alternative engines, the Daimler-Benz DB601 inline and the B.M.W. 139 radial, the latter being selected to power the prototype on account of its assumed higher power development potential. Detail design commenced under the leadership of Oberingenieur Blaser and the first prototype was flown by test pilot Hans Sander at Bremen on 1 June 1939.

The first two aircraft featured large, low-drag ducted spinners but these were soon discarded as they were thought to cause engine overheating, and after the B.M.W. 139 had been abandoned the Fw 190A entered production with the B.M.W. 801 14-cylinder radial with fan-assisted cooling. The first nine pre-production Fw 190A-0s featured small wings of 161.46 sq ft (15.00 m²) area, but the definitive version had larger wings of 196.99 sq ft (18.30 m²) area.

Service trials at Rechlin went ahead in 1940 without undue problems, although Luftwaffe pilots suggested that the proposed armament of the Fw 190A-1 (four synchronized 7.92-mm/0.31-in MG 17 machine-guns) would meet with spirited criticism in combat service. Production of the 100 Fw 190A-1s at Hamburg and Bremen was completed by the end of May 1941, and these were powered by 1,600-hp (1194-kW) B.M.W. 801C engines which bestowed a top speed of 388 mph (624 km/h). The aircraft were flown by Erprobungsstelle at Rechlin and 6./JG 26, the latter based at Le Bourget in August. The following month the first combats were reported with RAF Supermarine Spitfire Vs, showing the German fighters to be markedly superior, albeit lacking in weapon punch.

New armament

Already, however, the early gun criticisms had led to the Fw 190A-2 version with two wing root-mounted synchronized 20-mm MG FF cannon and two MG 17 guns; with a speed of 382 mph (614 km/h), this up-gunned version still had the edge over the Spitfire V. By the end of March 1942 JG 26, commanded by Adolf Galland, was fully equipped with Fw 190A-2s. Thirty Fw 190As had accompanied the escort forces during the famous Channel break-out by the battle-cruisers *Scharnhorst* and *Gneisenau* in February, Fw 190A-2s of III/JG 26 being involved in the one-sided action against Lieutenant Commander Eugene Esmonde's Fairey Swordfish torpedo strike.

As the RAF desperately sought to introduce an answer to the Fw 190, production of the German fighter was stepped up as Focke-Wulf factories at Cottbus, Marienburg, Neubrandenburg, Schwerin, Sorau and Tutow joined the programme, as well as the Ago and Fieseler plants. The Fw 190A-3, with 1,700-hp (1268-kW) B.M.W. 801Dg, four 20-

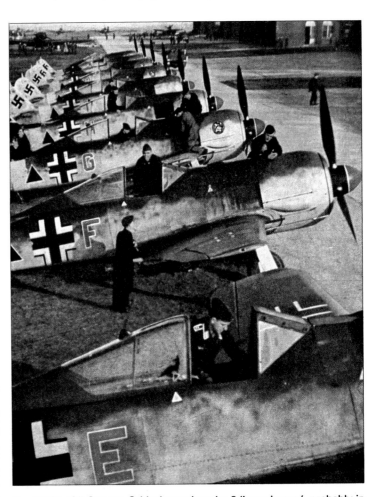

Fw 190Gs of II Gruppe, Schlachtgeschwader 2 'Immelmann', probably in mid-1943. The unit, commanded by Major Heinz Frank, had been the first to equip with this ground-attack version in North Africa but moved to the Eastern Front (note the yellow theatre panels).

Focke-Wulf Fw 190

Specification

Focke-Wulf Fw 190A-8
Type: single-seat fighter and fighter-bomber
Powerplant: one 2,100-hp (1567-kW) B.M.W. 801D-2
Performance: maximum speed (clean) 408 mph
(654 km/h); initial climb 2,363 ft (720 m)/min; normal
range 500 miles (805 km); service ceiling 37,400 ft
(11400 m)
Weight: empty 7,000 lb (3170 kg); maximum loaded
10,800 lb (4900 kg)
Dimensions: span 34 ft 5½ in (10.5 m); length
29 ft 0 in (8.84 m); height 13 ft 0 in (3.96 m); wing area
196.98 sq ft (18.3 m²)
Armament: (A-8/R2) two 7.9-mm MG17 machine-
guns, four 20-mm MG151/20 cannon, one 1,100-lb
(500-kg) and two 550-lb (250-kg) bombs, or one
66-Imp gal. (300-litre) drop tank

Major production version of the Focke-Wulf Fw 190 was the A-8
'Panzerbock', shown here in its basic configuration with the ETC 501
centreline store rank moved forward 7.9 in (20 cm) and carrying a 66-Imp
gal (300-litre) drop tank. Armed with four long-barrelled MG 151/20 20-
mm cannon in the wings and two MG 17 machine-guns in the nose, 'Red
19' was flown by Unteroffizier Ernst Schröder of 5.Staffel,
Jagdgeschwader 300, in 'Defence of the Reich' operations during October
and November 1944. II (Sturm) Gruppe of JG 300 had been formed with
Fw 190A-8s in July 1944 under Major Kurd Peters (awarded the Knight's
Cross in October that year), and was one of the fighter units opposing the
Western Allies during the invasion of Europe, adopting *Wilde Sau* night-
fighting tactics during the autumn. Staffelkapitän of 5.Staffel was
Oberleutnant Klaus Bretschneider, also a Knight's Cross holder, of whose
31 combat victories 14 were gained during *Wilde Sau* sorties, and who
was shot down and killed in combat with P-51s on 24 December 1944.

mm and two 7.92 mm (0.31-in) guns, joined II/JG 26 in
March 1942 and shortly afterwards the only other Luftwaffe
fighter Geschwader in the West, JG.2.

Thus by the time the RAF was ready to introduce its new
Spitfire IX and Typhoon fighters to combat over the Dieppe
landings in August 1942, the Luftwaffe could field some 200
Fw 190As in opposition. Unfortunately not only had the
RAF underestimated the number of these fighters available
but were unaware that a new version, the Fw 190A-4, had
appeared with a water-injected 2,100-hp (1567-kW) B.M.W.
801D-2 engine and a top speed of 416 mph (670 km/h), and
that a bomb-carrying variant, the Fw 190A-3/U1, was in
service. (The suffix U indicated *Unrüst-Bausatz*, or factory
conversion set.) The result was a stinging defeat for the RAF,
which lost a total of 106 aircraft including 97 to Fw 190s. As
a result largely of mismanagement, neither the Spitfire IX
nor the Typhoon had been able to redress the balance.

It would have been of little comfort had the RAF known
that the Germans had for many months devoted all their Fw
190 resources to the Channel front, such was the esteem held
for the Spitfire V. Indeed, despite the ferocious tempo of
battle on the Eastern Front, which had opened in June 1941,
no Fw 190A fighters fought on that front until well into 1942
when I/JG 51 received Fw 190A-4s. Fw 190A-3s and A-4s
were also issued to IV/JG 5 and to JG 1 for home defence and
protection of German fleet units in Norway. A reconnaissance
version of the Fw 190A-3 was first flown by 9.(H)/LG 2 in
March 1942 on the Russian Front. The Fw 190A-4/U4 reconnaissance fighter joined NAufklGr 13 in France, and Fw
190A-4/Trop ground-attack fighter-bombers appeared in
North Africa with I/SG 2 during 1942. Before the end of that
year Fw 190A-3/U1s and A-4/U8s of SKG 10, each able to
carry a 1,100-lb (500-kg) bomb, had embarked on a series of
day-light low-level 'tip and run' attacks against cities and

Focke-Wulf Fw 190

Pale grey Fw 190A-6/R11 of 1./NJG 10 flown by Oberleutnant Hans Krause from Werneuchen in August 1944. The pilot's insignia consisted of his nickname 'Illo' beneath the *Wilde Sau* emblem. Note *Neptun* radar arrays and two-shade grey on upper wing surface. Krause was later awarded the Knight's Cross.

'Defence of the Reich' Fw 190A-8 (note red fuselage band) of I Gruppe, Jagdgeschwader 1, based at Twenthe in the Netherlands in December 1944. An aircraft with white 'double chevrons' was being flown by Major Hans Ehlers, the Gruppenkommandeur, when he was shot down and killed on 27 December 1944.

ports in southern England, forcing Fighter Command to deploy disproportionately heavy fighter defences to counter the threat. Some measure of the dependence now placed on the Fw 190 may be judged from the fact that more than 1,900 Fw 190A-3s and A-4s had reached the Luftwaffe in 1942 (compared with 500 RAF Typhoons and Spitfire IXs).

Rocket launchers

Early in 1943 there appeared the Fw 190A-5 with slightly lengthened engine mountings, and with it a much increased range of *Rüstsätze* (field conversion kits), including the R6 that enabled the Fw 190A-5 (in modified form Fw 190A-5/ R6) to carry two under-wing WG21 8.27-in (21-cm) rocket-launchers for use against the growing Boeing B-17 and Consolidated B-24 bomber fleets operated by the USAAF. The Fw 190A-5/U2 night bomber could carry a 1,102-lb (500-kg) bomb and two 66-Imp gal (300-litre) drop tanks, the Fw 190A-5/U3 carried up to 2,205 lb (1000 kg) of bombs, the Fw 190A-5/U12 was a heavily armed fighter with six 20-mm MG 151/20 cannon and two MG 17s, while the Fw 190A-5/U15, of which three examples were built in November 1943, was equipped to carry a 2,094-lb (950-kg) LT950 torpedo (a torpedo-carrying Fw 190A-5/U14, a lighter version of the U15 torpedo-fighter, is said to have been flown in action by Hauptmann Helmut Viedebannt of SKG 10).

The Fw 190A-6, in its standard form with reduced wing structure weight, was armed with four fast-firing 20-mm

Focke-Wulf Fw 190A-3 cutaway drawing key

1 Rudder fixed tab	44 Flat-bottomed (equipment bay floor support) frame	79 Control column
2 Tail navigation light	45 First-aid kit	80 Seat pan
3 Leads	46 Optional camera (2 × Rb 12) installation (A-3/U4)	81 Starboard control console (circuit breakers)
4 Rudder hinge/attachment	47 Control runs	82 Underfloor linkage
5 Tailwheel extension spring	48 Access hatch (port side)	83 Electrical junction box
6 Tailwheel shock-absorber leg retraction guide	49 Electrical leads	84 Rudder pedal assembly
7 Tailfin spar	50 Distribution panel	85 Instrument panel sections
8 Rudder post assembly	51 Canopy channel slide cut-outs	86 Screen support frame
9 Rudder frame	52 Canopy solid aft fairing	87 Two 7.9 mm MG 17 machine-guns
10 Rudder upper hinge	53 Aerial	88 Ammunition feed chute
11 Aerial attachment	54 Head armour support bracket	89 Panel release catches
12 Tailfin structure	55 Aerial attachment/take-up pulley	90 Fuselage armament ammunition boxes
13 Canted rib progression	56 Equipment/effects stowage	91 Forward bulkhead
14 Port elevator fixed tab	57 FuG 7a/FuG 25a radio equipment bay	92 Inboard wing cannon ammunition boxes
15 Port elevator	58 Battery	93 Engine mounting lower attachment point
16 Mass balance	59 Cockpit aft bulkhead	94 Cooling air exit louvres
17 Port tailplane	60 Control runs	95 Engine mounting upper attachment point
18 Tailplane incidence motor unit	61 Cockpit floor/centre-section main structure	96 Oil pump assembly
19 Tailwheel retraction pulley cables	62 Wingroot fillet	97 Engine mounting ring
20 Tailplane attachment	63 Underfloor aft fuel tank (64 Imp gals/291 litres)	98 Fuselage MG 17 ammunition cooling pipes
21 Starboard tailplane structure	64 Underfloor forward fuel tank (51 Imp gal/232 litres)	99 Machine gun front mounting brackets
22 Elevator fixed tab	65 Cockpit sidewall control runs	
23 Starboard elevator frame	66 Seat support brackets	
24 Mass balance	67 Armoured bulkhead	
25 Tailplane front spar	68 Pilot's seat	
26 Semi-retractng tailwheel	69 Canopy operating handwheel	
27 Drag yoke	70 14-mm armoured backplate	
28 Tailwheel recess	71 Pilot's headrest	
29 Tailwheel locking linkage	72 Canopy	
30 Access panel	73 Windscreen frame assembly	
31 Actuating link	74 Armoured-glass windscreen	
32 Push-pull rod	75 Revi gunsight	
33 Rudder cables	76 Instrument panel shroud	
34 Rudder control differential linkage	77 Throttle	
35 Fuselage/tail unit join	78 Port control console	
36 Elevator control differential		
37 Fuselage lift tube		
38 Elevator control cables		
39 Bulkhead (No. 12) fabric panel (rear fuselage equipment dust protection)		
40 Leather grommets		
41 Rudder push-pull rods		
42 Fuselage frame		
43 Master compass		

First of the 190 series to be powered by the 1,660-hp (1238-kW) B.M.W. 801C-0 engine were the Fw 190 V5k and V5g, the former with small wing (161.46 sq ft/15.0 m² area), illustrated here, and the latter with enlarged wing (196.98 sq ft/18.3 m² area). The latter was chosen for production on account of superior manoeuvrability.

Displaying the black-white-black 'Defence of the Reich' bands of Jagdgeschwader 4, 'White Eleven' was an Fw 190A-8 of the Geschwader's I Gruppe, based at Delmenhorst during the winter of 1944–5. Painting of the Geschwaderzeichen on the engine cowling was fairly rare at this late, hectic stage of the war.

'Blue Eight' of Schlachtgeschwader 4 during Unternehmen 'Bodenplatte' of 1 January 1945. This Fw 190-F8 with *Spiralschnauze* (spiral nose) markings was based at Köln-Wahn and featured the blue Staffel colour characteristic of bomber units.

100 Machine gun breech blister fairings
101 Port split flap section
102 Flap actuating electric motor
103 Port outer 20-mm MG FF cannon
104 Aileron control linkage
105 Aileron fixed tab
106 Port aileron
107 Aileron hinge points
108 Port detachable wingtip
109 Port navigation light
110 Front spar
111 Wing lower shell
112 MG FF muzzle
113 Port mainwheel leg fairing
114 Aileron link assembly
115 Fuselage MG 17 muzzles
116 Muzzle troughs
117 Upper cowling panel
118 Fuselage MG 17 electrical synchronizing unit
119 Exhaust pipes
120 Cowling panel ring
121 BMW 801D-2 radial engine
122 Former ring
123 Upper panel release catches
124 Forward cowling support ring
125 Oil tank armour
126 Oil tank (10 Imp gal/ 45.5 litres)
127 Annular oil cooler assembly
128 Cooler armoured ring
129 Engine twelve-blade cooling fan
130 Three-blade propeller
131 Propeller boss
132 Oil cooler airflow track
133 Airflow duct fairing (to rear cylinders)
134 Lower panel release catches
135 Cowling lower panel section
136 Wingroot fairing
137 Centre-section wheel covers
138 Inboard 20-mm cannon muzzle
139 Wheel cover operating cable
140 Starboard wheel well
141 Mainwheel leg rib cut-out
142 Undercarriage retraction jack
143 Locking unit assembly
144 Inboard 20-mm cannon spent cartridge chute
145 Front spar inboard assembly
146 Ammunition feed chute
147 Fuselage/front spar attachment
148 Ammunition box bay
149 Starboard inboard 20-mm MG 151 cannon
150 Breech blister fairing
151 Fuselage/rear spar attachment
152 Rear spar
153 Starboard flap assembly
154 Inboard solid ribs
155 Rotating drive undercarriage retraction unit
156 Radius rod hinge
157 Outboard 20-mm cannon muzzle
158 Mainwheel leg strut mounting assembly
159 Undercarriage actuation drive motor
160 Starboard outboard 20-mm MG FF cannon
161 Front spar assembly
162 Ammunition drum
163 Rib cut-out
164 Aileron control linkage
165 Aileron fixed tab
166 Starboard aileron frame
167 Aileron hinge points
168 Rear spar

169 Wing lower shell outer 'floating ribs'
170 Wing undersurface inner skinning
171 Starboard detachable wingtip
172 Starboard navigation light
173 Leading-edge assembly
174 Nose rib attachment lips

175 Mainwheel leg fairing
176 Mainwheel leg
177 Brake lines
178 Fairing
179 Torque links
180 Axle hub assembly
181 Mainwheel fairing
182 Starboard mainwheel
183 Pitot head
184 Ventral bomb-rack aluminium aft fairing
185 Ventral bomb-rack carrier unit
186 ETC 500 ventral bomb-rack (A-3/U1)
187 SC 500 optional bomb load

Participating in the great tank battle of Kursk in July 1943, this Fw 190A-4/U3 of the Gefechtsverband Druschel (II/SG 1) features yellow theatre panels, fighter arm staff marks (forward black bar), Gruppe marks (aft black bar) and 4.Staffel (red) individual letter. Oberst Alfred Druschel, one of the most experienced assault pilots in the Luftwaffe, was killed on 1 January 1945.

Temporarily painted matt black, an Fw 190 A-5/U8 of I Gruppe, Schnellkampfgeschwader (SKG) 10, with centreline bomb rack and wing drop tanks, during the Jabo attacks on southern England during summer 1943. Based at Poix in France, this unit virtually obliterated all national insignia in the interests of camouflage.

'Yellow Nine' of II Gruppe (denoted by the yellow horizontal bar), Jagdgeschwader 54 'Grünherz' was an Fw 190A-5 flown by Leutnant Helmut Sturm at Petseri in Estonia during June 1944. The yellow panels indicate the theatre.

guns inside the wings (in addition to the two MG 17s in the nose); the Fw 190A-6/R1 carried six 20-mm guns in underwing packs; and the Fw 190A-6/R6 mounted four 30-mm MK 108 cannon in these packs, making it the most heavily-armed single-seater of the war. The Fw 190A-6/R4 with turbocharged B.M.W. 801TS had a top speed of 424 mph (683 km/h) at 34,450 ft (10500 m). Fighter-bomber versions of the Fw 190A-6 were able to carry a 2,205-lb (1000-kg) bomb under the fuselage.

The greatest single victory by Fw 190A-6s of JG1, JG5, JG 26, JG51 and JG 54 was gained on 14 October 1943, when they decimated the US 8th Air Force's daylight bombers attacking Regensburg and Schweinfurt, destroying 79 and damaging 121 out of the force of 228. Had it not been for the introduction of superlative American close-escort fighters, particularly the North American P-51 Mustang, the Fw 190-equipped Jagdflieger must have decisively suppressed American daylight bombing attempts early in 1944.

Notwithstanding these successes, the changing fortunes of war forced the Luftwaffe to adopt a wholly defensive stance, of an increasingly desperate nature. As the RAF night bomber offensive increased in weight the Luftwaffe employed Fw 190As (in particular Fw 190A-5/U2s) in the night-fighting role on moonlit nights, and the 'Wild Boar' tactics of Hajo Hermann's 30 Jagddivision, with three Geschwäder, are reckoned to have accounted for some 200 RAF heavy bombers during the latter half of 1943.

While Fw 190A fighter-bombers were in action in the Mediterranean theatre, there appeared the Fw 190A-7 with a pair of 20-mm cannon in the nose decking (in addition to the various wing gun combinations), and the Fw 190A-8 with GM-1 nitrous-oxide power-boosting and all the adaptability afforded by earlier Rüstsatz additions. The Fw 190A-8/U1 was a two-seat version, of which three examples were produced to assist the conversion training of Junkers Ju 87 pilots to the Fw 190 for the ground-attack squadrons on the Eastern Front. The Fw 190A-8/U3 was the upper component of the Mistel (Mistletoe) composite weapon, riding the back of explosive-packed, unmanned Junkers Ju 88 aircraft. The Fw 190A-8/U11 anti-shipping strike aircraft, with a BT700

The unarmed Focke-Wulf Fw 190 V1 (first Prototype, D-OPZE) with fan-cooled B.M.W. 139 and ducted spinner, at the time of its first flight on 1 June 1939. Numerous other differences from subsequent production versions are evident, including small tail-wheel, absence of fuselage wheel doors, and the hinged door covers on the wheel leg.

Early Focke-Wulf Fw 190A-1s undergoing final assembly at Bremen in 1941. Particularly evident in this picture is the exceptionally wide-track main landing gear and the large number of hinged panels providing access to the compact B.M.W. 801 radial engine. Just visible are the pair of nose-mounted MG 17 machine-guns.

'Black Twelve', an Fw 190D-9 (with early-style cockpit canopy) of 10.Staffel, Jagdgeschwader 54 'Grünherz'. Participating in Unternehmen 'Bodenplatte' on January 1, 1945, the aircraft crashed at Wemmel, Belgium. The yellow panels possibly indicate an aircraft withdrawn from the Eastern Front for the occasion.

Displaying pale blue-grey finish with dark grey dappling, this Fw 190D-9 of III/JG 2 'Richthofen' was based at Altenstadt in December 1944. Note the absence of white on fuselage and fin markings.

1,543-lb (700-kg) torpedo-bomb, was flown in attacks against the Russian Black Sea Fleet in February 1944. The Fw 190A-9, with armoured wing leading edge, was powered by a 2,000-hp (1490-kW) B.M.W. 801F (although the Fw 190A-9/R11 had a turbocharged B.M.W. 801TS). The Fw 190A-10, of which only prototypes were completed, featured provision for an increased range of bombs. Among the purely experimental versions of the Fw 190A were the Fw 190V74 with a seven-barrelled 30-mm SG117 Rohrblock cannon aimed by a Revi 242 gunsight, and the extraordinary Fw 190V75 with seven 17.72-in (45-cm) downward-firing mortars intended for low-level anti-tank use from a height of about 30 ft (10 m). Another interesting experiment was the use of large *Doppelreiter* overwing fuel tanks on the Fw 190A-8, evaluated by Erprobungskommando 25 under Major Georg Christl in July 1944.

New power

The arrival of the Spitfire IX in Fighter Command and its threat to combat domination by the Fw 190A led to the development of the Fw 190B series with GM-1 power-boosted B.M.W. 801D-2 engine and pressure cabin, but trouble with the latter led to the abandonment of this version after only a few prototypes had been produced. The Fw 190C series, of which five prototypes were completed with DB603 inline engines, annular radiators, Hirth 9-2281 superchargers and four-blade propellers, was also abandoned early in 1944.

The Fw 190D, with 1,770-hp (1320-kW) Junkers Jumo 213A-1 engine and annular radiator in a much-lengthened nose (necessitating increased fin and rudder area), proved very successful after it had first flown at Langenhagen in

May 1944. The first production Fw 190D-9s (so termed as they followed the Fw 190A-8s at the factories, and widely known as Dora-Nines in the Luftwaffe) joined III/JG 54 in September 1944 to defend the jet base of Kommando Nowotny. Among the sub-variants of the Fw 190D series was the Fw 190D-10 with a single 30-mm MK 108 cannon located between the engine cylinder banks and firing through the propeller hub. The Fw 190D-12/R21, a ground-attack version of the hub-gunned Fw 190D-10 and power-boosted with MW50 water-methanol injection, was almost certainly the fastest of all Fw 190s with a top speed of 453 mph (750 km/h) at 36,090 ft (11000 m). Dora-Nines equipped most of the Luftwaffe's fighter units during the last fateful months of the Third Reich, but in combat with the P-51s and Spitfire XIVs were frequently overwhelmed. The problems centred on fuel shortage which allowed only small formations with battle-hardened veteran pilots. For instance, when JG 6 (commanded by Major Gerhard Barkhorn, who had a record of 301 air victories) in April 1945 took delivery of 150 new Dora-Nines, it could only fly patrols of four against massed Allied fighters.

The Fw 190F and Fw 190G series were essentially ground-attack versions, the Fw 190F ('Panzer-Blitz') armoured assault aircraft appearing in the spring of 1944. Externally similar to the Fw 190A series, but with a bulged hood, this version featured gun armament reduced to two MG 17s and two 20-mm cannon, but had the ability to carry the 2,205-lb (1000-kg) bomb plus two 110-lb (50-kg) fragmentation bombs. Most important sub-variant was the Fw 190F-8, which could carry 14 8.27-in (21-cm) rocket bombs, six 11.02-in (28-cm) rocket-launchers or 24 R4M unguided rockets; Fw 190F-8s first joined III(Pz)/KG 200 in the autumn of 1944.

First of several torpedo-carrying versions of the Fw 190 was the A-5/U14 (c/n 871), shown here carrying an LT F5b torpedo. It probably saw action with SKG 10. The rack fairing of this version was deeper than that on the U15 which carried an LT 950 2094-lb (950-kg) weapon. Note the considerably lengthened tailwheel assembly.

Second unarmed prototype for the proposed high-altitude Fw 190C-series was the V18, shown here in its U1 guise with DB 603A-engine (which replaced the earlier DB 603G), four-blade propeller and Hirth 9-2281 turbocharger. Inclusion of a pressure cabin is evidenced by strengthening members on the canopy.

Captured at Marienburg, East Prussia, by the advancing Russians, this Fw 190D-9 flew with an IAP of the Red Banner Baltic Fleet Air Force in the spring of 1945. The addition of a ventral mast presumably indicates the inclusion of Soviet radio equipment.

The Fw 190G series actually entered operational service long before the Fw 190F, the first aircraft being sent to North Africa, joining SG 2 at Zarzoun, Tunisia, following the 'Torch' landings in November 1942. The majority, however, went to the Eastern Front where they played an active part at the great tank battle of Kursk in early July 1943. The Fw 190G-1 version, with greatly strengthened undercarriage, could lift a 3,968-lb (1800-kg) bomb.

Long-nose derivative

Mention must also be made of a development of the Fw 190, the Ta 152 (its designation finally reflecting Kurt Tank's overall design responsibility). This 'long-nose' derivative of the Fw 190D series retained the hub-firing 30-mm gun but introduced increased electrical systems. Various prototypes of the Ta 152A, B and C variants were produced, but it was the Ta 152H-1 version with one 30-mm and two 20-mm guns and a maximum speed of 472 mph (760 km/h) at 41,010 ft (12500 m) that was selected for operational service; only about a dozen aircraft of this type had been completed and delivered to JG 301 when the war ended. A total of 26 Ta 152

prototypes and 67 pre-production and production aircraft was completed.

Having regard to the nature of the Luftwaffe's defensive operations during the last 30 months of the war, it is scarcely surprising that production assumed impressive proportions, no fewer than 20,087 Fw 190s (including 86 prototypes) being produced during the 1939–45 period, the peak daily production rate of 22 aircraft per day being reached early in 1944.

By the same token many Luftwaffe pilots achieved remarkable combat feats at the controls of Fw 190s (not forgetting that of Josef Würmheller who shot down seven Spitfire Vs in one day over the Dieppe beaches – despite concussion and a broken leg suffered in a recent accident). Pride of place must go to Oberleutnant Otto Kittel, the Luftwaffe's fourth highest scoring pilot, of whose 267 air victories some 220 were gained in Fw 190A-4s and -5s. Other very high scorers in Fw 190s included Walter Nowotny, Heinz Bär, Hermann Graf and Kurt Bühligen, all of whose scores included more than 100 victories gained with the guns of the aptly named Butcher Bird.

Focke-Wulf Fw 190 and Ta 152 variants

Fw 190V1 to V80 (plus six others): prototypes and progressive development aircraft, 1939–44; served as prototypes for Fw 190A to G series and some Ta 152s
Fw 190A-0: nine aircraft with small wings, remaining 11 with large wings; B.M.W. 801C-1; four 7.92-mm (0.31-in) guns
Fw 190A-1: four 7.92-mm (0.31-in) guns
Fw 190A-2: two 20-mm and two 7.92-mm (0.31-in) guns; B.M.W. 801C-2

Fw 190A-3/U4 reconnaissance fighter

Fw 190A-3: four 20-mm and two 7.92-mm (0.31-in) guns; B.M.W. 801D-2; also U1 fighter-bomber, U3 ground-attack fighter, U4 reconnaissance fighter and U7 fighter-bomber; 'Trop' sub-variants

Fw 190A-4/U8 with SC500 bomb and underwing tanks

Fw 190A-4: FuG16Z radio; B.M.W. 801D-2 with MW50 injection; U1 and U8 fighter-bombers, U4 ground-attack fighter, R6 bomber-destroyer; 'Trop' sub-variants; introduced *Rüstsatz*

Fw 190A-5/U14 with LT F5b torpedo

Fw 190A-5: slightly lengthened mounting for B.M.W. 801D-2; U2 night ground-attack aircraft, U3 similar with increased bombload, U4 reconnaissance aircraft, U6 and U8 fighter-bombers, U11 bomber-destroyer, U13 ground-attack fighter, U14 and U15 torpedo-fighters, U16 bomber-destroyer, U17 was prototype for Fw 190F-3; 'Trop' sub-variants

Fw 190A-6/R1 with four underwing 20-mm cannon

Fw 190A-6: FuG16Ze and FuG125 radio; lighter wing structure; R1 to R4 bomber-destroyers, R4 with B.M.W. 801TS; R6 bomber-destroyer with underwing rockets; 'Trop' sub-variants

Fw 190A-7: two 20-mm and two 13-mm (0.51-in) guns; *Rüstsatz* conversions as for Fw 190A-6

Fw 190A-7: two 20-mm and two 13-mm (0.51-in) guns; *Rüstsatz* conversions as for Fw 190A-6

Fw 190A-8/U1 two-seat conversion trainer

Fw 190A-8: FuG16ZY radio; GM-1 power boosting; *Rüstsatz* conversions R1 to R6 as for Fw 190A-6; R7 had armoured cockpit; R11 all-weather fighter had PKS12 and FuG125 radio; R12 similar but with two 30-mm guns; U1 two-seat trainer; U3 upper component of Mistel weapon; U11 fighter/torpedo-bomber
Fw 190A-9: B.M.W. 801F; *Rüstsatz* conversions similar to Fw 190A-6, but R11 had B.M.W. 801TS, and R12 similar but with two 30-mm guns
Fw 190A-10: numerous prototypes only; B.M.W. 801TS/TH; three bomb or drop tank stations; four 20-mm and two 13-mm (0.51-in) guns
Fw 190B-0: three prototypes modified from Fw 190A-1s; various wing planforms; failure of pressure cabin caused discontinuation; one Fw 190B-1 not completed

Fw 190V18/U1 with DB 603A-1 engine

Focke-Wulf Fw 190C high altitude fighter project

Fw 190C-0: six prototypes, including one modified Fw 190A-0; various engines with Hirth supercharger; development abandoned
Fw 190D-0: 10 aircraft converted from Fw 190A-7s; Junkers Jumo 213A engines with annular radiators; first 'long-nose' Fw 190s
Fw 190D-9: Jumo 213A; two 20-mm and two 13-mm (0.51-in) guns; most aircraft had bulged hoods; R11 all-weather fighter with FuG125 radio
Fw 190D-10: two prototypes converted from Fw 190D-0s; single 30-mm hub-gun replaced guns in nose decking
Fw 190D-11: seven prototypes only; two 20-mm and two 30-mm guns; R20 with PKS12 radio; R21 with FuG125 radio
Fw 190D-12: one 30-mm and two 20-mm guns; armoured Jumo 213F, R5 ground-attack fighter; R11 all-weather fighter; R21 with MW50 injection; R25 with Jumbo 213EB
Fw 190D-13: Jumo 213EB; three 20-mm guns; R5, R11, R21 and R25 as for Fw 190D-12
Fw 190D-14: DB603A; two prototypes converted from Fw 190D-9 and Fw 190D-12
Fw 190E: reconnaissance fighter project; not built
Fw 190F-1: armoured fighter-bomber; one ETC501 and two ETC50 bomb racks; bulged canopy

Fw 190F-2 with centreline ETC501 and ER-4 racks

Fw 190F-2: similar to Fw 190F-1 but additional ER4 adaptor bomb rack
Fw 190F-3: provision for underwing drop tanks; R3 with two underwing 30-mm guns

Fw 190F-8/U14 carrying LT 950 torpedo

Fw 190F-8 with Sg 113A Förstersonde 45-mm Sabot-firing weapons

Fw 190F-8: provision for variety of rockets and anti-personnel weapons; U1 was proposed two-seat trainer; U2 and U3 had provision to carry various torpedo-bombs and U14 was torpedo-fighter; R1, R2, R3, R5, R8, R11, R14, R15 and R16 all provided for various armament combinations

Fw 190F-8/U2 with Bt 700 torpedo bomb

Fw 190F-9: armoured version of Fw 190A-9 and produced in parallel; B.M.W. 801TS
Fw 190F-10 to F-14: unbuilt projects
Fw 190F-15: one prototype; Fw 190A-8 wing; B.M.W. 801TS/TH
Fw 190F-16: one prototype; increased armour
Fw 190G-0: two 20-mm guns; maximum bombload 2,205 lb (1000 kg)
Fw 190G-1: strengthened undercarriage; one 3,968-lb (1800-kg) bomb; Junkers bombrack
Fw 190G-2: as above but Messerschmitt bombrack
Fw 190G-3: as above but Focke-Wulf bombrack; R5 could carry four fragmentation bombs under the wings
Fw 190G-4: three ETC503 bombracks
Fw 190G-7: was intended to carry single 198-Imp gal (900-litre) drop tank
Fw 190G-8: B.M.W. 801D-2, otherwise similar to Fw 190A-8, R4 had GM1 power boost
Fw 190H-1: proposed high-altitude fighter with DB603G, but not built
Ta 152A-1: unbuilt project similar to Fw 190D-9 with FuG24 radio
Ta 152A-2: unbuilt project as above but with four 20-mm guns
Ta 152B-1, Ta 152B-2: unbuilt projects
Ta 152B-3: armoured ground-attack fighter project
Ta 152B-4: heavy fighter project; R1 with two 13-mm and two 20-mm guns; R2 with three 30-mm and two 20-mm guns
Ta 152B-5: one prototype built (Fw 190V53); three 20-mm guns; R11, three prototypes built (Ta 152V19, V20 and V21)
Ta 152C: three prototypes built; DB603L
Ta 152C-0 and C-1: three prototypes completed; DB603L; many gun combinations proposed
Ta 152E-1: photo-reconnaissance aircraft; two prototypes completed
Ta 152E-2: high-altitude version of Ta 152E-1; one prototype (Ta 152V26) completed
Ta 152H: high-altitude fighter; Jumo 213E; three modified Fw 190 prototypes (Fw 190V29, V30 and V32)
Ta 152H-0: 20 pre-production aircraft built at Cottbus in 1944; Jumo 213Eb; R11, R21 and R31 variants with engine boost and radio variations
Ta 152H-1: one prototype (Ta 152V26) modified from Ta 152E-2 and about a dozen production examples
Ta 153: one prototype (Fw 190V32) modified from Ta 152H prototype to include very high aspect ratio wing

Ilyushin Il Shturmovik

Outside the USSR the Ilyushin Il-2 and Il-10 remain, almost unbelievably, a lesser-known type, even to young enthusiasts. But more were built than of any other aircraft in history. And Stalin said: 'They are needed by the Red Army like it needs air or bread'.

For every Hurricane built there were three Il-2s, and for every Lancaster or Mosquito there were five. No flying machine of man's creation has ever poured off assembly lines at such a sustained high rate as the Il-2, despite its immense manufacturing problems. And the most serious of these problems centred on the fact that the Il-2 was almost a flying tank, with better armour protection than any previous production aircraft. Remarkably, apart from this crucial factor of armour, the Il-2's specification was almost identical to that of the UK's disastrous Fairey Battle, which was shot down in droves. The big difference was that the Battle was conceived as a level day bomber, whereas the Il-2 was a specialized armoured ground-attack aircraft.

Until recently the USSR has generally regarded air power as an adjunct to ground forces, and in the 1930s it paid much more attention than any other country to creating survivable close-support and attack aircraft. In addition to numerous

technically fascinating prototypes, its large air armament organization, NII-AV, managed the development of the world's best air weapons, including excellent large-calibre guns, heavy recoilless cannon, hollow-charge armour-piercing bombs and similar warheads fitted to air-launched rockets. From 1929 a succession of heavily armed attack aircraft appeared, and in 1935 the Kremlin issued a requirement for a BSh (*Bronirovanyi Shturmovik*, or armoured attacker) aircraft specifically for knocking out armoured vehicles and ground strong-points. Polikarpov's team built a potentially outstanding twin-engined attacker, the VIT-1, with great speed and four 37-mm cannon, but this pro-

Il-2s depart from a forward base on a combat mission, probably in 1942. These are quite early single-seaters, though the nearest aircraft has VYa cannon whose barrels were longer than those of the ShVAK. Note the twin-oleo main landing gears with low-pressure tyres.

83

Ilyushin Il-2/Il-10

Specification

Ilyushin Il-10

Type: two-seat attack and anti-armour aircraft

Powerplant: one 2,000-hp (1492-kW) Mikulin AM-42 inline piston engine

Performance: maximum speed at sea level 319 mph (513 km/h); initial climb rate 1,970 ft (600 m) per minute; range 621 miles (1000 km)

Weight: empty 9,921 lb (4500 kg); maximum take-off 14,409 lb (6536 kg)

Dimensions: span 43 ft 11 in (13.4 m); length 36 ft 8¾ in (11.2 m); height 11 ft 5¾ in (3.50 m); wing area 323.0 sq ft (30.0 m²)

Armament: in this example, four 23-mm NS-23 and one 20-mm cannon, plus four wing bomb cells for total of 2,205 lb (1000 kg) or external carriage of bombs up to 1,323-lb (600-kg) size, plus eight RS-82 rockets on underwing launch rails

Il-2/Il-10 variants

TsKB-55: original two prototypes, both two-seaters with AM-35 engine

TsKB-57: third prototype, single-seater with AM-38 engine and better protection and armament; basis for initial production aircraft

BSh-2: designation of original production aircraft, with numerous detail refinements, deliveries from April to May 1941

Il-2: designation of BSh-2 under revised 1941 policy of designating according to design team rather than by function.

Il-2M: first modified version with revised structure to save aluminium

Il-2M2: second modified version with VYa-23 guns and AM-38F engine

Il-2M3: third modified version with rear gunner and other changes including improved protection; remained in production with successive refinements to reduce drag and increase flight performance

Il-2U: tandem dual-control trainer with glasshouse canopy over two pilots both facing ahead

Il-2T: torpedo-carrier with reduced armour and firepower but 21-in (533-mm) torpedo

Il-8: revised design with improved airframe and 2,000-hp (1492-kw) AM-42 engine

Il-10: succeeded Il-2 in production in 1944; completely new airframe, AM-42 engine and improved armament and systems; also **Il-10U** trainer

Il-16: prototype with AM-43 engine

Subject of the three-view illustration, the Il-10 was greatly cleaned up compared with the Il-2, and also differed greatly in airframe shape, structure and systems. The fuselage was deeper and better streamlined, the armoured cockpits closer together and the gunner had a 20-mm gun in a better mounting with a glazed cupola fairing. Though heavier, the Il-10 had simpler main landing gears, with single legs and wheels that rotated to lie flat inside the wing. The Il-10, operated by the Soviet tactical air force in Germany in 1945, had four 23-mm wing guns, a choice often associated with a single or twin UB at the rear.

gramme ground to a halt, partly because the VIT and derived designs could not safely fly from short front-line airstrips. By 1938 the need was even more urgent, and the OKBs (design bureaux) of Sergei V. Ilyushin and Pavel O. Sukhoi were set in head-on competition. Sukhoi was overloaded, but Ilyushin put a strong team on the project at once, though he personally was handicapped by being injured in a crash.

Both designers adopted a conventional low-wing single-engined configuration, but in the spring of 1939 Ilyushin's was ready much quicker. Designated TsKB-55, with the service designation BSh-2, it was powered by a large 1,350-hp (1007-kW) AM-35 liquid-cooled engine, and seated the pilot and radio operator/rear gunner/observer in tandem.

Colour schemes of Soviet aircraft in World War 2 were often irregular or non-standard. One of these Il-2s appears to be in white winter garb, while the nearer machine is probably green and fawn. Both are single-seaters of the pre-1943 type, with ShVAK cannon and eight rocket rails under the broad metal-skinned wings.

Each main landing gear had twin shock struts and retracted backwards into an underwing container. The wing, hydraulic flaps and tail were of light alloy, but the fuselage comprised a challenging forward section with a light alloy and steel-tube structure above, and a lower part made up of 1,543 lb (700 kg) of armour which covered the underside of the engine, coolant pipes, radiator, fuselage tanks and cockpits, other parts being attached directly to it (thus the armour was a structural part of the aircraft). The rear fuselage was wood. Four 7.62-mm (0.3-in) guns were mounted in the wings outboard of the main landing gear legs, with a fifth in the rear cockpit, and four compartments in the centre sections housed up to 1,323 lb (600 kg) of bombs.

Crash programme

Ilyushin was dissatisfied with the poor armament, and on test in the hands of Vladimir K. Kokkinaki the TsKB-55 showed, as predicted, poor stability. An improved second prototype, with the centre of gravity shifted forward and a larger tailplane, flew on 30 December 1939, but NII (State) testing in the summer of 1940 considered the good features outweighed by poor stability, range and general performance. Ilyushin therefore launched a 'crash programme' which in four months produced the TsKB-57. This was fitted with the 1,600-hp (1194-kW) AM-38, had an extra fuel tank instead of a rear cockpit, thicker and better distributed armour, two of the wing guns replaced by 20-mm ShVAK cannon and new underwing rails for eight RS-82 rockets. This was a much better machine, which reached 292 mph (470 km/h) and had good agility. All that now had to be done was improve the engine and oil cooling, raise the seat, redesign the canopy and cut-down rear fuselage, and refine the engine installation for better airflow, better access and flame-damping ejector exhausts. Very large scale production was then put in hand at three factories, in Moscow, at Fili to the north and at Voronezh to the south.

The Il-2M3 is also seen in one of the accompanying photographs. It was by no means uncommon to remove the rear cockpit canopy to give the gunner a free field of fire. It was also common for the gunner to have twin UB guns, though with reduced ammunition. The slogan *mstitel* painted on the side means 'Avenger'.

Taken in the latter part of 1944, this photograph shows Il-2M3 two-seaters on the Eastern Front, which by this time had almost everywhere been pushed beyond the frontiers of the Soviet Union and into Poland, Romania and other countries.

The Russian national insignia assumed many forms, including stars with circles in the centre, or with dark/light shades in each of the five arms, or with a yellow (less often, white) border when on a dark background. This unidentified Il-2M3 on the Stalingrad front in early 1943 had stars without borders.

This Il-10 was captured from the People's Republic of North Korea during the Korean War in 1951, and was photographed at Wright Field after its armament had been removed. It was found to handle extremely well, but of course was generally thought to be obsolescent. The use of the Skyraider in Vietnam questions this assessment.

This photograph shows the Czech-built dual-control pilot trainer version of the Il-10, with Czech designation of BS-33. The cockpits were spaced farther apart, the rear seat (occupied by the instructor) in this case of course facing ahead. Most BS-33s retained most of the armour, but this example appears to be unarmed.

When the Germans invaded on 22 June 1941, 249 had been delivered and a few were in service; but this was far below target. The director of the Kirov works at Leningrad, whence came the vital steel armour, tried to exonerate himself by showing Stalin a large drawing that had been used at a design conference and covered with doodles by Ilyushin, saying: 'How can I work from such shoddy drawings?' Stalin was naive enough to be taken in by this crude trick, and struck fear into Ilyushin with a telephone call telling him he would be 'brought to account'. Eventually Stalin was told the true state of affairs; the Kirov director was replaced, and Ilyushin's 2nd-class Stalin Prize was upped to 1st-class. In October the Moscow and Fili plants had to be closed and their tooling and workers evacuated far to the east, the chief new production centre being at Kuybyshyev. But output was slow to build up, and Stalin (by this time left in no doubt of the crucial value of the Il-2) sent a telegram to the factory directors telling them their performance was 'an insult'. He went on: 'The Red Army needs the Il-2 as it needs air or bread. I demand more. This is my last warning!'

This really put a spurt into the output, but, as well as the evacuation and the onset of winter, the aircraft itself still needed changes. Major parts of the outer wings and tail were redesigned in wood, to save aluminium, and in early 1942 the ShVAK guns were replaced by the much harder-hitting 23-mm VYa. Later in 1942 the designation changed to Il-2M2 with the introduction of the 1,750-hp (1306-kW) AM-38F engine, which improved all-round performance even with an increase in armour to 2,094 lb (950 kg). But losses to fighters were severe, and it was not practical to provide adequate armour against fire from above and behind. Many front-line regiments had taken the matter into their own

hands and fitted a rear cockpit for a gunner, who was usually one of their own ground crew. Despite Stalin's reluctance to sanction any further modifications, Ilyushin was authorized to produce prototypes with a rear gunner, and these flew in March 1942. The gunner had a 0.5-in (12.7-mm) UB with 150 rounds and, differently from original TsKB-55, was separated from the pilot by the amidships fuel tank. Production was eventually sanctioned in October 1942 as the Il-2M3; this new two-seater was in action with the Central Front by the end of October, and with the Stalingrad Front by November.

Streamlining modifications

Losses were immediately sharply curtailed, while casualties among Luftwaffe fighters increased. Production by this time was running at close to 1,000 per month, despite the introduction of a succession of minor changes which in the main were aimed at improving flight performance, which had fallen to a maximum speed of 251 mph (404 km/h). No detailed record was kept of these changes, but 18 have been identified in photographs in the West, and there were probably others. Almost every part that could be better streamlined was modified if it could be done without disrupting production, and among the more obvious were the windshield, cowling panels, radiators and ducts, wing roots, main-gear pods, tailwheel, and control-surface gaps and hinges. By mid-1943 maximum speed had improved to 273 mph (439 km/h) despite continuing growth in weight.

Part of the weight growth was due to increased armament, which benefitted from the superb products of the air weapon design staff. Most important was the new family of 37-mm guns, unrelated to earlier weapons of this calibre and firing high-velocity ammunition fully capable of penetrating Pzkpfw V (Panther) and Pzkpfw VI (Tiger) tanks, except in a head-on attack (these big guns are still in widespread use, notably on Su-7 series attack aircraft). Additional types of bombs could be carried in the wing cells, while underwing loads were expanded to include the large (132-mm/5.2-in calibre) RS-132 rocket and boxes of 200 small PTAB anti-armour bombs.

In 1942 Engineer-Colonel Alexei Sidorov, who had managed two-seat conversions of several fighters including the Hawker Hurricane Mk II, led a small team (curiously, at naval aviation workshops) which produced the first dual-control Il-2. Several were produced by field conversion, and by 1943 small numbers were factory-built as the Il-2U, most

This Il-2M3 was serving at the end of World War 2 with the 3rd Attack Regiment (*Szturmowego Pulk*) of the Polish 1st Mixed Air Corps, one of the first non-Soviet units to be equipped with these aircraft. This aircraft was replaced by the Il-10 in about 1947 or possibly early 1948, the Poles again being some of the first foreign recipients.

with reduced armament. Another field modification resulted in the Il-2T torpedo-carrier, which with the greatest ease carried a 21-in (533-mm) torpedo. The VMF (today the separate AV-MF, or naval air force) used this version operationally, though it is not known if they were factory-built. There were countless local modifications, notably various kinds of tug and several semi-standard reconnaissance conversions with either one or two cameras in the rear fuselage. It also became common practice to use the Il-2 as a front-line passenger transport with one passenger or casualty lying in the rear fuselage, loaded through the rear cockpit, and two in the main-gear pods, the pilot having to remember to leave the wheels extended throughout the flight!

Altogether at least 36,163 Il-2s had been built when production switched to the Il-10 in August 1944. By that time monthly acceptances were running at the record level of 2,300, almost 16,000 being delivered in the eight months of 1944, the figure for the whole year of 1943 being 11,200. Where before it had been difficult to gather Il-2s to form a trained regiment, by 1944 they were operating in corps strength, as many as 500 being committed at a time on a single localized area and generally leaving no vehicle able to move. The usual method of attack was a follow-my-leader orbit which gave a long firing run from the rear of heavy armour, while individual aircraft dropped cluster bombs, 100-kg (220-lb) HE bombs or anti-armour PTABs from above on armour or Flak (anti-aircraft) vehicles. To the Soviet forces the Il-2 was commonly the *Ilyusha*, but to the invaders it was soon the *schwarz Tod* (Black Death).

In 1943 the first foreign unit, the 3rd Regiment of the 1st Polish Mixed Aviation Division, received Il-2 equipment. Subsequently an estimated 3,000 were supplied to Polish, Czech, Yugoslav and even turncoat Bulgarian regiments, while large numbers were supplied to China and North

Ilyushin Il-2M3 cutaway drawing key

79 Starboard oil tank (total capacity 17.8 Imp gal/81 litres)
80 Ejector exhausts
81 Mikulin AM-38F engine
82 Radiator intake

1 Rear navigation light
2 Elevator tab
3 Elevator tab hinge
4 Starboard elevator frame
5 Non-retractable tailwheel
6 Wooden tailplane structure
7 Tailwheel leg assembly
8 Elevator torque tube
9 Tailwheel shock-absorber
10 Tail cone fairing
11 Rudder tab
12 Rudder tab actuating rod
13 Rudder frame
14 Rudder hinge
15 Rudder post
16 Rudder upper hinge
17 Rudder mass balance
18 Aerial attachment
19 Wooden tailfin structure
20 Tailfin spars
21 Rudder control cables
22 Fuselage aft frames
23 Elevator internal mass balance
24 Tailplane spar/fuselage attachment
25 Fuselage intermediate frame
26 Strengthened wooden frame
27 Plywood skinning
28 Elevator control rods
29 Rudder control cable pulleys
30 Aerial lead-in
31 Aerial
32 Fuselage frame
33 Provision for camera (portside window) or DAG-10 grenade launcher
34 Wingroot fairing
35 Armour protection (13-mm) for rear gunner
36 Ammunition tank (150 rounds)
37 Ammunition feed
38 Gun mounting post
39 12.7-mm Berezin UBT machine gun
40 K-8T sight
41 Canopy aft frame
42 Starboard-folding canopy section
43 Gunner's station

44 Gunner's canvas seat cradle
45 Cockpit area side armour (6-mm)
46 CO_2 fire extinguisher
47 Fuselage main fuel tank (63 Imp gal)286 litre capacity)
48 Fixed canopy centre section
49 RSI aerial mast
50 Pilot's armoured (13-mm) headrest and turnover pylon
51 8-mm armourglass side panels
52 Aft-sliding canopy section
53 Canopy track
54 Pilot's seat (vertically adjustable)
55 ESBR-ZP selection panel for rockets (forward) and bombs (aft)
56 Control column (incorporating brake lever, bomb and rocket release buttons, cannon and machine gun firing buttons)
57 Rudder pedal assembly
58 Instrument panel
59 Forward fuel tank (38.5 Imp gal/175 litre capacity)
60 55-mm armourglass windscreen (embodying VV-1 sight)
61 Aileron control linkage
62 Port aileron outer hinge
63 Port aileron
64 Port wingtip
65 Port navigation light
66 Wooden outer panel wing structure
67 Leading edge
68 Rocket launching rails
69 RS-82 rocket projectiles (RS-132 optional)
70 Landing lamp
71 VV-1 external front sight
72 Fuel filler access
73 Foam suppressant tank
74 Intake duct
75 Engine bearer attachment
76 Cowling panel
77 Engine accessories
78 Cooling louvres

83 Intake cowling trough
84 Armoured (6-mm) engine cowling
85 Cowling forward frame
86 Expansion tank
87 Auxiliary side intakes
88 Spinner armoured (6-mm) backplate
89 Propeller hub assembly
90 Spinner
91 Hucks-type starter dog
92 AV-57-158 three-bladed constant-speed propeller
93 Auxiliary intake
94 Underside armour (9-mm) protection
95 Engine support bearer
96 Bearer attachment
97 Port mainwheel
98 Filter intake
99 Intake duct

100 Radiator assembly
101 Radiator ventral intake
102 Exhaust trunking
103 Fuselage underfloor fuel tank (59 Imp gal/269 litre capacity)
104 Wing inboard bomb bay (for two 220-lb/100-kg bombs or cannisters of PTAB 5.5-lb/2.5-kg hollow-charge bombs)
105 Mainspar
106 Aileron control cable/rod transition

107 Flap actuating cylinder
108 Starboard flap inboard section
109 Flap outboard section profile
110 Aileron tab
111 Tab hinge
112 Starboard aileron
113 Aileron profile
114 Starboard wingtip assembly

After World War 2 many Soviet aircraft supplied to Yugoslavia were subjected to local modifications. One example was the Il-2M3, which (as in this case) was sometimes rebuilt as a dual-control trainer with both seats facing ahead and with a streamlined canopy. Note the repositioned radio aerial mast.

Korea in the post-war era. Several countries, including Poland and Czechoslovakia, applied their own local designations, while many Il-2s were modified in various ways with different equipment, weapons or (in Yugoslavia) a rear fuselage of fabric-covered welded steel tubes. At least six are preserved, four being on public view in Moscow (2), Warsaw and Prague.

Fundamental improvements

Like so many aircraft, the Il-2 was the best that could be done at the time, and it is only with hindsight that one can say: 'Why was it not designed like the Il-10?' The Il-10 was the aircraft that replaced it on the production line in August 1944, and it was a total redesign, though superficially similar. It was the end result of a large Moscow conference held in early 1942 attended not only by engineers, staff officers and Ilyushin and his team, but also by front-line *Shturmovik* pilots who were encouraged to think of possible improvements. Most of the improvements were not possible without more power, and that is a good answer to the question posed above, because more powerful engines simply were not available (though many were running on testbeds). One Il-2 was flown with the 1,700-hp (1268-kW) ASh-82 radial; it was good, but not really worth disrupting the production line. The ideal engine was Mikulin's AM-42, but this did not become available until December 1943.

Around this fine engine, driving a four-blade propeller to absorb its 2,000 hp (1492 kW), Ilyushin designed the Il-8 with an all-metal stressed-skin airframe, considerably greater fuel capacity, neater main gears with single legs folding flat under the wings with the large soft-tyred wheels turning 90° to lie in wing compartments, and greatly cleaned-up cowling with radiators in the wing roots. Armament was increased to 2,205 lb (1000 kg) of bombs or up to eight RS-132s, and guns comprised two VYa-23s and two ShVAK-20s, plus a UB at the rear. In parallel the bureau designed the Il-10 in which the same engine installation (with three-blade propeller) and landing gear were fitted to a completely redesigned airframe with a wing of different profile and planform, an improved tail, and a new cockpit for the pilot and a gunner immediately behind him in a turret. Both prototypes were on test in the spring of 1944, and though both were markedly better than the Il-2, the Il-10 was in a class of its own. While the Il-8 handled like an Il-2 (rather sedate, and hard work) the Il-10 could almost tangle with a Yak or La-5 if competently handled!

If only the 36,000 Il-2s could have been Il-10s, victory in the East could have come a little sooner and at much less cost. An absolute winner, the Il-10 was ordered into immediate production, and the first regiments were equipping in October 1944. Standard armament comprised two NS-23s and two small ShKAS machine-guns for sighting, plus a 20-mm cannon at the rear. Some had N-37 guns instead of the 23-mm NS-23s, and a few had four NS-23s with only a UB in the rear cockpit. Curiously, though it weighed the same as its predecessors and had a much smaller wing, the Il-10 had about the same top speed as the Il-8 and the same landing speed as both the Il-8 and Il-2. Its great advantages lay in agility, efficiency and much faster and simpler rearming and servicing. About 3,500 were built in the six months from November 1944 and, despite the emergence of the more powerful AM-43-powered Il-16 in 1945, production of the Il-10 continued at a low rate for about eight further years to a total of 4,966, plus another 1,200 built as B-33s by Avia in Czechoslovakia. The trainer version was the Il-10U, the Czech designation for this being BS-33. Small numbers were built of the Il-10M with redesigned square-tipped wings and other changes, one of the Il-10Ms having a booster rocket engine in the tail.

Ilyushin persisted with more powerful *Shturmoviki*, the next major type being the lumpy Il-20 powered by a 2,700-hp (2014-kW) AM-47F piston engine, followed by the Il-40 in which the same well-proven armoured two-place cockpit was fitted into a twin-jet air-frame. What killed off the *Shturmoviki* was the decision that the general ground-attack role could be fulfilled more efficiently and at less cost by the versatile MiG fighter-bombers. This policy has been followed for over 25 years, but now is again giving way to specialist *Shturmovik* aircraft (perhaps triggered by the USAF A-10A), the first of which, said to be a design from the OKB named for the late P. O. Sukhoi, was serving in numbers in Afghanistan.

115 Starboard navigation light
116 Wing outer rib
117 Aileron outer hinge
118 Wooden wing structure
119 Flap control linkage
120 Wing ribs
121 Aileron tab control
122 Flap rods
123 Wing centre/outer section joint/capping strake
124 Wing attachment points

125 Undercarriage retraction cylinder
126 Forward extremity of weapons bay
127 ShKAS 7.62-mm machine gun
128 Machine-gun barrel support
129 Cannon barrel fairing
130 Volkov-Yartsev VYa-23 23-mm cannon
131 Ammunition access panel
132 Magazine for starboard VYa-23 cannon (150 rounds)
133 Forward spar
134 Leading edge panels
135 Alternative pitot head positions

136 Undercarriage retraction linkage
137 Mainwheel leg cross-brace
138 Undercarriage fairing doors
139 Starboard mainwheel
140 Axle
141 Undercarriage oleo legs
142 Barrel of VYa-23 cannon
143 Undercarriage pivot point
144 Fairing nose section
145 Starboard bomb load comprising three (two internal and one external) 220-lb (100-kg) bombs which could be released singly or in salvo
146 Alternative main armament (Il02 Type 3M) of 37-mm Nudelman-Suranov NS-11-P-37 (NSK-OKB-16) cannon

This Mitsubishi A6M5 was restored in 1980 by the Fame Museum in Chino, California, and is one of the very few examples still flying. It was used by the 261st Kokutai of the Japanese Naval Air Force in Saipan during the war.

Mitsubishi A6M 'Zero'

Built in far greater numbers than any other Japanese aircraft, the A6M was a sudden terrible shock to the Allies from Pearl Harbor onwards. But once the Allies had armed themselves properly, the once-feared 'Zero' was on the defensive.

When the Japanese Navy struck at Pearl Harbor on Sunday, 7 December 1941, the Americans already possessed files on the A6M in the form of detailed combat reports from Colonel Claire Chennault in far-off Chungking, China. Nobody had bothered to disseminate the information, and for a second time this agile and well-armed fighter caused a great shock and made mincemeat of the motley collection of aircraft that opposed it. In six months the Sentais (fighter groups) equipped with A6M had so dominated the sky that the Imperial forces had conquered over 12 million square miles (37.3m km²), a far greater area than had ever previously been overrun by one nation. The A6M kept appearing in places where Japanese fighters had been judged 'impossible', sometimes almost 1,000 miles (1609 km) from the nearest advanced Japanese airbase or carrier. In combat it could outmanoeuvre practically every Allied fighter, and its firepower was also superior.

The A6M came to symbolize the previously unappreciated fact that Japanese weapons were not made of bamboo and rice-paper, nor were they inferior copies of Occidental ones. In its own homeland it was the focal point of a part-religious belief in Nipponese invincibility. The name of Jiro Horikoshi was better-known in Japan even than that of Reginald Mitchell in the UK, because he was the genius who had created the miraculous fighter that decimated its enemies.

Of course the A6M was not really miraculous. Back in 1937 the British Gloster company had flown a prototype fighter that almost precisely paralleled the A6M in size, shape, weight, power and performance – and it was not even accepted for the RAF. At that time Horikoshi was making the first drawings of his new fighter to try to meet a newly issued Imperial Navy specification that called for a shipboard

This frame from a Japanese ciné film shows an A6M2 (foreground) and B5N2 torpedo bombers ranged on the deck of a 1st Koku Kantai carrier early on Sunday 7 December 1941: destination, Pearl Harbor. The US Navy caption gives the carrier as the Hiryu but the insignia are not those of the 2nd Sentai.

Mitsubishi A6M Reisen

Specification

Mitsubishi A6M5c Reisen
Type: carrier-based fighter-bomber
Powerplant: one 1,130-hp (843-kW) Nakajima NK1F
Sakae 21 radial piston engine
Performance: maximum speed 351 mph (565 km/h);
cruising speed 230 mph (370 km/h); climb to 19,685 ft
(6000 m) in 7 minutes; service ceiling 38,520 ft
(11740 m); maximum range 1,194 miles (1922 km)
Weights: empty 4,136 lb (1876 kg); maximum take-off
6,025 lb (2733 kg)
Dimensions: span 36 ft 1 in (11.00 m); length
29 ft 11¼ in (9.12 m); height 11 ft 6 in (3.50 m); wing
area 229.27 sq ft (21.3 m²)
Armament: one 0.52-in (13.2-mm) Type 3 heavy
machine-gun in the fuselage decking (breech in the
cockpit), two 20-mm Type 99 cannon in the wings and
two 0.52-in (13.2-mm) Type 3 guns in the wings
outboard of the cannon, plus two 132-lb (60-kg)
bombs under the wings (suicide mission, one 551-lb/
250-kg bomb)

The subject of this illustration was
one of the rare late-war stop-gap
variants which tried to stem the
tide of Allied air power until the
A7M Reppu could be cleared for
production. An A6M5c of the 210th
Kokutai, it combined the non-
folding rounded wingtips and thick
wing skins, separate exhaust
stacks and other improvements of
the basic A6M5 (Model 52) with
heavier firepower from two 0.52-in
(13.2-mm) guns added in the wings
outboard of the cannon. Most had
better protection, with rear armour
and self-sealing wing tanks, but the
crucial fault of inadequate power
was not rectified and only 93 of this
model were built. Note the absence
of a white border to the Hinomaru
insignia.

210-118
B

Typical of the early A6M2 Reisens that administered a paralysing shock to the Allied aircraft in the Pacific in the first half of 1942, this example served aboard the carrier *Hiryu* with the 2nd Sentai (two blue bands) of the 1st Koku Kantai (air fleet). Ruling colour was sky grey, with matt black engine cowling.

A mainstream production Reisen, this A6M2 was based at Rabaul, New Britain, with the 6th Kokutai in late 1942. By this time the grey had been sprayed with blotches of dark green, requiring a white outer ring around the Hinomaru (the red disc representing the rising sun). Over 500 Reisens were lost in this region.

fighter with the manoeuvrability of his earlier A5M (one of the most agile aircraft ever built) despite the burden of two 20-mm cannon as well as the two machine-guns carried by the A5M, two 132-lb (60-kg) bombs, full radio, an engine to give a speed of 311 mph (500 km/h) and an endurance of eight hours with a drop tank. (It should be noted that the Imperial Navy measured speeds in knots, so that required of the new fighter was 270 knots.)

The result was wholly conventional, with stressed-skin structure, split flaps, wide-track inwards-retracting landing gear and a radial engine driving a variable-pitch propeller. After some argument a sliding canopy was added over the cockpit, and the newly demanded cannon (Type 99 Model 1, derived from the Oerlikon) were fitted in the wings, outboard of the propeller disc. Its designation was naturally A6M, A for carrier-based fighter and 6M for the sixth such type by Mitsubishi. Its popular name was Reisen (Rei-sen, zero fighter), from the Japanese year 2600 (1940 A.D.). The first A6M1, with a 780-hp (582-kW) Mitsubishi Zuisei 13 engine, flew at Kagamigahara on 1 April 1939, and showed outstanding qualities except in its speed of 304 mph

Few air-to-air photographs survive from Japanese air operations in World War 2. This picture was taken a year before Pearl Harbor as pre-series A6M2 fighters were blooded in combat over China with the 12th Rengo Kokutai. Nobody today knows what happened to the reports of the new fighter that were sent to Washington from Colonel Claire Chennault, who saw them in combat in Chungking.

(489 km/h), which just missed the target. A constant-speed propeller gave an increase in all-round performance, but more power was needed and on 28 December 1939 the third prototype, designated A6M2, flew with the 925-hp (690-kW) Nakajima Sakae 12. This prototype exceeded all expectations, and by July 1940 the A6M2 had been cleared for production. It was decided to send 15 to China to test them in action with the 12th Rengo Kokutai. They got their first victim on 13 September 1940, and though two A6M2s were shot down by ground fire their air combat record was a remarkable 99 victories for no losses before they were redeployed for the war in the Pacific.

Countdown to 'Zero'

From the 22nd A6M2 the rear spar was strengthened, and from the 65th the outermost 20 in (50.8 cm) of the wings was hinged to fold upwards manually. In June 1941 the A6M3 had these tips omitted, and with the 1,130-hp (843-kW) Sakae 21 engine offered higher speed and more rapid roll, though turn radius was slightly worsened. At Pearl Harbor the Imperial Navy had 328 A6Ms embarked aboard carriers, and from the start they achieved complete mastery over the Curtiss P-40, Curtiss-Wright CW-21A, Brewster Buffalo, Hawker Hurricane I and other opponents. For example the hapless Buffaloes of the RAF, RAAF, RNZAF and Dutch East Indies were so outflown their 0.5-in (12.7-mm) guns were replaced by 0.303-in (7.62-mm weapons), ammunition was cut by half and fuel by more than one-third, and still they could not bring their guns to bear over the more agile and much harder-hitting A6M.

Not knowing what the fighter was called, the Allies named it 'Ben' then 'Ray' and finally 'Zeke'. The clipped-wing model was called 'Hap', until someone recalled that that was the nickname of the USAAF Chief of Staff, General H. H. Arnold, when it became 'Hamp'. When the type was recognized as merely another version of the 'Zeke' it was called 'Zeke 32'. But desperate attempts to gather even pieces of the almost supernatural fighter proved elusive, until suddenly US troops found a perfect A6M2 in the Aleutians. Petty Officer Koga had taken off from the carrier *Ryujo* on 3 June to attack Dutch Harbor, but two bullets had

Mitsubishi A6M

One of the very first Reisens to reach the Imperial Navy, this pre-series A6M2 operated with brilliant success against the Chinese in the second half of 1940 with the 12th Rengo Kokutai (combined naval air corps) in the Hankow region. These aircraft lacked folding wingtips and numerous other small refinements.

severed the fuel supply pipe and he had glided in to the uninhabited island of Akutan. Landing on marshy ground, the A6M had somersaulted and Koga had broken his neck. The valuable prize was soon on test at NAS North Island, San Diego, where the myths were blown away and the A6M's numerous shortcomings revealed.

For one thing, it is possible to do only so much on 1,130 hp (843 kW). The A6M airframe was lightly built, and the vital parts were by Western standards deficient in armour. Tactics were worked out to gain superiority in combat, but at least as important was the first flight, on the other side of the United States, of the first Grumman F6F Hellcat in June 1942. Larger and heavier than the A6M, this US Navy fighter had a 2,000-hp (1492-kW) engine: this enabled it to be stronger, tougher and better protected and yet outfight the A6M in a dogfight. Another US Navy and Marines fighter, the bent-wing Vought F4U Corsair, was even more formidable, and the US Army's P-38 was not only much faster but could stay with an A6M at all heights above 10,000 ft (3050 m) despite being much larger. And all these Allied fighters had firepower that could actually cause an A6M to break up into pieces.

Off Okinawa in April 1945 hundreds of aircraft of the Imperial Navy were lost trying to stem the Allied advance. About half were suicide (so-called Kamikaze) attacks by various fighter and attack aircraft carrying bombs. Here an A6M5 just fails to reach the deck of the USS *Missouri* on 28 April 1945, glancing off the side.

Later in the war many Imperial Navy aircraft were painted dark green over the entire upper surface and sides, often with a black forward upper decking or engine cowling. This A6M2 was based with the 402nd Chutai (squadron) of the 341st Kokutai (the basic naval air unit of some 150 aircraft) at Clark Field, Manila.

Seaplane variant

In autumn 1940 an Imperial Navy specification called for a fighter seaplane to operate over isolated beachheads and beyond the range even of the A6M, and, while the powerful Kawanishi N1K1 (which in turn was eventually to lead to a formidable land-based fighter) was developed, the Nakajima company was instructed to build a seaplane A6M. The resulting A6M2-N flew on the day of Pearl Harbor and was soon in action. Though as neat a conversion as could be imagined, it was inevitably inferior to Allied fighters and though 327 were delivered, the last in September 1943, they did not achieve very much. Another off-mainstream variant was the tandem dual-control A6M2-K advanced trainer, which was the responsibility of the 21st Naval Air Arsenal, at Sasebo. No even started until 1943, the first two-seater flew in November that year, and eventually 515 were built in two versions, with cannon and landing-gear doors removed to save weight. At Mitsubishi, Horikoshi had from 1940 pressed for a successor to the A6M, with his company's 2,200-hp (1641-kW) MK9 engine, but this was repeatedly delayed, and the old A6M had to be kept in production, both at the parent firm and (in even greater numbers) by Nakajima.

A 1943 attempt to improve performance at medium and high altitudes came to nothing: the 1st Air Technical Arsenal

Mitsubishi A6M2 'Zero' cutaway drawing key

1 Tail navigation light
2 Tail cone
3 Tailfin fixed section
4 Rudder lower brace
5 Rudder tab (ground adjustable)
6 Fabric-covered rudder
7 Rudder hinge
8 Rudder post
9 Rudder upper hinge
10 Rudder control horn (welded to torque tube)
11 Aerial attachment
12 Tailfin leading-edge
13 Forward spar
14 Tailfin structure
15 Tailfin nose ribs
16 Port elevator
17 Port tailplane
18 Piano-hinge join
19 Fuselage dorsal skinning
20 Control turnbuckles
21 Arrester hook release/retract steel cable runs
22 Fuselage frame/tailplane centre-brace
23 Tailplane attachments
24 Elevator cables
25 Elevator control horns/torque tube

26 Rudder control horns
27 Tailwheel combined retraction/shock strut
28 Elevator trim tab
29 Tailwheel leg fairing
30 Castored tailwheel
31 Elevator frame (fabric-covered)
32 Tailwheel outer hinge
33 Tailplane structure
34 Forward spar
35 Elevator trim tab control rod (chain-driven)
36 Fuselage flotation bag rear wall
37 Arrester hook (extended)
38 Arrester hook pivot mounting
39 Elevator trim tab cable guide
40 Fuselage skinning
41 Fuselage frame stations
42 Arrester hook position indicator cable (duralumin tube)
43 Elevator cables
44 Rudder cables
45 Trim tab cable runs
46 Arrester hook pulley guide
47 Fuselage stringers
48 Fuselage flotation bag front wall
49 Fuselage construction join
50 Wingroot fillet formers
51 Compressed air cylinder (wing gun charging)
52 Transformer
53 'Ku'-type radio receiver
54 Oxygen cylinder (starboard); CO_2 fire-extinguisher cylinder (port)
55 Battery
56 Radio tray support
57 Radio transmitter
58 Canopy/fuselage fairing
59 Aerial mast support/lead-in

60 Aerial
61 Aerial mast (forward raked)
62 Canopy aft fixed section
63 Aluminium and plywood canopy frame
64 Crash bulkhead/headrest support
65 'Ku'-type D/F frame antenna mounting (late models)
66 Canopy track
67 Turnover truss
68 Pilot's seat support frame
69 Starboard elevator control bell-crank
70 Aileron control push-pull rod
71 Wing rear spar/fuselage attachment
72 Fuselage aft main double frame

73 Aileron linkage
74 Landing-gear selector level
75 Flap selector level
76 Seat adjustment lever
77 Pilot's seat
78 Cockpit canopy rail
79 Seat support rail
80 Elevator tab trim handwheel
81 Fuel gauge controls
82 Throttle quadrant
83 Reflector gunsight mounting (offset to starboard)
84 Sliding canopy

Mitsubishi A6M Reisen variants

Mitsubishi A6M1: first two prototypes, powered by the 780-hp (582-kW) Zuisei 13 engine
Mitsubishi A6M2: initial production version, powered by the 940-hp (701-kW) Sakae 12 engine, with an armament of two 20-mm and two 0.303-in (7.7 mm) guns, span 39 ft 4½ in (12.00 m) and normal take-off weight 5,313 lb (2410 kg); initial aircraft of the batch, up to c/n 21, had an unreinforced rear spar, aircraft from c/n 22 onwards had the reinforced rear spar (both sub-types being designated **Model 11**), and from c/n 65 the wingtips were capable of manual folding
Mitsubishi A6M3 Model 32: improved production model powered by the 1,130-hp (843-kW) Sakae 21; from the fourth aircraft 20-mm cannon ammunition was increased, and later aircraft had square-tipped wings of 36 ft 1-in (11.00-m) span compared with the **A6M3 Model 22**'s rounded tips of 39 ft 4½ in (12.00 m); normal take-off weight 5,609 lb (2254 kg)
Mitsubishi A6M4: unsuccessful experimental variant with turbocharged Sakae engine
Mitsubishi A6M5 Model 52: improved A6M3 with thicker wing skins, rounded wingtips and thrust-augmenting exhaust stacks; normal take-off weight 6,025 lb (2733 kg)
Mitsubishi A6M5a Model 52A: derivative of the A6M5 with thicker skin and improved Type 99 Model 2

Mark 3 cannon
Mitsubishi A6M5 Model 52B: improved A6M5a with extra protection, fire extinguishing system for the fuel tanks, and one 0.303-in (7.7 mm) machine-gun replaced by a 0.57-in (13.2 mm) Type 3 weapon
Mitsubishi A6M5c Model 52C: yet further improved model, with two 0.52-in (13.2 mm) Type 3 machine-guns added outboard of the cannon, armour behind the pilot, extra fuel capacity, and racks for eight 22-lb (10-kg) unguided air-to-air rockets
Mitsubishi A6M6c Model 53C: improved A6M5c with 1,210-hp (903-kW) Sakae 31 plus methanol/water boost, and self-sealing wing tanks
Mitsubishi A6M7 Model 63: dive-bomber version of the A6M6c intended for use from small carriers; centreline provision for one 551-lb (250-kg) bomb and underwing points for two 77-Imp gal (350-litre) drop tanks
Mitsubishi A6M8 Model 64: uprated model with 1,560-hp (1164-kW) Kinsei 62 engine, no fuselage guns, better protection, and normal take-off weight 6,945 lb
Mitsubishi A6M2-K: dual-control trainer version of the A6M2
Mitsubishi A6M5-K: d/c version of the A6M5
Nakajima A6M2-N: floatplane version of the A6M2 with single main float and two underwing stabilizing floats; normal take-off weight 5,423 lb (2460 kg)

206
207
208
205
210
209
211
201
212
213
214
216
215
217

The A6M3 not only had a reduced span but also reduced fuselage fuel necessitated by the installation of the Sakae 21 engine, with two-speed supercharger, which pushed the firewall 8 in (20 cm) further aft. This A6M3 served on Kyushu, Japan, with the 251st Kokutai in late 1942. It is shown with the 72.6-Imp gal (330-litre) drop tank.

85 Plexiglass panels
86 Canopy lock/release
87 Windscreen
88 Fuselage starboard 0.303-in (7.7-mm) machine gun
89 Control column
90 Radio control box
91 Radio tuner
92 Elevator control linkage
93 Rudder pedal bar assembly
94 Cockpit underfloor fuel
95 Wing front spar/fuselage attachment
96 Fuselage forward main double frame
97 Ammunition magazine
98 Ammunition feed
99 Blast tube
100 Cooling louvres
101 Fuselage fuel tank, capacity 34 Imp gal (155 litres)
102 Firewall bulkhead
103 Engine bearer lower attachment
104 Engine bearer upper attachment
105 Oil tank, capacity 12.7 Imp gal (58 litres)
106 Bearer support struts
107 Cowling gill adjustment control
108 Machine gun muzzle trough
109 Barrel fairing
110 Oil filler cap
111 Fuselage fuel tank filler cap
112 Port flap profile
113 Port fuselage machine gun
114 Port wing gun access panels
115 Port inner wing identification light
116 Port wing flotation bag inner wall
117 Wing spar joins
118 Aileron control rods
119 Port aileron (fabric-covered)
120 Aileron tab (ground adjustable)
121 Aileron external counter-balance
122 Control linkage
123 Wing skinning
124 Port outer wing identification light
125 Port navigation light lead conduit
126 Wingtip hinge
127 Wing end rib
128 Port wing flotation bag outer wall
129 Wingtip structure
130 Port wingtip (folded)
131 Port navigation light
132 Port wingtip hinge release catch
133 Pitot head
134 Wing leading-edge skinning
135 Wing front spar
136 Port wing gun muzzle
137 Port undercarriage visual indicator
138 Undercarriage hydraulics access
139 Nacelle gun troughs

173 Starboard inner wing identification light
174 Starboard wing 20-mm machine gun
175 Access panels
176 Ammunition magazine (underwing loading)
177 Landing-gear hydraulic retraction jack
178 Hydraulic lines
179 Starboard undercarriage visual indicator
180 Landing-gear pivot axis
181 Undercarriage/spar mounting
182 Starboard wing gun muzzle
183 Starboard undercarriage leg
184 Oleo travel
185 Welded steel wheel fork
186 Wheel uplock latch
187 Starboard mainwheel
188 Wheel door fairing ball and swivel closure
189 Mainwheel door fairing
190 Axle hub
191 Access plate
192 Hinge
193 Left fairing attachments
194 Brake line
195 Leg fairing
196 Leg fairing under flap
197 Wing gun barrel support collar
198 Wing nose ribs
199 Cartridge ejection chute
200 Wing spar joins
201 Wing outer structure
202 Front spar outer section
203 Inter-spar ribs
204 Rear-spar outer section
205 Aileron control access
206 Aileron (ground adjustable)
207 Starboard aileron frame
208 Aileron external counter-balance
209 Control linkage
210 Starboard wingtip (folded)
211 Starboard outer wing identification light
212 Aileron outer hinge
213 Starboard wing flotation bag outer wall
214 Wing end rib
215 Starboard wingtip hinge release catch
216 Wingtip structure
217 Starboard navigation light

140 Cowling gills
141 Fuselage gun synchronization cable
142 Bearer support strut assembly
143 Carburettor
144 Exhaust manifold
145 Cowling panel fastener clips
146 925-hp Nakajima Sakae 12 radial engine
147 Cowling inner ring profile
148 Cowling nose ring
149 Three-blade propeller
150 Spinner
151 Propeller gears
152 Hub
153 Carburettor intake
154 Port mainwheel
155 Oil cooler intake
156 Exhaust outlet
157 Starboard mainwheel inner door fairing
158 Engine bearer support brace
159 Oil cooler
160 Wingroot fasteners
161 Starboard mainwheel well
162 Front auxiliary spar cut-outs
163 Auxiliary fuel tank, capacity 74 Imp gal (337 litres)
164 Cockpit air intake
165 Intake trunking
166 Front main spar
167 Starboard wing fuel tank capacity 43 Imp gal (195 litres)
168 Fuel filler cap
169 Rear main spar
170 Flap actuating cylinder
171 Access cover
172 Starboard flap structure

These A6M2-N fighter seaplanes appear to be on the catapult of a surface warship, but this is a false impression. They are on the slipway of a surface base, perhaps at Tulagi, heavily lashed down and with control locks in place. Fighter seaplanes were generally outclassed and had little impact on operations in World War 2.

One of the best wartime photographs of Japanese Reisen operations, this scene shows A6M5c or A6M6c fighters of the Genzan Kokutai at Wonsan in the final weeks of the war. The 5c and 6c were the ultimate members of the Reisen family to see combat duty; they were crippled by being forced to use a low-powered engine.

at Yokosuka fitted two A6M2s with turbocharged Sakae engines, but these were gravely unreliable. Nothing could be done but hastily to contrive an interim improved version, the A6M5; and, like so many hasty interim fighters, such as the Spitfire Mk IX, it was made in greater numbers than all the others. The chief modification was a new wing, with fixed rounded tips of 36 ft 1 in (11.00 m) span and thicker skins to enable the new version to dive at much higher speeds; previously limitations in diving speed had made the Zero easy to catch. This added 416 lb (189 kg) to the weight, and did nothing for manoeuvrability, but a slight improvement in performance resulted from fitting individual or paired exhaust pipes to the 14 cylinders with nozzles arranged to give forward thrust at full power. Together with a careful detail refinement all this added up to a significantly better fighter, and when it reached combat units in numbers in the autumn of 1943, the A6M5 did something to redress the balance which had rather quickly tilted towards the US Navy with the entry to combat duty of the F6F Hellcat.

If any one aircraft can be said to have destroyed the myth of Japanese invincibility in the air, that aircraft was the F6F. In fact, in a pure test of turn radius, the F6F would be hard-pressed to hold any A6M that was skilfully flown, but that was not the end of the story. Sheer lack of power in the Japanese fighter meant that it was far behind its opponent in armour and firepower, and in its ability to withstand battle damage. Lack of power was also the reason for the rate of climb falling off, compared with the lighter earlier versions, to levels below that of the heavyweight F6F. Even with thicker wing skins the A6M could not escape by diving away; in fact faced with an F6F, F4U or Spitfire Mk VIII there was no way an A6M pilot could survive except by exceptional flying, amazing luck or shooting down his opponent. And, as 1943 proceeded, this became more and more difficult.

Fortune turns

For one thing, the Allied fighters were not only getting dramatically superior but they were arriving in floods that completely overwhelmed the Japanese. Even in 1941–2 the Zeros had been outnumbered, but they had been deployed in concentrated groups that gained total local control and inflicted catastrophic losses, while the motley collections of Allied machines were scattered and often under no central direction. By 1943 the US Navy, US Marines, US Army Air Force and British Commonwealth forces were all co-ordinated and enjoyed numerical superiority everywhere. Not least of the Imperial Navy's problems was its rapid attrition in aircraft-carriers. Even as early as the Battle of Midway in June 1942 – often regarded as the start of the turnaround in fortunes in the Pacific war – the great carriers *Akagi*, *Hiryu*, *Kaga* and *Soryu* were all sunk; the light carrier *Shoho* had been sunk a month earlier, and *Ryujo* went to the bottom in August 1942. These crippling losses in seagoing air power gravely restricted the Imperial Navy's ability ever again to achieve command of the sky, at any place or at any time.

There was yet a further serious problem which had as much effect as all other factors combined. In air combat the man is every bit as important as the machine. Even flying an inferior aircraft, in the rather primitive days of World War 2, a brilliant and courageous pilot could often run up strings of victories over opponents flying faster or better-armed aircraft. In 1941 the Imperial Navy pilots had been well trained, and were aggressive and in most cases experienced. Many had seen a year or more of actual fighting in China or against the USSR, and in their hands a Zero was deadly. By 1943 hardly any of these pilots were still alive, and their replacements were by comparison ineffectual. The home-based training programme was wholly inadequate, and by autumn 1944 the once-dominant Sentais were being re-organized into kamikaze (suicide) squads in a desperate attempt to stem the tide of Allied advance.

Improved armament

Throughout the war the need for long range had been manifest, but whereas at the start the A6M had been supreme in this regard, especially after its experienced pilots had learned correct long-range cruise techniques at high boost pressure but low crankshaft revolutions, by 1943 the Sakae 21 had resulted in smaller fuselage tankage (in part rectified by adding two small 9.9-Imp gal/45-litre tanks in the outer wings) and appreciably higher fuel consumption. Crucial need to keep weight down precluded heavier armament, though the Type 99 cannon was improved through several versions with a longer barrel and higher muzzle velocity, rate of fire increased from 490 to an eventual 750 rounds per

The most important of all Imperial Navy fighters in the final year of the war, the A6M5 was identifiable by its ejector exhaust stacks and fixed rounded wingtips. This colourful example served as a combat trainer with the Genzan Kokutai at Wonsan, Korea (later to be in North Korea and scene of bitter fighting a decade later).

minute, and a 125-round belt in place of the original 100-round drum. The greater muzzle velocity had the possibly important effect of extending the effective range (typically from 2,624 ft/800 m to 3,281 ft/1000 m). This was one factor where the A6M could have scored over the US fighters that relied on the 0.5-in (12.7-mm) Browning. In practice, Japanese pilots lacked the shooting skill to open fire accurately at long ranges, and at normal air-combat distances the much more rapid rate of strikes from the typical US armament of six 0.5-in (12.7-mm) guns proved decisive.

When fitted with the long-barrel belt-fed cannon the A6M5 became the A6M5a, available from production in the spring of 1944. Within weeks the A6M5b was coming off the line, and this partly rectified one of the type's gravest shortcomings, lack of protection. The A6M5b had improved armour, automatic fire-extinguishers in the main fuel tanks and a slab of bullet-proof glass behind the windscreen. A small increase in firepower resulted from substituting the 0.52-in (13.2-mm) Type 3 heavy machine-gun for one of the rifle-calibre weapons ahead of the windscreen. Hundreds of A6M5a and A6M5b fighters took part in the great battles around the Marianas and Philippines in the summer of 1944, but the first major engagement of the A6M5b was such a slaughter at the hands of F6Fs that US pilots called it 'The Marianas Turkey Shoot'. To a considerable degree this was because of the superior skill of the American pilots.

Two of the aircraft in this line-up are A6M2 Reisen fighters; the rest are A6M2-K dual trainers, 515 of which were delivered from the end of 1943 onwards. Their unit appears to be the Kasumigaura Kokutai, and the colour dark green, with black cowls. The small strakes on the rear fuselage improved spin recovery.

This debacle spurred the Imperial Navy into a further desperate attempt to improve the A6M, a requirement being issued for racks for underwing rockets, extra 0.52-in (13.2-mm) guns outboard of the cannon, a large additional fuel tank behind the cockpit and a fully armoured pilot seat. If the A6M had needed extra power beforehand, it doubly needed it now, but permission to fit a larger engine was not granted. After building 93 with the improvements demanded Mitsubishi did receive some Sakae 31 engines, with extra power gained by injecting water/methanol to prevent detonation at full throttle, but most of these engines were retained by the maker, Nakajima, which went into production with the resulting A6M6c at the end of 1944. This was the final model of Reisen to see action, and it could not do more than earlier models to hold back the overwhelming advance of the Allied land, sea and air forces towards Japan.

The A6M7 was equipped to carry a 551-lb (250-kg) bomb as well as outer-wing drop tanks. The A6M8 at last had a more powerful engine, the 1,560-hp (1164-kW) Mitsubishi Kinsei 62, resulting in a slightly larger cowling and removal of the machine-guns previously fitted above it. This did not fly until May 1945 and no production aircraft could be completed. There were many experimental forms of armament and special equipment fits, but by far the most important were the kamikaze lash-ups with, usually, a 551-lb (250-kg) bomb hung on the rack normally used for the centreline drop tank.

Total production of the A6M was about 10,449 (3,879 by Mitsubishi and 6,570 by Nakajima), and these were complemented by 327 Nakajima-built A6M2-Ns, and 515 A6M2-Ks and A6M5-Ks (236 by Dai-Nijuichi Kaigun Kokusho and 279 by Hitachi Kokuki KK).

Messerschmitt Me 262

The Me 262 was not just a revolutionary engine in a conventional airframe. The design of its wings, tail unit and firepower was years ahead of its time; it was a winner and, unlike some predecessors it was a joy to fly.

Young German gunners, huddled around their light 20-mm and 37-mm Flak weapons, could be excused for a slight lack of attention to their task at their first sight of the Messerschmitt Me 262s on the snow-covered expanses of Rheine-Hopstein air base in the autumnal sleet of 1944. In every sense the sleek shark-like fuselages, mottled ochre and olive green, and beset with razor wings from which hung the huge turbojets, were a portent of the future. The noise, the high-pitched whine and howl, of the Jumo 004B-1 turbines, the swirls of snow, the hot paraffin-tainted blast: all were of a different time. But this was the present: beset by Allied

Messerschmitt Me 262B-1a/U1 under test with the USAAF coding of FE-610 (Foreign Evaluation) at Wright Field in 1946. The aircraft was captured by the British following possible service with the 10./NJG 11. The armament installed was two 30-mm MK 108A-3s and two 20-mm MG 151/20 cannon: AI radar was an FuG 218 (Neptun V).

air superiority on all sides, the skies over Westphalia were dangerous elements for operations of the Luftwaffe's dwindling strength. Black-helmeted pilots, crouched forward in the narrow cockpits of their Messerschmitt Me 262A-2a fighter-bombers, anxiously scanned the overcast for the first signs of the diving Hawker Tempests, North American P-51s or Supermarine Spitfires, as they coaxed throttles and jabbed brakes prior to take-off. Flak gunners trained their pieces along the approach paths, watched for the red Very lights that would bring them to instant action, and heard the

thunder of the departing jets. With such machines, how could Germany lose the war in the air? Such a thought must have raced through minds. But the job of a Flak gunner is humble, and he and his comrades could have had no insight into the extraordinary train of events and decisions that were instrumental in the denial in quantity of Germany's most potent air weapon of World War 2. In the heady days of 1941, when the Messerschmitt Me 262 series was born, no one person in the Third Reich could foresee the need, the desperate need, for an outstanding aircraft with which to wrest air supremacy from the hands of the enemy.

The Heinkel concern

was already deeply involved in the development of a fighter powered by the new reaction-turbine engines when, on 4 January 1939, the Augsburg-based Messerschmitt AG received orders from the German air ministry (RLM, or Reichsluftfahrtministerium) to produce specifications for a similar type of aircraft. Two plans were drawn up by a team led by Dipl.Ing. Waldemar Voigt, one for a twin-boom configuration and the other for a pod-and-boom design. Neither of the two existing turbojet designs was considered to be powerful enough for a single-engine fighter, and as a result Voigt was forced to turn to the design of a twin-engine aircraft.

Heinkel had already turned to twin engines with the development of the promising He 280 series powered by the six-stage axial-flow BMW P 3302 engines, and Germany's first definitive jet fighter, the Heinkel He 280 V2 prototype, lifted off from Rostock-Marienehe's runway at 15.18 on 30

March 1941 with Fritz Schafer at the controls. And within six weeks of this maiden flight the UK too flew her first jet aircraft: powered by a Whittle-designed W1X centrifugal-type turbojet of 860-lb (390-kg) thrust, the Gloster E.28/39 took to the air on 15 May. Back at Augsburg work had proceeded slowly on the design of what at first bore none of the hallmarks that graced the Heinkel product, or gave any hint of the fineness of line that was a characteristic of Messerschmitt's piston-engine fighters. The design was termed the Messerschmitt P 1065 VI and, in the absence of its twin jet engines, was fitted with a 730-hp (545-kW) Junkers Jumo 210G driving a two-blade propeller. This ugly duckling was then renamed the Messerschmitt Me 262 V1, and was taken into the air for the first time on 18 April 1941. Test pilots Karl Baur and Fritz Wendel reported no vices on subsequent flight programmes: no urgency was attached

Messerschmitt Me 262A-1a cutaway drawing key

1 Flettner-type geared trim tab
2 Mass-balanced rudder
3 Rudder post
4 Tail fin structure
5 Tailplane structure
6 Rudder tab mechanism
7 Flettner-type servo tab
8 Starboard elevator
9 Rear navigation light
10 Rudder linkage
11 Elevator linkage
12 Tailplane adjustment mechanism
13 Fuselage break point
14 Fuselage construction
15 Control runs
16 FuG 25a loop antenna (IFF)
17 Automatic compass
18 Aft auxiliary self-sealing fuel tank (132 Imp gal/600 litre capacity)

19 FuG 16zyR/T
20 Fuel filler cap
21 Aft cockpit glazing
22 Armoured aft main fuel tank (198 Imp gal/900 litre capacity)
23 Inner cockpit shell
24 Pilot's seat
25 Canopy jettison lever
26 Armoured (15-mm) head rest
27 Canopy (hinged to starboard)
28 Canopy lock
29 Bar-mounted Revi 16B sight (for both cannon and R4M missiles)
30 Armourglass windscreen (90-mm)
31 Instrument panel
32 Rudder pedal
33 Armoured forward main fuel tank (198 Imp gal/900 litre capacity)

34 Fuel filler cap
35 Underwing wooden rack for 12 R4M 55-mm rockets
36 Port outer flap section
37 Frise-type aileron
38 Aileron control linkage
39 Port navigation light
40 Pitot head
41 Automatic leading-edge slats
42 Port engine cowling

43 Electrical firing mechanism
44 Firewall
45 Spent cartridge ejector chutes
46 Four 30-mm Rheinmetall Borsig MK 108 cannon (100 rpg belt-fed ammunition for upper pair and 80 rpg for lower pair)
47 Cannon muzzles
48 Combat camera
49 Camera aperture
50 Nosewheel fairing
51 Nosewheel leg
52 Nosewheel
53 Torque scissors
54 Retraction jack

55 Hydraulic lines
56 Main nosewheel door (starboard)
57 Compressed air bottles
58 Forward auxiliary fuel tank (37 Imp gal/170 litre capacity)
59 Mainwheel well
60 Torque box
61 Main spar
62 Mainwheel leg pivot point
63 Mainwheel door
64 Mainwheel retraction rod
65 Engine support arch
66 Leading-edge slat structure
67 Auxiliaries gearbox
68 Annular oil tank
69 Riedel starter motor housing
70 Engine air intake
71 Hinged cowling section
72 Junkers Jumo 004B-2 axial-flow turbojet
73 Starboard mainwheel
74 Wing structure
75 Automatic leading-edge slats
76 Mainspar
77 Starboard navigation light
78 Frise-type ailerons
79 Trim tab
80 Flettner-type geared tab
81 Starboard outer flap section
82 Engine exhaust orifice
83 Engine support bearer
84 Starboard inner flap structure
85 Faired wing root

to the flight development of the Me 262 V1 during that summer, for indeed little priority was deemed necessary. Of far greater import for the Messerschmitt concern were the improvements to the Bf 109 and Bf 110 combat types, and the development of their replacements.

The engines for the Me 262 V1 eventually arrived from Spandau in mid-November 1941: these were BMW 003s each of 1,213-lb (550-kg) static thrust. But on this first flight with the BMW 003s Wendel suffered a double flame-out shortly after take-off, and was forced to put PC + UA down

Messerschmitt Me 262 variants

Me 262 V1: first prototype (PC + UA) with single Junkers Jumo 210G piston engine; later fitted with two BMW 003 turbojets
Me 262 V2: test airframe for fitment of two BMW 003 turbojets
Me 262 V3: test airframe (PC + UC) with two Junkers Jumo 004 turbojets; first prototype to be flown by service test pilots; fourth prototype
Me 262 V4: (PC + UD) of similar configuration
Me 262 V5: fitted with two Jumo 004s, this PC + UE differed in having a fixed nosewheel, whereas previous prototypes have conventional tail wheels
Me 262 V6: definitive prototype (VI + AA) with lighter Jumo 004B-1 turbojets, and retractable tricycle landing gear; the **Me 262 V7** (VI + AB) was similar but with re-designed cockpit canopy and cockpit pressurization; many subsequent *Versuchs* prototypes evolved for testing of engines, radio, radar, and weapons systems
Me 262A-0: pre-production airframes based on the Me 262 V7 configuration; 23 units produced, and passed to test-centre at Rechlin and to service trials detachment (EKdo 262) in late April 1944
Me 262A-1a: standard interceptor fighter configuration with twin Jumo 004B-1 turbojets, four Rheinmetall-Borsig MK 108A-3 30-mm cannon, Revi 16.B gunsight, and FuG 16zY radio; the **Me 262A-1a/U1** designation covered three trials units with two MG 151, two MK 103 and two Mk 108 cannon
Me 262A-2a: standard fighter-bomber configuration, similar to Me 262A-1a but with two Schloss 503A-1 bomb

racks for two 551-lb (250-kg) bombs, and armament normally reduced to two 30-mm MK 108 cannon; the **Me 262A-2a/U2** was a trials development with Lotfe 7H bomb-sight, glazed nose, and accommodation for prone bomb-aimer
Me 262A-3a: trials models intended for close-support role
Me 262A-5a: reconnaissance-fighter with either twin nose-mounted Rb 50/30 oblique cameras, or single Rb 20/30 or Rb 75/30; adapted to the reconnaissance role the **Me 262A-1a/U3** was used by a number of units
Me 262B-1a: conversion trainer with dual flight controls under redesigned canopy; deletion of rear main fuel tank necessitated carriage of two 66-Imp gal (300-litre) drop-tanks on Schloss 503A-1 Wikingschiff racks
Me 262B-1a/U1: interim two-seat night-fighter with FuG 218 *Neptun V* airborne interception radar and FuG 350 ZC (*Naxos*) passive homer; fewer than a dozen in service by 1945
Me 262B-2a: definitive night-fighter with lengthened fuselage to contain additional fuel tanks; two produced
Me 262C-1a: point-defence interceptor fighter with twin Jumo 004B-1s supplemented by tail-mounted Walter RII-211/3 (HWK 509) bi-fuel rocket motor to give outstanding rates of climb; one trials aircraft produced
Me 262C-2b: point-defence interceptor; twin BMW 003R power units, each consisting of a BMW 003A turbojet and a BMW 718 bi-fuel rocket, fitted in place of conventional motors; one produced

with some damage. Fortunately, an alternative to the touchy BMWs was available. This was the Junkers Jumo 004 which had been developed by Dr Anselm Franz's team since its award of a contract as far back as July 1939 for a development specification. In their adherence to axial compressors, German engine designers showed much courage and foresight: this type of compressor was difficult to construct and balance, and was susceptible to vibration and could be damaged far more easily than the tough centrifugal type of compressor. But it became apparent that the acceleration rates, fuel efficiency, power output, and drag coefficients of axial-flow turbojets far exceeded the figures produced by the tougher, and sometimes more reliable, centrifugal types. By August 1941 the Jumo 004 was giving 1,323-lb (600-kg) static thrust, and many of the earlier problems had been cured.

Jumo 004s were installed on the Messerschmitt Me 262 V3 (PC + UC), and this aircraft, bereft of the piston engine and still with tailwheel landing gear, left Leipheim's runway on the morning of 18 July 1942 in Wendel's experienced hands. It looked correct in every way, and it flew beautifully, and henceforth the fortunes of the Messerschmitt Me 262 were to rise at the expense of its nearest rival, the Heinkel He 280, which suffered a series of setbacks until its eventual cancellation in March 1943.

In the Luftwaffe's interest
Service test pilots of the Erprobungsstelle (test establishment) at Rechlin showed interest in the Me 262 from its earliest days. It was largely at their instigation that Messerschmitt received contracts to produce a number of prototypes for weapons and engine tests. The experienced Major Wolfgang Späte had already reported his enthusiastic findings when the General der Jagdflieger, Adolf Galland, flew the Me 262 V4 on 22 May 1943, to become unequivocal in his constant praise for this revolutionary aircraft. At a conference in Berlin on 25 May it was suggested that the piston-engine Messerschmitt Me 209A be cancelled, and that all efforts be directed to the production of the Me 262: three days later a

production order for 100 was made. But other events now took a hand. On 17 August 1943 the US 8th Air Force's attack on Regensburg destroyed much of the embryonic Me 262 production lines, forcing Messerschmitt AG to move its jet development centres to Oberammergau, near the Bavarian Alps. The delay occasioned by the move was increased by a chronic shortage in the supply of skilled labour and production slipped by many months.

In the meantime the Me 262 V5 introduced the tricycle landing gear that was to become standard, only on this prototype the nose-gear was fixed. The definitive Me 262 V6 (Jumo 004Bs) flew on 17 October 1943: the VI + AA featured a retractable tricycle landing gear, gun bays and blast ports, the electrically operated tailplane, and the beautiful high-speed wing with automatic leading-edge slats and trailing-edge flaps.

Can it carry bombs?
By the autumn of 1943 Germany was on the defensive in the USSR and Italy, and was being subjected to furious aerial assault by day and by night: not least of Hitler's concerns was when and where the Allies would strike in north west Europe. During the amphibious invasions in North Africa, on Sicily, and recently of Italy at Salerno and Reggio, Allied air power had kept the Luftwaffe and the German naval forces at bay, and had thus prevented the loss of shipping that could have jeopardized the entire extent of these operations. Therefore nobody could have been surprised when

Aerial photograph of an Me 262A-1a of III Gruppe of Ergänzungs-Jagdgeschwader Nr 2 (III/EJG 2). This powerful conversion unit, based at Lechfeld, flew many sorties against Allied aircraft in the spring of 1945, with Leutnant Bell downing a P-38 Lightning with this particular aircraft on 21 March 1945. The EJG 2 was formed on 2 November 1944.

Messerschmitt Me 262A-2a Jagdbomber (Jabo) of 1./KG 51, based at Achmer in March 1945. By the spring of 1945 the Me 262s of I and II/KG 51 were operating energetically from airfields in the Rheine complex, with a predilection for low-level skip-bombing attacks at dawn and dusk on the Allied front line.

many senior commanders, including Hitler himself, mooted the concept of the Messerschmitt Me 262 as a fighter-bomber as opposed to an interceptor: the idea was tactically sound. It was at Insterberg, in East Prussia, on 26 November 1943 that Hitler watched the dove-grey VI + AA being put through its party tricks by the able Gerd Linder. Present was Professor Willy Messerschmitt to answer the inevitable query from the fascinated Hitler: yes, indeed, the Me 262 could carry up to

In the quest for maximum rates of climb for point-defence work some Messerschmitt Me 262s were modified for development programmes with liquid-fuelled Walter rockets. Illustrated is the Me 262C-1a first flown by Gerd Linder on 27 February 1945. The type arrived too late to enter service, although Major Heinz Bär of III/EJG 2 claimed a P-47 in this Me 262C-1a in the spring of 1945.

2,205-lb (1,000-kg) of bombs with uncomplicated conversion work completed within two weeks per unit! So from this day the Messerschmitt Me 262 was destined to play a dual role: that of a fighter-bomber and that of a pure air-superiority fighter. Neither the role nor the aircraft could by now have had any influence on the outcome of the war. It was too late to start a major production scheme: oil and aviation kerosene, precious alloys, and skilled airframe and engine specialists were at a premium. The Messerschmitt Me 262 had been recognized in its full potential, but too late in the war.

In service

Service conversion of the Me 262 was placed under Hauptmann Werner Thierfelder's Erprobungskommando 262 at Lechfeld, to where the unit moved on 21 December 1943: pilots were drawn from 8. and 9./ZG 26. The EKdo 262 was given a batch of pre-production Me 262A-0 aircraft, and finally got into the swim of operations in the early summer of 1944. Thierfelder was killed in combat with 15th Air Force Mustangs over Bavaria on 18 July, and his place was taken by Hauptmann Neumeyer. The RAF brought back its first confirmation of the Me 262's existence on 25 July, when a de Havilland Mosquito of No. 544 (PR) Squadron was intercepted near Munich.

Messerschmitt Me 262A-2a of 1./KG 51, the 9K + FH (Nr 111625). Command of Kampfgeschwader Nr 51 came under Major Wolfgang Schenk in November 1944: during the summer of that year Schenk took his Kommando into action with Me 262s on the Normandy war front.

Equipped with Messerschmitt Me 262A-2a fighter-bombers, the Einsatzkommando Schenk (Major Wolfgang Schenk) was formed at Lechfeld in July, before posting to the Normandy invasion front: the unit was based at Châteaudun, Etampes and Creil, before pulling back to Juvincourt, near Reims, in late August. It was on 28 August 1944 that Allied fighter pilots downed the first ME 262 to be lost in combat. Operations by Einsatzkommando Schenk continued in a desultory manner until its incorporation into the I Gruppe of Kampfgeschwader Nr 51, which began combat operations from

Messerschmitt Me 262A-2a/U1 fighter-bomber of Erprobungskommando Schenk in the summer of 1944: this was the first Luftwaffe unit to take the Me 262 fighter-bomber into action. Normal bomb load was two SC250 (551-lb) bombs, but for attacks on troop positions and transports the Me 262 carried two AB250 containers.

Messerschmitt ME 262

Specification

Messerschmitt Me 262A-1a

Type: single seat air-superiority fighter

Powerplant: two Junkers Jumo 004B-1, -2, or -3 axial-flow turbojets each rated at 1,984-lb (900-kg) static thrust

Performance: maximum speed 514 mph (827 km/h) at sea level, 530 mph (852 km/h) at 9,845 ft (3000 m), 540 mph (869 km/h) at 19,685 ft (6000 m) and 532 mph (856 km/h) at 26,245 ft (8000 m); initial climb rate 3,937 ft (1200 m) per minute; service ceiling above 40,000 ft (12190 m); range 652 miles (1050 km) at 29,530 ft (9000 m)

Weights: empty 8,378 lb (3795 kg); empty equipped 9,742 lb (4413 kg); maximum take-off 14,080 lb (6387 kg)

Dimensions: span 40 ft 11½ in (12.50 m); length 34 ft 9½ in (10.58 m); height 12 ft 7 in (3.83 m); wing area 234 sq ft (21.73 m²)

Armament: four 30-mm Rheinmetall-Borsig MK 108A-3 cannon with 100 rounds per gun for the upper pair and 80 rounds per gun for the lower pair, and aimed with Revi 16.B gunsight or EZ.42 gyro-stabilized sight, plus provision for 12 R4M air-to-air rockets under each wing

Messerschmitt Me 262A-1a fighter in the colours of the 9.Staffel Jagdgeschwader Nr 7, based at Parchim in early 1945 under 1.Jagddivision of I Jagdkorps in the defence of the Reich. After capture at the end of the war this particular aircraft, Nr 500491, was given the code FE-111 by the technical branch of the USAAF for evaluation. In the course of 1979 the aircraft was stripped down, refurbished and rebuilt in over 6,000 hours of work, and placed on display at the National Air and Space Museum, Washington DC, where it remains to this day. The illustration accentuates the Me 262's sleek lines: the airframe alone, in particular the wing design, was considered by the Allies to be far ahead of their own attainments in the field of high-speed flight.

Rheine-Hopsten under Major Umrau in October 1944. The value of the Me 262 as a reconnaissance aircraft was soon recognized, and a few went to the Einsatzkommando Braunegg, and to Nahaufklärungsgruppen 1 and 6.

Hitler's firm insistence on the Messerschmitt Me 262 being the property of the General der Kampfflieger (Marienfeld) denied Galland the opportunity of forming the first fighter unit until September 1944. One of Germany's finest fighter pilots, Major Walter Nowotny, formed the Kommando Nowotny based at Achmer and Hesepe near Osnabrück, to fly its first mission against Allied bombers and fighters on 3 October 1944. The Messerschmitt Me 262A-1a (two Jumo

III Gruppe was formed from the survivors of Kommando Nowotny, while the I/JG 7 was later formed at Parchim. Four additional bomber units were formed on 30 January 1945: these were KG(J)6, KG(J)27, KG(J)54 and KG(J)55. Of these only I/KG(J)54 at Giebelstadt, II/KG (J) 54 at Kitzingen and III/KG(J)6 at Prague-Ruzyne played any part in operations. The only occasions on which Jagdgeschwader Nr 7 made any impact were during the battles of 18–21 March 1945 when, using Oranienburg and Parchim, a daily average of some 40

Many Messerschmitt Me 262s were captured by Soviet forces in Prague airfield complex in May 1945. Alias an Me 262A-1a, this Czechoslovakian Avia-assembled S-92 Turbina was operated by the 5th Fighter Squadron (5.stihaci letka) of the Czech air force in 1950–1. One Avia S-92, coded V-34, is now on display at the Narodni Technical Museum in Prague.

Third Messerschmitt Me 262 prototype. The Me 262V3 was the first prototype to fly on turbojet power alone, the date being 18 July 1942. It was transferred to the German Aviation Experimental Establishment (DVL) in April 1944 for high-speed flight testing, and written off on 12 September 1944 following damage in an air attack.

004B-1 turbojets) formed the establishment of around 30. The armament was exceptionally potent and consisted of four Rheinmetall-Borsig MK 108A-3 30-mm cannon; the pilot was protected by 9-mm back armour, and a 90-mm armour-glass windscreen. With a maximum speed of 531 mph (855 km/h) at 26,245 ft (8000 m), the Me 262A-1a could outrun anything that the Allies had in their inventory.

Kommando Nowotny disbanded shortly after the death of its leader on 8 November 1944. The potent jet, the presence of which thoroughly alarmed Allied intelligence in the West, continued to be used in penny packets on bombing attacks (with AB250 containers) on Allied front lines, reconnaissance missions, and an occasional foray against enemy fighters. In mid-November Oberst Johannes Steinhoff formed the nucleus of Jagdgeschwader Nr 7 at Brandenburg-Briest:

or more sorties was put up against American bombers. A new unguided air-to-air weapon, the R4M rocket, was used on Me 262A-1a fighters for the first time during these encounters. Final day operations fell to Generalleutnant Galland's Jagdverband 44 (JV 44) at München-Riem, to the aforementioned units, and to the night-fighting Messerschmitt Me 262B-1a/U1 aircraft of 10./NJG 11 at Burg.

Over the period March 1944 to 20 April 1945 the Luftwaffe took delivery of 1,433 Me 262s, but for the Allies the impact of this fine aircraft was largely psychological. After the war they acknowledged that in design the Messerschmitt Me 262 was years ahead of those of other nations, and its secrets permitted the Russians and the Anglo-Americans to accelerate development of jet fighter and bomber aircraft to the magic of Mach 1.0 and beyond over the ensuing years.

Boeing B-29 Superfortress

No other aircraft ever combined so many technological advances as the B-29. Designed for a specific strategic task, it later spawned the double-deck Stratocruiser airliner, the KC-97 tanker/cargo aircraft, the swollen Guppies and the entire lineage of modern heavy aircraft from the Soviet Tupolev bureau.

It is probable that a detailed analysis of the Soviet 'Blackjack' swing-wing bomber of the 1980s would unearth design features that can be traced right back to the B-29. And the Boeing B-29 Superfortress was started more than three years before the USA entered World War 2, in October 1938. In one of his last acts before he was killed in a crash at Burbank the US Army Air Corps Chief of Staff, General Oscar Westover, had officially established a requirement for a new super-bomber to succeed the Boeing B-17, at a time when the B-17 itself was being denied funds by the Congress. Despite totally negative reaction from the War Department, procurement chief General Oliver Echols never gave up in his fight to keep the super-bomber alive, and it had the backing of 'Hap' Arnold, Westover's successor. The bomber was to be pressurized to fly very fast at high altitude: the figures for

Dave's Dream was built as B-29-40-MO 44-27354, but it is pictured here with Major W. P. Swancutt in command heading for Bikini atoll on 1 July 1946, where the modified aircraft dropped the first post-war nuclear weapon. The 509th Composite Group named the aircraft for bombardier Dave Semple, killed in a B-29.

speed (390 mph/628 km/h), range (5,333 miles/8582 km) and military load were staggering.

At the Boeing Airplane Company in Seattle they did at least have experience of large pressurized aircraft, unlike all other companies, but there seemed no way to reconcile the conflicting factors. For most of 1939 the answer seemed to be to fit Pratt & Whitney's slim sleeve-valve liquid-cooled engines inside the wing, but newly hired George Schairer soon pointed out that as the biggest drag item was the wing, the best course was to make the wing as small as possible and not try to put engines inside it. (Thus began a basic philosophy which saw sharp contrast between the Boeing B-47 and the British V-bombers, and has continued to today's Boeing Models 757 and 767.) How does one pressurize a fuselage containing enormous bomb doors? The answer here was to make the colossal bomb bays unpressurized and link the front and rear pressure cabins by a sealed tunnel. Chief engineer Wellwood Beall was first to crawl through the mock-up tunnel in January 1940.

By March 1940 the demands had increased, including 16,000 lb (7258 kg) of bombs for short-range missions,

Boeing B-29
Superfortress

Specification

Boeing B-29 Superfortress

Type: 10-seat long-range strategic bomber/ reconnaissance aircraft

Powerplant: four 2,200-hp (1641-kW) Wright R-3350-23-23A/-41 Cyclone 18 turbocharged radial piston engines

Performance: maximum speed 358 mph (576 km/h) at 25,000 ft (7620 m); cruising speed 230 mph (370 km/h); service ceiling 31,850 ft (9710 m); range 3,250 miles (5230 m)

Weights: empty 70,140 lb (31815 kg); maximum take-off 124,000 lb (56245 kg)

Dimensions: span 141 ft 3 in (43.05 m); length 99 ft 0 in (30.18 m); height 29 ft 7 in (9.02 m); wing area 1,736 sq ft (161.27 m²)

Armament: two 0.50-in (12.7-mm) guns each of four remotely controlled power-operated turrets, and three 0.50-in (12.7-mm) guns or two 0.50-in (12.7-mm) guns and one 20-mm cannon in the tail turret, plus a bomb load of up to 20,000 lb (9072 kg)

Allocated to the 500th Bomb Group of the 73rd Bomb Wing (Very Heavy), 20th Air Force, this B-29 Superfortress operated from the island bases in the Marianas group. Operating by night and at low altitude, the Superfortress fleets dumped tons of incendiaries on the highly combustible cities of Japan, so reducing them to ash.

Boeing B-29 Superfortress

The very first Superfortress was XB-29 no. 41-002, design of which took place in 1939-40, ready for a first flight on 21 September 1942. Olive-drab and grey, it had three-blade propellers, no defensive turret system and numerous details which were later altered, yet the basic airframe was almost identical to production B-29s.

were going to be needed instead of rivets, yet every part of the exterior had to be smooth as glass, with no projections. Nobody knew yet how to make the remote-control gun turrets, or even the multi-ply tyres.

Funds from USAAC

As the BEF was rescued from the beaches at Dunkirk the new bomber was designated the B-29, and in August the US Army Air Corps provided funds for two (later three) prototypes. Work was rushed ahead, but nobody knew how to stop guns and propeller mechanisms from freezing at far over 30,000 ft (9145 m), which Boeing was confident the aircraft could reach. The intense wing loading was all

powered turrets, and far more protection including armour and self-sealing tanks. Weight had already leapt in stages from 48,000 to 85,000 lb (21773 to 38556 kg), and with the fresh demands the design finally rounded out at a daunting 120,000 lb (54432 kg). With just 1,739 sq ft (161.55 m²) of wing, the wing loading was going to be 69 lb/sq ft (336.9 kg/m²), about double the figure universally taken in 1940 as the desirable limit. Test pilot Eddie Allen was happy that the Boeing Model 345 would be flyable (just) if it had the biggest and most powerful high-lift flaps ever thought of, to reduce take-off and landing speeds to about 160 mph (257 km/h), which was about double the equivalent speed of such familiar machines as the B-17 and Supermarine Spitfire. Structurally it meant the wing skins were going to be more than three times as thick as any seen before. Precision bolts

Boeing B-29 variants

XB-29: Boeing Model 345 prototypes (41-002, 41-003 and 41-18335)
YB-29: service-test aircraft with armament (41-36954/36967); total 14
B-29: main production by BW (Boeing Wichita), BA (Bell Airplane) and MO (Martin Omaha); total 1,620 BW, 357 BA and 204 MO
B-29A: span 142 ft 3 in (43.36 m), R-3350-57 or -59 engines, and four-gun forward upper turret; built at Boeing Renton (BN); total 1,119
F-13A: conversions as strategic reconnaissance aircraft with large camera installations and long-range tanks; total 117
RB-29A: redesignation in 1948 of F-13A
TB-29A: conversions as crew trainers
ETB-29A: TB-29A modified for parasite attachments of F-84 jet fighters at wingtips (44-62093)
B-29B: R-3350-51 engines, defensive armament removed except tail turret; built by Bell (BA); total 311
EB-29B: conversion to launch XF-85 Goblin parasite jet from trapeze (44-84111)
B-29D: ex-XB-44, later became B-50
XB-29E: conversion to test different electronic defensive fire-control
B-29F: Arctic conversions of six aircraft
XB-29G: conversion (44-84043) to test experimental turbojets in pod extended below bomb bay
XB-29H: conversion of B-29A for different defensive armament
YB-29J: conversions (six) to test commercial R-3350 powerplants
RB-29J: conversions (two YB-29J) as multi-sensor reconnaissance aircraft; also called FB-29J
YKB-29J: conversions (two YB-29J) for tests of Boeing Flying Boom inflight-refuelling system
CB-29K: conversion to military cargo aircraft
B-29L: original designation of B-29MR
KB-29M: major programme of rebuilds as inflight-refuelling tankers (92) with British looped hose method
B-29MR: conversions (74) as receivers to link with inflight-refuelling hose
KB-29P: major programme of conversions (116) as inflight-refuelling tankers with Flying Boom for SAC
YKB-29T: single conversion of KB-29M (45-21734) as triple-point tanker
DB-29: various conversions as drone and target directors
GB-29: conversions to launch the XS-1, X-1, X-2 and X-3 supersonic research aircraft

QB-29: conversions to remotely piloted target vehicles
SB-29: conversions as ASR (air/sea rescue) platforms with British airborne lifeboat
WB-29: weather reconnaissance aircraft with various air sampling systems
XB-39: conversion of YB-29 with four Allison V-3420 double liquid-cooled engines
XB-44: conversion with 3,000-hp (2238-kW) Wasp Major R-4360-33 engines; became B-29D
P2B-1: conversions (four) for US Navy patrol duty, later rebuilt as P2B-1S radar picket (AEW) platforms and
P2B-2S carrier aircraft for D-558-II Skyrocket, with one transferred to NACA for research
B-50A: production version of B-29D with new wing material, tall vertical tail and reversible propellers; total 79
TB-50A: conversions (11) as crew trainers
B-50B: increased gross weight and modified systems; total 45
EB-50B: conversion to test tandem ('bicycle') landing gear for B-47
RB-50B: conversions as strategic reconnaissance aircraft with 583-Imp gal (2650-litre) underwing tanks; total 44
YB-50C: planned prototype of next generation B-54; not completed
B-50D: definitive bomber with frameless nose, 583-Imp gal (2650-litre) underwing tanks, new forward upper turret etc; total 222
DB-50D: conversion to launch vehicles in Bell XB-63 Rascal programme
KB-50D: conversion as prototype of later tankers
TB-50D: conversions (11) as unarmed crew trainers
WB-50D: conversions (36) as weather reconnaissance platforms
RB-50E: conversions of RB-50B, new sensors; total 14
RB-50F: conversions (a different 14) with SHORAN navigation radar
RG-50G: conversions (15) with air/ground mapping radar, new navaids and B-50D-type nose
TB-50H: new-build programme of unarmed crew trainers; total 24
WB-50H: weather conversion of TB-50H
KB-50J: major conversion programme for inflight-refuelling tankers with Flight Refuelling A-12B hose drum unit at wingtips and in rear fuselage, plus extra tankage and new observation stations: rebuilds by Hayes Aircraft which then added 5,800-lb (2631-kg) thrust General Electric J47-23 booster jet pods under the outer wings; conversions of all RB-50E, RB-50F and RB-50G plus seven B-50D aircraft
KB-50K: conversions to KB-50J standard of all TB-50Hs

Boeing B-29 Superfortress cutaway drawing key

1 Temperature probe
2 Nose glazing
3 Optically flat bomb aiming panel
4 Bombsight
5 Windscreen panels
6 Forward gunsight
7 Bombardier's seat
8 Pilot's instrument console
9 Control column
10 Co-pilot's seat
11 Pilot's seat
12 Side console panel
13 Cockpit heating duct
14 Nose undercarriage leg strut
15 Steering control
16 Twin nosewheels
17 Retraction struts
18 Nosewheel doors
19 Underfloor control cable runs
20 Pilot's back armour
21 Flight engineers station
22 Forward upper gun turret, four 0.5-in (12.7-mm) machine-guns 500-rpg
23 Radio operator's station
24 Chart table
25 Navigator's instrument rack
26 Fire extinguisher bottle
27 Forward lower gun turret, two 0.5-in (12.7-mm) machine-guns, 500-rpg
28 Ventral aerial
29 Navigator's seat
30 Hydraulic system servicing point
31 Access ladder
32 Forward cabin rear pressure bulkhead

33 Armoured bulkhead
34 Pressurized tunnel connecting front and rear cabins
35 Astrodome observation hatch
36 Forward bomb racks
37 Bomb hoisting winches
38 Catwalk
39 Bomb rack mounting beam
40 Pressurized tunnel internal crawlway
41 D/F loop aerial
42 Radio communications aerials
43 Starboard main undercarriage wheel bay
44 Wing inboard fuel tanks, 1,415-US gal (5356 litres)
45 Starboard inner engine nacelle
46 Intercooler exhaust flap

against the designers, but using four monster Wright R-3350 Duplex Cyclones, each with not one but two of General Electric's best turbochargers and driving 16 ft 7 in (5.05 m) Hamilton Standard four-blade propellers, the propulsion was equal to the task. The crew finally rounded out at 10, with the pilot and co-pilot riding in the extreme nose surrounded by Plexiglas windows with the bombardier between them, the navigator facing ahead behind the pilot, the flight engineer (often two) facing aft behind the co-pilot and the radio operator farther aft.

Behind this nose section were two giant bomb bays, from which an electric sequencing system released bombs alternately from front and rear to preserve the centre of gravity position. Between the two bays was a ring forming the structural heart of the aircraft and integral with the main wing box, the strongest aircraft part built up to that time.

On the wing were four monster nacelles, which Schairer showed to have less drag than engines buried in a bigger wing. After four main gears had been studied, a way was found to fold simple two-wheel gears into the inboard nacelles. Fowler flaps were screwed out electrically to add 21 per cent to area of the wing, fighting a wing loading which by September 1940 reached 71.9 lb/sq ft (351.1 kg/m²) and climbed to a frightening 81.1 lb/sq ft (396.0 kg/m²) by the time of the first combat mission.

Behind the wing the rear pressure cabin had three sighting stations linked to two upper and two lower turrets, each with twin 0.5-in (12.7-mm) machine-guns. The electric fire control was normally set so that the top station controlled either or both the upper turrets, the side stations the lower rear turret, and the bomardier the forward lower turret, but control could be overridden or switched (because gunners

47 Engine cooling air outlet flaps
48 Engine cowling panels
49 Hamilton Standard 4-bladed constant-speed propellers, 16 ft 7 in diameter
50 Propeller hub pitch change mechanism
51 Starboard outer engine nacelle
52 Exhaust stub
53 Wing outboard fuel tanks, 1,320-US gal (4991 litres) maximum internal fuel load 9363-US gal including bomb bay ferry tanks
54 Wing bottom skin stringers
55 Leading edge de-icing boots
56 Starboard navigation light
57 Fabric-covered aileron
58 Aileron tab
59 Flap guide rails
60 Starboard Fowler-type flap
61 Flap rib construction
62 Inboard nacelle tail fairing
63 Life raft stowage
64 Wing panel centreline joint
65 Wing/fuselage attachment main frames
66 Pressurization ducting
67 Heat exchanger
68 Centre section fuel tank, 1,333-US gal (5046 litres)
69 Cabin heater
70 Pressurization control valve
71 Fuselage framing
72 Rear bomb bay, 4 × 2000-lb bombs shown
73 Bomb rack
74 Access door
75 Rear cabin front pressure bulkhead
76 Radio aerial mast
77 Upper gun turret sighting hatch
78 Upper gunner's seat
79 Remote gun controller
80 Radio and electronics racks
81 Upper gun turret, two 0.5-in (12.7-mm) machine-guns, 500-rpg
82 Rear pressure bulkhead
83 Fin root fillet
84 Starboard tailplane
85 Starboard elevator
86 Leading edge de-icing boots
87 Tailfin construction
88 HF aerial cable
89 Fin tip fairing
90 Fabric-covered rudder construction
91 Rudder tab
92 Tail gunner's pressurized compartment
93 Armoured glass window panels
94 Tail gun camera
95 20-mm cannon, 100-rounds
96 Twin 0.5-in (12.7-mm) machine-guns, 500-rpg
97 Remotely controlled ball turret
98 Elevator tab
99 Port fabric-covered elevator construction
100 Tailplane leading edge de-icing boot
101 Tailplane construction
102 Fin/tailplane attachment joints
103 Tail turret ammunition boxes
104 Retractable tail bumper
105 Oxygen bottles
106 APU fuel tank
107 Rear ventral turret, two 0.5-in (12.7-mm) machine-guns, 500-rpg
108 Auxiliary power unit (APU)
109 Oblique camera
110 Vertical camera
111 Crew entry door
112 Batteries
113 Pressure bulkhead access door
114 Crew rest bunks
115 Toilet
116 Radio communications tuning units
117 Remote gunsight
118 Gun aiming blister
119 Gunner's seat, port and starboard
120 Voltage regulator
121 Bomb door hydraulic jacks
122 Rear bomb bay doors
123 Port Fowler flap
124 Flap shroud ribs
125 Rear spar
126 Outer wing panel joint
127 Aileron tab
128 Fabric-covered aileron construction
129 Wing tip fairing
130 Port navigation light
131 Wing stringers
132 Outer wing panel ribs
133 Front spar
134 Leading edge nose ribs
135 Leading edge de-icing boots
136 Port wing fuel tank bays
137 Engine nacelle firewall
138 Nacelle construction
139 Engine mounting frame
140 Twin mainwheels
141 Main undercarriage leg strut
142 Mainwheel leg pivot mounting
143 Port mainwheel bay
144 Hydraulic retraction jack
145 Nacelle tail fairing
146 Self-sealing oil tank, 85 US gal (322 litres)
147 Hydraulic reservoir
148 Mainwheel doors
149 Exhaust stub
150 Exhaust driven turbo-supercharger
151 Intercooler
152 Engine cooling air exit flaps
153 Exhaust collector ring
154 Wright cyclone R-3350-57A, 18-cylinder, two-row radial engine
155 Engine intake ducting
156 Forward bomb bay doors
157 20 × 500-lb (227-kg) bombs, maximum bomb load 20,000 lb (9072 kg)

could be knocked out in action). In the extreme tail was another gunner driving a turret with two 0.5-in (12.7-mm) guns and a 20-mm cannon. Combat experience with B-17s in 1942 showed the need for more forward firepower and the upper forward turret was later replaced by a four-gun model, but this required a larger magazine which obstructed the interior.

In any case over 2,000 B-29s were to be built before this turret could come on production, because immediately after Pearl Harbor a colossal manufacturing programme was organized, involving vast new plants across the nation. Major parts were made in over 60 new factories, the enormous nacelles, each as big as a P-47, coming from a new Cleveland facility operated by the Fisher Body Division of General Motors. Final assembly was organized at three of the world's largest buildings, Boeing at Wichita, Martin at Omaha and Bell at Marietta (today the same building houses the Lockheed-Georgia Company). Later yet another line was set up at Boeing Renton. All this had been organized before the olive-drab XB-29 (41-002) had even flown, but from the first flight, on 21 September 1942 (initially using three-blade propellers), it was clear that the B-29 was going to be a winner. It could so easily have been what test pilots then called 'a dog'; and one of the firms delegated to build B-29s was convinced Boeing's figures were far too optimistic and that the whole programme was a giant mistake. What made the B-29, by 1942 named Superfortress, now vitally important was that it was obviously going to be the only aircraft with the range to attack Japan.

Incorporating the Boeing-designed 'flying boom' refuelling unit, the KB-29P was first delivered to SAC in March 1950. With it is shown a North American RB-45C Tornado. As can be seen, the air-refuelling tanker version had its armament removed, but an extra observation station was added at the rear.

Externally indistinguishable from the B-29, the Tupolev Tu-4 made its public debut at the 1947 Soviet Aviation Day held at Tushino, Moscow. This photograph of the original aircraft was taken in 1983 at Monino, which was closed to the public shortly afterwards.

To say that the good results of ship 41-002 were a relief would be an understatement. Far more money (three billion dollars) had been invested in the B-29 programme long before its wheels left the ground than in any other project in the history of any nation. At the same time the technical snags were severe, and multiplied. Many, such as power-plant fires and runaway propellers, were highly dangerous, and three months into the flight programme the prototypes had logged just 31 of the 180 hours scheduled. The low point in the programme was 18 February 1943 when Eddie Allen and his crew of 11, plus 19 meat-packers on the ground, were killed when blazing 41-002 just failed to make it to the runway. Underlying it all was the certain knowledge that the lost B-29 had ushered in a new capability in aviation.

Even when the Superfortresses trickled and then poured off the lines, they were so complex that nobody in uniform fully understood them. All went to a modification centre at Salina, Kansas, where over 9,900 faults in the first 175, urgently needed for the new 20th Bomb Wing, were bull-dozed right by a task force of 600 men in 'The Battle of Kansas'. Sheer manpower and the USA's mighty industrial power forced the obstacles out of the way, and the B-29s not only began racking up the hours but their baffled crews gradually learned how to manage them, how to fly straight and level in a goldfish bowl without continuously using instruments, and above all how to get something faintly resembling the published range with heavy bombloads. Air miles per pound of fuel were improved by exactly 100 per cent between January and March 1944. And the complex systems grew reliable in the ultra-cold of 33,000 ft (10060 m).

On 5 June 1944 the first combat mission was flown from Kharagpur, India, to Bangkok; the worst problem was an unexpected tropical storm. On 15 June the first of the raids on Japan was mounted, from Chengtu (one of many newly bulldozed B-29 strips in China) to the Yawata steelworks. The specially created 20th Air Force grew in muscle, and in October 1944 the first B-29s arrived on newly laid runways on the Marianas islands of Tinian, Saipan and Guam, just taken from the enemy. Swiftly the numbers grew as the mighty plants back home poured out B-29s and B-29As with 12 in (0.30 m) more span and the four-gun front turret, while Bell added 311 B-29Bs with all armament stripped except that in the tail, making a great difference in reduced weight

One of very few surviving pictures of 'parasiting', this photograph was taken during trials in 1949–51 to see if a bomber really could tow fighters over long ranges. ETB-29A-60 44-62093 was much more modified for Project Tom Tom, towing F-84D-1 Thunderjets 48-641 and 48-661. Another B-29 carried the XF-85 Goblin.

and complexity. The B-29B was made possible by the patchy fighter opposition, and many Superfortresses were similarly stripped in the field.

Moreover, the commander of the XXI Bomber Command, Major General Curtis LeMay, boldly decided to bomb Tokyo by night from low level, with a full load of incendiaries. There were many reasons for this, but the chief ones were that it promised much greater bombloads and the elimination of bombing errors attributable to jetstream winds. This policy, totally at variance with the idea of high-altitude day formations, resulted in the greatest firestorms the world has ever seen, and the biggest casualties ever caused by air attack. They were far greater than the 75,000 of Hiroshima, hit by the 20-kiloton 'Little Boy' atom bomb dropped on 6 August 1945 from Colonel Paul Tibbetts' B-29 *Enola Gay*, or the 35,000 of Nagasaki hit by the 20-kiloton 'Fat Man' dropped

with 583-Imp gal (2650-litre) underwing tanks), 222 of the definitive B-50D and finally 24 TB-50H crew trainers.

In the 1950s hundreds of B-29s kept flying, almost all modified for different roles but including 88 ordinary B-29 bombers handed to the RAF and used as the Boeing Washington by Bomber Command's Nos 15, 35, 44, 57, 90, 115, 149, and 207 Squadrons. In the USAF the jet-assisted KB-50J went on tanking until the last pair were struck off charge in Vietnam in 1963. But this is not really the end of the story.

Back in 1943 Josef Stalin began a major campaign to get B-29s. He never succeeded, and work began on a Soviet copy, though smaller and without the complex armament. Then out of the blue, on 29 July 1944, a B-29 made an emergency landing in the Soviet Union near Vladivostok after bombing Japan. Two more arrived later (one of them was the *General H. H. Arnold Special*, the 175th to be built

Together with Consolidated C-87s and other modified B-24s, the B-29 was pressed into service as a tanker to bring to Chinese B-29 airbases the fuel needed for the missions over Japan. Many were permanently modified as tankers, an example being B-29-1-BW 42-6242, one of the first production block, which served with the 486th BG.

Eighty-eight ex-USAAF B-29As were supplied to the RAF to meet the UK's long-range bombing requirements of the 1950s; the aircraft were known as 'Washingtons'. An aircraft of No. 90 Sqn based at Marham, Norfolk, is shown. This squadron won the Sassoon and Laurence Minot trophies for visual bombing and gunnery in 1952.

on 9 August from *Bock's Car*. The war ended five days later. Only by the incredibly bold decision to go into the biggest multi-company production programme ever organized long before the first flight did the B-29 manage to make so large a contribution to World War 2. By VJ-Day more than 2,000 were actually with combat crews, and though 5,000-plus were cancelled days later the manufacturing programme was slowed progressively, and did not close until May 1946, by which time 3,960 B-29s had been built. Hundreds were modified for different tasks, and many were launched on new careers as air/sea rescue aircraft, turbojet test-beds or tankers, which kept them busy for another decade or more. Back in 1942 Boeing had begun to work on the Model 367 transport version with a much larger upper lobe to a 'double bubble' fuselage, the first XC-97 flying on 15 November 1944. Various improved bomber versions were cancelled but the B-29D, with new engines, was continued and became the B-50.

A B-29A (42093845) was flown with the 28-cylinder Pratt & Whitney R-4360 Wasp Major engine in early 1944 as the XB-44 and the 3,000-hp (2238-kW) engine made such a difference that other changes were made, including a wing made of 75ST aluminium alloy giving much greater strength with 650 lb (295 kg) less weight, and a taller vertical tail. There were many systems changes, and the propellers were made reversible. The new bomber, the B-29D, went into production at Renton in July 1945. Manufacture continued, at a reduced pace, with the changed designation B-50. The first production B-50A finally emerged in June 1947, and Boeing built 79, followed by 45 strengthened B-50Bs (all but one being rebuilt as unarmed RB-50B reconnaissance aircraft

and picked out on the Wichita line by the USAAF chief of staff, who said 'This is the one I want as soon as you can build it; it will complete our first Bomb Group'), and within weeks they were all being carefully taken apart. In an operation without parallel, the Russian technicians studied every part of the B-29 to the extent of preparing their own production drawings, establishing material specifications, manufacturing tolerances and production procedures. The vast Tupolev bureau finally went into production, trying to short-cut some areas by buying tyres and brakes in the USA. These purchases did not succeed, but they did make the US government believe the previously incredible rumours of what the Soviets were doing.

First the Tupolev bureau built much simpler aircraft, the big-bodied Tu-70 and Tu-75 transports, both of which incorporated the complete wing and many other parts of the 'captured' B-29s. The Tu-70 flew on 27 November 1946. On Aviation Day, 3 August 1947, three Soviet copies of the B-29, designated Tu-4 by the VVS (air force), thundered over Moscow. They were followed by over 300 others. Like the B-29 four years earlier, the Tu-4 test programme in 1947–9 was marked by plenty of problems, but the Tu-4 eventually matured and not only comprised the core of a formidable nuclear strike force but, to a far greater extent than the B-29 itself, led to versions of much greater power and capability including the Tu-80 and Tu-85 which represented the all-time pinnacle of piston-engine bomber development to the traditional formula. Very considerable amounts of B-29 technology were carried straight across to the Tu-88 (Tu-16 'Badger') and Tu-95 (Tu-20 'Bear'), and small features can no doubt be distinguished in today's Tu-22M 'Backfire'.

This EC-121D, derived from the Super Constellation, is shown here patrolling over the Gulf of Tonkin in November 1969. It was used to monitor the skies over Vietnam and was intended as an early warning aircraft against Russian MiGs *(Photo: US Air Force)*.

Lockheed Constellation

Though it initially suffered from protracted technical problems, the 'Connie' became the best-loved piston-engine airliner of all, and, in its maker's words, was 'Queen of the Skies'. Finally, while commercial Connies were slowly rotting away, military examples of a dozen species were working unnoticed around the clock.

In its day the Lockheed Constellation was the biggest, most powerful and most expensive of all airliners. But it avoided joining the list of unsuccessful giants, because at first its capacity was not so great as to frighten the airlines. The 'Connie', as it was affectionately known, was made possible by the development of engines of great power, and this power was used for speed, and to lift fuel for long range while cruising in pressurized comfort at high altitude. Once the basic type was established, Lockheed met the demand for greater capacity by introducing one of the first and greatest of all 'stretching' programmes to yield the 'Super Connie', seating up to 100 or more.

But in 1938 this could not be foreseen. On 23 June of that year the McCarran Act had transformed US commercial aviation, and the manufacturing industry had rationalized into the same three names that dominate it today, Boeing, Douglas and Lockheed. The first two had already built the big four-engine DC-4 and pressurized Model 307 Stratoliner, but Lockheed was overloaded with small twins and the military Hudson and P-38, and its promising Excalibur remained a succession of mock-ups. This was tough, because Lockheed had a strong leaning towards powerful, fast aircraft, and had pioneered pressure cabins with the XC-35 flown in May 1937. Nothing much could be done until

suddenly on 9 June 1939 the company was visited by the famed Howard Hughes, who had secretly bought most of the stock of TWA, and Jack Frye, whom he had appointed president.

Hughes had lately given Lockheed a giant boost by flying a Model 14 airliner around the world in record time. TWA was in severe trouble with money and route competition, and Hughes urged the development of a new super-luxury transport that could fly nonstop coast-to-coast across the continental USA. The specifications sounded out of this world (empty weight 52,300 lb/24132 kg, four 2,200-hp/1641-kW engines, cruising speed over 300 mph/483 km/h and the ability to fly from New York to London nonstop), and all Lockheed's rivals gave Hughes a thumbs-down. But Lockheed's Bob Gross called in his top designers, Hall L. Hibbard and Clarence L. 'Kelly' Johnson, and said 'Come up with something'. Long meetings were held at a secret Hughes place on Romaine Street, Hollywood, and before the end of

Known to Lockheed as the Model 749-79-38, the C-121A was a properly designed military transport, the C-69s having mainly been converted airliners. USAF No. 48-616 is seen here in MATS (Military Air Transport Service) markings, flying as a PC-121A passenger aircraft. Engines were 2,500-hp (1864-kW) R-3350-75 Duplex Cyclones.

US Army Air Force no. 42-94553 was a Model 049-39-10, ordered pre-war by TWA but built as a C-69-5. It is shown in May 1946 finish without olive-drab paint, and with the 'buzz number' CM-553. Later it was struck off the Army strength and sold to TWA, with civil registration N52414. All early models had circular porthole-type windows.

HI-328, registered to Aerolineas Argo SA of the Dominican Republic. An L-749A, she served with several operators before going to Dominica, which was a final stronghold of old Connies until Argo – an all-cargo airline – ceased flying in 1983.

the year a formal meeting took place at which Hughes asked the price and was told $425,000. He rocked back and forth like an Indian at a pow-wow and said 'Hell, TWA can't pay, the damn airline's broke. Go ahead and build 40, I'll have to pay for them myself.'

C-69 for the US Army

Wartime pressures delayed the Model 49 Constellation, but eventually Lockheed hired pilot Eddie Allen to take the first one aloft on 9 January 1943. No commercial production was allowed after Pearl Harbor, and TWA's idea of a commercial lead with a super dream-ship evaporated as PanAm came in alongside; and in the event all production went to the US Army. But even in olive drab the C-69, as it was now called, was quite something. Its wing was a scaled-up version of the wing of the P-38, with giant area-increasing Fowler flaps. The fuselage was curved like the body of a fish and ended in a triple tail. The circular-section cabin seated 64 passengers, though Hughes was bemused that the US Army could take out all the luxury and still contrive to make the C-69 heavier than the Model 49. All flight-control surfaces were hydraulically boosted. Not least, the height of the Constellation off the ground was unprecedented. In two respects, however, the civil registered NX67900, or Lockheed ship no. 1961, was conventional: it had normal cockpit windows instead of once-planned perfectly streamlined nose, and the engines were also fairly conventional instead of being in perfectly streamlined nacelles with reverse-flow cooling from inlets in the leading edges.

During the war the USAAF received 22 Constellations, comprising nine ex-TWA and 13 of a contract for 180 signed in 1942. At VJ-Day the military contract was cancelled. Lockheed shut down the Burbank plant for five days to plan its future. It almost decided to start again with an even newer Constellation, but finally elected to buy back surplus government tooling, parts, materials and unfinished C-69s. This resulted in the commercial Model 049 having an 18-month lead over the DC-6 and Stratocruiser, and even more over the Republic Rainbow, and within nine days 103 Constellations valued at $75.5 million had been ordered by eight airlines. TWA at last got the first of 27 Model 049s in November 1945. CAA certification followed on 11 December. Commercial services followed in early February 1946, TWA flying the New York–Paris and PanAm the New York–Bermuda routes.

The USAAF sold its surplus C-69s to airlines in 1946, and the in-service record built up so fast that by July 1946 over 200 million passenger miles had been flown without anyone suffering injury. This was despite numerous engine fires and both engine and propeller failures, but on 11 July 1946 a TWA training flight crashed at Reading, Pennsylvania, because the pilots could not see from the smoke-filled cockpit. A six-week grounding followed, in which 95 modifications were made to the powerplant and systems. There was light at the end of the tunnel (and the DC-6 and other rivals were grounded too): on 19 October 1946 the first definitive post-war Model 649 took the air, so luxurious and with such good air-conditioning and soundproofing it was called the 'Gold Plate Connie'. Eastern worked on the specification and was first to use it, one of its features being a Speedpak external cargo pod under the belly.

Post-war civil success

Ten airlines then bought nearly 100 Model 749s in which 2,700-hp (2014-kW) engines enabled gross weight to rise to 102,000 lb (46267 kg), with a long-range tank in each outer wing to give an extension of range of 1,000 miles (1609 km) without any reduction in payload. Payload/range was further enhanced by the Model 749A at 107,000 lb (48535 kg), with Curtiss paddle-blade propellers. The USAAF (now the USAF) again adopted the Constellation, buying 10 Model

This historic photograph was taken at Burbank on 9 January 1943 when the very first Constellation, painted in US Army olive drab, took off for the first time. It was to suffer its fair share of technical problems, but it opened up a new plateau in air transport range, speed and comfort.

The final variant of the Super Constellation was the L-1049H, which featured a mixed passenger/cargo configuration. The speed and ease of conversion from one role to the other was a prime requirement of this last variant of the 'Queen of the Skies'.

KLM Royal Dutch Airlines was one of the first operators of the Turbo-Compound engined L-1049C, which was placed in use on the North Atlantic in August 1953. Just a year later KLM took delivery of this tip-tanked L-1049G, PH-LKE, which could fly the Amsterdam–New York route much better with less frequent stops for refuelling.

With a maximum range of 4020 miles (6469 km), uprated Wright TC-18-DA3 Turbo-Compound engines and an increased cabin length of 56 ft (17.06 m), the L-1049G proved the most successful Super Constellation model in sales terms. Shown here is Lufthansa's D-ALUB. The airline flew its first intercontinental service from Hamburg to New York on 8 June 1955.

749s as C-121s of various sub-types, two of which were General MacArthur's *Bataan* and General Eisenhower's *Columbine*. Later another of this batch (48-610) was used as *Columbine II* when Eisenhower became President. The US Navy, which in 1945 had used two R7O-1 transports off the US Army line, purchased two Model 749s as its first dedicated radar picket (AEW) aircraft, initially designated PO-1W and later WV-1. Initially flown in June 1949, these were the first aircraft in the world bought from the start as high-flying radar stations, if one discounts modified single-engine Grumman TBM-3 Avengers. Their giant radars were served by aerials (antennae) above and below, but despite the grotesque appearance the addition of extra height to the fins resulted in a very tractable aircraft, and the success of these first two examples led to massive orders of no fewer than 27 distinct subsequent versions for various electronic purposes.

The unexpected USAF and USN sales helped carry the commercial line through a bad patch, and spurred Lockheed into the striking 'stretch' which turned the Constellation into the Model 1049 Super Constellation. By 1950 the whole programme, under Carl M. Haddon, was poised for its second generation, backed by Lockheed Aircraft Service which had begun at Idlewild in 1949 spurred by the Berlin Airlift, in which C-121s flew almost six million passenger miles from Westover AFB to Rhein-Main. But the big news was the L-1049, in which Hibberd injected rational sense with a straight passenger tube of constant section, it having been realized that an airliner in which the body section varied continuously was a mistake.

The first L-1049, the old no. 1961 rebuilt, flew on 13 October 1950. There were many minor changes, but the most obvious one apart from the 18 ft 4 in (5.59 m) extra length was the switch from port-holes to rounded square windows, removing what had become another outdated feature despite the better fatigue resistance of rings to squares. TWA was behind the Super Constellation, though it was pipped to the post by Eastern which got the new transport, able to seat 99, on the Miami run on 15 December 1951. The largely new engine installations worked well, as did the improved de-icing systems and the larger cockpit windows, integrally stiffened wing skins machined in the newly opened 'Hall of Giants' at Burbank, and better environmental systems.

The L-1049B was a cargo model with integrally stiffened floor and two large loading doors. Lockheed was requested by the US Navy to switch to the complex new Wright Turbo-Compound engine derived from the existing R-3350 used in all previous Constellations, and the 3,250 hp (2425 kW) available from each engine not only promised more speed but also a jump in gross weight to 133,000 lb (60329 kg), representing a further great advance in payload/range. Though the Turbo-Compound engine predictably took a long time to mature, it also totally removed the slight sluggishness which

One of the last European airlines to continue flying the Super-G was Iberia, the national airline of Spain (though it withdrew them long before its last cargo DC-4!). EC-AMP is shown on test near Burbank prior to delivery in 1956. One can almost imagine the deep rumble of those Turbo-Compound engines and mighty propellers!

In its day – it first flew in December 1954 – the L-1049G, or 'Super G', was the greatest airliner in the world. Structural changes enabled it to carry large tip tanks (tested on the original company-owned L-1049 prototype) which combined with the Turbo-Compound engines to give the greatest range of any Constellation up to that time, despite capacity for 71 first-class or 95 'coach' passengers. One of the chief operators of the 99 examples built of this model was TWA, which had sponsored the original Constellation before World War 2. With these fine aircraft the airline

pioneered trans-Atlantic and other long-haul services including its luxury Ambassador class, patronized chiefly by businessmen and using special private suites at the airports. In the plan view the dark apertures above the trailing edge between the engines are the air-conditioning heat exchanger exhausts. Behind the black line of the rear spar just inboard of these can be seen the big doors of the life raft bays. The black bands on the leading edges are the pulsating rubber de-icers.

118

Lockheed Constellation

Specification

Lockheed L-1049G
Type: long-haul passenger airliner
Powerplant: four 3,250-hp (2423-kW)
Wright R-3350-DA3 Turbo Compound 18-
cylinder turbine-boosted piston engines
Performance: cruising speed 354 mph (570
km/h) at 22,600 ft (6890 m); range with
maximum fuel and full reserves 5,100 miles
(8200 km)
Weights: equipped empty (typical) 79,700
lb (36152 kg); maximum take-off 145,000 lb
(65772 kg)
Dimensions: span (over tanks) 126 ft 2 in
(38.47 m); length 116 ft 2 in (35.42 m);
height 24 ft 9 in (7.54 m); wing area 1,654 sq
ft (153.66 m²)
Accommodation: flight crew, usually five;
variable cabin crew for maximum of 95
passengers

had crept into the original Model 1049, which cruised at barely 300 mph (483 km/h). In addition to 57 US Navy R7V-1s, of which 32 were transferred to the USAF as C-121Gs, Lockheed sold 33 C-121Cs to the USAF. The C121C was cleared to 135,000 lb (61236 kg), and the others introduced the uprated 3,500-hp (2611-kW) R-3350-34 engine and could take off at 145,000 lb (65772 kg). Subsequently the USAF and US Navy variants of the Model 1049 far outnumbered the commercial versions, as the variants list shows.

Comfort and capability

Seaboard & Western bought a commercial version of the Model 1049B, but the passenger version was the Model 1049C, first put into service by KLM on the New York–Amsterdam route in August 1953. Increasingly the airliner models were fitted with weather radar, which added 3 ft (0.91 m) to the length, as in the military variants. This helped improve passenger comfort, especially on US coast-to-coast trips, and such was the capability of the Model 1049C that from 19 October 1953 TWA at last opened a nonstop service between Los Angeles and New York, rivalling that opened by American with the similarly powered DC-7. This was a time when the British de Havilland Comet was blazing the trail of the airline jet. The Constellation's Mach 0.58 was less impressive, but history was to show that the US industry, greatly aided by the unfortunate collapse of the original Comet programme, was able to fend off this new competition with its fundamentally old generation piston-engine machines, with the Model 1049 in the forefront. Unit price, typically $1 million for a Model 749, rose to $1.25m with the first Model 1049s, and more than doubled with later Model 1049 versions.

The Model 1049D was an improved cargo aircraft, and the Model 1049E a corresponding passenger version, but most Model 1049E aircraft were actually completed as Model 1049Gs, which were among the most important of all commercial versions. Improved climb ratings from the R-3350-DA3 Turbo-Compound enabled gross weight to reach 137,500 lb (62370 kg), which among other things enabled 600-US gal (2271-litre) tip tanks to be added. The Model 1049G entered service with Northwest in January 1955. A convertible passenger/cargo model was the Model 1049H, of which 54 were built. The very last Constellation was an L-1049H delivered in November 1958.

Piston-engine pinnacle

Before then, one final model had been designed, flown and built in quantity; but the quantity was small, and this was the only version to prove unprofitable to Lockheed, because its development cost over $60 million. The model 1649A Starliner was launched in 1954 to meet the severe competition of the DC-7C Seven Seas on ultra-long routes, especially the nonstop North Atlantic services. No Model 1049 was really a nonstop Atlantic aircraft (certainly not westbound)

and TWA for the last time decided to push Lockheed into a further development of what had by this time become an old aeroplane. In going for long range Lockheed capitalized on the one thing the Super Constellation could offer in competition with the new Comet 3: lower fuel consumption, though of course it was 115/145 grade gasoline. Fitting Turbo-Compounds had inevitably resulted in severe noise and vibration in an airframe originally planned for about half this power, and it was ultimately decided to out-do Douglas by designing a totally new wing, of great span and high aspect ratio, which would give unrivalled cruising efficiency, house more fuel and enable the engines to be moved well away from the fuselage to reduce noise and propeller vibration.

The Model 1649A first flew on 10 October 1956. It was a beautiful aircraft, and can be regarded as the final pinnacle

Acting as relay stations for signals from ground sensors in Project 'Igloo White', 30 ex-USN EC-121Ks and EC-121Ps proved invaluable to the US Air Force's intelligence operations during the Vietnam war.

This Lockheed L-1049G served for 10 years from 1955 with Air India as VT-DJX on the airline's trunk routes. Eight Super-Gs were then passed on to the Indian Air Force, where for a further decade they flew not only transport but also maritime reconnaissance missions with No. 6 Sqn. Radar was retained, but the tip tanks were removed.

Lockheed L-1049C Super Constellation cutaway drawing key

1 Nose cone
2 Landing and taxiing lamps
3 Front pressure bulkhead
4 Hydraulic brake accumulator
5 Radio mast
6 Nosewheel leg door
7 Steering jacks
8 Twin nosewheels
9 Nosewheel leg strut
10 Retraction linkages
11 Pitot tube mast
12 Rudder pedals
13 Instrument panel
14 Instrument panel shroud
15 Windscreen wipers
16 Windscreen panels
17 Co-pilot's seat
18 Control column
19 Pilot's seat
20 Flight deck floor level
21 Radio operator's station
22 Flight engineer's station
23 Starboard crew door
24 VOR aerial
25 Engineer's instrument panel
26 Radio racks
27 Cockpit bulkhead
28 Navigator's chart table
29 Underfloor battery bay
30 Nosewheel doors
31 Forward entry door
32 Cabin bulkhead
33 Crew rest area

34 Radio aerial mast
35 Overhead luggage racks
36 Starboard emergency exit window
37 Forward cabin seating
38 Forward underfloor freight hold, total freight hold volume 728 cu ft (20.61 m³)
39 Radio altimeter
40 Ventral freight door
41 Port emergency exit windows
42 Ventral ADF sense aerial
43 Toilet compartments, port and starboard
44 Wardrobes
45 Main cabin four-abreast seating
46 Cabin wall trim panels
47 Starboard inner engine nacelle

48 Starboard wing integral fuel tank, total fuel capacity 6,550 US gal (24760 litres)
49 Supercharger oil cooler
50 Starboard outer engine nacelle
51 Detachable engine cowling panels
52 Spinner

53 Hamilton Standard three-bladed propeller
54 Leading edge de-icing boots
55 Fuel system piping
56 Outer wing panel joint rib
57 Outboard integral fuel tank
58 Starboard navigation light
59 Static dischargers
60 Starboard aileron
61 Aileron balance weights
62 Fuel venting system piping
63 Aileron control hydraulic booster
64 Aileron tab
65 Fuel jettison pipe
66 Starboard Fowler-type flap
67 Flap guide rails
68 Starboard air conditioning plant

69 Fuselage centre section construction
70 Wing/fuselage attachment main frames
71 Centre section bag-type fuel tanks
72 Central flap control motor
73 Cabin floor panels
74 Fresh-air distribution ducting

75 Air conditioning system overhead ducting
76 Heating system overhead ducting
77 Cabin roof air distribution duct
78 Cabin partition
79 Lounge area
80 VHF aerial
81 Galley
82 Wardrobe
83 Aft cabin seating
84 Fuselage frame and stringer construction
85 Cabin attendants' folding seats
86 Wardrobes, port and starboard
87 Port and starboard washrooms
88 Cabin pressurization valves
89 Rear pressure bulkhead
90 Tailcone construction
91 Elevator mass balance weight
92 Fin/tailplane fillets
93 Starboard tailplane
94 Rudder control rods
95 Leading edge de-icing boots
96 Starboard fin
97 Fabric-covered rudder

98 Rudder trim tab
99 Lower rudder segment
100 Starboard elevator
101 Elevator trim tab
102 Centre fin construction
103 Centre rudder
104 Tail navigation light
105 Port elevator construction
106 Elevator tab
107 Port fin construction
108 Static dischargers
109 Port rudder construction
110 Tailplane tip fairing
111 Leading edge de-icing boots
112 Tailplane construction
113 Rudder and elevator hydraulic boosters
114 Tailplane attachment frame
115 HF aerial cable
116 Aft toilet compartments port and starboard
117 Rear underfloor freight hold
118 Rear cabin emergency exit window
119 Ladder stowage
120 Passenger entry door
121 Entry lobby
122 Folding table
123 Wing root fillet construction
124 Cabin heater unit
125 Port flap shroud panels
126 Life raft stowage bays
127 Port air conditioning plant
128 Heat exchange air exhaust ducts
129 Port Fowler-type flap

130 Flap shroud ribs
131 Fuel jettison pipe
132 Aileron tab
133 Port aileron construction
134 Static dischargers
135 Wing tip construction
136 Port navigation light
137 Leading edge de-icing boots
138 Port outboard fuel tank bay
139 Outer wing panel main spar
140 Outer wing panel joint rib
141 Rear spar
142 Wing rib construction
143 Engine nacelle construction
144 Air conditioning system turbine
145 Oil cooler air duct
146 Oil cooler
147 Engine mounting ring
148 Carburettor intake duct fairing
149 Twin mainwheels
150 Leading edge nose ribs
151 Front spar
152 Wing stringer construction
153 Main undercarriage leg strut
154 Retraction linkage
155 Main undercarriage wheel well
156 Mainwheel doors
157 Engine firewall
158 Exhaust collector ring
159 Wright R-3350-DA1 Turbo-Compound, 18-cylinder two-row radial engine
160 Propeller hub pitch change mechanism
161 Hamilton Standard three-bladed propeller
162 Carburettor intake duct
163 Engine oil tank
164 Main undercarriage mounting ribs
165 Inner wing integral fuel tank
166 Leading edge construction
167 Hydraulic reservoir
168 Cabin fresh air intake

The first modern airborne early-warning aircraft to fly, with rotating rotodome-type aerial arrays, was this WV-2E of the US Navy first flown in 1956, with the new AN/APS-82 surveillance radar. In 1962 it was redesignated EC-121L, by which time several other rotodome-equipped C-121s were flying. They led to today's Boeing E-3A Sentry.

reached by the piston-engine airliner. The wing box, which had acute dihedral from the roots, was wholly skinned in gigantic machined planks. The body was slightly stretched, and the redesigned nacelles housed the most powerful civil piston engines ever used, driving Hamilton Standard three-blade propellers with synchrophasers to keep their speeds exactly synchronized. TWA, which called the Model 1649 the Jetstream, began services on the North Atlantic on 1 June 1957, but by then the jet era was only weeks away and at last the old Constellation had begun to lose its once powerful appeal. Only 44 of this vastly improved final version were sold, and all were withdrawn in the 1960s while basically older models kept at work, several occasionally trucking odd cargoes around the Caribbean and Dominica.

Far more important in the post-1960 era was the profusion of technically intriguing military versions, packed with unusual devices mainly of an electronic nature, which thundered faithfully all over the globe until 1980 despite concerted efforts made from 1975 to eliminate everything calling for 115/145 gasoline. In the 1960s Super Constellations of the USAF and the US Navy flew more than 600,000 hours, though by this time the basic type ceased to appear in books

on US military aircraft. Total production of all Constellation models was 856 (one XC-69, 233 Constellations, 578 Super Constellations and 44 Starliners).

On 15 April 1969 a US Navy Connie piloted by Lieutenant Commander James Overstreet was attacked by two North Korean MiG-17 fighters over the Sea of Japan and shot down. The loss of EC-121M no. 135749 from electronics squadron VQ-1, and of all 31 American crew members – the only loss in anger of a US military Constellation – highlights the special role of this aircraft type in reconnaissance, intelligence-gathering, and airborne early warning (AEW).

This role was first undertaken when the ubiquitous old 1961 was converted – again! – by Lockheed/Burbank for trials as an AEW platform. Modifications to accommodate radar and other gear gave the Connie a tall, narrow dorsal hump and a large under-fuselage bulge. This configuration was first seen operationally on the US Navy's PO-1W and PO-2W (later designated WV-1 and WV-2) weather-reconnaissance and AEW machines based respectively on the 749 and 1049 airliners.

Later, other duties were added to the AEW role, including electronic eavesdropping and countermeasures. The variety of humps, bumps and bulges protruding from various 'spook' Connies in the C-121 series became, itself, an encyclopedia-length subject. A one-off variant, the WV-2E, later called EC-121L, carried its antenna in a saucer-like disc evocative of today's Boeing E-3A Sentry.

In these Constellations, large crews could journey for up to 30 hours far from the Fleet or from shore, relief crews replacing each other while searching for air or sea threats. Initially, with the purpose of extending the range of ground and ship radars, USAF Constellations were used off American coasts by the Air Defense Command. In Vietnam, under the 'College Eye' programme, USAF Constellations stood off the enemy coast and reported MiG activity to endangered US combat pilots. In South Vietnam, the USAF's EC-121R, camouflaged and devoid of bulges, copied enemy radio transmissions for Intelligence. More than a dozen designations were eventually applied to 'spook' Connies (see Variants list), and today one of the most beautiful of these preserved machines is the US Navy's EC-121K no. 141292, from squadron VAQ-33, on display at the Air and Space Museum in Florence, South Carolina.

Lockheed Constellation variants

Model 049-39-10: pre-war TWA/PanAm aircraft with four 2,200-hp (1641-kW) R-3350-35 after being taken over by USAAF prior to completion; first aircraft (Lockheed no. 1961) completed as **XC-69** in olive drab, civil registration NX67900, later NX25600, later AAF 43-10309; remaining aircraft AAF **C-69-1** (43-10310/10317) and **C-69-5** (42-94549/94561); total 22

C-69C: conversion of 294550 as VIP transport, later **ZC-69C**

XC-69E: conversion of first prototype with 2,000-hp (1492-kW) R-2800 Double Wasp engines

Model 049 Constellation: initial new-build commercial model with 2,200-hp (1641-kW) R-3350-BA1 engines, gross weight 86,000 lb (39010 kg), later 90,000 lb (40824 kg) and later 96,000 lb (43546 kg); nos 2023/88, total 66

R70-1: initial US Navy counterpart of Model 049-46, used by VPB-101, BuAer nos not assigned

Model 649: commercial transport with 2,500-hp (1865-kW) R-3350-BD1 engines, gross weight 98,000 lb (44453 kg); total 14, later brought up to L-749 standard

Model 749: long-range tanks in outer wings; gross weight 105,000 lb (47628 kg); the **Model 749A** had stronger spars and main legs; gross weight 107,000 lb (48535 kg); total 111

C-121A (Model 749A-79-38): 2,500-hp (1865-kW) R-3350-75 engines as USAF passenger transports (48-609/617); at one time designated **PC-121A**, for passenger transport; total 9

VC-121A: VIP conversions, 48-610 as *Columbine II*, 48-613 as *Bataan* and 48-614 as *Columbine I*

VC-121B: special long-range VIP aircraft (48-608); total 1

Model 1049 Super Constellation: stretched version with 2,700-hp (2014-kW) R-3350-CA1 engines, gross weight 120,000 lb (54432 kg); prototype was conversion of no. 1961, redesignated N6201C; square windows retained but tip tanks deferred until the Model 1049G; total 24 (nos 4001/4024)

R7V-1: US Navy **Model 1049B**, first with 3,250-hp (2425-kW) R-3350-91 Turbo-Compound engines; weather radar lengthened nose 3 ft (0.91 m); total 51 (BuAer nos 128434/128444, 131621/131629, 131632/131659, 140311/140313); see **C-121G** and **C-121J**

PO-1W: see WV-1

WV-1: first AEW radar picket version, based on Model 749, height-finder radar above fuselage, plan surveillance radar below; crew 22; BuAer nos 124437/124438, total 2 and ordered as PO-1Ws

WV-2: production AEW model, later named **Warning Star**; based on Model 1049, 3,400-hp (2536-kW) R-3350-34 or -42 Turbo-Compounds, improved radars and data links, crew 26; BuAer nos 126512/126513, 128323/128326, 131387/131392, 135746/135761, 137887/137890, 141289/141333, 143184/143230, 145924/145941, total 142

WV-2E: conversion of BuAer no. 126512 with APS-82 radar using rotating dish 'rotodome'

WV-2Q: conversions (16-plus) as high-power ECM warning, D/F and jamming platforms

WV-3: weather reconnaissance variant, also called Warning Star, same basic airframe as WV-2 but totally different interior and equipment, no tip tanks, crew 8; BuAer nos 137891/137898, plus conversion of 141323, total 9; became WC-121N, but two to USAF as EC-121R

R7V-2: US Navy **Model 1249** high-speed transports to evaluate turboprop propulsion, restressed airframe for high speeds (437 mph/703 km/h); four P&W YT34-12A driving broad paddle-blade propellers; BuAer nos 131630/131631, 131660/131661, total 4

C-121C: standard USAF long-haul passenger transport for MATS derived from Model 1049, weather radar, 3,500-hp (2611-kW) R-3350-34 Turbo-Compounds; 54-151/183, total 33

EC-121C: see RC-121C

JC-121C: two C-121C (54-160, 54-178) and one RC-121C (51-3841) converted as systems (mainly electronics) test aircraft

RC-121C: first USAF AEW radar picket version, based on C-121C airframe with dorsal and ventral radars similar to WV-2; 51-3836/3845, total 10; in 1962 became EC-121C

TC-121C: nine RC-121Cs converted as AEW radar trainers; subsequently became EC-121C

VC-121C: conversions as VIP executive transports total 4 (54-167/168, 54-181/182)

EC-121D: see RC-121D

RC-121D Warning Star: improved long-range AEW&C (airborne early warning and control) version, tip tanks and other changes, equipped second AEW&C Wing (551st), basis for many other versions; 52-3411/3425, 53-533/556, 53-3398/3403, 54-2304/2308, 55-118/139, total 72; most became **EC-121D**

VC-121E: ex-USN R7V-1 (131650) transferred to USAF as 53-7885 as Presidential *Columbine III*

YC-121F: last two R7V-2 transferred to USAF as 53-8157/8158, later re-engined with T34-P-6

C-121G: transferred US R7V-1s to USAF for MATS use, renumbered 54-4048/4049; total 32

TC-121G: conversions as crew trainers; 54-4050/4052 and 4058, total 4

VC-121G: VIP conversion of 54-4051

EC-121H: rebuild of 551st AEW&C Wing EC-121Ds with SAGE data-links, large airborne computer, new navaids and other equipment; total 42

C-121J: transfer of C-121G (54-4079) back to USN as 140313; later became NC-121K

EC-121J: updates of EC-121Ds with extra equipment (classified); 52-3416 and 55-137, total 2

EC-121K: redesignation of WV-2

YEC-121K: conversion of WV-2 128324 for classified 'Ferret' Elint

JC-121K: conversion of EC-121K 143196 for classified Army test programme(s)

NC-121K: conversions (21-plus) for special tests, including C-121J and EC-121K 145925 for Project 'Magnet' mapping Earth's field

EC-121L: redesignation of WV-2E

EC-121M: redesignation of WV-2Q

WC-121N: redesignation of WV-3

EC-121P: conversions (13-plus) of EC-121K with ASW sensors and special overwater navaids; 143184, 143199, 143200 to USAF with numbers as before omitting initial 1

JEC-121P: four of above transfers (189/199/200) later on special USAF test

EC-121Q: conversions (unknown number) of EC-121Ds with augmented and updated AWACS systems

EC-121R: conversions (total 30) for Project 'Igloo White' in Vietnam, serving as airborne data-relay stations (67-21471/21500)

EC-121S: near-total rebuild of five C-121Cs (54-155, 159, 164, 170, 173) as Ec-121Q

EC-121T: classified conversions (25-plus) of EC-121D, H and J as Elint electronic intelligence platforms

Model 1049C: conversions with Turbo-Compounds (3,250-hp/2425-kW R-3350-DA1), strengthened wing, extra fuel; total 49

Model 1049D: cargo version of Model 1049C; total 4

Model 1049E: improved passenger model; total 18

Model 1049G: major upgrade of commercial aircraft with DA3 engines, tip tanks and other improvements; total 104

Model 1049H: corresponding long-range restressed cargo aircraft; total 53

Model 1649 Starliner: ultra-long-range model with new long span wing, slightly stretched body and many other improvements; total 44

Vickers Viscount

Between 1935 and 1965 American dominance of the world market for airliners encountered only one formidable competitor. This was the smooth Viscount, the first aircraft designed for turboprop propulsion.

With most aircraft, and no less so with engines, it takes a touch of genius to get the design right: too clever, and it takes too long to achieve reliability and the costs go through the roof; too crude, and it will be uncompetitive. With the Dart engine Rolls-Royce appeared to have erred on the side of crudity: in 1966 Rolls-Royce chief executive Sir Denning Pearson called the engine 'agricultural machinery', but he also commented that at that time nobody had ever junked a Dart-engined aeroplane. In fact mating four of these engines with the Viscount airframe proved so successful that in 1955 Convair, the immediate rival, tried to compete by offering the airlines a look-alike called the Convair Dart. It was never built, because the customers kept buying Viscounts.

Towards the end of World War 2 the UK tried hard to make up for lost ground by reconvening the Brabazon Committee to make specific proposals on which types of civil transport should be built when peace returned. It was rightly believed the nation had a world lead in gas-turbine engines, and though for the immediate future the industry had to make do with 'interim' airliners converted from bombers, for the longer term it was planned to design 'clean sheet of paper' aircraft which, where appropriate, would have turboprop or turbojet engines.

One of the most important requirements was the Brabazon Type II, intended to produce a major short-haul airliner for

European routes, and clearly with global sales prospects. It was split into Type IIA (piston) and Type IIB (turboprop) concepts. The former category was filled by Arthur Hagg's aerodynamically outstanding Airspeed Ambassador, with two Centaurus engines. BEA bought 20, but for reasons not unconnected with de Havilland's takeover of the Airspeed company this remained the only order. The Type IIB clearly posed a higher technical risk, so the Ministry of Supply ordered prototypes of two rival types, the Armstrong Whitworth A.W.55 Apollo and Vickers-Armstrongs VC2. The latter appeared to be the result of careful studies at Weybridge started in mid-1944 to design a successor to the VC1 Viking, an interim DC-3 type machine derived from the Wellington bomber. First ideas centred on a stretched Viking with tricycle landing gear and stressed-skin wings carrying four 1,000-hp (745.7-kW) turboprops, but by January 1945 double-bubble pressurized drawings began to appear. In April 1946 the Type IIB specification (8/46) was published, calling for 24 seats, a 7,500-lb (3402-kg) payload and 1,000-mile (1609-

Stretching the V.630 into the V.700 did wonders for the Viscount's appearance. Here the first V.700, G-AMAV, is seen early in its career in 1950. It never belonged to BEA, though in 1953 it was named *Endeavour* as a member of the airline's 'Discovery' class, and with race number 23 on the tail took part in the race to Christchurch, New Zealand.

F-BGNK was the first Viscount to be built and the first to be exported, flying as a V.708 on 11 March 1953 and being delivered to Air France on 18 May. It was one of the very few Viscounts to crash fatally; during a crew training flight on 12 December 1956 it dived into the ground near Paris, killing the five Air France crew. The flight-deck windows were common to all early aircraft (though not quite the same as on the V.630 and 663); TCA asked for larger vertical windows with pull-in direct vision, and this became standard. Under the rear fuselage is the cabin air system ram inlet.

Vickers Viscount

Specification

Vickers Viscount V.708

Type: 49 (later 65) seat passenger airliner

Powerplant: four 1,400-shp (1044-kW) Rolls-Royce Dart 504 turboprops (later 700s: 1,600-shp/1193-kW Dart 510)

Performance: cruising speed 311 mph (501 km/h); take-off to 50 ft (15 m) at maximum weight 4,050 ft (1234 m); range with maximum 12,500 lb (5670 kg) payload, 940 miles (1513 km) (later versions up to 2,450 miles/3943 km).

Weights: empty 32,330 lb (14,665 kg); maximum 52,500 lb (23814 kg) (later versions up to 72,500 lb/32886 kg)

Dimensions: span 93 ft 8.5 in (28.56 m); length 81 ft 2 in (24.74 m) (later 700s: 81 ft 10 in, 24.94 m); height 26 ft 9 in (8.05 m); wing area 963 sq ft (89.47 m²)

AIR FRANCE

F-BGNK

Vickers Viscount

Originally the second Viscount 701 to be delivered to British European Airways in February 1953, G-ALWF flew as part of the airline's 'Discovery' class until transfer to Channel Airways. Subsequent operators were British Eagle and Cambrian Airways, the latter's colour scheme being shown here. The aircraft is now on show at the Imperial War Museum, Duxford.

TCA's order in November 1952 was most significant: for the first time a British company realized that an operator outside Britain might be able to improve the product and make it more acceptable in the world market. CF-TGK was no. 3 for TCA, delivered on 4 February 1955, and finally scrapped by Air Canada in July 1970.

km) range. In September Rex Pierson was promoted to be chief engineer, so his place as chief designer (Weybridge) was filled by G. R. Edwards. Sir George Edwards, as he became, was probably the most important leader the British aircraft industry has ever had, and he was to direct the Viscount, Valiant, Vanguard, VC10, TSR.2 and Concorde with the skill and confidence lacking from most other British companies but to be found in abundance in their American rivals. Without him the Viscount would almost certainly never have happened, because most British managements would have reacted differently at several crucial points in the programme.

For a start he decided to design for not 24 but 32 seats. He decided against a double-bubble and went for an almost circular fuselage, but with the cockpit roof added as an extra section built separately and attached on top. The wing was derived from that of the Wellington, via the Viking, with a single main spar but all stressed-skin structure, and with thermal de-icing and double-slotted flaps. The four engines were to be in pencil-slim nacelles, in turn calling for main gears each with two small wheels (which even then would be bulkier than the engines). Unlike de Havilland with the Comet, Vickers took great care to avoid any small-radius corners in the fuselage cut-outs, and both doors and windows were elliptical neutral holes. In later years the giant windows were to be highly popular with passengers, and Fokker adopted them for the F.27 Friendship along with many other Viscount parts including the engines and propellers.

At first the best engine seemed to be the Armstrong Siddeley Mamba, an advanced turboprop with an axial compressor. This was naturally picked for the rival Apollo, because both were Hawker Siddeley companies. When the Ministry placed its order on 9 March 1946 it specified two Mamba-powered VC2s (now the Vickers Type 609 and

named Viceroy, G-AHRF/RG), with Vickers to build a third at its own expense. The third was possibly to have the Rolls-Royce Dart engine, a seemingly more primitive turboprop with two centrifugal compressors derived from the Griffon supercharger and seven can-type combustion chambers around the outside. Edwards talked with Lionel Howorth, the Dart designer, and with Lord Hives, who assured him of Rolls-Royce's commitment to the engine. Because of the reliability of the centrifugal compressor and the fact that at that time the whole turbine experience had been with this type of engine, Edwards decided in March 1947 to pick the Dart. The designation with this engine was changed to V.630, and manufacture began at the secure experimental centre at Foxwarren of the two V.630s plus, to a later schedule, G-AJZW funded by Vickers, the V.640 with four 1,500-hp (1118.6-kW) Napier Naiads. In August 1947 India gained independence and the name Viceroy was changed to Viscount (names that hardly assist marketing, and in 1954 Capital Airlines was to print thousands of very necessary stickers saying 'Pronounced Vi-Count').

Success and failure

G-AHRF was flown by 'Mutt' Summers and 'Jock' Bryce from Wisley on 16 July 1948. The results could hardly have been better. The radical new engines ran like sewing machines, and the aircraft proved beautiful to fly. Edwards was just daring to believe that he might have a world-beater when, on 22 September 1948, BEA ordered its fleet of 20 Ambassadors. To say this was a body-blow is to understate the case; with loss of the prime customer there seemed little point in continuing. The third prototype was cancelled and work on the second slowed down. The existing machine was repainted in Ministry markings as VX211, but continued in low key to fly outstandingly well to gain a restricted certificate

The V.630 prototype appeared in numerous civil and Ministry colour schemes, and is seen here over Poole Harbour in January 1949 in Vickers house livery, with civil registration. A few months later it was VX211, but still in Vickers livery; then it carried a subdued BEA title, and by early 1950 had been repainted in full BEA airline livery.

One of the numerous ministerial nonsenses of the immediate post-war period was Britain's failure to use the world-beating Nene and Tay turbojets. The only British Tay-powered aircraft was the second Viscount, the V.663. Like its predecessor the Nene-Viking, it had four main landing gears, retracting on either side of the jetpipes.

of airworthiness on 19 August 1949. Meanwhile Edwards had been informed of the RDa.3 rating of 1,400 hp (1044 kW) compared with 990 hp (738.2 kW), and he then obtained from Peter Masefield and Bob Morgan of BEA an indication of renewed interest in the Viscount provided it continued to prove reliable and could be stretched to take advantage of the greater power. By this time the 32-passenger specification could be seen to be still too small, and in late 1948 Edwards cleared drawings for the RDa.3-powered V.700 version with a 47-seat fuselage lengthened by 88 in (2.23 m), and with 30 in (762 mm) added to the root of each wing, not only to increase lift but also to give larger propeller/fuselage clearance to reduce noise.

The second airframe had been diverted as a Ministry research aircraft powered by two Rolls-Royce Tay turbojets, each of 6,250-lb (2835-kg) thrust (it was the only British aircraft to use this engine). Serialled VX217, it was put on trials to support the Vickers Valiant bomber, being leased to Boulton Paul Aircraft for work on powered flight controls and then to Louis Newmark and Decca Navigator, overall spending eight years pioneering FBW (fly-by-wire) control systems. Its type number was V.663. As for the V.630, this

Lufthansa began using a number of Vickers Type 814s on its European routes in the late 50s and early 60s.

received clearance on 27 July 1950 for one month of scheduled airline operation, and on 29 July it took off from London Northolt in the hands of Captain H. R. 'Dickie' Rymer on a regular service to Paris Le Bourget. This was the first-ever airline service with any form of turbine power, and it was a revelation. G-AHRF made 35 further Paris trips, followed by eight to Edinburgh. The passenger reaction, and total reliability, confirmed BEA in its decision to buy the stretched version.

The prototype of the latter, the V.700 G-AMAV, was Ministry-funded and greatly speeded by using parts from the cancelled G-AJZW and bringing in other Vickers-Armstrongs factories such as Itchen (Southampton) for the wings and South Marston (Swindon) for the fuselage. Thus G-AMAV was able to fly from Weybridge on 28 August 1950, and it proved every bit as good as had been hoped. Despite the increase in size, and in gross weight from 40,000 to 50,000 lb (18144 to 22680 kg), performance was considerably enhanced and operating economics were much better. The turning

The VP-YNC was a version of the V.748 for CAA (Central African Airways) and the 100th Viscount to be built. It bore the name *Mlanje* and was delivered in 1956. After the Central African Federation was broken up on 1 January 1968 it was transferred to Air Rhodesia. Air Zimbabwe bought the aircraft in 1979.

This V.794 was one of the last short-bodied Viscounts. When it left the factory at Hurn it was numbered 431, and as TC-SES it was delivered to the Turkish airline THY in October 1958. Later it was transferred to the Turkish Air Force, where for a long time the three V.794s were used as troop transporters.

Typical of the smaller airlines that have recognized the value offered by the Viscount is Manx Airlines, an operator of relatively recent origin that leased this particular V.813 aircraft from British Midland Airways; the aircraft has seen over 25 years of operational flying.

point came on 3 August 1950 when at last BEA confirmed an order for 20 (later increased to 26) of the V.701 type with one class seating for 47 or 53 and augmented freight capacity both below and (at the rear) above the floor. The first V.701 (G-ALWE) flew on 20 August 1952. On 11 February 1953 Lady Douglas named it *Discovery*, all subsequent members of the class being named for famous explorers. By this time gross weight had been cleared at 56,000 lb (25402 kg), a full certificate of airworthiness was granted on 17 April 1953, and regular service started on the following day on the route from London Heathrow, via Rome and Athens, to Nicosia.

This was effectively the true start of the turbine age on the world's airlines (the jet Comet suffering a major hiccup), and orders began to come in as never before for a British airliner. First to sign were Air France and Aer Lingus, followed by TAA of Australia (which already used the immediate rival, the Convair-Liner). During 1952 Canada's TCA (now Air Canada) had begun discussions at Weybridge. The airline's list of engineering change orders soon exceeded 100 (one, for an on-board potable water dispenser, appearing in Weybridge documents as 'portable water'). A few years earlier a self-centred British industry might have declined to bother, but Edwards knew that to do the impossible and crack the North American market would demand a much more 'North American' aircraft, in many ways a better aircraft. It had much greater electrical power, two-pilot cockpit, new fuel system, provision for cold-weather operation and a revised interior, the specification being agreed as the V.724, and 15 were ordered in November 1952. This was just the start; TCA came back for V.757s of the V.700D family with 1,600-hp (1193-kW) Dart 510 engines and a gross weight of 60,000 lb (27216 kg), and altogether bought 51 Viscounts. In Washington Capital Airlines staked its whole operation on the British aircraft and took delivery of 60.

In October 1953 a race was flown from London to Christchurch, New Zealand. BEA considered that, though the Viscount was a short-hauler, it could get favourable publicity from entering. G-AMAV, still on Ministry charge, was fitted with a big rectangular fuel tank in the cabin, given the 'Discovery' name *Endeavour* and, under Captain W. Baillie and with chief executive Peter Masefield in the crew, averaged 290 mph (467 km/h) over the 11,795 miles (18982 km), which did nothing to harm either BEA or the Viscount. On the other hand Hughes Tool Company was one of the customers which flocked to Weybridge in 1953, Howard Hughes himself having a personal interest. The specification for the single V.763 was the longest ever drawn up, and a resident team of Hughes men inspected every part and

almost every rivet. Eventually the V.763 had to be shunted to one side, because it was getting in the way of the production line, and three years later it was re-registered YS-09C and sold to TACA of El Salvador, Hughes by this time being interested in Bristol Britannias and Boeing 707s.

The Dart 510 (RDa.6 rating) clearly made possible further increases in capability. Some V.700D aircraft had slipper tanks outboard of the outer engines for increased range, the first such being the fifth V.720 for TAA. More significant was

Vickers Viscount variants

V.630: G-AHRF prototype, 990-hp (738.2-kW) Dart 502/RDa.1, span 88 ft 11 in (27.1 m); length 74 ft 6 in (22.7 m); gross weight 40,400 lb (18325 kg); 32 seats
V.663: VX217, Tay (jet) second prototype
V.700: G-AMAV, 1,400-hp (1044-kW) Dart 505/RDa.3, span 93 ft 8.5 in (28.56 m); length 81 ft 2 in (24.74 m); gross weight 50,000 lb (22680 kg)
V.701: first production series, 1,400-hp (1044-kW) Dart 506/RDa.3, as V.700 but weight 60,000 lb (27216 kg); 13 similar versions
V.700D: aircraft fitted with 145-Imp gal (660-litre) slipper tanks, cleared to 62,000 lb (28123 kg)

V.745: uprated model with 1,600-hp (1193.1-kW) Dart 510/RDa.7 engines, 64,500 lb (29257 kg); 32 similar versions
V.802: stretched model, 85 ft 8 in (26.11 m) long, up to 77 seats, Dart 510/RDa.6, 63,000 lb (28576 kg); 10 similar versions
V.806: as V.802 but Mk 520/RDa.7 engines, 64,500 lb (29257 kg); four similar versions
V.810: as V.806 but 2,100-ehp (1566-kW) Dart 525/RDa.7/1; weight 72,500 lb (32885 kg), up to 77 seats; 19 similar versions

Vickers Viscount 810/840 Series cutaway drawing key

1 Radome
2 Weather radar scanner
3 Radar tracking mechanism
4 Front pressure bulkhead
5 Ranome hinge panel
6 Nose section construction
7 Pressurization relief valve
8 Control system linkage
9 Rudder pedals
10 Pneumatic system air bottle
11 Nosewheel doors
12 Forward retracting twin nosewheels
13 Nosewheel steering jack
14 Pitot head
15 Cockpit floor level
16 Seat mounting rails
17 Conditioned air delivery duct
18 Nosewheel steering control
19 Control column handwheel
20 Instrument panel
21 Weather radar display
22 Instrument panel shroud
23 Windscreen wipers
24 Windscreen panels
25 Overhead systems switch panels
26 Co-pilot's seat
27 Direct vision opening side window panel
28 Pilot's seat
29 Cockpit rear bulkhead
30 Cockpit pressure dome
31 Folding observer's seat
32 Cockpit doorway
33 Windscreen de-icing fluid reservoir
34 Wing and engine inspection floodlight
35 Radio and electronics equipment racks
36 Underfloor autopilot controllers
37 Cockpit section frame construction
38 Folding airstairs
39 Folding handrail
40 Entry lobby
41 Forward entry doorway
42 Starboard side baggage compartment

43 HF aerial mast
44 Hydraulic equipment compartment
45 Cabin front bulkhead
46 Cockpit pressure dome aft fairing
47 Forward passenger compartment
28 Four-abreast passenger seating
49 Forward entry door, open
50 Door latch
51 Door hinge link
52 Forward 'pull-out' emergency exit-window
53 Underfloor cargo hold, 250 cu ft (7.08 m³) capacity
54 Toilet compartments, port and starboard
55 Ventral cargo hold door, starboard side
56 Toilet compartment doors
57 Magazine rack
58 VHF aerial
59 Starboard engine nacelles
60 Engine cowling panels
61 Propeller spinner
62 Rotol four-bladed constant speed propeller
63 Propeller blade root de-icing
64 Starboard wing central fuel cells; total fuel system capacity 1,916 Imp gal (8710 litres)
65 Fuel system piping
66 Outboard fuel cells
67 Overwing fuel filler cap
68 De-icing air outlet louvres
69 Retractable landing taxiing lamp
70 Leading edge hot air de-icing
71 Starboard navigation light
72 Wing tip fairing with hot-air exhaust
73 Static dischargers
74 Starboard aileron
75 Aileron trim tab

76 Starboard double-slotted Fowler-type flap (down position)
77 Flap guide rails
78 Flap operating torque shaft and chain drive
79 D/F loop aerials
80 Fuselage frame and stringer construction
81 Floor beam construction
82 Main cabin passenger seating
83 Control rod runs
84 Front auxiliary spar attachment main frame
85 Main cabin 'pull-out' emergency exit windows
86 Main spar centre-section carry-through
87 Spar boom bolted joints
88 Cabin wall soundproof lining
89 Electrical system static inverters
90 Central flap drive motor
91 Main spar attachment double frame
92 Cabin trim panelling
93 VHF aerial
94 Overhead air conditioning ducting
95 Rear auxiliary spar attachment main frame
96 Cabin window panels
97 Main cabin four-abreast passenger seating, 52-seat layout (alternative 65-seat tourist or 75-seat coach class layouts)
98 Fresh air ducting
99 Individual passenger service units

100 Overhead coat/light luggage racks
101 Cabin rear bulkhead
102 Fin root fillet construction
103 Starboard tailplane
104 HF aerial cable
105 Starboard elevator
106 Elevator trim tab
107 Fin rib construction
108 Leading edge double skin de-icing air duct
109 VOR/ILS aerial
110 Fin tip fairing with hot-air exhaust
111 Rudder tab
112 Rudder construction
113 Tailcone
114 Tail navigation light
115 Spring tab
116 Anti-balance tab
117 Static dischargers

118 Port elevator construction
119 Tailplane rib construction
120 Leading edge de-icing air duct
121 Tailplane attachment main frame
122 Rudder and elevator control linkages
123 Rear pressure bulkhead
124 Wardrobe
125 Lounge compartment
126 Buffet/galley units, port and starboard
127 Rear entry/service door open

128 Cabin attendant's folding seat
129 Rear entry/service doorway, port and starboard
130 Fuselage skin panelling
131 Cabin floor panelling
132 Underfloor air conditioning plant
133 Wing trailing edge root fillet
134 Flap rib construction
135 Flap shroud ribs
136 Port double-slotted Fowler-type flap
137 Flap down position
138 Optional fuel jettison pipe
139 Port aileron rib construction

140 Aileron hinge control
141 Aileron tab
142 Static dischargers
143 Port wing tip fairing with hot-air exhaust
144 Port navigation light
145 Outer wing panel rib construction
146 Retractable landing/taxiing lamp
147 Leading edge de-icing hot air duct
148 Leading edge double skin panelling
149 Outer wing panel fuel tank bays
150 Rear auxiliary spar
151 Main spar
152 Outer wing panel spar joints
153 Petal-type engine cowlings, open position
154 Engine bearer struts
155 Main engine mounting ring frame
156 Engine annular air intake
157 Spinner
158 Intake lip de-icing

159 Oil cooler air intake
160 Forward retracting twin mainwheels
161 Main undercarriage leg strut
162 Rear drag strut
163 Central fuel tank bays
164 Inner wing panel rib construction
165 Main undercarriage hydraulic retraction jack
166 Mainwheel leg breaker joint
167 Engine nacelle mounting rib
168 Wheel bay door operating link
169 Engine fire extinguisher bottle
170 Mainwheel bay
171 Air ducting to conditioning system
172 Inboard fuel cells
173 Water/methanol tank, port and starboard, total capacity 75 Imp gal (340 litres)
174 Leading edge air ducting
175 Engine-driven cabin air compressor (three)
176 Engine accessory equipment gearbox
177 Jet pipe
178 Engine bearer struts
179 Fireproof bulkhead
180 Accessory gearbox drive shaft
181 Engine flame tubes
182 Oil cooler
183 Rolls-Royce Dart RDa.7/1 (Mk 525) turboprop engine
184 Propeller hub pitch change mechanism
185 Rotol or DH four-bladed constant speed propeller

Vickers Viscount

G-AOYV was the prototype for the ultimate V.810 series, and was painted in the markings of the first customer (for the V.812). G-AOYV flew in December 1957 and spent over a year on company research from Wisley, in the course of which it was fitted with massive water spray rigs and a dummy Vanguard fin for de-icing certification trials.

ZS-CDT was no. 346 off the line and the first of seven V.813s for South Africa; SAA added a V.818 bought from Cubana. All had extremely long and successful careers, this particular machine, *Blesbok*, being sold eventually to BMA in 1972 as G-AZLP. All the British Midland fleet saw extensive prior service with other operators.

the decision to stretch the fuselage, in partnership with BEA. At first the V.801 was studied with a massive stretch, but it was then found that, by moving back the rear pressure bulkhead, a 111-in (2.82-m) internal stretch could be achieved with a fuselage only 46 in (1.17 m) longer. On 14 April 1954 BEA ordered 12 (later 24) of these longer V.802 aircraft, still sticking to names of discoverers. As before, many customers followed suit, but Rolls-Royce was by this time ardently developing the trusty Dart and kept offering increased power. In 1954 the 1,700-shp (1267.7-kW) Dart 520 (RDa.7) led to the V.806, with unchanged 320-mph (515-km/h) economical cruising speed but gross weight raised to 64,500 lb (29257 kg). In 1955 the Dart 525 (RDa.7/1) of 1,800-shp (1342.3 kW) led to the considerably revised V.810 series with structure restressed for greater weights and higher indicated airspeeds. The only visible change was a simpler rudder aerodynamic balance, but in fact gross weight was cleared to 72,500 lb (32885 kg) and cruising speed to 360 mph (579 km/h).

Healthy sales and production

The V.810 prototype flew on 23 December 1957, by which time Viscounts were flooding off the assembly lines, the V.800 series all being assembled at a newly established factory at Hurn. The V.700 was by this time in Vickers hands and it was re-engined with RDa.7s to speed Viscount V.810 series certification. At the end of this programme in 1963 it was unceremoniously given to the Fire School at Stansted, which was sad because the original V.630 prototype had been written off at Khartoum in 1952.

The plan in 1956 had been to offer a V.840 series with RDa.8 engines of 2,500 ehp (1864.3 kW), for a cruising speed of 400 mph (644 km/h). When Robert F. Six of Continental signed for 14 V.812s he intended to re-engine them later, and several other customers were interested in the '400-mph

Viscount', but it was never built. This was partly because with Boeing 707s in service 400 mph (644 km/h) was less impressive and partly because the engine-out certification would have required a substantial redesign of the rear fuselage and tail. As it was, the V.810 family kept selling very healthily, until the very last order was received from CAAC of the People's Republic of China (that country's first purchase from a Western source). The 444th and last Viscount was first flown on 2 January 1964, 438 of these being regular aircraft sold to customers. Several were bought new by executive owners (the first being the Canadian Department of Transport in 1954) and air forces (the first being the Indian Air Force, again in 1954). In 1955 United States Steel bought three, specially equipped for luxurious inflight conferences. When ex-airline Viscounts came on to the second-hand market every single example was snapped up by other customers, many of them being scheduled operators but including an increasing proportion of corporate customers.

Four aircraft with long lives in the UK included two ex-Capital V.745s used by the Empire Test Pilots School and two stretched examples (an ex-Ghana V.838 and ex-Austrian V.837) which did sterling work for the Royal Radar (now Royal Signals and Radar) Establishment. Several countries have used Viscounts as flying test-beds for radars and other systems, and in February 1982 a Canadian aircraft began flight testing the new PW100 turboprop (ironically a Dart replacement) with the new engine mounted far ahead of the original nose. In January 1985 at least 139 Viscounts were still active, including 93 with scheduled airline operators, the largest surviving fleet being that of British Air Ferries (14 plus two leased to Jersey). To the passenger the Viscount is still a very pleasant way to travel, in no way inferior to the short-haulers now being built. It will be some time before its distinctive sound disappears from the scene.

9G-AAU came very near the end of the line as no. 446, being delivered to Ghana Airways on 26 November 1961. Note the rectangular doors swinging aft on parallel arms which on the stretched 800-series replaced the original elliptical type to improve freight loading. Subsequently no. 446 was G-BCZR with Field, BMA, Southern International and Dan-Air. Viscount construction numbers included undelivered or unfinished aircraft, no. 446 being in practice no. 431.

The Vickers Viscount was not greatly harmed by the jet age. Because it was so cheap to run there are still many machines like this V.806 in use. British Air Ferries used it for flights to Germany and Holland. (*Photo: Austin J. Brown/APL*)

Boeing B-52 Stratofortress

What is the greatest aircraft of all time? If one accepts a military type, few can rival the monster B-52 long-range bomber, which was designed to drop nuclear bombs from the stratosphere and is in service almost 30 years beyond its planned retirement date.

Today we are no longer amazed to find military aircrew flying aircraft older than they are themselves, but the B-52 (to later generations of its crews the Buff, politely translated as the Big Ugly Fat Fella) is one of the few aircraft that can properly be called a legend in its own time. Before it flew it was regarded as impossible to create, unless it had propellers. Unlike the other great bombers of USAF Strategic Air Command (SAC), its production was divided into eight versions, each significantly more capable than its predecessor. By the late 1950s the general view was that it was impossible to invent an externally carried load that would prove too much for it. By the 1960s it was being flown round the clock

on gruelling 'airborne alerts', while simultaneously forced down into the harsh turbulent air at the lowest safe levels at which so large an aircraft could be flown. By the 1970s sums far exceeding the original purchase price were being spent keeping the tired structures each in one piece and packing them with ever more extensive new avionic systems. Today,

An unidentified 'Big Belly' B-52D, probably of the 43rd BW, parked between missions at Andersen AB, Guam, in 1969. In these harsh trucking missions engines were invariably started at 452,000 lb (205023 kg) gross weight, 2,000 lb (907 kg) beyond the B-52D's safe structural limit. Note the stacked 750-lb (340-kg) bomb triplets on the left.

One of the last B-52Cs in service was 54-2672 (note 0-prefix denoting that the aircraft is over 10 years old) serving with the 7th BW at Carswell AFB, Fort Worth. The tail emblem is that of the 2nd Air Force, which no longer exists; today the 7th BW has been incorporated into the 19th Air Division within the 8th Air Force.

even though they have radar cross-sections bigger than the proverbial 'barn door', the tough old birds face many years of front-line duty, all much more severe than the serene stratospheric cruise for which they were intended.

The US Army Air Force set out its first specification for a turbine-engined (not necessarily jet) bomber to replace the B-36 in April 1945. There was then no prospect of achieving the required range with a jet, and there was no obvious turboprop (Northrop offered competition with its all-wing B-35 proposals powered by its own Hendy Turbodyne XT37 engine of 10,400 hp/7758 kW). The figures were refined in January 1946, and again all the jet projects failed by wide margins to meet the radius of 5,000 miles (8047 km) with a 10,000-lb (4536-kg) bombload. So when Boeing won the Phase I contract in June 1946 it was with the Model 462, which resembled an enlarged B-50 with six Wright XT35 Typhoon turboprops. By 1947 this had developed into a series of Model 464 studies which were even bigger and soon featured swept wings and tail. Inflight-refuelling then enabled size to be reduced, but there was plenty of opposition from the US Navy and even the commander of SAC, and the XB-52 was cancelled in January 1948.

On 24 June 1948 the Russians began their campaign to starve the Allies out of West Berlin, and just 24 hours later the B-52 was resurrected. Boeing received a Phase II award for two prototypes, serialled 49-230 and 49-231, to be ready

in 1951; but nobody liked the prospect of giant gearboxes and propellers, and few people believed they could be readied by 1951. On the other hand Pratt & Whitney, General Electric and Westinghouse were developing new turbojets offering more power with much lower specific fuel consumption. Boeing cut armament to tail guns only, pared the range and improved the aerodynamics, and armed themselves with truckloads of research data. Over 40,000 man-hours had been devoted in early 1948 to a parallel study for a medium bomber with a bombload of 20,000 lb (9072 kg) and with four of the new turbojets each at an assumed rating of 8,500 lb (3856 kg); never built, it would have been broadly in the class of the Model 367-80 (prototype of the Model 707/717 series).

On 21 October 1948 six of Boeing's top engineers, led by Ed Wells, George Schairer and Maynard Pennell, arrived at Wright Field, Ohio, for a last presentation of the final design, the Model 464-350-0 turboprop. To their astonishment Colonel Pete Warden pre-empted their presentation by asking if they could let him have an updated proposal for a jet.

The team went back to their rooms in the Van Cleve Hotel in nearby Dayton and worked nonstop from the next day (Friday) until the morning of the following Monday, when at 8 a.m. they were back in Warden's office. They brought with them a total preliminary design of the B-52 as we know it today, with full performance specifications, weight breakdowns, costings and development schedules, plus a neatly finished desk-top model made in balsa from a nearby hobby shop and carrying USAF markings. To a large extent this staggering accomplishment was made possible by the existence of the medium-bomber study. To create the new jet B-52 the team scaled up the same design to have two engines in each pod instead of one.

A rare portrait of two B-52 prototypes flying together. Externally almost identical, they differed from later models in having tandem-pilot cockpits and no tail armament. The YB-52 (49-231) in the rear was the first to fly, in April 1952. It had flaperons and six spoiler sections above each wing for roll control.

A picture taken in February 1956 by the co-pilot of a B-52B of the 93rd BW, the original operator at Castle AFB, of an RB-52B (52-8715). This was one of the early B-52B/B-52D models with MD-5 rear fire control for two 20-mm cannon. By 1956 the A-3A with four 0.5-in (12.7-mm) guns had supplanted this installation.

The fifth B-52 ever built became *The High and Mighty One*, painted white, as an NB-52A at the AF Flight Test Center. It was the parent ship for the X-15 hypersonic aircraft, but is seen here on 4 October 1973 after release of the Martin Marietta X-24B lifting-body research aircraft.

The first flight

Maximum effort was immediately put behind this Model 464-49 project, and soon afterwards all turboprops were abandoned. By late 1950 the bomber had become the Model 464-67, and it was to this standard that the two prototypes were built. The second (49-231) had to be designated YB-52 because money was so tight that Logistics Command had to help pay for it, and that command is not empowered to fund experimental (X-prefix) aircraft! In the event, though the XB-52 was the first to leave the plant, on the night of 29 November 1951, it was the YB-52 that was the first to fly, on 15 April 1952. The colossal silver ship had already completed thunderous taxi runs, its eight YJ57 engines spewing black smoke and disturbing half Seattle. Now Tex Johnston, in leather wartime jacket, boarded through the small hatch under the whale-like nose and put on his yellow bonedome

Taken on 31 May 1956, this night scene shows a reconnaissance capsule being winched into an RB-52B. The capsule contained provisions for four to six cameras and/or various items of ECM and other electronics, as well as two human operators. The concept of convertible bomber/reconnaissance B-52s was dropped in the same year.

Boeing B-52G Stratofortress cutaway drawing key

1 Nose radome
2 ALT-28 ECM antenna
3 Electronic countermeasurers (ECM) equipment bay
4 Front pressure bulkhead
5 Electronic cooling air intake
6 Bombing radar
7 Low-light television scanner turret (EVS system), infra-red on starboard side
8 Television camera unit
9 ALQ-117 radar warning antenna
10 Underfloor control runs
11 Control column
12 Rudder pedals
13 Windscreen wipers
14 Instrument panel shroud
15 Windscreen panels
16 Cockpit eyebrow windows
17 Cockpit roof escape/ejection hatches
18 Co-pilot's ejection seat
19 Drogue chute container
20 Pilot's ejection seat
21 Flight deck floor level
22 Navigator's instrument console
23 Ventral escape/ejection hatch, port and starboard

B-52G 58-0239 even had eyes painted on its chin blisters at the 1974 Giant Voice bombing contest, as well as its *Loring Moose Gooser* emblem indicative of flight at little more than moose-antler height with the 69th BS, 42nd BW, from Loring AFB, Maine. It has since received OAS updating and may have got MRASM missiles.

24 Radar navigator's downward ejection seat, navigator to starboard
25 Access ladder and hatch to flight deck
26 EWO instructor's folding seat
27 Electronics equipment rack
28 In-flight refuelling receptacle, open
29 Refuelling delivery line
30 Electronic warfare officer's (EWO) ejection seat
31 Rear crew members escape/ejection hatches
32 EWO's instrument panel
33 Gunner's remote control panel
34 Gunner's ejection seat
35 Navigation instructor's folding seat
36 Radio and electronics racks
37 Ventral entry hatch and ladder
38 Lower deck rear pressure bulkhead
39 ECM aerials
40 ECM equipment bay
41 Cooling air ducting
42 Upper deck rear pressure bulkhead
43 Water injection tank, capacity 1,200 US gal (4542 litres)
44 Fuselage upper longeron
45 Astro navigation antenna
46 Tank access hatches
47 Leading edge 'strakelets' fitted to identify cruise missile carriers
48 Forward fuselage fuel tank
49 Air conditioning plant
50 Forward starboard main undercarriage bogie
51 Landing lamp
52 Forward port main undercarriage bogie
53 Torque scissor links
54 Steering jacks

55 Main undercarriage door
56 Main undercarriage leg strut
57 Wing front spar/fuselage/ main undercarriage attachment frame
58 Main undercarriage wheel bay
59 Doppler aerial
60 Central electronic equipment bay
61 Air conditioning intake duct
62 Front spar attachment joint
63 Wing root rib
64 Wing panel bolted attachment joint
65 Centre section fuel tank bay
66 Wing centre section carry-through
67 Starboard wing attachment joint
68 Vortex generators
69 Starboard wing integral fuel tank bays; total fuel system capacity (includes external tanks), 48,030 US gal (181813 litres)
70 Engine ignition control unit
71 Bleed air ducting
72 Starboard engine nacelles
73 Nacelle nylons
74 Fixed external fuel tank, capacity 700 US gal (2650 litres)
75 Tank pylon
76 Fuel venting channels
77 Tip surge tank
78 Starboard navigation light
79 Wing tip fairing
80 Fixed portion of trailing edge
81 Starboard outrigger wheel, stowed position
82 Hydraulic equipment bay
83 Roll control spoiler panels, open

84 Outboard single-slotted, Fowler-type flap, down position
85 Inboard fixed trailing edge segment
86 Chaff dispensers and flare launchers
87 Inboard single slotted flap, down position
88 Flap guide rails
89 Flap screw jacks
90 Flap drive torque shaft
91 Life raft stowage
92 Wing centre section/ longeron ties
93 Central flap drive motor
94 Rear spar attachment joint
95 AGM-69 missile environmental control unit
96 Bomb bay rotary missile launcher

97 AGM-69 SRAM, air to ground missiles
98 Bomb bay rear bulkhead
99 Rear fuselage bag-type fuel tanks
100 Rear fuselage longeron
101 Fuel delivery and transfer piping
102 Fuselage skin panelling
103 Fuselage fuel system surge tank
104 Data link antenna
105 Rear fuselage frame construction
106 Rear equipment bay air conditioning plant
107 Ram air intake

108 Starboard tailplane
109 Vortex generators
110 Starboard elevator
111 Fin spar attachment joint: fin folds to starboard
112 Tailfin rib construction
113 VOR aerial
114 Lightning isolator
115 Fin tip aerial fairing
116 Rudder
117 Rudder tab
118 Hydraulic rudder control jack
119 Rudder aerodynamic balance
120 Rear ECM and fire control electronics pack
121 ECM aerial fairing
122 Brake parachute stowage
123 Parachute and door release mechanism
124 ALQ-117 retractable aerial fairing
125 AN-ASG-15 search radome
126 ALQ-117 and APR-25 ECM radome
127 Four 0.5-in (12.7-mm) machine-guns
128 AN-ASG-15 tracking radome
129 Remote control gun turret
130 Ammunition feed chutes
131 Ammunition tanks, 600 rounds per gun
132 Elevator tab
133 Port elevator
134 ALQ-153 tail warning radar
135 All-moving tailplane construction
136 Tailplane carry-through box section spar
137 Elevator aerodynamic balance
138 Centre section sealing plate

139 Tailplane trimming screw jack
140 Air conditioning ducting
141 Fuel system venting pipes
142 Ventral access hatch
143 Rear fuselage ECM equipment bay
144 ECM aerials
145 Strike camera compartment
146 Rear main undercarriage wheel bay
147 Bomb/wheel bay box section longeron
148 Main undercarriage mounting frame
149 Hydraulic retraction jack
150 Rear main undercarriage bogie units
151 Flap shroud ribs

152 ECM dispensers
153 Fixed portion of trailing edge
154 Port flaps, down position
155 Outboard single slotted flap
156 Port roll control spoiler panels
157 Hydraulic reservoir
158 Outrigger wheel bay
159 Fixed portion of trailing edge
160 Glass-fibre wing tip fairing
161 Port navigation light
162 Outer wing panel integral fuel tank
163 Port outrigger wheel
164 Fixed external fuel tank
165 Fuel tank pylon
166 Outrigger wheel retraction strut
167 Outer wing panel attachment joint
168 Engine pylon mounting rib
169 Pylon rear attachment strut
170 Engine pylon construction
171 Pratt & Whitney J57-P-43WB turbojet engine
172 Engine oil tank, capacity 8.5 US gal (32 litres)
173 Accessory equipment gearbox
174 Generator cooling air duct
175 Oil cooler ram air intakes
176 Engine air intakes
177 Detachable cowling panels
178 Leading edge rib construction
179 Front spar
180 Wing rib construction
181 Rear spar
182 Port wing integral fuel tank bays
183 Inboard pylon mounting rib
184 Leading edge bleed air and engine control runs
185 Weapons bay doors, open (loading) position
186 Bomb doors, open
187 Wing mounted cruise missile pylon
188 Boeing AGM-86B Air Launched Cruise Missiles (ALCM), six per wing pylon, stowed configuration
189 AGM-86B missile in flight configuration
190 Retractable engine air intake
191 Folding wings
192 AGM-69 SRAM, alternative load
193 Missile adaptors
194 Nacelle pylon
195 Port inboard engine nacelles
196 Central engine mounting bulkhead/firewall
197 Bleed air ducting
198 Generator cooling air ducting
199 Fuselage bomb mounting cradle
200 Free-fall 25-megaton nuclear weapons (four)

Boeing B-52
Stratofortress

USAF no. 55-0677 is a B-52D-25-BW, delivered from Wichita in 1958. It is pictured as it looked in 1972 during the gruelling 'Linebacker' missions in the face of intense SAM defences, with the standard load of 42 bombs each weighing 750 lb (340 kg) in the 'Big Belly' bomb bay and 24 weighing 500 lb (227 kg) on the wing pylons. Two years later it had been transferred from Guam's 43rd Strategic wing to the 2nd AF's 7th BW, 20th BS, with the winged '2' on the tail and the name *City of Fort Worth*, plus a map of Texas under the SAC badge on the nose.

Specification

Boeing B-52D-25-BW

Type: six-seat strategic bomber

Powerplant: eight 12,100-lb (5489-kg) thrust Pratt & Whitney J57-P29WA turbojets

Performance: maximum speed at low level about 415 mph (668 km/h); cruising speed at height 555 mph (893 km/h) or Mach 0.84; range 7,370 miles (11861 km); operating height from 500 to 45,000 ft (152 to 13716 m)

Weights: empty typically 189,000 lb (85730 kg); maximum 450,000 lb (204120 kg)

Dimensions: span 185 ft 0 in (56.39 m); length 156 ft 7 in (47.727 m); height 48 ft $3\frac{2}{3}$ in (14.724 m); wing area 4,000 sq ft (371.6 m²)

Armament: maximum 108 conventional bombs or four nuclear free-fall bombs (no SRAM, ALCM or MRASM) plus four 0.5-in (12.7-mm) tail guns helmet in the front cockpit. Behind him at a higher level, a red bonedome denoted the presence of Lieutenant Colonel Guy M. Townsend. It was one of the most successful first flights ever, and instead of being a brief shakedown the YB-52 was put through three hours of intensive testing, clearing more than the first month's planned work on the first flight, before landing at flight-test base at Larson AFB, Moses Lake.

Nobody needs to have the B-52 described, but it is worth noting that the type abounded in novel features. Fuel capacity was greater than in any previous production aircraft at 38,865 US gal (147112 litres), compared with 21,000 US gal (79493 litres) for the B-36, giving a maximum take-off weight of 405,000 lb (183708 kg). On the ground the aircraft rested on four twin-wheel trucks, all of which were steerable and which could be slewed in unison to allow cross-wind landings to be made with the wings level and the aircraft crabbing diagonally on to the runway. Small outrigger wheels near the wingtips were pressed hard on the ground by a maximum fuel load, but at light weights the vast 35°-swept wings were arched upwards leaving these outrigger wheels high in the air. The gigantic fin, only the very trailing edge of which was hinged to form a rudder, could be power-folded to the right to allow the B-52 to enter standard USAF hangars. As not even the enormous power of the variable-incidence tailplane could be used to rotate the bomber on take-off the wing was set at an incidence of 8° for a fly-away with the fuselage horizontal. Thickness was mostly 8 to 10 per cent, but at the root the upper surface rose and was swept sharply forward to give a value of 15 per cent at the side of the body, where each wing was bolted to a bridge truss that was the strongest structural item ever built into any aircraft. Perhaps the most extraordinary of many odd features in the on-board systems was that all accessory power was taken from the engines in the form of high-pressure bleed air, ducted through stainless-steel pipes (under their thermal lagging these glowed cherry-red with the heat) to small high-speed turbines which screamed and hissed in every part of the aircraft driving alternators, hydraulic pumps, cabin-conditioning and everything else.

B-52G-105-BW no. 58-0231 looks rather tired, with numerous local patching and repainting after something like 12,000 hours of hard flying. It still lacks the OAS update and ALQ-153 pulse-doppler tail-warning radar. When cruise missiles are added these aircraft are given distinctive wing-root fairings.

Pre-flight orders

Even before first flight Boeing had a letter of intent for 500 B-52s and a vast nationwide production programme was organized. Many companies contributed major systems and equipment, while the airframe was assigned to Goodyear (centre fuselage, wing centre section, fuel tanks and internal floors and fuel decks), Aeronca (all bomb/wheel/crew doors and movable panels, rudder, elevators, spoilers and ailerons), Fairchild (outer wings, rear fuselage jointly with Temco, top panels, fin and tip-protection gears). Cessna (tailplane) and Rohr (aft fuselage, engine pods, pylon struts and external tanks). Aeronca also built the pressurized reconnaissance capsules, packed with cameras, other sensors and large ECM systems as well as two crew in downward-ejecting seats. The intention was that aircraft should fly with either the capsule or with maximum bombload depending on mission requirements, but in fact no capsules were flown on combat missions.

In May 1951 the final mock-up review accepted a new cockpit with airline style side-by-side seating for the pilots, which offered many advantages. This was to be introduced at the 14th production aircraft, but in fact Boeing got it on the very first B-52A, flown on 5 August 1954. Subsequent versions are listed separately. Production built up rapidly, and in September 1953 Boeing Wichita was named as second-source producer, and eventually Wichita took over the whole programme to leave Seattle to churn out tankers and commercial Model 707s at rates which today seem astronomic.

The B-52B was cleared for combat duty on 29 June 1955 (more than six months earlier than the UK's Vickers Valiant, first of the V-bombers). The first units were both at Castle AFB, California: the 93rd Bomb Wing and the 4017th

138

Combat Crew Training Squadron. In its first year the B-52 had plenty of problems. Turbos exploded to cause fire or wreck sections of fuselage (they were shrouded in flak curtains), main-gear trucks tried to swivel left and right simultaneously or jammed at the maximum 20° slewed position, the pneumatic-system air ducts suffered high-frequency vibration and failed in fatigue to spew 750°F air, and the giant Fowler-type flaps cracked and broke under the intense sonic buffeting caused by repeated take-offs with the engines at full power with water injection. Indeed in February 1956 the 78 aircraft in service were grounded while the danger of exploding air turbos was removed. Much later the turbo system was abandoned (on the B-52F), it having finally been determined that conventional shaft drives resulted in more miles per gallon! The vast navigation/bombing and tail defence schemes were completely re-thought three times, while with the B-52G the entire aircraft was redesigned to have a lighter structure with less drag, six crew all grouped together in a much better pressurized compartment, with remote tail guns, and much greater internal fuel capacity (raised from 35,550 to 46,575 US gal/134571 to 176305 litres) with integral-tank wings. This model also introduced inboard-wing pylons (for the Hound Dog cruise missile), and on the unexpected extra version, the B-62H, these pylons were tailored to pairs of Skybolt missiles (later cancelled and replaced by Hound Dog or SRAM) while the engines were changed for TF33 turbofans giving much greater range and less noise. The 744th and last B-52 was delivered to Minot AFB on 26 October 1962.

Last of the B-52 variants, the B-52H model is powered by visibly larger TF33 turbofans derived from the original J57 turbojet, and offering much greater take-off thrust, without the need for water, with less noise and much reduced specific fuel consumption. The B-52H carried the Hound Dog missile until 1976.

By this time the B-52B had been withdrawn and the SAC bomb wings were feverishly learning low-flying while simultaneously maintaining an airborne alert with live nuclear weapons. Things were not helped by a succession of inflight structural failures, leading to extremely far-reaching and costly rebuild programmes, and to the Palomares incident of 17 January 1966 in which a B-52 and KC-135 collided fatally over a Spanish fishing village plunging four multi-megaton bombs on to land and sea (the search for the fourth bomb was an epic of deep-ocean technology). In January 1968 another B-52 with four H-bombs on board crashed on sea ice near Thule AFB, Greenland, and that was the end of airborne alerts with live thermonuclear weapons.

In its place came a totally different sort of mission: 9 or 10-hour 'trucking' with conventional 'iron' bombs from the slippery, algae-coated switchback runway at Guam to the featureless forests of Vietnam in which Viet Cong were thought to be lurking. The B-52 had been designed to carry nuclear bombs, and the limit for conventional weapons was 27 1,000-lb (454-kg) bombs. For the war in South East Asia Boeing-Wichita was awarded a 1966 contract for increased capability in the conventional role. The B-52F was given inner-wing pylons which, with long beams carrying four tandem triplets of bombs, added 24 bombs of up to 750-lb (340-kg) size (actual mass 825 lb/374 kg). The B-52D was given not only these wing racks but also the so-called Big Belly modification which, while not altering the volume of the internal bomb bays, rebuilt them structurally to house up to 84 bombs of nominal 500-lb (227-kg) size (actual mass 580 lb/263 kg), thus increasing total load from 27,000 lb the (12247 kg) to approximately 70,000 lb (31750 kg).

Today all B-52s have been retired except some of the B-52Ds and all of the B-52G and B-52H series, the newest and in most respects the best of all versions. A few major improvements, such as the totally new all-digital ASQ-48 nav/bomb system, are still being applied to the B-52D, some

One of the first Wichita-built B-52s was B-52D no. 55-0069, seen as it was at the height of the Vietnam war when it was burdened by 400 lb (181 kg) of camouflage and black while operating from Guam with the 60th BS in the 43rd Strategic Wing. The 43rd was the last user of the B-52D, still at Guam.

Another early withdrawal from combat duty was the B-52F, one of which, Wichita-built 57-169, is seen when it was *Thunder Express* with 68 missions recorded with the 320th BW operating from Andersen AB, Guam. In 1986 320th still flew B-52s as part of the 15th AF's 14th Air Division at Mather AFB.

of which serve in the training role on Guam. The B-52G and B-52H, however, have already cost more than four times their extremely low original purchase price (about $6 million for a B-52D or B-52E and $9 million for a B-52G) on various update programmes, and plenty more are to come by mid-1990. Most of the modification funds in the 1960s went on the structure. In the 1970s the main effort was on adding SRAM (AGM-69A attack missile) of which two tandem triplets can be carried on each wing pylon plus another eight

on an internal rotary dispenser, the EVS (Electro-optical Viewing System) whose twin blisters can be seen under the nose, one for infra-red and the other for low-light TV), and quick-start capability to allow aircraft to scramble from air bases under attack by ICBMs or SLBMs. Many new avionic items are being added, and in December 1982 the first SAC unit became operational with the AGM-86B cruise missile, which by 1987 (as AGM-86C) equipped all 173 B-52Gs and possibly 96 of the B-52H version. Each aircraft carries 12 missiles on the wing pylons, and late in the 1980s may be modified internally to house a long eight-round dispenser. A 'strakelet' fairing on each leading edge, visible for treaty reasons to Soviet satellites, shows aircraft thus converted.

The Boeing B-52 was used for tactical bombing in Vietnam. This was a long way from the purpose the plane was originally designed for, but it proved to be extremely effective.

Boeing B-52 variants

XB-52 (Model 464-67): prototype (49-230); 8,700-lb (3946-kg) thrust YJ57-3 engines, crew five, 10,000-lb (4536-kg) bombload, no defensive guns, three spoilers per wing lus small servo-tab ailerons, water in 125-US gal (473-litre) tank under fin

YB-52: prototype (49-231), as XB-52 but six spoilers per wing plus flaperons, later rear turret with gunner and two 20-mm guns

B-52A (Model 464-201-0): three aircraft (52-001/003), side-by-side pilots, 9,000-lb (4082-kg) thrust J57-1W or J57-9W engines, internal fuel reduced to 35,550 US gal (134571 litres) plus 2,000 US gal (7571 litres) externally, operative inflight-refuelling receptacle and cross-wind landing gear

NB-52A: third aircraft rebuilt as parent aircraft of X-15 aircraft

B-52B (Model 464-201-1/3/4): total 50, comprising 23 **B-52B-35** bombers (53-373/376 and 380/398), first 10 initially with J57-1W engines, all later with 12,100-lb (5489-kg) thrust J57-19W or J57-29W engines, full combat equipment; 27 additional (52-004/013, 52-8710/8716, 53-366/372 and 377/379) ordered as **XR-16** reconnaissance aircraft, redesignated **RB-52B** and converted to bomber

NB-52B: aircraft 52-008 rebuilt as parent aircraft of X-15

B-52C (Model 464-201-6): total 35(53-399/408 and 54-2664/2688), cleared from 420,000 lb (190512 kg) up to 450,000 lb (204120 kg) external fuel up from 2,000 to 6,000 US gal (7571 to 22712 litres) in giant underwing

tanks, water moved to 125-US gal (473-litre) tank in each wing root, tail guns four 0.5-in (12.7-mm) with MD-9 fire control

B-52D (Model 464-201-7): total 170 (101 Seattle-built, 55-068/117 and 56-580/630; 69 Wichita-built, 55-049/067, 55-673/680 and 56-657/698), J57-29W engines; basically as B-52C but provision for reconnaissance capsule deleted

B-52E (Model 464-259): total 100 (42 Seattle-built, 56-631/656 and 57-014/029; 58 Wichita-built, 56-699/712 and 57-095/138), ASQ-38 nav/bomb system

B-52F (Model 464-260): total 89 (44 Seattle-built, 57-030/073; 45 Wichita-built, 57-139/183), 13,750-lb (6237-kg) thrust J57-43W, WA or WB engines, water in four tanks in leading edge next to pylon struts

B-52G (Model 464-253): total 193, all built at Wichita (57-6468/6520, 58-158/258 and 59-2564/2602), new integral-tank wing, fuel 46,575 US gal (176305 litres) internally plus 1,400 US gal (5300 litres) externally, weight 488,000 lb (221357 kg), J57-43WB engines, ASG-15 rear defence with gunner relocated in main crew compartment, short fin and complete structural redesign, ailerons eliminated, fully powered elevator/rudder; weapon bay configured for launching two ADM-20 Quail ECM decoy missiles, inner-wing pylons for two AGM-28 Hound Dog missiles; subsequently modifed to carry up to 20 SRAM or ALCM

B-52H (Model 464-261): total 102, all built at Wichita (60-001/062 and 61-001/040), 17,000-lb (7711-kg) thrust P & W TF33-1 or -3 turbofan engines, water eliminated, gross weight 505,000 lb (229068 kg) for take-off and 566,000 lb (256738 kg) after maximum inflight-refuel, ASG-21 rear defence with 20-mm T-171 gun

de Havilland Comet

In May 1952 a de Havilland Comet left London for Johannesburg to open the jet age for the world's airlines. So far ahead of all competition was the Comet at this time that no rival even had any firm idea what to build. Amazingly, this lead was later completely lost, but the Comet was developed out of all recognition and was also used as the basis for today's Nimrod sub-hunter and AWACS-type platform.

At the height of World War 2, in late 1941, the UK took the farsighted step of appointing a special group of experts to study what commercial transport aircraft should be planned for use after final victory. In May 1943 the Second Brabazon Committee had its first meeting, and towards the end of that year issued a series of recommendations, one of which, called Type IV, was for a jet-propelled transport. It is paradoxical that, whereas in the USA several large jet bombers were then being planned, without the slightest thought of a jet airliner, in the wartime UK the reverse was true. A major factor was that in the pre-war era the United States had come to dominate the world airliner market, and it was rightly felt that the only way to compete after the war would be to take bold technological leaps.

The various Brabazon recommendations quickly became associated with particular companies, and Type IV went to de Havilland. This enterprise had both an Aircraft company, with a design team led by R. E. Bishop and R. M. Clarkson, and an Engine company whose top engineers were F. B. Halford and J. S. Moult. In early 1944 both de Havilland teams studied the Type IV, and after many possibilities had been examined they were given authority to go ahead with the D.H.106 in February 1945. Even then the design remained fluid, ranging from a twin-boom Vampire-like machine with three Goblin engines, via a canard to a tailless swept-wing machine scaled up from the D.H.108. British Overseas Airways Corporation (BOAC) found it hard to make up its mind what was wanted, and the D.H.106 hovered between a 14-passenger short-hauler and a nonstop North Atlantic mailplane carrying a few sacks of letters plus two VIP passengers.

Fortunately de Havilland managed to persuade BOAC and the government that a more conventional transport would be more useful; the company also recognized that trans-Atlantic range was unattainable. The design at last went ahead in September 1946, when the Ministry of Supply ordered two prototypes. BOAC had said in 1944 it would need 25, but it had second thoughts and the first production order, in January 1947, was for eight. British South American Airways then ordered six, but this airline was merged into BOAC who cancelled the BSAA order but increased its own purchase to nine. The name Comet was announced in December 1947.

Because of the dramatically advanced nature of the new Comet, parallel research programmes were launched to provide a basis of proven hardware. The new Ghost engine was tested in the outer nacelles of Avro Lancastrian VM703 and in a special high-altitude de Havilland Vampire TG278. The Lockheed Servodyne powered flight controls were exhaustively tested at Farnborough on Lancaster PP755, while control components were flown on a D.H.108 and a Hornet.

RAF Comet C. Mk.2 aircraft served No. 216 Sqn flawlessly from 1956 until April 1967, fully modified with reskinned fuselages, oval windows and many other changes for military operations. XK697, the 32nd Comet and intended to be G-AMXJ, was named *Cygnus* from October 1959. The legend later read Air Support Command.

de Havilland Comet

Specification

D.H.106 Comet 4B

Type: medium-range passenger transport

Powerplant: four Rolls-Royce Avon turbojets, originally 10,500-lb (4763-kg) Mk 542; later Mk 525B

Performance: maximum cruising speed 532 mph (856 km/h); typical field length 7,000 ft (2134 m); range with maximum payload (initial weight) 2,300 miles (3701 km), (final weight) 3,350 miles (5391 km)

Weights; empty 73,816 lb (33483 kg); maximum (initial) 152,500 lb (69174 kg) subsequently 156,000 lb (70762 kg) and finally 162,000 lb (73483 kg)

Dimensions: span 107 ft 10 in (32.87 m); length 118 ft 0 in (35.97 m); height 28 ft 6 in (8.69 m); wing area 2,059 sq ft (191.28 m²)

Accommodation: flight crew of three or four and normal seating for (initially) 101 passengers; (Dan-Air) 119 passengers

One of the best-looking Comet variants, the short-span 4B was derived for British European Airways from the stillborn 4A for the US operator Capital Airlines. Longer than all other versions, it was planned for short-haul European operations, but natural growth in certificated weight endowed it with such range that BEA Airtours and the final operator of the type, Dan-Air, found it an excellent vehicle for long charters and inclusive-tour flights. The aircraft shown was the fifth of BEA's initial batch of six, to which eight more were later added, the only other initial customer being Olympic with four. Interesting features include the bogie main gears with dimpled tyres retracting into bays bulged on the underside, the fatigue-resistant windows and ADF aerials (two black ovals above the forward fuselage), outward-swept jetpipes with Greatrex-type noise-reducing nozzles, and reversers on the outer engines only.

de Havilland Comet

G-ALYP – *Yoke Peter* – was the first production Comet I (roman numerals were used originally) and the third Comet built. She first flew on 9 January 1951 and on 2 May 1952 operated the world's first scheduled jet service. She piled up the hours, cracking insidiously until she burst open near Elba on 10 January 1954.

Even the streamlined nose was tested on an Airspeed Horsa glider, mainly to verify pilot vision in rain. Construction of the prototypes moved rapidly, and the first, unpainted and bearing Class B registration G-5-1, was rolled out at Hatfield on 25 July 1949 and flown by John Cunningham two days later.

A revolution in design

Though the Comet was less radical than it might have been, it nevertheless broke new ground in almost every part of its aerodynamics, structure, propulsion and systems. Basically, it had a low wing of substantial area whose 20° sweep resulted mainly from taper; the tail was unswept. The three widely separated spars passed through the fuselage under the floor, the inboard part of the wing on each side being bulged to house the 5,050-lb (2291-kg) thrust Ghost 50

One of the first air-to-air photographs ever taken of a Comet, G-ALVG is here seen in late 1949 after the addition of BOAC's Speedbird badge and a Union Jack on the fin. Later, G-ALVG had the full BOAC white-top livery then current, though it never served with the airline. It was scrapped after fatigue testing.

A view of the cabin of a British European Airways Comet 4B with its 86 seats, 22 First Class (front) and 64 Economy (rear). Below, the cockpit of a Comet 4B with British Airways. The instrumentation is comparatively simple, like the Mk 1, and there are dual controls for first and second pilot, with places behind for engineer and navigator. Each seat has instruments, duplicates of the other position, engine instruments are centred.

F-BGNX was the first of three Series 1A Comets for Air France (they were preceded by two for another French carrier, UAT), making its first flight on 6 May 1953. The airline opened Paris–Rome–Beirut services on 26 August 1953, but after the Certificate of Airworthiness was withdrawn in April 1954 Air France never again used Comets.

First of two Series 1A aircraft for CPA, CF-CUM had 7,000 gal (31823 litres) of fuel and water-methanol injection for full-load take-offs. After the destruction of her sister in a take-off crash she was passed to BOAC, where she served as G-ANAV. Photographed on 15 August 1952, she was the 13th Comet to be built.

turbojets, with plain oval inlets in the leading edge and long jetpipes projecting just behind the trailing edge. Large plain flaps were fitted, with split flaps under the jetpipes. The leading edge was fixed, with a small fence well outboard, ahead of the inner end of the powered aileron. Narrow perforated airbrakes could be raised ahead of the outer flap sections. Thickness ratio was 11 per cent, and the first Comet had a lower stalling speed and was easier to fly than most contemporary airliners with piston engines!

With a diameter of 10 ft (3.05 m), the circular tube fuselage was pressurized to 8.25 lb/sq in (0.58 kg/cm^2), to give an 8,000-ft (2440-m) interior when flying at 40,000-ft (12190 m). This was double the pressure of any previous airliner, and a further factor was that outside temperatures of minus 70°C had a profound effect on materials throughout the aircraft. Not least of the innovations was the use of Redux metal-to-metal bonding throughout the structure. In effect a glueing process, Redux had never before been used on such a scale or on such highly stressed parts. The de Havilland engineers conducted extensive tests to prove the strength of many critical parts, and also pressure-tested large fuselage sections. One of the latter exploded, the shattered pieces making it hard to pinpoint the source of the original crack, a fact that was later to be very significant. Its main result was to cause the company to switch to underwater pressure testing, where failures did not cause such explosive release of stored energy.

Secrecy worthy of a military project was maintained throughout. This applied especially to the quite simple engine installations, which were backed up by a neat stored-liquid rocket motor, a 5,000-lb (2268-kg) thrust de Havilland Sprite, between the jetpipes on each side to maintain take-off thrust in hot or high conditions. In sharp contrast with previous British aircraft, the Comet was planned to house all the fuel that could be packed in, virtually the whole wing apart from the engine and landing-gear bays forming a giant sealed integral tank with a capacity of 6,050 Imp gal (27503 litres), some three times that of a Lancaster. Another new feature was pressure fuelling, the large hose being attached in the underside of the wing to feed at the rate of one ton per minute. The cabin pressurization boldly took bleed air from the engines, while other bleed air was used to de-ice the wings and tail.

Overall technical risk was very great, and it is greatly to the credit of de Havilland that the company went ahead on the basis of an order for eight aircraft at a fixed price of £250,000 each. It rightly judged there would be many more orders once this revolutionary airliner had entered service. Passenger accommodation was on the basis of pairs of seats on each side of the aisle, and at the initial gross weight of 105,000 lb (47627 kg) it was possible to carry 36 passengers, eight in facing pairs in a 'smoking room' forward and 28 in the main cabin at what today seems the princely seat pitch of 45 in (1.14 m), the rearmost seats being in line with the jet nozzles. The limited underfloor space resulted in the main

G-APYC was the 37th of the 'New Comets' and was originally flown from Chester as SX-DAK of Olympic Airways, the only customer for the short-span 4B version other than BEA. She is depicted in Channel livery (1970–2), and finally found her way (like most surviving Comets) to Dan-Air in April 1972.

SU-ALC was the 39th of the 4/4B/4C series, being delivered as the first of nine 4Cs for Misrair. She is shown after repainting in the livery of UAA, Misrair's successor, with whom she was lost after 10 years of use in an accident near Tripoli on the second day of 1971. (Biggest export buyer was Aerolineas.)

Originally planned for 58 passengers, the Comet 4 was late in life regularly seating 106. G-APDR was the 18th of 19 Series 4 aircraft ordered by BOAC. She is seen here on pre-delivery testing in July 1958. Later she was sold to Mexicana and ended her days somewhat ignominiously – but usefully – in 1972 at the Standard Fire School.

The 45th Comet 4 series was this 4C for Middle East Airlines of the Lebanon. OD-ADR, along with sisters ADQ (no. 46) and ADS (no. 48), was destroyed in the Israeli attack on Beirut Airport on 28 December 1968. Altogether Comet 4, 4B and 4C aircraft flew almost exactly 2,000,000 hours, ending in December 1979.

baggage bay being above the floor, aft of the capacious flight deck laid out for two pilots, an engineer and a navigator.

Inevitably, every overseas trip by the prototype broke records, and it was established that full payload could be carried over a range of 1,750 miles (2816 km) cruising at 490 mph (788 km/h). The top of the fuselage was painted white, BOAC livery applied and civil registration G-ALVG bestowed, the certificate of airworthiness being issued as early as 21 April 1950. In December of that year the ungainly single-wheel main gears were replaced by neat four-wheel bogies (which could not retract in G-ALVG), and these were standard on the production machines. The latter also did not have the take-off rockets, though provision for them was retained.

The first production aircraft flew on 9 January 1951, and an unrestricted passenger-carrying certificate of airworthiness was awarded on 22 January 1952, ready for the start of regular service on 9 May. The initial route was from London to Johannesburg via Rome, Beirut, Khartoum, Entebbe and Livingstone, the end-to-end time being just under 24 hours. Thus, as Concorde was to do 25 years later, the Comet halved the effective size of the world; but in addition it utterly transformed air travel, the traditional thumping and lurching progress through bad weather being replaced by a totally effortless and virtually silent progress far above any turbulence, vibration or any kind of unpleasant environment. The world airline industry was naturally cautious, but could not overlook the fact that passengers who had flown in BOAC's Comet disliked any other kind of air travel.

Thus other customers slowly began to emerge, and de Havilland upgraded the basic aircraft to Comet 1A standard with weight raised to 115,000 lb (52163 kg), with extra fuel, 44 seats and water/methanol injection to maintain hot/high engine thrust. The first sale was to Canadian Pacific Airlines, followed by Air France, UAT and the Royal Canadian Air Force. For the next generation de Havilland switched to the Rolls-Royce Avon engine in the Comet 2, and early Avons flew the Comet 2X prototype on 16 February 1952. BOAC asked for 11 Comet 2s, using almost the same airframe as the Series 1 but with a 3-ft (0.91-m) stretch giving an extra passenger window on each side. After them came British Commonwealth Pacific, Japan Air Lines, LAV and Panair do Brasil, as well as the Comet 1A customers Air France, UAT and CPA. Suddenly de Havilland ran out of available capacity, because every inch of floorspace was already bursting with production on many other types, and Shorts at Belfast were brought in with a duplicate Comet 2 assembly line.

Developments and setbacks

At the 1952 Farnborough air show de Havilland announced the Comet 3. The power of later Avon engines enabled gross weight to jump to 145,000 lb (65772 kg), transforming the 44-seat 1,750-mile (2816-km) Comet 1 into a really capable and efficient airliner that could carry 76 passengers 2,700 miles (4345 km), and at slightly higher speed. With a fuselage stretch of 18 ft 6 in (5.639 m), the Comet 3 also looked a truly modern jetliner, and the Hatfield company was deluged with

enquiries. Sales were quickly made to BOAC, Air India and Pan Am, and plans were drawn up for a third Comet assembly line at the company's Chester factory. The Comet 3 prototype flew on 19 July 1954, by which time six BOAC Comet 2s had been completed, and shown their capability by flying nonstop to Khartoum, 3,064 miles (4930 km) in 6½

de Havilland Comet 4 cutaway drawing key

1 Radome
2 Radar scanner
3 Front pressure bulkhead
4 Windscreen framing
5 Windscreen wipers
6 Instrument panel coaming
7 DME aerial
8 Rudder pedals
9 Cockpit roof construction
10 Co-pilot's seat
11 Control column
12 Pilot's seat
13 Engineer's control panel
14 Emergency escape hatch
15 Radio rack
16 Engineer's work table
17 Engineer's swivelling seat
18 Navigator's seats
19 Navigator's worktable
20 Nosewheel bay construction
21 Nosewheel leg strut
22 Twin nosewheels
23 Nosewheel door
24 Crew entry door
25 Crew's wardrobe
26 Forward galley
27 Galley supplies stowage boxes
28 Radio and electrical equipment bay
29 Forward starboard toilet compartment
30 Forward port toilet compartment
31 Wash basin
32 Air conditioning duct
33 Toilet servicing panel
34 Cabin window panel
35 First class cabin seats
36 Twin ADF loop aerials
37 Air conditioning grilles
38 Floor beams
39 Forward freight and luggage hold
40 Freight hold door
41 Control cable runs
42 Fuselage keel construction
43 Overhead hat rack
44 Cabin dividing bulkhead
45 Air distribution duct
46 Emergency escape window
47 Air conditioning plant
48 Hydraulics bay

49 Starboard wing integral fuel tanks
50 Flow spoilers
51 External fuel tank
52 Tank bumper
53 Fixed slot
54 Outer wing fuel tanks
55 Navigation light
56 Wing tip fuel vent
57 Static dischargers
58 Starboard aileron
59 Aileron tab
60 Flap outer section
61 Airbrake (upper and lower surfaces)
62 Fuel dump pipes
63 Fuel vent
64 Flap inboard section
65 Inboard airbrake (upper surface only)
66 Fuselage frame and stringer construction
67 Wing centre section fuel cells
68 Emergency escape hatch
69 Aileron servo controls
70 Main fuselage frame
71 Aft tourist class cabin
72 Rear freight hold/luggage compartment
73 Floor beam construction
74 HF aerial cable (port and starboard)
75 Overhead hat rack
76 Tourist class cabin seats
77 Aft galley
78 Starboard service door
79 Aft starboard toilet compartment
80 Aft radio rack
81 Rear pressure bulkhead
82 Anti collision light
83 Dorsal fin fairing

84 Starboard tailplane
85 ILS aerial
86 Starboard elevator
87 Leading edge de-icing ducts
88 Fin construction
89 HF blade aerial
90 Rudder balance weight
91 Rudder
92 Elevator hinge controls
93 Elevator tab
94 Port elevator
95 Tailplane construction
96 ILS aerial
97 Leading edge de-icing
98 Tailplane attachment
99 Fuselage fin frame
100 Tail bumper/fuselage vent
101 Rudder and elevator control rods
102 Access hatch to control bay
103 De-icing air supply duct
104 Rear freight hold

hours. But other things had happened by this time that crippled the programme.

The first accident came on 26 October 1952 when G-ALYZ failed to become airborne at Rome and was damaged beyond repair, though without injury to the 42 passengers and crew. On 3 March 1953 exactly the same thing happened to CF-CUN of CPA making a maximum-weight take-off in hot air at Karachi, and on this occasion all on board were killed. The cause was hauling back on the yoke too early, causing the aircraft to proceed down the runway with the wing stalled, the high drag preventing acceleration and the inlet angle reducing thrust. The answer was to droop the leading edge and refrain from hauling the aircraft off until a proper rotation speed had been reached.

More serious was the inflight destruction of G-ALYV while climbing out of Calcutta on the first anniversary of BOAC services on 2 May 1953. Tragically there was plenty of monsoon turbulence, and no enquiry was made to see whether or not the structural break-up might have been due to a weakness in the aircraft. But when the famed G-ALYP,

de Havilland Comet variants

D.H.106 Comet: two prototypes (G-ALVG and G-ALZK) with Ghost 50 engines and large single mainwheels; provision for Sprite rockets
Comet 1: nine production aircraft for BOAC with bogie main gears, Ghost 50-1 engines and no rockets (G-ALYP/S and G-ALYU/Z)
Comet 1A: 10 aircraft with more fuel (6,906 Imp gal/31395 litres) and water/methanol injection, for CPA, AF, UTA and RCAF
Comet 1XB: two RCAF (later CAF) Series 1As (nos 5301/5302) after structural rework in 1957
Comet 2X: one aircraft (G-ALYT), test-bed with Avon 501 engines
Comet 2: planned production civil transport with slightly longer fuselage (96 ft/29.26 m instead of 93 ft/28.35 m) and Avon 503 engines; 36 intended for BOAC and seven other operators; none delivered
Comet 2E: two ex-Comet 2s (G-AMXD and G-AMXK) used by BOAC for route-proving with modified airframes and Avon 524s in the outer positions; G-AMXD later rebuilt as radar and navaid laboratory for use by RAE as XN453
Comet 2(RAF): three aircraft (G-AMXA, G-AMXC and G-AMXE) transferred to RAF as XK655, 659 and 663; later designated **Comet E.Mk 2** for use as Elint platforms

Comet C.Mk 2: 10 aircraft begun as BOAC Series 2 but rebuilt for RAF; XK669 *Taurus*, XK670 *Corvus*, XK671 *Aquila*, XK695 *Perseus*, XK696 *Orion*, XK697 *Cygnus*, XK698 *Pegasus*, XK699 *Sagittarius*, SK715 *Columba* and XK716 *Cepheus*; XK669 and XK670 were initially **Comet T.Mk 2** trainers
Comet 3: one prototype (G-ANLO) with stretched fuselage and Avon 523 engines; later Avon 523, then (1958) rebuilt as Series 3B
Comet 3B: rebuild of G-ANLO as prototype of Series 4B with clipped wing, Avon 525 and other changes, finally rebuilt as blind-landing and avionics laboratory for RAE/BLEU with serial XP915
Comet 4: production fleet for BOAC, total 19 (G-APDA/DT) with revised airframe, Avon 524 engines and increased fuel
Comet 4A: planned short-haul version for Capital, not delivered
Comet 4B: short-haul version for BEA (14, G-APMA/MG, G-ARCO/CP, G-ARGM, G-ARJK/JN) and Olympic (SX-DAK/DAL/DAN/DAO) with Avon 525B engines and clipped wing
Comet 4C: final production model with long fuselage and large wing, total 30; last two completed as XV147 Nimrod with Avons and XV148 Nimrod with Speys, XV148 finally being avionics test-bed at Pershore/Bedford

105 Tailplane servo controls
106 Mail locker
107 Aft port toilet compartment
108 Passenger entry door
109 Door frame construction
110 Steward's seat
111 Tourist class passenger seating
112 Wing fillet construction

113 Life raft stowage
114 Inboard tailpipe duct
115 Exhaust silencer nozzles
116 Outboard tailpipe
117 Thrust reverser (outboard only)
118 Inboard flap section
119 Fuel vent
120 Fuel dump pipes
121 Flap jack
122 Flap connecting links
123 Port airbrake (upper and lower surfaces)
124 Outboard flap section
125 Flap construction

126 Aileron tab
127 Port aileron
128 Aileron hinge controls
129 Aileron construction
130 Static dischargers
131 Wing tip fuel vent
132 Port navigation light
133 Outer wing construction
134 Outboard fuel tank bays
135 Fuel tank access panels
136 Wing stringer construction
137 External fuel tank
138 Tank bumper
139 Fixed slot
140 Wing rib construction

141 Leading edge de-icing ducts
142 Four wheel bogie unit
143 Wing skin joint strap
144 Undercarriage well
145 Main undercarriage leg mechanism
146 Wing integral fuel tank
147 Rolls-Royce Avon R.A.29 engine
148 Inboard engine bay (engine omitted)
149 Engine mounting frame
150 Intake duct construction
151 Landing lamp
152 Engine intakes
153 Ram air intake
154 Heat exchangers
155 Taxi lamp

de Havilland Comet

Not included in the two million hours flown by Comet 4 variants are the RAF and Ministry versions. These are three of the latter, XV814, ex-BOAC G-APDF, has a dorsal fin to balance the equipment gondola; XN453 was a Comet 2E G-AMXD used on navaid research; XP915 was the Mk 3 G-ANLO, used on blind landing research.

which had flown the first scheduled service, disappeared on 10 January 1954 outward bound from Rome, with no radio transmission from the crew, the Comet 1 was grounded and all available aircraft were subject to a detailed examination. Nobody knew what flaw to look for, but a month later a Royal Navy salvage team found the wreckage near Elba and began the laborious process of recovering every fragment. There were many theories as to what had happened, and after various small modifications the Comet 1s resumed services, but on 8 April G-ALYY disappeared while climbing out of Rome in the opposite direction. This time the Comets stayed grounded, causing great difficulties to BOAC, Air France, UAT and the RCAF.

There followed the biggest technical investigation up to that time, culminating in the certain knowledge that G-ALYP's fuselage had ripped open from a fatigue crack started at the corner of one of the rectangular cut-outs for the ADF aerials in the top skin. Another fuselage, that of G-ALYU, was tested in a giant water tank and after 1,830 simulated flights also ripped open, from the corner of a passenger window. Why de Havilland should have used straight-sided cut-outs in the most highly pressurized fuselage then attempted remained a mystery. For many months the whole Comet project hung in the balance. All export orders were terminated, and all Comet 1As were returned, except for those of the RCAF which without fuss were suitably modified with stronger skins and oval cut-outs and served with No. 412 Squadron until late 1964. The other Comet 1s and Comet 1As were used up in test programmes or simply scrapped. The Comet 2s were rebuilt with oval cut-outs in thicker skins and delivered from June 1956 to RAF Transport Command, whose 216 Sqn achieved a perfect record in intensive operation until April 1967. The assembly lines at Belfast and Chester were abandoned.

Two Comet 2s were passed to Rolls-Royce for use in developing the more powerful Avons being used in France's Sud Caravelle, and for BOAC route-proving, while three others with the original fuselage and with pressurization removed served as electronic-warfare 'ferret' platforms with RAF No. 51 Squadron at Wyton. But the big question was whether de Havilland could ever succeed in selling a completely redesigned derivative of the Comet 3, or whether the image was so damaged that the Comet had become unsaleable to the airlines and to the public. The answer came in February 1955 when BOAC announced it would buy 19 Comet 4s, similar to the Series 3 (which from the start had oval windows) but with even greater fuel capacity and range, with a weight up to 156,000 lb (70762 kg), which later grew to 162,000 lb (73483 kg). This at last resulted in a capable mainliner, but it was clear the new model would emerge into a world dominated by the Boeing 707 and Douglas DC-8. Thus, for narrow competitive reasons, the Comet 4's service life began on the North Atlantic on 4 October 1958, beating Pan Am's Model 707s into service by 22 days, though the type had never been intended for this route. BOAC's own Model 707-420s replaced the Comet on the Atlantic after little over a year.

The BOAC fleet of 19 Comet 4s demonstrated that at last de Havilland had created a safe airliner, and none were sold until 1965, and even then there were plenty of customers for the second-hand airliners. The first export order, in 1956, was for four Series 4 and 10 of a new clipped-wing long-body short-haul model, the Series 4A, for Capital Airlines of Washington DC. The Series 4A was specially strengthened for high speed at low levels, and it was a major blow when Capital was taken over by mighty United, which cancelled the order. But by this time BEA had become interested, and (to the disgust of the French, who said the Caravelle did the same job on two of the identical engines instead of four) in April 1958 the British airline ordered six Comet 4Bs, later increased to 14. Olympic ordered four. This version had clipped wings and even better payload, and without effort could carry over 100 passengers for 3,350 miles (5390 km), which a Caravelle certainly could not do. They put up a fine record, and de Havilland ended the programme by merging the long body with the large pinion-tanked wing to produce the Comet 4C.

The Comet 4C was the most successful model of all, being bought initially by Mexicana, Misrair (Egyptair), Aerolineas Argentinas, MEA, Sudan and Kuwait. Altogether 30 of this series were made, 23 of them at Chester, bringing total production to 113, the final examples being made speculatively and finally going to King Ibn Saud of Saudi Arabia, five for No. 216 Squadron RAF, one for the A&AEE at Boscombe Down and the last two being passed to Hawker Siddeley Manchester for use as starting points for the first Nimrods.

Some ex-BOAC Comet 4s were snapped up by the British Ministry of Aviation for research and trials purposes, notable examples being G-APDF which became the much-modified XV814, and G-APDS which grew a Nimrod AEW radome. Most, however, went to other airlines, all over the world. Malaysia Singapore purchased seven, but by far the most important operator after 1966 was the UK's Dan-Air. Having no doubts of the reliability and practicability of the now ageing Comet, the British independent purchased no fewer than 47 of various (Series 4, 4B and 4C) types, though never more than one-third were in use at any one time. Dan-Air really showed what Comets could do, even after the 1973 fuel crises trebled the price of kerosene, and it put 106 seats in its Series 4s and 119 into the Series 4Bs and 4Cs. Its scheduled and inclusive-tour Comet services finally ceased on 3 November 1980.

XR399 was built as a Comet C.Mk 4 for the RAF, almost at the end of the Chester line and first flown in March 1962. Usually fitted with 94 aft-facing seats, XR399 was the last of the five C.Mk 4s (basically 4Cs) which operated without any problems with No. 216 Sqn from RAF Lyneham. In 1975, with commendably few hours, she was sold to Dan-Air, being re-registered as G-BDIX.

Boeing 707

In 1954 Boeing risked more than the company's net worth to build the first Boeing 707. It seemed a desperate gamble, and possible sales were counted on the fingers. Nobody guessed that the same airframe would still be in production in 1983.

Though the British de Havilland Comet was the pioneer jetliner, it paid the penalty of being first. It remained an attractive exception to the mainstream of civil air transport, and its main effect was to show the enormous passenger appeal of a vehicle that got there in half the time after a trip that, in comparison with the noisy, vibrating piston-engined machines, was like being wafted by an angel. Could this rather small and supposedly uneconomic machine threaten the almost total grip of US industry on the world transport-aircraft market? The answer was clearly to meet the competition with an American jet, but how could it be financed? The only way seemed to be with federal aid, but after arguing the matter throughout 1949 the US Congress eventually in 1950 threw out a bill to fund a US jet prototype.

Douglas and Lockheed studied the problem intently and published a few brochures, but only Boeing (very much an also-ran in the civil transport aircraft business) had actually built large modern jets. By the autumn of 1950 the Seattle-based company could see that to meet its global range needs, the US Air Force would have to use inflight-refuelling not only with its Boeing B-47 bombers but also with the giant new Boeing B-52. Boeing was building the tankers as well, in the form of KC-97s; but these were piston-engined, and to hook up with them the bombers had to slow down and lose almost half their altitude. Surely, reasoned Boeing, the answer was a jet tanker?

Boeing began by proposing a swept wing, jet-propelled KC-97 in March 1951. After much argument the idea was rejected by the USAF on 17 August 1951. Yet Boeing were convinced both the airlines and the US Air Force would eventually buy jet transports, and that the tanker and the civil liner could be basically the same design. But in the absence of airline orders, government prototype funds or even US Air Force interest, Boeing had to do it the hard way. It had to tighten its belt and produce a prototype with its own money. After the

Seen here at Mauritius, this Boeing 707-465 typifies hundreds of the type that will carry on flying with third-world operators well into the 1990s. By that time many may have logged 100,000 hours, setting new records for longevity, despite the unmatched light weight of the original airframe.

Boeing 707

One of the most gaily painted civil airliners flying, this aircraft was built as a 707-321B of Pan American, and subsequently flown to Israel, like many other 707s. There it was overhauled and equipped for all-cargo operation and supplied by the Israeli Atasco organization to Ecuatoriana, the national airline of Ecuador, whose Boeings are all provided with Israeli engineering, technical and commercial support. Scheduled and charter cargo services are flown from Quito and Guayaquil to major centres in the Americas, and on rare occasions across the Atlantic. Like most 707s today it has no underfin but the tall vertical tail. It is shown as it would appear when on routine maintenance, with main landing-gear doors open. Note vortex generators on wing and tailplane.

Specification

Boeing Model 707-321B converted to Dash-320C (cargo)
Type: long-range narrow-body transport
Powerplant: four 18,000-lb (8164-kg) thrust Pratt & Whitney JT3D-3B turbofans
Performance: maximum speed 627 mph (1010 km/h); normal cruising speed 550 mph (886 km/h); sea level take-off to 35 ft (10.7 m) 10,620 ft (3240 m); range with maximum fuel 7,510 miles (12086 km), with maximum cargo 3,925 miles (6317 km)
Weights: empty 133,874 lb (60725 kg); maximum cargo 96,126 lb (43603 kg); maximum take-off 332,000 lb (150590 kg)
Dimensions: span 145 ft 9 in (44.42 m); length 152 ft 11 in (46.61 m); height 42 ft 5 in (12.93 m); wing area 3,010 sq ft (279.64 m²)

HC-BGP

Cathay Pacific's colourful livery adorns Boeing airframe no. 18888, delivered in May 1965 as a 707-351C to Northwest Orient and sold in August 1974 to the Hong Kong carrier, with registration VR-HHE.

Boeing Model 707 variants

Model 367-80: company prototype; first flown 15 July 1954 and subsequently used in numerous research programmes

Model 707-102: four 13,500-lb (6124-kg) JT3C-6 engines; initial production version, with fuselage increased in width and length, gross weight raised to 225,000 lb (102060 kg) and finally 257,000 lb (116575 kg)

Model 707-120B: four 17,000-lb (7711-kg) JT3D-1 engines, aerodynamic improvements for Mach 0.91 cruise

Model 707-138: short-body model for Qantas, 10 ft (3,048 m) shorter

Model 707-220: as model 707-120 but four 15,800-lb (7167-kg) JT4A-3 engines

Model 707-320: first intercontinental version; all-round increase in size; four JT4A engines (various ratings); gross weight 312,000 lb (141520 kg)

Model 707-320B: aerodynamic improvements, four 18,000-lb (8165-kg) JT3D-3 engines; includes **VC-137C**; optional gross weight 333,600 lb (151321 kg)

Model 707-320C: as Model 707-320B but equipped for passengers (up to 202) or cargo

Model 707-420: as Model 707-320 (not Model 707-320B) but with 17,500 lb (7945-kg) or 18,000 lb (8165-kg) Rolls-Royce Conway 508 or 508A turbofans

Model 720: derivative of Model 707 series with lightweight structure and shorter fuselage tailored to short/medium-range operations

Model 720B: turbofan-engined version of Model 720

VC-137A: USAF version of Model 707-120 for VIP transport

VC-137B: designation of VC-137A after re-engining with JT3D; gross weight 258,000 lb (117025 kg)

VC-137C: Presidential (often 'Air Force One') aircraft, as Model 707-320B with various special equipment; gross weight 322,000 lb (146055 kg)

E-3A Sentry: AWACS platform; 21,000 lb (9525-kg) TF33-100/100A engines; gross weight 325,000 lb (147400 kg)

---

most searching evaluation, the company's board met on 22 April 1952 (exactly one week after the successful first flight of the B-52) and took the big decision. It would cost not less than $15 million.

Essential ingredient

One essential ingredient was the Pratt & Whitney JT3 engine, the lightweight commercial verson of the fuel-efficient J57 used in the B-52. But, whereas the giant bomber used eight of the 10,000-lb (4536-kg) thrust engines, the transport would need just four, hung in single pods below and ahead of the 35°-swept wing. The fuselage would not be that of the C-97 but larger, and with a more streamlined nose tipped by radar. (Even creating the radome would mean solving a completely new set of technical problems.) Gross weight worked out to 190,000 lb (86184 kg), and though the military model would have an interior configured for cargo and fuel, the commercial passenger aircraft could seat 130. Because it could fly at 600 mph (966 km/h), the jetliner promised to do three times the work of either the military KC-97 or a commercial type such as the Douglas DC-7 or Lockheed Super Constellation. But the airlines and US Air Force never showed more than polite interest as the prototype took shape at the Renton (Seattle) plant.

In fact the correct Boeing model number for the prototype was 367-80, and the company-owned prototype was to become popularly known as the Dash-80, but that was because the years of study had been numbered as suffixes to the same Model 367 number of the original piston-engined C-97. Numbers in the 500 series were reserved for gas turbine engines and in the 600 series for Boeing missiles, and aircraft numbers began again at 700. When the Model 367-80 finally became a flyable aircraft it was given the new designation Model 707. Subsequently Boeing deliberately capitalized on this memorable sequence by making their subsequent jet transports the Models 717, 727, 737, 747, 757 and 767.

Boeing E-3A Sentry cutaway drawing key

1 Weather radar scanner
2 Glide-slope aerial
3 Forward pressure bulkhead
4 Pilot's station
5 Central control console
6 Co-pilot's station
7 Flight engineer's station
8 Observer's supernumerary
9 Navigator's table
10 Navigator's overhead panel
11 Flight deck door
12 In-flight refuelling receptacle
13 Communication consoles (one unmanned TAC)
14 Forward entry door
15 Nosewheel hydraulic actuator
16 Nosewheel box
17 Twin nosewheels
18 Nosewheel doors
19 Forward cargo hold equipment bay
20 Flight essential avionics
21 Communications
22 Data processor functional group
23 Computer operator console
24 Bailout jettison mechanism
25 Bailout chute
26 DC power
27 Power distribution
28 Multi-purpose consoles (nine-off)
29 VHF aerial
30 Engine intakes
31 Secondary inlet doors
32 Turbocompressor intakes
33 Turbocompressor outlets
34 Nacelle pylons
35 Leading-edge wing flap
36 Main tank No. 3 (4,069 US gal/15400 litres each wing)
37 Fuel system dry bay
38 Main tank No. 4 (2,323 US gal/8791 litres each wing)
39 Reserve tank (439 US gal/1660 litres each wing)
40 Vent surge tank
41 HF antenna
42 Starboard outboard aileron
43 Tab
44 Starboard outboard spoiler (extended)

58-6970 was one of the early civil 707-153 transports purchased by the US Air Force and remodelled with a 22-seat VIP interior and extremely comprehensive communications for use as an airborne command post (designation VC-137A). It is shown in its 1959 configuration; later it was re-engined as a VC-137B.

This 707 is a Dash-338C used for many years as a mainline vehicle of Qantas and with over 35,000 hours sold in 1979 to the Royal Australian Air Force as its first long-range jet. The RAAF has two such aircraft, both on the strength of No. 37 Sqn, based at Richmond, near Sydney, NSW. The RAAF has no tanker capability.

MILITARY AIR TRANSPORT SERVICE

U.S. AIR FORCE

MATS
86970

ROYAL AUSTRALIAN AIR FORCE

45 Starboard outboard flap
46 Flap tracks
47 Aileron/spoiler linkage
48 Starboard inboard aileron
49 Control tab
50 Starboard inboard flap
51 Starboard inboard spoiler (extended)
52 Emergency overwing escape
53 Duty officer station (TAC)
54 Fuselage frame/production break
55 Front spar pick-up point
56 Landing lights
57 Front spar

58 Fuel tank end rib
59 Inboard wing stringers
60 Centre-section fuel tank (10,193 US gal/38582 litres)
61 Wing top skin
62 Floor support members
63 Rear spar pick-up point
64 Mainwheel bay
65 Keel beam
66 Radar receiver and signal processor

67 Radar maintenance station
68 Radar transmitter equipment
69 Rear cargo hold equipment bay
70 Access door (starboard)
71 Communications
72 Navigation and identification
73 Radome support struts
74 Radome
75 Westinghouse surveillance radar antenna array

76 Forged rotodome bearing
77 Turntable rotary joint
78 Antenna ancillary equipment
79 Centre section
80 TADIL C/IFF antenna
81 IFF window
82 Crew rest area
83 Bunks
84 Fin fillet
85 Starboard tailplane
86 VOR antenna
87 Removable fin leading edge
88 Fin construction
89 HF probe antenna
90 HF receiver No. 2
91 LORAN
92 Rudder

93 Rudder control tab
94 Rudder anti-balance tab
95 Internal balance panel
96 Rudder trim tab
97 Tail cone
98 Tailplane actuator tab
99 Elevator control tab
100 Port elevator
101 Port tailplane
102 Internal balance panel
103 Tailplane centre-section
104 Fin/fuselage joints
105 Tailplane jack screw
106 Rear pressure bulkhead
107 Toilet
108 Spare survival equipment
109 Rear entry door
110 Galley
111 Bunks
112 Screen
113 Bailout chute

114 Underfloor APU
115 Fuselage frame/strut support members
116 Radar transmitter equipment
117 Wingroot/fuselage fairing
118 Fillet flap
119 Port inboard flap
120 Port inboard spoilers
121 Landing gear trunnion
122 Side strut
123 Torsion links
124 Four-wheel main landing gear
125 Vortex generators
126 Nacelle pylon
127 Turbocompressor
128 Pratt & Whitney TF33-P-100A turbofan
129 Fan thrust reverser doors
130 Engine fuel pump
131 Starter
132 Primary thrust reverser cascade vanes

133 Leading-edge wing flap
134 Rear spar
135 Control tab
136 Port inboard aileron
137 Integral wing fuel (see items 36, 38, 39)
138 Port outboard spoilers
139 Port outboard flap
140 Pylon/wing joint
141 Tab
142 Port outboard aileron
143 Wing skin
144 Exhaust
145 Strut attachment
146 Nacelle construction
147 Access doors (port and starboard)
148 Nacelle nose cowl

Boeing 707

This Boeing 707-358C was one of the last of the type to be built (though beaten in this respect by the IIAF tanker shown on p. 157). With Boeing hull number 20897 and registration ST-AFA, it was delivered new on 17 June 1974 to Sudan Airways, with whom it has since operated on the trunk route to London with the individual name *Blue Nile*. Its partner, ST-AFB, is *White Nile*.

Question marks

The designation Model 717 was assigned to the proposed USAF tanker, but by 1954 the Korean War had ended, money was tight, and strong forces favoured a cheaper turboprop tanker, or even modified Convair B-36s or B-47s. There was still nothing certain about the programme when the Dash-80, painted in a rich company livery of chocolate-brown and chrome yellow, rolled out in a ceremony on 15 May 1954. The question marks loomed larger when, during taxi tests six days later, the left main gear smashed its way up through the wing and left the vital prototype lying crippled on its left outer engine pod. It was not until 15 July 1954 that Tex Johnston and Dix Loesch were able to fly the aircraft that was to keep the United States the world leader in civil transports.

By this time the USAF had told Boeing it wanted a new-build jet tanker, a great relief after the company had already spent not only $15 million on the prototype but half as much again on design and tooling for production machines. In October 1954 the first tanker order came through, for 29 aircraft, launching a gigantic programme of KC-135 and C-135 versions. This underpinned the commercial Model 707, but in 1954 Boeing did not enjoy the same clout with the airlines as mighty Douglas, and the announcement of the DC-8 on 5 June 1955 meant Boeing was going to have to fight every inch of the way. Moreover, on a run of 50 aircraft Boeing could see no way of pricing the 707 below $5.5 million, far above what the airlines would pay.

Nor was this all. To meet the competition of the DC-8, Boeing decided to do one of the costliest modifications possible: change the body cross section. It remained a figure-8 with smoothly faired sides but the upper lobe was increased in width by 4 in (10.16 cm) to 140 in (3.556 m), beating Douglas by 2 in (5.08 cm) and enabling a triple seat unit to be installed on each side of the aisle, for up to 150 passengers. A new form of fatigue-proof window structure was devised, with two small windows per seat row and chemically machined panels running the whole length of each side of the fuselage to double up on the original skin

This aircraft, one of the hardest-worked of all 707s, was built as a Dash-330C for Lufthansa, and registered D-ABUA. Delivered in 1965 it logged over 35,000 hours before being handed in April 1977 to German Cargo, a Lufthansa subsidiary, after complete gutting and conversion as a windowless freighter. It has since operated with high utilization on long-haul cargo charters throughout the world.

and frames. Boeing learned a great deal from the British investigation into Comet fatigue problems, as did other US builders. Fuel capacity was increased, with various arrangements of flexible cells inboard and integral tanks outboard, and the first models offered were the Model 707-120 series with a length of 144 ft 6 in (44.04 m) and the special Model 707-138 which was 10 ft (3.048 m) shorter. The standard launch engine was the JT3C-6, rated at 13,500-lb (6124-kg) thrust with water injection, and fitted with a large noise-suppressing nozzle with 20 separate tubes (which soon became covered with soot from wet take-offs).

Predictably the first airline customer was Pan American, which bought 20 Model 707-121s; but, to Boeing's consternation, it also signed for 25 DC-8s on the same day (13 October 1955) in a $296 million deal. Later in the same month United chose 30 DC-8s, and Douglas announced a longer-ranged DC-8 with the big JT4A engine. Boeing had to respond with a long-range Model 707, and unlike Douglas

N70700 lifted off from Renton on 15 July 1954 to open the world-wide era of jet transportation. After many years of valued research by Boeing, which involved several startling modifications, this historic aircraft was rebuilt in its original form for permanent preservation.

History was made when the Boeing 707-121 of Pan American World Airways opened the 'Big Jet' era on 26 October 1958 with a scheduled service from New York to Paris. Since that time the US grip on the air-transport industry has been almost total.

The Boeing 707-384B, *Mycenae*, belonging to Olympic Airways, has four Pratt & Whitney JT3D-3B engines. It was built in 1968 and was still in use in 1986. International noise regulations mean that all Boeing 707s now have to be fitted with sound absorbers.

Aircraft 72-7000 is perhaps the most senior aircraft in the US Air Force, because when the President is aboard it becomes Air Force One. Basically a civil 707-320C, it lacks the latter's underfin, and of course has a custom-built interior and very special navigation and communication installations for global self-sufficiency.

(whose aircraft were all the same size) decided to make it larger. Braniff, in fact, was odd man out in buying the Model 707-220, which was the original size but had the JT4A, rated at 15,800-lb (7167-kg) thrust, for sprightly take-off at hot-and-high airports on routes to South America. But it was American's order for 30 Model 707-123s on 8 November 1955 that clinched the go-ahead and took Boeing to the 50 mark. Subsequently Boeing at least level-pegged Douglas. In the UK BOAC, having said it had no interest in jets and so getting the Vickers VC 7 cancelled, began talking with Boeing only four months later.

Rolls-Royce power
BOAC, like PanAm, was interested in Boeing's bigger longer-range model, the Model 707-320 Intercontinental. This had a new high-efficiency wing of 11 ft 7 in (3.53 m) greater span, a fuselage 8 ft 5 in (2.57 m) longer seating up to 189 passengers, much greater fuel capacity, and an initial gross weight of 312,000 lb (141520 kg). Launch engine was the JT4A at the increased rating of 16,800 lb (7620 kg), but Rolls-Royce's Conway bypass turbojet (a turbofan of very low 0.3:1 bypass ratio) fitted perfectly and offered greater power, lower installed weight and much better fuel consumption, and was selected by a small minority of airlines including BOAC and Lufthansa. The considerably greater capability of the Intercontinental quickly made this the standard type of Model 707, while the original size was developed into a new shorter-range family initially marketed with the same Model 717 number as the tanker but in 1959 renumbered as the Model 720.

The first of many military 707s was this 707-153, delivered on 4 May 1959 to the USAF as a VC-137A, operated by the 1298th Air Transport Squadron with a 22-seat VIP interior convertible as an airborne command post. The engine pods with multi-pipe nozzles were typical of early JT3C aircraft. Later the three VC-137As were converted to VC-137B standard with JT3D (TF33) engines, for the 89th Military Airlift Wing.

The first production Model 707, Boeing no. 17586, was flown at Renton on 20 December 1957, but was actually numbered as the second of the initial batch of 20 Model 707-121s for PanAm, N708PA, the second production machine having the specially chosen registration N707PA. Flight development was generally trouble-free, and FAA certification was awarded on 23 September 1958. The world airline industry was poised on the brink of a new era. Some thought the prospect disastrous; one important expert said it was 'an industry gone mad'. Bristol, trying to sell Britannia turboprops, had insisted the Model 707 was technically impossible, and would need six engines. Even jet enthusiasts admitted that the Boeing monster was almost impossibly big, heavy, capacious, expensive to buy, needed runways longer than those available, could gobble up passenger-miles at a rate that seemed astronomic, and might indeed bankrupt the airlines (either those that bought it or those that stayed with propellers). The voices which predicted that what had become known as The Big Jets would result in a gigantic expansion of the air-transport business were muted and uncertain. Those that predicted an era of unknown profitability, and freedom from reliance on government subsidies, were hardly heard at all.

PanAm opened scheduled services between New York and Paris on 26 October 1958. New York and London and other European capitals soon followed. On these routes the Model 707-121 was marginal. It had not been designed for the North Atlantic, and the flight crews had to learn fast about correct take-off procedures and how to get the most air-miles per pound of fuel. Had noise certification been in force the operations would have been impossible. As it was,

The main display and control interfaces with the human crew of the E-3A are provided by these nine MPCs (multi-purpose consoles), plus three auxiliary display units. The normal mission crew comprises 13 AWAC (airborne warning and control) specialists, plus a flight crew of four to fly the aircraft. Up front are communications and data-processing, and at the rear the navigation units and crew-rest bunks.

5-241

IIAF

Right at the very end of 707 production, in 1976–7, came a batch of 14 extremely well equipped 707-3J9C aircraft for the Imperial Iranian Air Force. They combined special communications for global operation with triple-point air refuelling, with tip-mounted hose/drogue installations and a Boeing high-speed boom driven by an operator in the rear fuselage. All were delivered before late 1977.

on westbound flights a refuelling stop was invariably needed at Iceland or one of the other wartime-built fields farther west. But these were the first halting steps of a revolution in global travel. On 25 January 1959 American began services with the Model 707-123 between New York and Los Angeles, and here there was no real problem.

Spurred by competition from the DC-8, CV-880 and European types, Boeing had been forced to embark on a programme of building ever-better jetliners. The original risk of $15 million had been left far behind. Now the risks were beginning to approach $100 million. What was still uncertain was whether or not the company would survive. The Model 707 was selling in dozens, but would it ever sell in hundreds? Pratt & Whitney met the competition of the Conway with a startlingly simple modification to the JT3C which replaced the first three stages of the compressor with two stages of enormous blades called a fan; and they coined the name turbofan, more descriptive than 'bypass turbojet' and easier to sell. Called the JT3D, the new engine began life at 18,000-lb (8172-kg) thrust and offered much better fuel economy and dramatically reduced noise as well as release from water injection. The result was a second generation of Model 707s characterized by a B suffix.

Before these were available, the big Model 707-320 Intercontinental flew as the 16th off the Renton line on 11 January 1959. It was certificated on 15 July the same year and entered service with PanAm a month later, sweeping away the Model 707-121 from trans-Atlantic routes with a replacement aircraft designed for the job, and able to carry a considerably greater payload non-stop even westbound. The UK's certification was held up while the ARB (today the CAA) studied the handling and stability in adverse circumstances and finally insisted on greater fin area. At first an underfin was added, with a tail bumper incorporated, but later this was

replaced by a much taller vertical tail which was retrofitted on almost all Model 707s and related military models. This cleared the way for the Conway-engined Model 707-420 family, which was approved in February 1960.

Boeing's bargain

In fact the first model to have the JT3D fan engine was the Model 707-120B. This stemmed from the Model 720, first flown on 23 November 1959, which looked like a Model 707-120 but in fact had a completely revised lightweight airframe matched to reduced weights for short/medium hauls, as well as aerodynamic improvements to the wing which resulted in better take-off and higher cruising speed. Sold at what was called a 'bargain basement' price, the Model 720 killed Convair's CV-880 stone dead even with JT3C engines, and 154 were quickly sold, most having the JT3D engine (either when built or as a retrofit) and styled Model 720B. When the extended-chord wing with high-lift leading-edge flaps was fitted to the Model 707-120 the result was the Model 707-120B, with fan engines, which needed less than half the runway length of the original Model 707-120, besides being quieter and making no visible smoke. American was first of many customers for this model which first flew on 22 June 1960. One oddball customer was Qantas, which bought the short-body Model 707-138 and later fitted fan engines to result in the Model 707-138B.

Last of the major variants was the Model 707-320C. Boeing had already fitted the fan engine to the Intercontinental to produce the Model 707-320B, and with it came a host of aerodynamic improvements including longer-span curved wingtips giving lower drag, and a high-lift leading edge with full-span flaps similar to those of the Model 707-120B and Model 720B. The Model 707-320B entered service with PanAm in June 1962, and a year later the same pioneer airline began using the Model 707-320C mixed-traffic version certificated for up to 202 passengers or 96,126 lb (43603 kg) of cargo, with special provisions for loading and positioning very large or heavy items. The Model 707-320C quickly became the standard model, and the customers kept coming.

In the 1950s the Model 707 and DC-8 had fought a pretty even battle. In the 1960s Boeing began to draw ahead, and when a DC-8 operator, Northwest Orient, bought a much bigger fleet of 26 Model 707-351Cs it looked as if the DC-8

Though the general level of serviceability in the Islamic Iranian Air Force is believed to be very low, the 707-3J9C is a very useful long-range aircraft and at least some of the original force of 14 are kept in operation. Since 1980 efforts have been made to maintain their capability as tankers, especially for the Grumman F-14As.

Boeing 707

This profile shows the first production Boeing E-3A Sentry, USAF 73-1674, which was preceded by two special test aircraft designated EC-137D (numbers 71-1407 and 71-1408). The latter were converted 707-320B airframes, with the JT3D (TF33-7) engine, whereas the production Sentry incorporates many refinements and is powered by the TF33-100A of 21,000 lb (9525 kg) thrust with large generators.

was finished. Douglas fought back with the stretched DC-8 Super Sixty series, but finally closed the DC-8 line at aircraft no. 556 in May 1972. But the Model 707 kept on selling, in slowly diminishing numbers. Many late customers were air forces, starting with the USAF which applied the designation C-137 (see variants). Canada and Iran were among customers for military models with inflight-refuelling capability by wing-tip hosereels and drogues. The total for all regular transport variants was 970, completed in 1986.

The remaining current aircraft using the Model 707 airframe is the E-3A Sentry, or AWACS (Airborne Warning and Control System). This impressive aircraft was planned with eight TF34 engines for greater endurance, but to save money was finally built with four TF33-100/100A engines, military versions of the JT3D. Packed with electronics, the E-3A's purpose is surveillance of the entire airspace within a radius

of some 250 miles (402 km), with a Westinghouse APY-1 radar whose main aerial rotates with a 30-ft (9.14-m) roto-dome rotating six times per minute. The USAF has since 1977 been building up a force of 34 E-3As, and NATO is deploying an additional 18 paid for by most NATO European nations, registered in Luxembourg, completed with a special avionic fit by Dornier at Oberpfaffenhofen and based at Geilenkirchen. Last is the E-8A, a platform for the Joint STARS attack radar.

Distinguished by a communications probe aerial at both wingtips, the NATO E-3A Sentries have been flown from Boeing Aerospace to the Dornier plant at Oberpfaffenhofen for final fitting-out with a third HF radio, a new data analysis and programming group and underwing hardpoints for self-defence weapons which initially include AIM-9L Sidewinders.

Starfighter: manned missile

'Missile with a man in it': such was Lockheed's slogan describing the F-104 Starfighter, visually perhaps the 'hottest' aircraft ever built. Its wing looks too small to be believable, and for just this reason it was never a good air-combat fighter. Large numbers were built, however, to fly attack, reconnaissance and stand-off intercept missions.

In the early 1950s the swept-wing North American F-86 Sabres of the US Air Force were having a hard time in combat with the unexpected Mikoyan-Gurevich MiG-15. The Soviet fighter was as good as the F-86 in almost all aspects of flight performance and in climb and ceiling it was definitely superior. Lockheed's C. L. 'Kelly' Johnson, then chief engineer and soon to be vice-president, visited the F-86 squadrons and listened to their plea for more speed, more climb, and more altitude. Back at the plant in Burbank, Los Angeles, he was well along with planning a new fighter to

Above Sidewinders are particularly prominent on this Royal Netherlands air force F-104G, with tanks instead of Sidewinders on the wingtips. The unit is No. 323 Sqn at Leeuwarden. Today the Starfighter, once the foremost Netherlands type, is becoming rare.

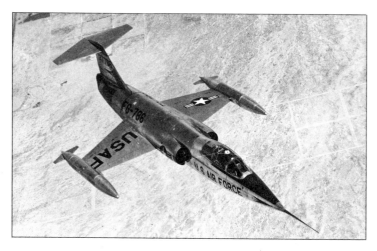

Above These Starfighters are two of the original F-104As (the more distant of the pair is the no. 2 production aircraft) photographed in the late 1960s after their return to active status with the very powerful J79-19 engine. They were briefly again used by Aerospace Defense Command after having previously been in the Air National Guard.

Left Seen here flying in the vicinity of Palmdale, California, USAF no. 53-7786 was the original Model 83, the first XF-104 prototype. It was lighter and less powerful than the F-104A, but the main recognition feature was the use of plain engine inlets. The engine was one of the rare afterburning J65 Sapphires.

159

Lockheed F-104-6

Specification

Lockheed F-104G
Type: single-seat fighter and attack aircraft
Powerplant: one General Electric J79-11A turbojet engine rated 15,800 lb (7167 kg) with full afterburner
Performance: maximum speed (clean) at 40,000 ft (12192 m) 1,300 mph (2092 km/h); service ceiling (clean) 55,000 ft (16764 m); mission radius (typical lo-lo conventional attack) 315 miles (507 km), (no bombs but four external tanks) 690 miles (1110 km)

Weights: empty 14,082 lb (6390 kg); maximum 28,779 lb (13054 kg)
Dimensions: span (no tanks or missile shoes) 21 ft 11 in (6.68 m); length 54 ft 9 in (16.69 m); height 13 ft 6 in (4.15 m); wing area 196.1 sq ft (18.22 m²)
Armament: usually one 20-mm M61A-1 gun; four underwing pylons for total load of 4,000 lb (1814 kg); pairs of Sidewinder AAMs may be carried on wingtips or fuselage pylons

Now replaced by a Panavia Tornado, this Lockheed F-104G served until early 1982 with Federal German Marineflieger wing MFG 1 based at Schleswig in northern Germany. MFG 1 is tasked in the anti-ship attack role, with secondary photo-reconnaissance duties. This aircraft is depicted with a centreline practice bomb carrier and two Kormoran anti-ship missiles under the wings. The plan view shows the access doors above the 'piccolo' power units for the ailerons, just 1 in (25.4 mm) deep. In the front view the single

M61 gun can be seen, as well as the levered-suspension main landing gears with Dowty-licensed Liquid Spring shock struts and landing lights inside the doors. The side elevation shows the airfield arrester hook and electrically de-iced engine inlets.

160

Lockheed F-104

Until 1967 the Aeronautica Militare Italiano was organized into large *aerobrigate* (air brigades) each with several *gruppi* (squadrons). This European-built F-104G served with the 4ª Aerobrigata's 9° Gruppo throughout the 1960s (note Ferrari-style prancing horse badge). The 9° Gruppo is now an F-104S fighter unit.

USAF no. 12341 (actually 62-12341) was one of a batch of 48 F-104Gs built by Canadair on MAP instructions and in this case allocated to the Royal Danish air force. It is shown in the light grey overall finish originally applied in 1964 when serving with Esk 723 at Aalborg in the interceptor role.

succeed the F-80 Shooting Star. What the front-line pilots told him convinced him to go for performance at all cost. The result was one of the most startling aeroplanes ever built. At times it has been the centre of furious controversy, and as a fighter for close combat it was never outstanding. But for moving at high speed in a straight line it has few rivals, and late in its life it blossomed forth as an exceptionally good attack machine.

Johnson did not just sit down and design the F-104: he was surrounded by parametric studies for fighters of all shapes and sizes, and until early 1952 had leaned heavily towards substantial aircraft powered by the new J57 or J67 (Olympus-derived) engines. To try to meet the demand for still greater performance he took one of the best J67-powered fighters, weighing 31,849 lb (14447 kg), and stripped it of everything removable. The weight came down to 28,100 lb (12746 kg) but the improvement in performance was hardly noticeable and as a fighter the stripped-down machine was inferior. After further study Johnson and his team decided to build a much smaller fighter, the Model 83, to meet the USAF requirement for Weapon System 303A (a supersonic day fighter). The Mach number chosen was 2.2, the practical limit for an airframe made of conventional aluminium alloys.

Aerodynamically the Model 83 was almost unique in having wings tailored purely to the supersonic regime, only 3 per cent thick and of extraordinarily small span and area, without sweep. Almost everything was packaged in the long circular-section body, tailored closely to the chosen engine, the superb new X-24A by General Electric, fed by lateral inlets leaving a long needle nose for radar if necessary. To reduce weight the canopy was made non-jettisonable and the seat was designed to fire downwards. One of the factors contributing to this potentially dangerous idea was that, after studying no fewer than 285 different tail arrangements, it was decided to use a powered slab tailplane at the very top of the fin in what has since become known as the T-tail

The Japan Air Self-Defense Force operates the F-104J single-seater in the interceptor role and also the F-104DJ trainer, built by Lockheed but assembled, like the F-104Js, by Mitsubishi. In the foreground is the fifth production aircraft parked next to a F-104DJ two-seater and with the fin and canopies of a Mitsubishi T-2 visible beyond.

Taiwan is another of the refuges of surviving Starfighters, though for several years a replacement (the F-16 has been favoured) has been unsuccessfully sought. These four F-104Gs serve with the 5th Wing, each carrying Sidewinders in the interceptor role. They carry nose numbers 4303, 4311, 4313 and (rear) 4354 plus buzz number FG-792.

configuration. It was considered that ejecting over this tail might be even more of a problem at the speeds to be reached by this aircraft.

Other novel engineering was found throughout the aircraft. Because the wing was so small, the maximum depth at the root being a mere 4.2 in (107 mm), it was difficult to fit anything inside it. All fuel had to be in flexible cells in the overcrowded fuselage. To drive the outboard ailerons Lockheed and the Bertea company devised so-called piccolo actuators containing a row of 10 small hydraulic rams in a solid block of aluminium fitting within the available depth

Below USAF no. 63-8455 was one of the fifth production block of TF-104G two-seaters made by Lockheed. Known as the Lockheed Model 583D-10-20, they usually had no gun but retained the NASARR radar and weapon delivery boxes. TF-104Gs used by the Luftwaffe at Luke AFB look identical except for red/white/blue tank fins.

of 1.1 in (28 mm). To enable the tiny wing to generate sufficient lift at reasonable take-off speeds, the leading edge was hinged to pivot downwards under electric actuation, in one of the world's first 'droop snoot' configurations. For landing, even more radical measures were necessary, and the F-104 was the first production application of the boundary-layer controlled blown flap which had just been devised by John D. Attinello: high-pressure air bled from the engine is blown at supersonic speed through narrow slits ahead of the upper surface of the flap, to prevent flow separation and generate powerful lift. The British Dowty company provided Liquid Spring shock struts (made under licence by H.M. Loud) small enough to cushion the shock of landing in small main landing gears pivoted to the fuselage and retracted forwards and inwards. Armament comprised the revolutionary new gun developed by General Electric as Project Vulcan, spewing out 6,000 shells a minute from six 20-mm barrels (and even today the standard gun of US fighters). Another new weapon, the simple Sidewinder air-to-air missile, could be carried on each wingtip in place of drop tanks.

The USAF liked the Model 83, and in March 1953 placed a contract for two prototypes, designated XF-104, numbers 53-7786/7787. Lockheed's name, Starfighter, was officially adopted. The General Electric engine was not even run on the test-bench until 8 June 1954, so Johnson planned the two XF-104s to have the lower-powered Wright XJ65-W-6, an afterburner-equipped derivative of the British Sapphire rated at 10,200-lb (4627-kg) maximum thrust. Plain sharp-lipped fixed inlets were used, and the nose gear retracted to the rear. Design and manufacture at Johnson's famed 'Skunk Works' were rapid, and Tony LeVier began taxi tests with the first aircraft at Edwards AFB in February 1954. On 28 February LeVier made a 300-ft (91-m) hop and on the morning of 4 March he accomplished a flawless first flight, with a non-afterburning J65 rated at 7,200-lb (3266-kg) thrust. With Herman 'Fish' Salmon and Joe Ozier also handling the test flights, LeVier explored the limits of handling and soon found severe pitch-up problems which took a long time to cure. Meanwhile Lockheed's main plant, especially Burbank's shop B-1, was busy with the revised design and manufacture of a pre-production run of 17 YF-104As, with significant changes.

Prototype roll-out

Called Lockheed Model 183, and with USAF numbers 55-2955/2971, all were powered by the YJ79-GE-3, rated with afterburner at 14,800-lb (6713-kg) thrust. For the first time in any aircraft the engine was combined with a fully variable duct system that could adapt itself to all the contrasting conditions from take-off to Mach 2.2 at high altitude. The inlets were greatly enlarged and fitted with half-cones to position the oblique shockwave formed at supersonic speeds. Instead of a series of auxiliary inlets and overboard bleeds, a very large secondary airflow was ducted around the

Below Canada was one of the chief participants in the F-104G production programme, the Canadian Armed Forces calling the type the CF-104. Aircraft no. 12854 was originally operated unpainted by the RCAF's (as the CAF air branch was then called) No. 441 Sqn at Marville, France. It is shown with the Vicom camera pod under the fuselage.

FX-31 was one of the 18 F-104Gs (plus two two-seat TF-104s) flown from 1963 until 1980 by the FAB's (Belgian air force) No. 350 Sqn at Beauvechain. With similarly based No. 349 Sqn they operated in the all-weather interceptor role, though the Starfighter was not really adequate for the job in European weather.

engine and discharged around the primary nozzle, and the nozzle itself was composed of fully variable ejector-profiled petals driven by hydraulic (lubricating oil) actuators to match nozzle area and shape to the flight Mach number and altitude. The fuselage was lengthened to accommodate five fuel cells, the nose gear was redesigned to retract forwards, the electrical system was more than doubled in power, and later modifications included the incorporation of operative flap-blowing and a ventral underfin at the tail.

The first YF-104A, still lacking numerous non-vital items, was rolled out on 23 December 1955, and on 17 February 1956 Salmon took it aloft. It was the first aircraft, apart from General Electric's XF4D-1 test aircraft, to fly on the power of a J79. Subsequent testing was exciting, punctuated by various incidents, and it took very much longer to clear the aircraft as an operational fighter than it had taken to design and build in the first place. The second XF-104 and three YF-104As were lost, but another YF-104A was saved when LeVier managed a dead-stick landing after the engine had been drenched in kerosene from a tank pierced by a shell-case that entered one of the engine inlets. General Electric introduced the J79-3A engine with a modulated afterburner, the gun (then designated T-171) became available, and Lockheed finally turned to the manufacture of 153 production F-104As for the USAF inventory.

On 17 April 1956 Lockheed organized a giant press ceremony at which the previously classified F-104 was unveiled by General Otto P. Weyland, commander of Tactical Air Command. The inlet geometry was still secret, so the inlets were covered by large streamlined fairings. Ten days later Mach 2 was exceeded, and later in 1956 there was added the MA-10 avionic system, comprising an ASG-14 gunsight ranging radar and a small infra-red detector for sighting at night. Basically the F-104A was a visual day fighter, with the gun and either two tanks or Sidewinders. Service clearance was received on 26 January 1958, and deliveries began to the 83rd Fighter Interceptor Squadron at Hamilton AFB, near San Francisco. Engine reliability was poor, and though dead-stick landings were accomplished at 275 mph (442 km/h) most pilots ejected, when the downward-fired seat proved deadly at low level. By April 1958 the F-104A was grounded, but aircraft still with the maker kept flying and USAF pilots set numerous world records including absolute speed at 1,404.19 mph (2259.83 km/h), zoom altitude at 91,249 ft (27813 m) and a series of time-to-height records up to 82,021 ft (25000 m).

Subsequently many F-104As were converted into other sub-types as shown in the variants list. This model was withdrawn from USAF duty in 1959, though many continued with the Air National Guard and a few were given the powerful J79-19 engine in 1968. Surplus aircraft were supplied to Taiwan (25), Jordan (36), Pakistan (12) and Canada (1).

The RF-104A was cancelled, so Lockheed next built 26 F-104B tandem trainers (Model 283) with reduced fuel, no gun and various other changes including a larger fin and

Though the Aeritalia F-104S is the most important Italian Starfighter variant the Aeronautica Militare Italiano also uses the RF-104G and, as seen here, the TF-104G two-seater. The aircraft illustrated is one of 28 supplied to the 20° Gruppo which shares Grosseto with an operational squadron, the 9° Gruppo (F-104S).

Lockheed (Aeritalia) F-104S Starfighter cutaway drawing key

1 Pitot tube
2 Radome
3 Radar scanner dish
4 R21G/H multi-mode radar equipment
5 Radome withdrawal rails
6 Communications aerial
7 Cockpit front bulkhead
8 Infra-red sight
9 Windscreen panels
10 Reflector gunsight
11 Instrument panel shroud
12 Rudder pedals
13 Control column
14 Nose section frame construction
15 Control cable runs
16 Pilot's side console panel
17 Throttle control
18 Safety harness
19 Martin-Baker IQ-7A ejection seat
20 Face blind seat firing handle
21 Cockpit canopy cover
22 Canopy bracing struts
23 Seat rail support box
24 Angle of attack probe
25 Cockpit rear bulkhead
26 Temperature probe
27 Nosewheel doors
28 Taxiing lamp
29 Nosewheel/leg strut
30 Nosewheel
31 Steering linkage
32 AIM-7 Sparrow avionics (replacing M-61 gun installation of strike model)
33 Inertial platform
34 Avionics compartment
35 Avionics compartment shroud cover
36 Cockpit aft glazing
37 Ram-air turbine
38 Emergency generator
39 Avionics compartment access cover
40 Fuselage frame construction
41 Pressure bulkhead
42 Ammunition compartment auxiliary fuel tank (101.5 Imp gal/462 litre capacity)
43 Fuel feed pipes
44 Flush-fitting UHF aerial panel
45 Anti-collision light
46 Starboard intake
47 Engine bleed air supply to air conditioning
48 Gravity fuel fillers
49 Fuselage main fuel tanks (total internal capacity 746 Imp gal/3391 litres)
50 Pressure refuelling adaptor
51 Intake shock cone centre body
52 De-iced intake lip
53 Port intake
54 Shock cone boundary layer bleed
55 Boundary layer bleed air duct
56 Auxiliary intake
57 Hinged auxiliary intake door
58 Navigation light
59 Leading edge flap jack
60 Intake trunking
61 Fuselage main longeron
62 Wing root attaching members
63 Intake flank fuel tanks
64 Wing-mounting fuselage mainframes
65 Control cable runs
66 Electrical junction box
67 Dorsal spine fairing
68 Starboard inboard pylon
69 Leading edge flap (lowered)
70 AIM-7 Sparrow AAM
71 Missile launch rail
72 Starboard outer pylon
73 Tip tank vane
74 Tip tank latching unit
75 Starboard wingtip tank
76 Fuel filler caps
77 Starboard aileron
78 Aileron power control jacks
79 Power control servo valves
80 Fuel lines to auxiliary tanks
81 Flap blowing duct
82 Starboard blown flap (lowered)
83 Engine intake compressor face
84 Intake spill flaps
85 Aileron torque shaft
86 Hydraulic reservoir
87 Air conditioning bleed air supply pipe
88 General Electric J79-GE-19 turbojet
89 Engine withdrawal rail
90 Starboard airbrake (open)
91 Fin root fillet
92 Elevator servo controls
93 Elevator/all moving tailplane hydraulic jacks
94 Push-pull control rods
95 Tailfin construction
96 Fin tip fairing
97 Tailplane rocking control arm
98 Starboard tailplane
99 One-piece tailplane construction
100 Tailplane spar
101 Tailplane spar central pivot
102 Fin trailing-edge construction

powered rudder. Next came 77 F-104C single-seat fighter-bombers for Tactical Air Command, with the more powerful J79-7 engine, operative flap-blowing, a removable inflight-refuelling probe and underwing and belly pylons for tanks, Sidewinder missiles or 1,000-lb (454-kg) bombs. These equipped the 479th TFW at George AFB from 16 October 1958 until 1965; subsequently many were camouflaged and sent to Vietnam where they operated with some success in the day-attack role. Production for the USAF was completed by 21 F-104D (Model 283) two-seaters based on the F-104C but without the gun. The two-seaters had two separate canopies, each hinged to the left, though downward-ejection seats were retained.

By mid-1957 Lockheed was left in no doubt the F-104 programme was going to be about one-tenth as large as it had expected, unless the company carried out extensive internal redesign and, moreover, found new customers. The key to further sales was West Germany's Luftwaffe, which not only required about 1,000 supersonic fighter-bombers, but also wanted to build them under licence to restore its once

mighty aviation industry. As early as 1956 Lockheed had begun the redesign process with a project designated F-104-7, but in late 1958 this was redesignated F-104G (for Germany). In a total about-face from the concept of a small, light and simple day fighter built solely for performance, the F-104G was planned as a heavy, complex and extremely effective attack aircraft, and in particular as a carrier of tactical nuclear weapons to point targets using advanced all-weather navigation and weapon-delivery systems.

The airframe was totally redesigned, with 36 large heavy-press forgings, 60 no-draft close-tolerance forgings, numerous machined and composite skin panels, Spraymat electrically

103 Rudder construction
104 Rudder power control jacks
105 Rudder servo valves
106 Exhaust shroud
107 Fully-variable afterburner exhaust nozzle
108 Fin attachment joints
109 Fin-carrying mainframes
110 Afterburner duct
111 Nozzle control jacks
112 Steel and titanium aft fuselage construction
113 Rear navigation lights
114 Aft fuselage attachment joint
115 Brake parachute housing
116 Port airbrake (open)
117 Airbrake scissor links
118 Fuselage strake (both sides)
119 Emergency runway arrester hook
120 Airbrake jack
121 Air exit louvres
122 Primary heat exchanger
123 Wing root trailing edge fillet
124 Flap hydraulic jack
125 Flap blowing slot
126 Port blown flap (lowered)

127 Aileron servo valves
128 Aileron power control jacks
129 Port aileron
130 Tip tank fins
131 Port navigation light
132 Port wing tip fuel tank (283 Imp gal/1287 litre capacity)
133 Fuel filler caps
134 Outboard pylon mounting rib
135 Wing multi-spar construction
136 Inboard pylon mounting rib
137 Main undercarriage leg door
138 Shock absorber strut
139 Swivel axle control rods
140 Port mainwheel
141 Leading edge flap (lowered)
142 Leading edge flap rib construction
143 Port outboard pylon
144 Missile launch rail
145 Port AIM-7 Sparrow AAM
146 Mk 82 500-lb (226-kg) bomb
147 Mk 83 1,000-lb (454-kg) bomb
148 Bomb-mounting shackles
149 Auxiliary fuel tank (163 Imp gal/740 litre capacity)
150 Port inboard wing pylon
151 Pylon attachments
152 LAU-3A 2.75 in (70 mm) FFAR pod (19 rickets)
153 AIM-9 Sidewinder AAM
154 Missile launch rail
155 Fuselage stores pylon adaptor

de-iced inlets, the large tail and powered rudder, improved blown flaps with an intermediate setting to enhance manoeuvrability, stronger landing gear with bigger tyres and high-capacity anti-skid brakes, a larger drag chute and, not least, the J79-11A engine. In the nose was the Autonetics F15A NASARR multi-mode radar, amidships was the first inertial navigation system ever to go into operational service in any aircraft (Litton LN-3) as well as various advanced

Looking distinctly tired after long service, and due for imminent replacement by a General Dynamics F-16, no. 17754 of the Danish air force was one of the last batch of F-104Gs built by Canadair on MAP (Military Assistance Program) account. Full USAF serial is 64-17754. Note the prominent fuselage pylons, added to take Sidewinders.

weapon-aiming subsystems, and in the cockpit Lockheed finally bowed to pressure and fitted the C-2 seat which ejected upwards. A total of 3,000 lb (1361 kg) of external weapons could be carried, including a 2,000-lb (907-kg) special store (nuclear weapon) under the fuselage.

During the heyday of the Luftwaffe's F-104G, each *Geschwader* (wing) was assigned eight tandem dual TF-104G trainers, able to undertake conversion and continuation training as well as fly operational sorties. This TF-104G flew with JG 32, based at Lechfeld during the 1970s.

Success with the Luftwaffe

There was plenty of competition, but Lockheed's F-104G (otherwise the Model 683-10-19) Super Starfighter beat the lot, because, even though it did not exist, it promised to fly all the missions the Luftwaffe wanted. Federal Germany signed on 18 March 1959; this triggered off Canada, Japan, the Netherlands, Belgium, the USAF for MAP customers, Italy and an additional USAF MAP buy, in that order. A gigantic European manufacturing programme was created, made up of Arge Nord (Hamburger, Weser, Focke-Wulf, Fokker and Aviolanda), Arge Süd (Messerschmitt, Heinkel, Dornier and Siebel) and a West Group (Avions Fairey and SABCA). Together these built respectively 350, 210 and 188 aircraft. Initially the Belgians were teamed with Italy, but finally the Italian group was separate (Fiat, Aerfer, Macchi, SIAI-Marchetti, Piaggio and SACA) and it assembled 229 F-104Gs. The Canadians made 200 Canadair CL-90 (CF-104) ground-attack and reconnaissance aircraft, and also shipped 121 sets of wings, aft fuselages and tails to Europe, 40 sets to Lockheed and 40 sets to Japan, and also delivered a further 110 MAP aircraft built to F-104G standard. In contrast the Japanese F-104J is configured for the air-to-air role, with the gun fitted and external armament of four Sidewinders; Mitsubishi, assisted by Kawasaki, built 207 of this model. The Japanese also received 20 Lockheed-built F-104DJ trainers. There are many sub-variants, as listed.

The first F-104G flew in Lockheed hands at Palmdale on 5 October 1960, as the first of 96 supplied by Lockheed to the Luftwaffe. The first Arge Süd aircraft flew on 10 August 1961, followed by the first Arge Nord aircraft on 11 November 1961. The first CF-104 was airlifted to Palmdale and flew on 26 May 1961, the first West Group aircraft on 4 December 1961 and the first Italian machine on 9 June 1962. The only major problem with this otherwise extremely potent attack aircraft was that the Luftwaffe pilots often lacked experience to cope with a mount that was totally unforgiving, and suffered a loss-rate which in 1963 reached 139 per 100,000 flight hours. The Luftwaffe had fought strongly for the Martin-Baker seat, having refitted its Republic F-84F and Canadair Sabre fighters with the British seat and noted the major improvement in reliability and pilot survival. But West Germany had no means of qualifying the alternative seat, and placed a contract with the USAF. The latter did all it could to prevent the British seat being fitted, and after 23 months of argument the Germans gave in and accepted the Lockheed C-2 seat, which at least ejected upwards. Fatalities continued at a serious level, despite urgent seat-modification programmes. The crafty Danes quietly fitted Martin-Baker

seats to their Canadair-built MAP aircraft, but it was not until 8 March 1967 that the US campaign to keep Martin-Baker out collapsed, and in 12 months the entire German and Italian F-104 inventories had the British GQ-7 seat. Martin-Baker made no announcement.

More than 25 F-104G developments never came to pass, among them V/STOL models, Spey-powered interdictors and the next-generation CL-1200 Lancer (USAF X-27). But the 1966 German/Italian proposal for the F-104S (S for Spey engine and also for Sparrow missile) did lead to a new sub-type. Planned as an all-weather interceptor, and thus marking a return to air fighting, the F-104S incorporates many large and small improvements including a new R21G/H multi-mode radar and radar-guided AAMs, either Sparrow or Italy's own Aspide. The US Defense Department managed to keep out the British engine, and the F-104S has the uprated J79-19. The main external distinguishing feature is the pair of small canted ventral fins, one on each side of the main ventral fin. Lockheed and Aeritalia shared development, but all production took place in Italy. Lockheed flew a pattern aircraft in December 1966 and Turin-assembled aircraft followed from 1969 until March 1979, when production was completed at 206 for Italy and 40 for Turkey. Since 1982 some Aeronautica Militare Italiano aircraft have been recycled for updating to improve look-down shoot-down capability, to enhance electronic-warfare capability and to enable attack missions to be flown accurately against ground targets at low level, in all weather.

Lockheed F-104 variants

XF-104: YJ65 engine, short fuselage, plain inlets (2 prototypes)

YF-104A: YJ79 engine, long fuselage, advanced inlet/nozzle system (17 service-test aircraft)

F-104A: J79-3A, fitted with gun, tip attachments and retrofitted with ventral fin (153 production aircraft)

NF-104A: rocket-boosted conversion for NASA Astronaut training, also designated **F-104N** (3F-104A conversions)

QF-104A: target-drone conversions (24YF-104A/F-104A conversions in various sub-types)

RF-104A: unarmed photo-reconnaissance version of F-104A (projected)

F-104B: tandem trainer with larger vertical tail (26 production aircraft)

F-104C: J79-7 engine, extra underwing and centreline pylons, inflight-refuelling probe, blown flaps (77 production aircraft)

F-104D: two-seat version of F-104C (21 production aircraft)

F-104DJ: Japanese version of F-104D with J79-IHI-11A made in Japan (20 production aircraft)

F-104F: two-seat trainer based on F-104D structurally but with F-104G avionics and C-2 seat (30 production aircraft)

F-104G: redesigned attack aircraft with new airframe, J79-11A engine, NASARR radar, inertial navigation and five stores attachments; most retrofitted with Martin-Baker seats (1,127 production aircraft)

CF-104: Canadian derivative for attack and (with multi-sensor pack fitted) reconnaissance (200 production aircraft)

CF-104D: Canadian two-seat derivative of CF-104 (38 production aircraft)

RF-104G: five sub-types all configured for tactical reconnaissance, with NASARR and either an external multi-sensor pod or camera pod, or with the gun removed and an internal pod (189 production aircraft)

TF-104G: two-seat version of F-104G with no gun or centreline pylon but retaining full avionics (220 production aircraft)

RTF-104G: two-seat multi-sensor reconnaissance aircraft, some configured for electronic warfare missions (projected)

F-104H: export version with simplified equipment, optical gunsight but no NASARR (projected)

TF-104H: two-seat version of F-104H (projected)

F-104J: J79-IHI-11A, Japanese fighter version (210 production aircraft)

F-104S: Italian all-weather interceptor, J79-19 engine, gun/AAM fit (245 production aircraft)

Sukhoi's Super-strikers

The Sukhoi Su-7 'Fitter' has for more than 20 years been one of the world's leading ground-attack aircraft. It could carry either bombs or adequate fuel, but not both at the same time, so was regarded as obsolescent by 1970. Today advanced swing-wing derivatives are still in production.

One of the fundamental features of Soviet procurement is that nothing is thrown away it if can be used (there are always masses of air and ground crews familiar with established hardware), and aircraft are kept in production in progressively improved versions to avoid the need to introduce completely new designs. Nothing better exemplifies this than the long series of tactical attack aircraft developed by the Sukhoi OKB (experimental design bureau), which remain in production despite the fact that almost 10 years ago they were joined by a totally new aircraft of greatly

A striking US Navy photo of a 'Fitter-J', one of the latest export variants of the Tumansky-powered Sukhoi swing-wing family, of the Libyan Arab air force in late summer 1981. This one is carrying two tanks and two 'Advanced Atoll' AAMs. The Libyans have received well over 100 swing-wing Su-17 and Su-77 aircraft.

increased capability, the formidable Su-24 'Fencer'. Transformed by swing-wings, new engines and improved sensor and weapon-delivery systems, the new members of the family, known by the reporting name 'Fitter' to NATO

Sukhoi Su-20 'Fitter'

Specification

Sukhoi Su-20/-22 'Fitter-J'
Type: single-seat attack fighter
Powerplant: one Tumansky R-29B augmented turbofan, rated at 27,502-lb (12475-kg) thrust with full afterburner
Performance: maximum speed, clean at high altitude about 1,450 mph (2335 km) or Mach 2.2, and at sea level as depicted about 699 mph (1125 km/h); service ceiling 59,055 ft (18000 m); combat radius with 4,409 lb (2000 kg) of weapons 450 miles (725 km)
Weights: empty about 24,250 lb (11000 kg); maximum take-off 41,887 lb (19000 kg)
Dimensions: span (28° sweep) 45 ft 11¼ in (14.00 m) (62° sweep) 34 ft 9½ in (10.60 m); length overall 62 ft 0 in (18.90 m); height 17 ft 0 in (5.18 m); wing area (28° sweep) 432 sq ft (40.1 m²)
Armament: two 30-mm NR-30 or related cannon, (70 rounds each) plus about 11,023 lb (5000 kg) of weapons and tanks carried on two tandem pairs of pylons under the fuselage, two inboard leading-edge pylons and two pylons under the main pivot fences

Though not in the same class as the Su-24 and similar advanced attack aircraft, either in the matter of payload/range or nav/attack avionics, the later members of the Su-17/20/22 family are formidable tactical machines deployed in large numbers throughout several Warsaw Pact air forces. This 'Fitter-J' (the designation of the prototype Su-17-20-22 series was S-22I or Su-

71G) is one of the Tumansky-powered models, with the enlarged dorsal spine and tall vertical tail. Shown in the markings of VVS Frontal Aviation, with only 'Advanced Atoll' AAMs and four tanks, it serves alongside a two-seat variant whose NATO code name has not yet been published.

Sukhoi Su-7

This ageing Su-7BMK is shown in the livery in which it was painted in 1978 when it was serving with a Frontal Aviation regiment in the Trans-Baikal Military District in eastern Siberia. Substantial numbers of older Sukhoi attack aircraft are still serving in advanced training units in less-sensitive Soviet regions.

personnel, make this the most prolific dedicated attack family since World War 2.

In World War 2 Pavel Osipovich Sukhoi had few successes, and his run of bad luck continued until his OKB was summarily shut by Stalin's order in 1949. After Stalin's death in 1953 Sukhoi applied for permission to reopen, and this was quickly granted. Lavochkin's OKB was unsuccessful and a strong rival was needed to offer competition to the Mikoyan/Gurevich team. The two latter designers and Sukhoi were all invited to the Kremlin later in 1953 and appraised of the two new shapes for future supersonic combat aircraft being refined at TsAGI, the national aerodynamics centre. One was a sharply swept (leading edge 62°) machine with a swept tailplane; the other was a pure delta, of just under 60° leading-edge sweep, also with a swept tailplane.

Two configurations

Furious efforts to apply the lessons of Korea to a new generation of warplanes were centred on these shapes, the Sukhoi OKB quickly confirming that while the delta showed lower drag and seemed better for an interceptor, the long swept wing gave better lift at low speeds and was clearly superior for attack aircraft. Sukhoi was authorized to expand his bureau rapidly and build prototypes for both missions. The first prototypes of both configurations flew in the spring and summer of 1955. The T-1 (T for *treoogol*, or three-angled) eventually led to numerous other types, including a long series of production interceptors with VVS (air force) designations Su-9, Su-11 and Su-15. The S-1 (S for *strelovidnosti*, or arrowed or sweptback) was first flown by Andrei Kochetkov in about May 1955 and led to the family of attack aircraft.

Even before the 1949 closure Sukhoi had worked closely with Arkhip L. Lyulka's turbojet OKB, and it was Lyulka who furnished the engine for all the first generation of new Sukhois. The Type 31 engine, designated AL-7 in VVS service, was a large and impressive single-shaft axial with initially eight and later nine compressor stages with supersonic flow, and variable stators, on the first two rows of blades. In the same size and thrust class as the American JT4 (J75) it was developed from 1952 and had an afterburner added by 1954. It was ideal for the Sukhoi aircraft, which were relatively large machines, much bigger than the rival MiG-21 and in the size class of the American Republic F-105 attack bomber and Convair F-106 interceptor.

From the start the S-1 handled extremely well, the OKB pilots Kochetkov, Korovushkin and Mikhailin releasing the prototype for preliminary NII (State scientific research institute) testing before the end of 1955 even though it had a primitive engine with two-position nozzle and fixed nose inlet. In 1956 pre-production prototypes began to appear, designated Su-7 by the VVS, and these incorporated the definitive AL-7F engine with fully variable afterburner and what may have been the first variable inlet in the Soviet Union, with a translating centrebody and various bleed and auxiliary inlet doors. With this powerplant installation the level Mach number rose to 2.05, compared with the figure of

1.71 demanded by the 1953 specification. It is also almost certain that even the very first S-1 had a single powered 'slab' tailplane, the first in the USSR and ahead of the introduction of such a tail to the well-established MiG-19.

By the time several S and T prototypes had briefly flashed over Tushino at the 1956 Aviation Day display, both had been selected for mass production at factories far from the Sukhoi bureau at distant Komsomolsk in eastern Siberia.

Sukhoi Su-7MBK 'Fitter-A' cutaway drawing key

1 Pitot tube
2 Pinch vanes
3 Yaw vanes
4 Engine air intake
5 Fixed intake centre-body
6 Radome
7 Ranging radar scanner
8 ILS aerial
9 Radar controller
10 Weapon release ballistic computer
11 Retractable taxiing lamp
12 SRO-2M 'Odd-rods' IFF aerials
13 Intake suction relief doors
14 Intake duct divider
15 Instrument access panel
16 Su-7U 'Moujik' two-seat operational training variant
17 Armoured glass windscreen
18 Reflector sight
19 Instrument panel shroud
20 Control column
21 Rudder pedals
22 Control linkages
23 Nose undercarriage wheel well
24 Nosewheel doors
25 Torque scissor links
26 Steerable nosewheel
27 Low pressure 'rough-field' tyre
28 Hydraulic retraction jack
29 Cockpit pressure floor
30 Engine throttle
31 Pilot's side console panel
32 Ejection seat
33 Canopy release handle
34 Parachute pack headrest
35 Rear view mirror
36 Sliding cockpit canopy cover
37 Instrument venturi
38 Radio and electronics equipment bay
39 Intake ducting
40 Air conditioning plant
41 Electrical and pneumatic systems ground connections
42 Cannon muzzle
43 Skin doubler/blast shield
44 Fuel system components access
45 Main fuel pumps
46 Fuel system accumulator
47 Filler cap
48 External piping ducts
49 Starboard main undercarriage leg pivot fixing
50 Shock absorber pressurization charging valve
51 Gun camera
52 Starboard wing integral fuel tank
53 Starboard wing fence
54 Outer wing panel dry bay
55 Wing tip fence
56 Static discharger
57 Starboard aileron
58 Flap guide rail
59 Starboard Fowler flap
60 Flap jack
61 Fuselage skin plating
62 Fuselage fuel tank
63 Wing/fuselage attachment double frame
64 Engine compressor face
65 Ram air intake
66 Engine oil tank
67 Bleed air system 'blow-off' valve
68 Fuselage break point, engine removal
69 Lyulka AL-7F-1 turbojet
70 Afterburner duct
71 Fin root fillet
72 Autopilot controller
73 Starboard upper airbrake, open
74 Rudder power control unit
75 Artificial feel unit
76 Tailfin construction
77 VHF/UHF aerial fairing
78 RSIU (very short wave fighter radio) aerial
79 Tail navigation light
80 Sirena-3 tail warning radar
81 Rudder
82 Brake parachute release tank
83 Brake parachute housing
84 Parachute doors

This rather attractive three-colour camouflage is used on most front-line aircraft of the Force Aérienne Algérienne (Algerian air force), which among other Soviet-supplied equipment has two squadrons dedicated to ground-attack operations using these Su-7BMs. The air-bleed port outside the engine is outlined in red.

85 Engine exhaust nozzle
86 Port all-moving tailplane
87 Static discharger
88 Tailplane anti-flutter weight
89 Tailplane construction
90 Pivot mounting
91 Tailplane limit stops
92 Variable area exhaust nozzle flaps
93 Nozzle control jacks
94 Fin/tailplane attachment fuselage frame
95 Afterburner cooling air intake
96 Rear fuselage frame and stringer construction
97 Insulated tailplane
98 Airbrake housing
99 Hydraulic jack

100 Tailplane power control unit
101 'Odd rods' IFF aerials
102 Port lower airbrake, open
103 Engine accessories
104 Jettisonable JATO bottle
105 Port Fowler flap
106 Port wing integral fuel tanks
107 Aileron control rod
108 Port aileron construction
109 Static discharger
110 Wing tip fairing
111 Port navigation light
112 Wing tip fence
113 Pitot tube
114 Wing rib and stringer construction
115 Port outer stores pylon

116 UV-16-57 rocket launcher pack
117 Auxiliary fuel tank, inner pylon
118 Port mainwheel
119 Low-pressure 'rough-field' main undercarriage
120 Inner stores pylon
121 Port wing fence
122 Mainwheel doors
123 Main undercarriage leg strut
124 Leg shortening link
125 Hydraulic retraction jack
126 Wing fuel tank filler cap
127 Port mainwheel bay
128 Main undercarriage up-lock
129 Aileron power control unit
130 Retractable landing lamp
131 Ammunition tank (70 rounds per gun)
132 30-mm NR-30 cannon

133 Cannon pressurization bottle
134 Ventral gun gas venting intake
135 Radar altimeter
136 Fuselage pylon, port and starboard
137 Twin fuselage mounted auxiliary fuel tanks
138 551-lb (250-kg) concrete piercing bomb
139 1,102-lb (500-kg) HE bomb

The original pre-production batch of Su-7s had been warmly received, and by 1957 numerous suggestions from the user had been added to improvements recognized as desirable by the OKB in the second batch of development aircraft designated S-2, S-21, S-22 etc. Unlike the delta interceptor, which worked its way through many further generations of development, the S-2 sub-family led straight to a production run of several hundred identical attack aircraft designated Su-7B. These entered service with the FA (*Frontovaya Aviatsiya*, or frontal aviation) before March 1959.

The aircraft were typically Russian, with the maximum design simplicity and robustness for troublefree service with minimal servicing in the harshest environments. The wing has no dihedral, a fixed leading edge with no dogtooth or slot, and only very modest fences at the inner and outer ends of the powered ailerons. Large flaps of modified Fowler type make a great difference at low speeds, and the all-round good handling has always made these aircraft perhaps more popular than their capability warrants. The cockpit is pressurized and air-conditioned, and offers an excellent all-round view thanks to the raised aft-sliding canopy. The levered-suspension landing gear cushions the roughest airstrips, and powerful multi-disc brakes, quadruple airbrakes on the removable rear fuselage and a ribbon parachute in a ventral box all assist quick stopping. The inbuilt punch comprised two of the extremely powerful NR-30 guns in the roots of the wing, fed by curved magazines between the engine duct and fuselage wall holding 70 (maximum 73) rounds per gun.

The wing was designed for four pylons, two rated at 1,653 lb (750 kg) ahead of the main gears and two at 1,102 lb (500 kg) just inboard of the inner fences. But on almost every mission the internal fuel capacity of 7,011 lb (3180 kg) was insufficient, and with the two side-by-side ventral drop tanks adding the necessary extra 2,094 lb (950 kg) the total weapon load had to be limited to an unimpressive 2,205 lb (1000 kg). To put this in perspective, it is no better than that of small fighters of World War 2, and much less than the bomb load of any modern respectable basic jet trainer.

Dual trainer

In 1961, when 21 Su-7Bs took part in the Tushino parade, the Su-7BKL entered service with numerous small changes including a nose pitot boom mounted on the upper right of the nose instead of at the top ahead of the windshield, and two prominent duct fairings along the upper sides of the centre fuselage. A tandem dual trainer, the Su-7U, went into production at about this time, with a rather clumsy arrangement of tandem clamshell canopies and a dorsal spine joining the rear canopy and fin. This was not positively identified in the West until 1967, when it was given the name 'Moujik'.

By 1966, if not earlier, deliveries had switched to the Su-7BM with the uprated (24,250-lb/11000-kg rather than 22,046-lb/10000-kg thrust) AL-7F-1 engine, larger blast panels in the fuselage skin beside the gun muzzles, twin braking parachutes repackaged in a long box under the

Starting the Lyulka engine of an early Su-7BMK close-support aircraft of the CL (Czech air force). Czechoslovakia at one time had 70 of these in front-line duty, with as many in reserve, but most have now been relegated to operational training. The twin drop tanks are an essential fit for most missions.

rudder and other changes including the first ECM (electronic countermeasures) suite. The new braking parachutes were for pulling up on short strips, and rough-field capability was further improved in the mass-produced Su-7BMK by fitting larger tyres of lower inflation pressure (also done to other VVS-FA types at this time), the nosewheel doors being blistered to clear the new tyre. Two large solid take-off assistance rockets could be clipped under the rear fuselage. In parallel the trainer moved into Su-7UM and Su-7UMK versions.

Well over 1,000 of the Su-7BM and Su-7BMK models were exported. Some 600 of these saw war service, suffering heavy losses in Egypt, Syria and India, the total of losses in action in these three countries in 1967–73 exceeding 240. A lot of blame can probably be attributed to inexperience and bad tactics, and the Egyptians never lost their high regard for even these primitive Sukhois. Production of these variants cannot have been less than 2,000, completed in about 1972.

During the early 1960s V/STOL was intensively studied by Soviet designers, and the rival merits of fuselage jet-lift engines and variable-sweep wings were evaluated. Jet lift was flown on an early Su-15 twin-jet interceptor, but not on a member of the Su-7 family where the problems were almost insuperable. But swing wings looked promising, and in partnership with TsAGI a scheme was drawn up for fitting pivoting outer panels to the existing airframe, though with a new wing centre section (much the same was done to other aircraft including the much larger Tupolev Tu-22). The S-22I (I for *Izmenyaemaya strelovidnostyu*, or variable-sweep) flew very successfully in 1966 and was displayed at the Aviation Day show in 1967. Though flown impressively at that show, and called 'Fitter-B' by NATO, the half-span pivot location and general air of improvization resulted in the Western assessment being a dismissal of the S-22I (also called Su-7IG, the suffix meaning variable-geometry) as an unimportant one-off of which nothing more would be heard.

Though some of the CL (Czech air force) tactical aircraft are uncamouflaged, most are now finished in the standard Warsaw Pact scheme for aircraft in this category, including this Su-7BMK, illustrated with tanks under the wings as well as the usual twin belly pair. No bombs can be carried in these circumstances.

Despite its remarkable age, the Polish air force still owed around 50 Su-7 'Fitter A's in combat service in the mid-1980s. Here the aircraft are being fitted with brake parachutes. (Photo: M. Taylor)

Sukhoi Su-7

This Lyulka-powered Su-20 of the Egyptian air force was originally assigned in 1977 to the 55th Strike Squadron. On the nose is the individual aircraft number 3536 in

Arabic numerals. Note the clamshell canopy with rear-view mirror, and the four tanks yet vacant inboard wing pylons for bombs or other stores of 1,000 lb (454 kg) each.

٣٥٣٦

A totally different species from earlier Sukhois, the final sub-family have many of the features of late-model MiG-21s with deep fuselage spines giving reduced drag yet increased internal fuel. This Su-20 'Fitter-J' of the Libyan Arab air force is one of the Tumansky-powered single-seaters which may represent the final development.

Single enormous fences were noted at the pivot location, their lower edges incorporating weapon or tank pylons. Small changes were seen in the ailerons, flaps and landing gear, and the new outer wings were fitted with full-span slats and inboard slotted flaps usable at minimum sweep only. There was some disagreement among Western analysts over the capability of the Su-7IG and the pessimists won, claiming it was not worth studying.

It was thus no small surprise when from 1971 production swing-wing 'Fitters' began to appear in the VVS and also in the Polish air force; less than two years later versions were in squadron strength in a growing number of Arab air forces. This prompted an urgent reappraisal which disclosed that the swing-wingers had the much more powerful AL-21F-3 engine (which in fact has a lower specific fuel consumption than the AL-7 and extends range) and a very much refined airframe, the most obvious change being the dorsal spine from the new clamshell canopy to the modified fin. Called 'Fitter-C', this machine, which is actually the basic Su-17 in VVS service, carries twice the bomb load of the Su-7BMK a distance 30 per cent farther from airstrips little more than half as long! The original appraisal had erred by more than 150 per cent.

By 1975 export versions were known to have the designation Su-20, and by 1977 Peru announced receipt of the Su-22, showing that the basic type was now regarded primarily as a bomber rather than a fighter (only fighters have odd service numbers). By 1980 it was realized that the VVS itself uses the Su-20 designation (attention to this may have been drawn by the correction of the supposed designation of Su-19 for the other and much larger Sukhoi bomber to the correct one of Su-24).

By 1975 the production Su-20 had improved air-data sensors on its pitot boom, with front and rear seats of cruciform relative-wind vanes. A year later a laser ranger and marked-target seeker began to look through a window cut in the underside of the inlet centre-body, and a small terrain-avoidance radar looked ahead from a new pod added along the underside of the nose. This version was dubbed 'Fitter-D' by NATO. About a year later the dorsal fin was enlarged to counter the degraded yaw stability of the under-nose fairing, though the original tails were not modified. Progressive advances in ECM fit occurred approximately each year, the overall fit reaching a very high standard by

1980. The first-generation swing-wing family included dual trainers, generally called Su-22U or 'Fitter-E' (instead of 'Moujik').

In the late 1970s it was suddenly noticed that production aircraft had a bulged rear fuselage, detailed study revealing the odd fact that this bulge is vertically asymmetric. Though full information is lacking, and much of what follows is partly speculative, it is known that most Su-20 and -22 aircraft built since 1978 have the Tumansky R-29B engine, the same as that used by the MiG-27, which offers a much more modern propulsion system with more thrust and reduced fuel consumption, lower installed weight and less smoke. In 1986, the Su-21 ('Fitter-F') and Su-22 ('Fitter-G' and 'J') had appeared, the 'Atoll'-armed 'J' going to the Libyan air force.

As the current production 'Fitter-H' has a new wing, new tail, new fuselage and new engine, not much remains of the Su-7 but the maker's name. Nevertheless, it has the advantage, much appreciated in the Soviet Union, of being a derivative instead of a new type. For this reason some 650–850 of the chief swing-wing versions are in front-line VVS service and the best part of another 100 with AVMF (naval aviation) regiments near the Baltic, despite the parallel production of the Su-24. The swing-wing variants have probably roughly doubled the total production from 2,000 to 4,000. Export customers include Algeria, Czechoslovakia, Egypt, India, Iraq, Libya, Peru, Poland, Somalia, Syria, Vietnam and North and South Yemen.

Sukhoi attack fighter variants

S-1: original swept-wing prototype, flown spring 1955
Su-7: pre-production series for VVS evaluation
S-2: first of series prototypes
Su-7B: series derivative of S-22, AL-7F engine rated at 19,840-lb (9000-kg) thrust with full afterburner
Su-7BKL: relocated instrument boom, fuselage duct fairings
Su-7BM: twin brake chutes at base of rudder, AL-7F-1 engine rated at 22,046-lb (10000-kg) thrust with full afterburner, larger gun blast panels
Su-7BMK: short rough airstrip model with low-pressure tyres and RATO rockets
Su-7U: first tandem dual trainer
Su-7UM, UMK: trainers corresponding to BM, BMK
Su-7IG, S-221: prototype with pivoted outer wings
Su-17 (SU020) 'Fitter-C': first swing-wing production version, AL-21F-3 rated at 24,700-lb (11200-kg) thrust with full afterburner, extra fuel and weapons, dorsal spine behind clamshell canopy, better sensors
'Fitter-D': lengthened nose, terrain-following radar in undernose pod, laser receiver in inlet centrebody

'Fitter-E': trainer version of 'Fitter-C' with right gun only and downward-drooped nose to improve view from rear cockpit ('Moujik' name dropped)
'Fitter-F': Tumansky R-29B engine rated at 25,350-lb (11500-kg) thrust with full afterburner in bulged rear fuselage; improved sensors and avionics, two guns
'Fitter-G': completely redesigned tandem two-seater, some dual trainers and others with combat pilot and systems operator, usually Lyulka engine; very deep dorsal spine, down-sloping nose, extra fuel, tall clean-cut fin with narrow square top and small ventral fin; right gun only; laser receiver but no TFR
'Fitter-H': corresponding single-seater, with deep dorsal spine behind down-sloped clamshell canopy and tail fin; small ventral fin, both guns, eight pylons and enhanced avionics
'Fitter-J': corresponding single-seater with R-29B engine
'Fitter-?': the reporting name has not been published for the R-29B two-seater, though this was first seen in early 1980

174

McDonnell Douglas Phantom

A name to strike terror into the heart of an enemy and inspire confidence in the minds of its pilots; an aviation trump card which for two decades assured victory in the air. And yet this multi-record-breaking fighter started life as a loser, rejected by service experts who eventually came to depend on it as the backbone of their airpower.

From the very outset, the F-4 Phantom II with its roaring engines and twin vapour trails was the greatest and most powerful American fighter plane, but it was also the fastest, with the highest operating ceiling and the longest range. Although the Soviet Union had bigger, heavier and more powerful fighters, they were, like all other machines of this class, inferior to the Phantom in terms of manoeuvrability and weapons capacity.

Fighters are supposed to seem small, sleek and agile; and many would say a great fighter has to be beautiful. In 1958 a new fighter thundered off the runway at Lambert Field, the St Louis Municipal Airport, that was none of these things. It was a great jagged-looking juggernaut, as big as a World War 2 bomber and with two seats, two engines and the bulkiest midriff in any plane of its size. One of its first users, an officer of the US Navy, described it as 'awkward as a goose with drooping tail feathers and middle-aged spread'. A pilot from the US Air Force thought it 'so ugly I wondered if it had been delivered upside down'. This fighter was the F-4 Phantom II. It was to smash every record open to a fighter to break, outperforming its many rivals in speed, climb, weapon load, radar power and even safe slow flying, to the extent that it became the yardstick against which every other contemporary and even later fighter was to be judged.

Phantoms poured off the St Louis assembly line for 23 years. In financial terms it was the top fighter in all history,

in any country. And it all happened because the McDonnell Aircraft Company (MAC) lost out to a rival in May 1953 in the seemingly vital contract for the US Navy's first supersonic fighter.

MAC's exceptionally talented engineers did not give up, but instead set about planning a better fighter. Picking up every scrap of information about the US Navy's thinking and possible future requirements, MAC in 1954 produced a mock-up of the F3H-G, with two Wright J65 engines, four cannon and no fewer than 11 weapon pylons for heavy and varied military loads. In November 1954 MAC's persistence paid off in a US Navy contract for two prototypes, designated AH-1, similar to the F3H-G but with two of the outstanding new General Electric J79 engines when these were ready. This much more powerful engine opened up exciting possibilities in higher performance, and MAC's team redesigned the inlets and nozzles so that they could be reshaped and controlled to match the airflow exactly to different speeds and Mach numbers up to and beyond Mach 2.

So impressive was the potential of the AH-1 multi-role

An RAF Phantom FGR.2 from No. 43 Sqn, 'The Fighting Cocks' from Leuchars, intercepts a Soviet long range reconnaissance Tu-95 'Bear' away from UK airspace. It is just one of the many tasks this versatile aircraft carries out for the nations that fly it.

McDonnell Douglas F-4E Phantom II

Specification

Type: two-seat multi-role fighter

Powerplant: two 17,900-lb (8119-kg) thrust General Electric J7?GE-17 afterburning turbojets

Performance: maximum speed (clean) 1,432 mph (2304 km/h) or Mach 2.17; initial climb (clean) 49,800 ft (15180 m) per minute; service ceiling 62,250 ft (18975 m); operating radius (four AIM-7F Sparrows, one Mk 28 and two tanks) hi-lo-hi 422 miles (680 km); ferry range 1,611 miles (2593 km)

Weights: empty 30,328 lb (13770 kg); maximum loaded 61,795 lb (28055 kg)

Dimensions: span 38 ft 4 in (11.68 m); length 63 ft 0 in (19.2 m); height 16 ft 5 in (5.00 m); wing area 530 sq ft (49.24 m²)

Armament: one M61A-1 20-mm gun with 639/640 rounds; four AIM-7E2 or -7F Sparrow III missiles recessed under fuselage; centreline pylon for any tactical store including 3,020-lb (1370-kg) M118 HE, nuclear, fire, cluster or other bombs, SUU-16/A or -23/A gun pods, spray tank, tow target or air-to-ground rockets; four wing pylons for Shrike, Standard ARM, Walleye, Harm or other missiles (inner pylons only can carry one Sparrow, or twin Falcon, or twin Sidewinder or other missiles); wide variety of ECM pods and tanks

The Phantom II is now nearly 35 years old, aged for a fighter. And yet its performance makes it still a front-line combat plane, able to handle contemporary missions in both ground attack and air-to-air combat. JV308 was an F-4E-35-MC, serial 67-308, delivered in late September 1968, and soon thereafter sent to South East Asia to help equip the 388th Tactical Fighter Wing, based at Korat Air Base, Thailand. It fought in that war from then on, subsequently being transferred to the 432nd TFW at Udorn before returning to the United States in 1973.

attack aircraft that the US Navy examined it in detail. In April 1955 a US Navy delegation came to St Louis and told MAC to replan it as a pure fleet defence fighter, the F4H-1. Ten of the 11 pylons were removed, leaving just the centre-line position to carry a large jettisonable fuel tank; the guns were removed and replaced by four of the new Sparrow II air-to-air missiles, carried semi-submerged on the flat underside of the amazingly broad fuselage; and the nose was given an even more powerful and versatile radar, specially designed by the Air Arm Division of Westinghouse, managed by a second crew-member.

The AH-1 contract was switched to two F4H-1 Phantom II fighters in May 1955, and the first of these, with Bureau of Aeronautics number 142259, made its maiden flight at St Louis on 27 May 1958. From the start it was clearly a fighter of extraordinary potential, and it quickly won over the XF8U-3 — an excellent aircraft built by Vought, the company that had beaten MAC in 1953 — and went into full production. The complex wing and flap-blowing system was operative on the sixth F4H-1, and other additions included a more bulged and pointed radome housing a radar with a larger scanner dish, an infra-red detector in a streamlined pod just beneath the radome, underwing pylons to carry a Sparrow or two close-range Sidewinder missiles on each side, and an inflight-refuelling probe. As for measured flight performance, this so consistently exceeded the guaranteed figures that the sum of all the plus and minus percentages where the actual figures differed from the calculated guarantees added up to an unprecedented +75 per cent!

By 1959 Phantoms had begun to set the greatest collection of world records ever gained by a single aircraft type. The first was the absolute height record, on 6 December 1959, at 98,557 ft (30040 m). Next came the 310.7-mile (500-km) closed-circuit record, set by the US Marine Corps on 5 September 1960 (the pilot was the famed Col. Tom Miller). This record fell at 15 minutes 19.2 seconds, officially 1,216.76 mph (1958.19 km/h) but actually — taking into account the distance round the large-radius turns — closer to about 1,315 mph (2116 km/h). This run meant almost half an hour in full afterburner mode, far beyond the capability of any other Western fighter. Three weeks later the 62.1-mile (100-km) circuit fell at a time of 2 minutes 40.9 seconds, or 1,390.24 mph (2237.4 km/h); actually the tightly banked circle was 65.2 miles (104.9 km) long, giving a true speed over 1,459 mph (2348 km/h). Records across the USA followed, for which air-refuelling was used. On 28 August 1961 the US Navy took the low-level speed record at 902.769 mph (1452.87 km/h) in the hot and turbulent air just above the desert. On 22 November 1961 the king of records fell to the Phantom: the high-altitude straight-line speed record was captured, the mean of two runs in opposite directions being 1,606.3 mph (2585 km/h), almost Mach 2.6; this was achieved by the second prototype, modified to have water injection to cool the air entering the engines. Many other records followed, including time-to-height records that no other aircraft could approach: the 10,000-ft (3048-m) level was

This historic photograph shows the first F4H-1 prototype tucking up its wheels on its first take-off on 27 May 1958 from St Louis Municipal Airport. No major modification was needed, and with 23 development aircraft (later styled F-4A) the new fighter was cleared for carrier service by 1960.

McDonnell Douglas F-4E Phantom II cutaway drawing key

1 Starboard tailplane
2 Static discharger
3 Honeycomb trailing edge panels
4 Tailplane mass balance weight
5 Tailplane spar construction
6 Drag chute housing
7 Tailcone/drag chute hinged door
8 Fuselage fuel tanks vent pipe
9 Honeycomb rudder construction
10 Rudder balance
11 Tail warning radar fairing
12 Tail navigation light
13 Fin tip antenna fairing
14 Communications antenna
15 Fin rear spar
16 Variable intensity formation lighting strip
17 Rudder control jack
18 Tailplane pivot mounting
19 Tailplane pivot seal
20 Fixed leading edge slat
21 Tailplane hydraulic jack
22 Fin front spar
23 Stabilator feel system pressure probe
24 Anti-collision light
25 Stabilator feel system balance mechanism
26 Tailcone cooling air duct
27 Heat resistant tailcone skinning
28 Arresting hook housing
29 Arresting hook, lowered
30 Starboard fully variable exhaust nozzle

31 Rudder artificial feel system bellows
32 Fin leading edge
33 Ram air intake
34 Fuselage No. 7 fuel cell, capacity 84 US gal (318 l)
35 Engine bay cooling air outlet louvres
36 Arresting hook actuator and damper
37 Fuel vent piping
38 Fuselage No. 6 fuel cell, capacity 213 US gal (806 l)
39 Jet pipe shroud construction
40 Engine bay hinged access doors
41 Rear AIM-7E-2 Sparrow air-to-air missile
42 Semi-recessed missile housing

43 Jet pipe nozzle actuators
44 Afterburner jet pipe
45 Fuselage No. 5 fuel cell, capacity 180 US gal (681 l)
46 Fuel tank access panels
47 Fuel system piping
48 Tailplane control cable duct
49 Fuselage No. 4 fuel cell, capacity 201 US gal (761 l)
50 Starboard engine bay construction
51 TACAN aerial
52 Fuselage No. 3 fuel cell, capacity 147 US gal (556 l)
53 Engine oil tank
54 General Electric J79-GE-17A turbojet engine
55 Engine accessories
56 Wing rear spar attachment
57 Mainwheel door
58 Main undercarriage wheel well
59 Lateral control servo actuator
60 Hydraulic accumulator
61 Lower surface airbrake jack
62 Flap hydraulic jack
63 Starboard flap
64 Honeycomb control surface construction
65 Starboard aileron
66 Aileron power control unit
67 Flutter damper
68 Spoiler housing

69 Wing tank fuel vent
70 Dihedral outer wing panel
71 Rear identification light
72 Wing tip formation lighting
73 Starboard navigation light
74 Radar warning antenna
75 Outer wing panel construction
76 Outboard leading edge slat
77 Slat control linkage
78 Slat hydraulic jack
79 Outer wing panel attachment
80 Starboard wing fence
81 Fuel vent system shut-off valves
82 Top of main undercarriage leg
83 Outboard pylon attachment housing
84 Inboard slat hydraulic jack
85 Starboard outer pylon
86 Mainwheel leg door
87 Mainwheel brake discs
88 Starboard mainwheel
89 Starboard external fuel tank capacity 370 US gal (1400 l)
90 Inboard leading edge slat, open
91 Slat hinge linkages
92 Main undercarriage retraction jack

93 Undercarriage uplock
94 Starboard wing fuel tank, capacity 315 US gal (1192 !)
95 Integral fuel tank construction
96 Inboard pylon fixing
97 Leading edge ranging antenna
98 Starboard inboard pylon
99 Twin missile launcher
100 AIM-9 Sidewinder
101 Hinged leading edge access panel
102 Wing front spar
103 Hydraulic reservoir
104 Centre fuselage formation lighting
105 Fuselage main frame
106 Engine intake compressor face
107 Intake duct construction
108 Fuselage No. 2 fuel cell, capacity 185 US gal (700 l)
109 Air-to-air refuelling receptacle, open
110 Port main undercarriage leg
111 Aileron power control unit
112 Port aileron
113 Aileron flutter damper

114 Port spoiler
115 Spoiler hydraulic jack
116 Wing fuel tank vent pipe
117 Port outer wing panel
118 Rearward identification light
119 Wing tip formation lighting
120 Port navigation light
121 Radar warning antenna
122 Port outboard leading edge slat
123 Slat hydraulic jack
124 Wing fence
125 Leading edge dog tooth
126 Inboard leading edge slat, open
127 Port external fuel tank, capacity 370 US gal (1400 l)

128 Inboard slat hydraulic jack
129 Port wing fuel tank, capacity 315 US gal (1192 l)
130 Upper fuselage light
131 IFF antenna
132 Avionics equipment bay
133 Gyro stabiliser platform
134 Fuselage No. 1 fuel cell, capacity 215 US gal (814 l)
135 Intake duct
136 Hydraulic connections
137 Starter cartridge container
138 Pneumatic system air bottle
139 Engine bleed air supply pipe
140 Forward AIM-7 missile housing
141 Ventral fuel tank, capacity 600 US gal (2271 l)
142 Bleed air louvre assembly lower
143 Avionics equipment bay
144 Variable intake ramp jack
145 Bleed air louvre assembly, upper

Final model of fighter Phantom, the F-4E introduced more power and fuel and a more modern radar, and was later given an internal gun and slats. This F-4E was assigned to the 32nd TFW at Camp Amsterdam (Soesterberg), Netherlands.

The RF-4E is the ultimate multi-sensor reconnaissance version of the Phantom and has the powerful Dash-17 series engine and No. 7 fuel tank in the rear fuselage. This example, built wholly by McDonnell, serves with JASDF No. 501 Hiko-Tai at Hyakuri, Honshu.

Distinguished by its big engine nozzles and fin-cap ECM installation, this Spey-engined Phantom FGR.2 was armed with the excellent Sky Flash missile. This aircraft from RAF No. 19 Sqn, Wildenrath, West Germany, bears the low-visibility colour scheme.

161 HOBOS 2000-lb (907-kg) guided bomb
162 Nosewheel door
163 AIM-7E-2 Sparrow missile semi-recessed housing
164 Forward formation lighting
165 Air conditioning plant
166 Battery
167 Pilot's starboard side console
168 Ejection seat safety harness
169 Engine throttles
170 Port intake front ramp
171 Forward cockpit canopy cover
172 Port inboard wing pylon
173 Pylon attachments
174 Triple ejector release unit
175 Mk 84 low profile 500-lb (227-kg) bombs
176 Extended bomb fuses
177 Windscreen panels
178 Pilot's lead computing sight
179 Instrument panel shroud
180 Control column
181 Rudder pedals
182 Cockpit front pressure bulkhead
183 Refrigeration plant
184 Communications antenna
185 Nosewheel jack
186 Nose undercarriage leg strut
187 Twin nosewheels
188 Nosewheel torque links
189 Landing and taxiing lamps
190 Air conditioning ram air intake
191 Angle of attack probe
192 Ammunition drum 639 rounds
193 Rain dispersal duct nozzle
194 ADF antenna
195 Gun bay frame construction
196 M61A-1 20-mm rotary barrel cannon
197 Cannon fairing
198 AN/APQ-120 fire control radar
199 Radar antenna mounting
200 Gun muzzle fairing
201 Radar scanner
202 Radome
203 Pitot tube

146 Radar operator's Martin-Baker ejection seat
147 Safety harness
148 Face blind seat firing handle
149 Rear cockpit canopy cover
150 Front canopy hinges
151 Inter-canopy bridge section glazing
152 Radar operator's instrument console
153 Canopy jack
154 Port intake
155 Pilot's Martin-Baker ejection seat
156 Intake front ramp
157 Starboard intake
158 Bleed air holes
159 Boundary layer splitter plate
160 ALQ-72 electronic countermeasures pod (replaces forward Sparrow missile)

passed on each climb roughly 30 seconds after the start of the take-off run. Perhaps the most impressive new record was that for the 98,425-ft (30-km) level that in fact went on to top 100,000 ft (30480 m).

Phantoms joined the US Navy and US Marine Corps in December 1960, having set wholly new standards in almost all aspects of mission capability. The designations were changed in 1962 and the original F4H-1F model, of which 45 were built, became the F-4A. It was identified by a straight top line from the canopy to the fin, and a small radome with 24-in (0.61-m) scanner. The first quantity-production model was the F-4B, with a raised canopy, improved inlets and larger ducts feeding J79-8 engines rated at 17,000-lb (7711-kg) thrust, and a larger radome housing the APQ-72 radar with a 32-in (0.81-in) dish. Tests proved this model could carry eight short tons (16,000 lb/7258 kg) of weapons on five pylons, far more than the US Navy's heaviest bomber and much more than any tactical fighter then in service with the US Air Force. MAC built 637 of this model, and hundreds served in Vietnam flying carrier-based attack, land-based bombing with the US Marines, air-combat sorties (such as MiG-CAP – MiG combat air patrol) and even FAC (forward air control) directing strikes from a position next to surface targets.

So impressed was the US Air Force that, after prolonged tests, it decided in March 1962 to buy the Phantom as the standard weapon system of most wings in TAC (Tactical Air Command). At first designated F-110, the US Air Force model was almost at once restyled F-4C. It was a minimum-change aircraft, though the US Air Force felt it had to have larger lower-pressure tyres, self-contained cartridge/pneumatic starters for J79-15 (Dash-15) engines, anti-skid brakes, a receptacle for the 'flying boom' refuelling system, dual controls and various avionics changes. MAC delivered 583 between 1963 and 1966, and these too played a major role in the South East Asia war.

So successful was the F-4C that it led immediately to two new models. One was the RF-4C, a dedicated reconnaissance platform for the most advanced tactical reconnaissance of its era. The APQ-72 radar was replaced by a small APQ-99 set for mapping, terrain-following and collision-avoidance, with the rest of the re-shaped nose filled with forward-oblique, lateral and panoramic cameras. In the underside was installed a large SLAR (sideways-looking airborne radar) giving a high-definition picture strip along the flight-path.

Further back was placed an IR (infra-red, or heat) line-scan system giving a clear thermal-image film picture of the same area. Masses of special communications and electronics were installed from nose to tail. The US Air Force bought 505 of these, and the US Marines converted 46 F-4B fighters into RF-4B models similar in equipment to the RF-4C.

Outwardly not easy to distinguish from the more common fighter version, the RF-4C carries no armament yet costs more because of its sophisticated reconnaissance sensors and communications systems. Here a pair of RFs from the USAF 363 TRW leave Nellis AFB during the 1981 Red Flag exercise.

Land-based variant

The other new model triggered off by the F-4C was the F-4D, the result of a relaxation of the law that the US Air Force had to accept the F-4B with minimal changes. The folding wing and some other naval features were retained, but the F-4D introduced many avionic items tailored specifically for land-based missions against ground targets. An inertial navigation system was installed, together with improved radar, a lead-computing optical sight, weapon-release computer and an impressive suite of EW (electronic warfare) equipment. More powerful electric generators were installed, and the F-4D was made compatible with 'smart' bombs, the Maverick air-to-surface missile, the Falcon air-to-air missile and, later, many other new ordnance items. Many F-4D models lacked the undernose pod for an IR sensor. MAC delivered a useful 825 of this series, and they flew more hours in Vietnam than any other fighter except the F-100.

As the ultimate US Air Force model the F-4E was planned with improved avionics; and in the course of design in 1966 it was decided to fit the most powerful J79, the 17,900-lb (8119-kg) Dash-17A, and use the extra thrust to handle an added seventh fuel tank at the tail. The main change was planned to be a new radar, and Westinghouse finally came up with the all-solid-state APQ-120 offering much more capability in a smaller and lighter package in a slimmer nose. New Martin-Baker seats with zero/zero (at rest on the airfield) capability were fitted, and the tailplanes were given the inverted leading-edge slat previously seen on other models (F-4J, K and M). Deliveries of the F-4E began in 1967, but five years later frequent stall/spin accidents in Vietnam – caused by pulling tight turns at very low level with many

Wearing the camouflage now standard on Japanese (JASDF) tactical combat aircraft, this RF-4EJ is one of the multi-sensor reconnaissance version supplied to Japan from St Louis, initially for No. 501 Sqn. The JASDF fighter Phantoms, styled F-4EJ, were manufactured under licence in Japan.

In conformity with modern ideas about low-visibility insignia, this RF-4B is painted in the current low-contrast markings of Navy and Marine Corps combat aircraft. This RF-4B also bears the muted insignia of VMFP-3 photo-recon squadron, based at El Toro, California.

West German industry gained an important slice of the overall F-4 production programme, a proportion which increased with Phantoms built for the Luftwaffe. Two wings are equipped with the RF-4E, a version slightly simpler than the RF-4C; this one is in the markings of AG (Aufklärungs Geschwäder) 52 at Leck, in 2nd ATAF.

The F-4C was the original 'minimum-change' model for the US Air Force. This 1963-funded example, with infra-red seeker under the nose, was in 1980 serving with the 171st FIS of the Michigan ANG

The F-4D was the first land-based model designed specifically for US Air Force requirements, with emphasis on attack on surface targets. This example, without the prominent infra-red seeker under the nose, was flying in 1970 with the Imperial Iranian AF's 306th Fighter Sqn.

tons of ordnance on board, something never asked for in the original design – led to a new wing leading edge with giant slats instead of the blown droop flaps. The slatted wing not only dramatically cut the number of fatal accidents but also significantly reduced the turn radius and thus made the F-4E a better dogfighter. After much argument another change rectified what had been the Phantom's chief shortcoming: lack of an internal gun. Cannon could previously be carried in external pods, but in 1967 an M61 multi-barrel 20-mm cannon was fitted under the nose, fed by a drum of 640 rounds. This was a godsend to the Phantom pilots in Vietnam who had previously had to throw away their long-distance kill capability while closing to positive visual identification range, at which distance they had no gun with which to shoot down enemies.

Phantoms join the Royal Navy

In 1964 the Royal Navy decided to buy the Phantom and, after long development, the F-4K became operational in 1968–9. This is powered by Rolls-Royce Spey afterburning

turbofans, fed by enlarged ducts and with shorter but larger nozzles. Despite giving 20,350-lb (9231-kg) thrust, these engines actually resulted in a deterioration in performance except in range. Called Phantom FG.1 by the Fleet Air Arm, the F-4K model also introduced folding nose radar, a double-extending nose leg for British catapult take-offs, an inverted slat on the tailplanes and British avionics and equipment. The RN took 24, and 28 more went to the RAF which also bought 118 of an uprated version designated F-4M and with the British title Phantom FGR.2. This has increased-capacity landing gears and anti-skid brakes, as well as a completely new nav/attack system and many other updated avionic items which from 1975 included an analog-controlled radar warning system with aerials in a long flat-topped extension added to the top of the fin. External loads could include a giant EMI multi-sensor reconnaissance pod carried on the centreline.

In 1963 the US Navy and US Marines planned a second-generation Phantom based as closely as possible on the F-4B, and this matured as the F-4J. It has 17,900-lb (8119-kg) Dash-10 engines, an integrated missile/weapons control system with new radar, a seventh fuel tank, the slatted tail, Martin-Baker zero/zero seats, stronger landing gears, drooping ailerons and uprated electric generation. MAC built 522 of this version, completing in 1972. The F-4N is a remanufactured

Outside the United States the largest user of the Phantom II is Israel, whose Heyl Ha'Avir received 204 F-4Es, similar to this example, plus 12 of the RF-4E reconnaissance version. They have seen prolonged combat duty, extending over south Lebanon and Syria up to the present day.

McDonnell Douglas F-4E Phantom

The F-4N is the remanufactured and updated F-4B, in many respects equal to the F-4J but not incorporating the wing slats now flying on the F-4S (rebuilt F-4J). This F-4N flew with one of the most famous Navy fighter outfits, VF-111 'The Sundowners'.

Most costly of all versions of the Phantom, the F-4G is the Wild Weasel II electronic-warfare platform, 116 of which were produced in 1975–81 by rebuilding F-4Es. This example served with 81 TFS, 52 TFW, at Spangdahlem AB, West Germany.

F-4B with extensive new equipment, 227 of these being produced. Likewise the F-4S is a remanufactured F-4J with stronger fatigue-resistant airframe, leading-edge slats and inboard leading-edge flaps, totally new outer wings and updated fire-control avionics. By 1981 there were 300.

Wild Weasel

An even larger rebuild, the F-4G Advanced Wild Weasel, is the US Air Force's standard tactical platform for suppressing hostile radars, especially those for guiding surface-to-air missiles. The F-4G can be produced by rebuilding an F-4D or F-4E, but most in 1981 were F-4Es. The main new subsystem is the APR-38 RHAWS (radar homing and warning system) with 57 aerials all over the aircraft, including new emitters and passive receivers in a pod on top of the fin. Apart from AAMs (air-to-air missiles) for its own defence, the F-4G can carry such anti-radar missiles as the Shrike (all versions), Standard ARM (anti-radar missile) and Harm (high-speed Arm). A force of 116 aircraft was rebuilt, starting in 1978.

This massive sustained manufacturing programme has been boosted by numerous exports. One of the first was a loan of 24 F-4Es to Australia pending delayed delivery to the

RAAF of the F-111C. The West German Luftwaffe purchased 88 of a simplified and slightly different unarmed reconnaissance version called EF-4E, which opened the way to useful participation by German companies in all subsequent Phantom manufacture. After 1970 the West German government signed contracts for a further 175 of a dedicated fighter model, the F-4F, which at one time was expected to be a single-seater but finally crystallized as a somewhat simplified F-4E. Another F-4E variant was made in Japan. The first two F-4EJ fighters were made by MAC and flown to Japan. These were followed by eight sent out in kit form, and after successfully assembling and testing these, Mitsubishi made a further 130 F-4EJ Phantoms at Nagoya.

Other planes went to Greece (56), Iran (177), Israel (216), South Korea (19), and Turkey (40). 14 RF-4Es were flown from St Louis to Japan, and 16 Phantoms of the same type ordered by Iran stayed on the tarmac in St Louis because of the Iranian Revolution.

The Israeli Air Force was upgrading its F4s in 1986. First prototypes were fitted with Kfir-type canard surfaces and new avionics include Elta pulse-Doppler radar and other sophisticated combat gadgetry.

McDonnell Douglas Phantom II variants

XF4H-1

XF4H-1: two prototypes

F-4A: two 15,000-lb (6804-kg) J79-GE-2 engines (later GE-2A), Westinghouse APQ-50 radar, four recessed Sparrow III missiles (21 pre-production and 24 production)
TF-4A: trainer conversion of F-4A without arrester hook or combat equipment (small number of conversions)
F-4B: two 17,000-lb (7711-kg) J79-GE-8A/8B engines, raised cockpits with higher canopy, Westinghouse APQ-72 radar (637 built)

F-4B

RF-4B: unarmed reconnaissance derivative of F-4B with basically same equipment and systems as RF-4C (12 built for US Marine Corps)

RF-4B of US Marine Corps

DF-4B: RPV control aircraft (drone mother ship), rebuild of F-4B
QF-4B: pilotless RPV drone (44 converted from F-4B)
F-4C: two 17,000-lb (7711-kg) J79-GE-15 engines with cartridge starters, wider low-pressure main tyres, completely revised avionics with APQ-100 radar, ASN-48

inertial system, AJB-7 bombing system, LADD timer and AGM-12B Bullpup control panel, dual flight controls and inflight-refuelling boom receptacle instead of probe (583 built for USAF, but 36 passed to Spain)

F-4C

RF-4C: multi-sensor reconnaissance derivate of F-4C with longer nose housing cameras, APQ-99 forward-looking radar, APQ-102 SLAR and (in fuselage underside) AAS-18A IR linescan, with augmented EW subsystems and communications including HF with flush shunt aerial in sides of fin (505 built)

RF-4C Nose Section

F-4D: developed from F-4C to meet full requirements of USAF with APQ-109 radar fire-control, ASG-22 servoed sight, ASN-63 inertial system, ASQ-91 weapon release computer, and uprated generators; IR seeker under nose often removed (793 built for USAF and 32 for Iran; 36 USAF aircraft transferred to South Korea)

F-4D

F-4E: two 17,900-lb (8119-kg) J79-GE-17 engines, seventh fuel cell, longer but slimmer nose with APQ-120 radar fire-control; later fitted with M61 20-mm gun under nose and later still with leading-edge slats in place of blown droop flaps and Tiseo electro-optical target viewing system on left wing (831 built for USAF, plus 538

for export to West Germany, Israel, Iran, Greece, Turkey, Japan and South Korea)

F-4E

F-4EJ: variant of F-4E for JASDF (Japan) with tail-warning radar and interfaces with AAM-2 missiles (140 built, including 138 assembled or manufactured in Japan)
RF-4E: reconnaissance variant of F-4E with equipment generally as RF-4C (130 built for export customers West Germany, Japan, Israel, Iran, Greece and Turkey)
F-4F: two 17,900-lb (8119-kg) J79-MTU-17A engines and generally as F-4E but without seventh tank, stabilator slat and certain classified equipment items (175 built for West Germany, with German-supplied airframe sections)
TF-4F: small number of dual trainer conversions of F-4F
F-4G: defunct designation of 12 F-4Bs fitted with ASW-21 digital data-link, subsequently modified to F-4B standard but not included in F-4B total
F-4G: currently active designation of F-4D (2) and F-4E (116) rebuilt as Wild Weasel II EW aircraft with APR-38 system and various missile provisions
F-4H: not used, to avoid confusion with original F4H-1
F-4J: two 17,900-lb (8119-kg) J79-GE-10 engines; updated US Navy/Marine aircraft with Westinghouse AWG-10 pulse-doppler fire control, slatted stabilator and drooping (16½°) ailerons, AJB-7 bombing system, uprated generators (522 built)

F-4K: two 20,350-lb (9231-kg) Rolls-Royce Spey 202/203 engines, with AWG-11 fire-control with double-hinged folding radome, drooping ailerons, slatted stabilator, fuselage and ducts widened to handle increased engine airflow, strengthened main gears and double-extending nose leg, much British avionic equipment (52 built for UK)

Royal Navy F-4Ks (Phantom FG.1s)

F-4M: development of F-4K for RAF with F-4C wheels/tyres/brakes, no stabilator slat, AWF-12 fire control, Ferranti nav/attack system, British airframe sections; later updated with ECM fin-cap installation and Sky Flash missiles (118 built for UK)

Royal Air Force F-4M (Phantom FGR.2) showing Sky Flash missiles

F-4N: updated F-4B with remanufactured structure and avionic updating (228 rebuilt)
F-4S: updated F-4J with F-4N improvements plus manoeuvring slats on outer wings only (302 rebuilt)
F-4CCV: experimental research CCV (control-configured vehicle) aircraft with fly-by-wire controls, canard foreplanes and outboard flaperons (single aircraft rebuilt)

F-4J

North-American X-15: the black bullet

More than 16 years after its last flight, the North American X-15 remains the world's fastest and highest-flying aircraft. Remarkably, this brilliant feat of engineering was obtained at the cost of only one fatal accident. In the course of 199 flights between June 1959 and October 1968, the X-15 made exceptionally valuable contributions to many scientific fields.

Midway through World War 2, a number of piston-engined aircraft broke the sound barrier when diving. But there were serious aerodynamic problems involved in doing so, because at speeds above Mach 0.8 the laws of hydrodynamics no longer apply. If the flow velocity of air exceeds the speed at which sound is transmitted, the basic laws affecting the compressibility of gases start to change, and localised disturbances such as compression shock occur. It was obvious that the turbojet and rocket engines under development at the time would soon be attaining even higher speeds and thus creating even bigger problems. So scientists all over the world were agreed that the problems with compressibility needed to be solved.

In the United States, this quest was spearheaded by the National Advisory Committee for Aeronautics (NACA, the forebear of today's National Aeronautics & Space Administration), with Dr William F. Durand, its chairman of the Special Committee for Jet Propulsion, suggesting on 18 December 1943 that the US Army, US Navy, NACA, and the

The three X-15s were used for research purposes by the American Air Force the Navy and NASA.

North American X-15

Specification

North American X-15 (with large rocket engine)

Type: single-seat research aircraft

Powerplant: one Thiokol (Reaction Motors) XLR99-RM-2 single-chamber throttlable liquid-propellant rocket engine, with a thrust rating of 57,000 lb (25855 kg) at 45,000 ft (13716 m)

Performance: maximum speed 4,104 mph (6605 km/h); maximum altitude 354,200 ft (107960 m); typical range 275 miles (440 km)

Weights: empty 15,000 lb (6804 kg); maximum launch 33,300 lb (15105 kg)

Dimensions: span 22 ft 4 in (6.81 m); length 50 ft 9 in (15.47 m); height 13 ft 0 in (3.96 m); wing area 200 sq ft (18.58 m²)

After sustaining serious structural damage during an all-but-uncontrolled landing on 9 November 1962, the second X-15 emerged in 1964 after a major rebuild as the X-15A-2. With a lengthened fuselage and jettisonable external tanks increasing propellant capacity by 13,500 lb (6130 kg) the aircraft's engine burn time rose from 86 to 145 seconds, allowing at least Mach 6.5 to be reached at 100 per cent thrust. In reality the aircraft, piloted by William J. Knight, reached Mach 6.72 (over 4,520 mph/7273 km/h) at 102,100 ft (31120 m) on 3 October 1967 after 141.4 seconds of engine burn – the fastest winged flight to date.

In lieu of the Reaction Motors-designed XLR99-RM-1 powerplant, the first X-15 was fitted with two uprated XLR11 rocket engines for the initial test flights. With a modest 8,000-lb (3632-kg) thrust per engine, the first powered flight on 17 September 1959 saw Mach 2.11 easily attained.

Neil Armstrong, Forrest Peterson, Joe Walker and John McKay were all X-15 test pilots. Armstrong became world-famous as an astronaut.

aircraft industry define jointly the specification for a research aircraft to explore high transonic and low supersonic speeds. Subsequently, inter-service rivalries scuttled this joint effort and the USAAF funded the Bell X-1 and X-2 programmes while the USN sponsored the Douglas D-558-1 and D-558-2 series, with NACA co-operating in both projects.

The USAAF and Bell were first out of the gate as the X-1, dropped at 27,000 ft (8230 m) from the belly of a Boeing B-29 flying over Pinecastle Field in Florida, made its first un-powered flight on 19 January 1946. The X-1 first fired its XLR-11-RM-3 rocket engine during its twelfth flight on 11 April 1947; three days later the turbo-jet-powered Douglas D-558-1 of the US Navy was first flown. Of the two, it was the X-1 which rightfully gained the greater fame as, during the aircraft's 31st flight on 14 October 1947, Captain Charles E. Yeager became the first pilot to fly supersonically when he reached Mach 1.06 at 43,000 ft (13106 m) over Muroc Field, the future Edwards AFB in California's Mojave Desert. (Contrary to the story in the popular movie *The Right Stuff*, this was Yeager's 12th flight in the X-1, not his first!)

These two types of pioneering research aircraft were followed in February 1948 by the D-558-2 (first flown with a turbojet, then from October 1949 with a turbojet and rocket, and finally from September 1950 without a turbojet but with a more powerful rocket), in July 1951 by the X-1D, in June 1952 by the Bell X-2, in February 1953 by the X-1A, in September 1954 by the X-1B, and in December 1955 by the

X-1E. With the availability of these more capable aircraft, military and NACA pilots were able to reach greater and greater speeds: Mach 1.45 with the X-1 on 26 March 1948, Mach 1.88 on 7 August 1951 and Mach 2.005 (the world's first Mach 2+ flight) on 20 November 1953 both with the D-558-2, Mach 2.44 with the X-1A on 12 December 1953, and Mach 2.87 with the X-2 on 23 July 1956. Finally, the first Mach 3+ (Mach 3.196) flight was made on 27 September 1956 by Captain Milburn Apt in the ill-fated X-2. Like-wise, higher altitudes were progressively obtained until 7 September 1956 when the Bell X-2 reached 125,907 ft (38376 m). However, a high price had been paid for these results as, in addition to Captain Apt, two test pilots were killed while six of the 14 research aircraft (six X-1s, two X-2s, and six D-558s) were destroyed.

In June 1952, 10 months after acquiring the modified second prototype of the D-558-2 (then the fastest aircraft but still 17 months away from flying at twice the speed of

This is the view from the B-52 motherplane prior to launch of the X-15. Extensive wind tunnel tests were carried out by NACA to ensure an effective X-15/B-52 launch procedure from the special launch pylon once sufficient height had been obtained. For the X-15 pilot, an ejection seat was provided for use up to Mach 4.

sound), NACA had urged that the research programme be expanded to explore flight characteristics at speeds of Mach 4 to 10 and altitudes of 12 to 50 miles (19.3 to 80.5 km). This ambitious programme was beyond the financial reach of a single agency, however, and following numerous research studies representatives of NACA, the US Air Force and the US Navy met on 9 July 1954 to discuss the need for a hypersonic research vehicle and the eventual joint sponsoring of its acquisition and testing. More discussions followed until late 1954 when NACA and the two services were ready to request proposals from the industry. The gestation period for the highly successful X-15 had begun.

Four manufacturers responded to this invitation: Bell submitted its D-171 design, Douglas its Model 684 D-558-3, North American its NA-240, and Republic its Model AP-76. Initially the US Air Force representatives favoured the North American entry while their US Navy colleagues, pleased with the results so far achieved with the D-558-2, leaned towards the Douglas Model 684. In the end, however, the joint selection team agreed in September 1955 that the NA-240 was 'the most suitable for research and potentially the simplest to make safe for the mission'. Contract AF-(600)-31693, calling for three X-15 research aircraft, was awarded to North American Aviation, Inc. by the USAF in June 1956.

Following contract award, design of the NA-240 was refined: the all-moving upper portion of the vertical tail surfaces were revised to improve directional control at high speeds, and the originally planned split trailing-edge speed brakes constituting the rear portion of the upper vertical tail surfaces were replaced by large surfaces at the base of the dorsal and ventral fins. The landing gear, which at first was to be comprised of twin nosewheel and retractable metal skids beneath the centre fuselage, was modified by relocating the landing skids to the aft end of the fuselage. Another design change initiated during this phase was the replacement of the encapsulated emergency escape system by a conventional ejector seat of advanced design usable by the pilot for emergency egress at speeds up to Mach 4.

To withstand temperatures of up to 1,200°F (649°C) caused by aerodynamically induced friction, the North American design team, under the direction of Harrison Storms and Charles Feltz, planned from the outset to use titanium and stainless steel for most of the internal structure, while Inconel X nickel alloy sheets were to be used as skin coverings. Other noteworthy design features included the selection of small trapezoidal wing surfaces of thin section

The relatively small size of the X-15 is apparent as it is carried aloft under the mother plane. On this, the first flight, the X-15 carried not rocket fuel but hydrogen peroxide for control system operation. Trouble was encountered during the approach, but a safe landing was just possible at Edwards AFB.

(5 per cent, or 2 in/5.08 cm at the root and 0.375 in/0.95 cm at the tip), the use of the all-moving tailplane for roll control, and provision for a three-stick control system. A conventional central stick was to be used to control the aircraft in pitch and roll during low-speed atmospheric flight, a side-mounted stick was for use during acceleration and re-entry, and another side stick actuated reaction jets during exoatmospheric flight. The cockpit, with dualpane heat resistant glass panels and Inconel X construction, was pressurized and refrigerated; in addition, the pilot was to wear an MC-2 full-pressure suit.

Like previous US supersonic research aircraft, with the notable exception of the D-558-2 in its original configuration, the X-15 was to be powered by a rocket engine and air-launched. Its weight and size, however, precluded the launch of the X-15 by existing Boeing B-29 and B-50 mother aircraft. After briefly considering the modification of a Convair B-36 for this role, the contractor and the government selected the Boeing B-52 as the X-15 launch aircraft. Accordingly, a B-52A (serial number 52-003) and a B-52B (52-008) were delivered to North American to be modified as an

The first X-15 streaks upwards towards the boundary of the atmosphere and beyond. Such was the aircraft's performance that a new NACA/USAF tracking network was created, a 485-mile (780-km) corridor 50 miles (80 km) wide over California and Nevada with emergency landing sites on various dry lakes.

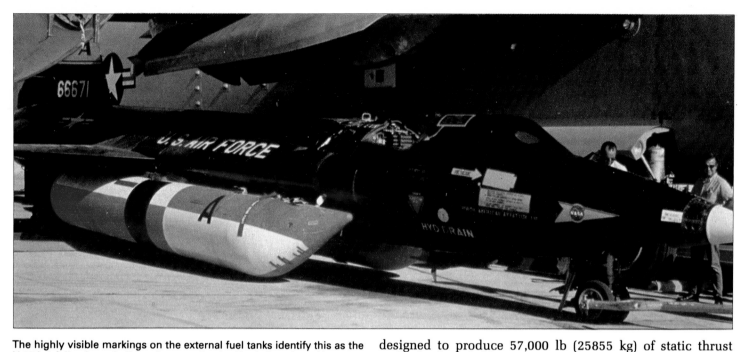

The highly visible markings on the external fuel tanks identify this as the X-15A-2 following rebuild and conversion by North American. Here the aircraft has left its ground pulley device and is about to be hoisted and attached to the underwing pylon visible immediately above.

NB-52A and an NB-52B respectively by installation of a launch pylon beneath the starboard wing, rocket fuel top-off tanks in the bomb bays, and observation and recording domes on the right fuselage side.

As originally proposed in 1955, the NA-240 was to have been powered by a Thiokol XLR30-RM-2 rocket, but during the detail design phase it was decided to replace this engine with a more powerful XLR99-RM-1. Burning a mixture of liquid oxygen and anhydrous ammonia, the XLR99 was

designed to produce 57,000 lb (25855 kg) of static thrust and to be throttled between 40 and 100 per cent. Its development, however, lagged behind that of the airframe. To avoid delaying the programme, North American proposed to start flight trials with two Reaction Motors XLR11s (improved versions of the rocket engine first used on the Bell X-1 in 1946). Even though the two XLR11s could generate a combined thrust of only 16,000 lb (7257 kg), only 28 per cent of that of the XLR99, the aircraft was still expected to reach a top speed of Mach 3.0. As this represented a worthwhile improvement over the then maximum speed of Mach 2.44 attained on 12 December 1953 by the Bell X-2, the contractor's proposal was endorsed by NACA and the two services.

Roll-out and flight trials
Component manufacturing for the first X-15 (US Air Force serial number 56-6670, constructor number 240-1) started in September 1956, and the aircraft was rolled out at the Inglewood plant 25 months later. Bearing US Air Force markings as this service was the contracting agency, the X-15 was trucked to Edwards AFB where preparations were made for the flight trials. To initiate these trials, North American

North American X-15A-2 cutaway drawing key

1 Hypersonic flow sensor
2 Nose cone
3 Power supply amplifier
4 Pitch control reaction jets
5 Yaw control reaction jets
6 Front equipment bay
7 Inconel-X skin plating
8 Heat insulating lining
9 Nosewheel bay
10 Undercarriage leg pivot
11 Nose undercarriage leg (shortens on retraction)
12 Free-fall nose undercarriage member
13 Twin nosewheels
14 Nosewheel door
15 Door air scoop
16 Pitot tube
17 Instrument panel shroud
18 Back of instrument panel
19 Rudder pedals
20 Antenna
21 Engine throttle control
22 Ballistic control column
23 Pilot's seat
24 Aerodynamic control column
25 Knife-edge cockpit canopy
26 Fused silica elliptical windows
27 Pilot's starboard side console
28 Safety harness
29 Port side console
30 Telescopic strut for ejection seat blast shield
31 Folded stabilizing vanes
32 Headrest
33 Cockpit canopy open position
34 Rocket powered ejection seat
35 Instrumentation inertia platform
36 Liquid nitrogen cooling system
37 Ventral antenna
38 Canopy insulation
39 Canopy hinge
40 Forward connecting link to NB-52 launcher pylon
41 Sprung doors to connectors
42 Stellar camera platform
43 Two oblique astronomical cameras
44 Two vertical astronomical cameras
45 Camera platform gimballed mounting
46 Systems equipment compartment
47 Control runs
48 Twin General Electric auxiliary power units
49 APU exhausts
50 Cooling system vent
51 Two APU generators
52 Starboard external fuel tank, anhydrous ammonia, 6,006 lb (2724 kg)
53 Starboard side fairing
54 Liquid oxygen vent
55 Liquid oxygen tank pressure bulkhead
56 Equipment cooling system liquid nitrogen tank
57 Reaction control jet HTP fuel tanks, port and starboard
58 Port external tank nose fairing
59 External tank front attachment
60 Recovery parachute
61 Parachute release link
62 Fuel tank pressurizing helium reservoir
63 Pipe runs in side fairing
64 Side fairing frames
65 Test and recording equipment
66 Liquid oxygen fuel tank
67 Fuel tank compartment bulkheads
68 Tank baffles
69 Welded Inconel-X fuel tank skins
70 Internal stiffeners
71 Liquid oxygen filler cap
72 Welded external tank stiffeners
73 Liquid oxygen supply pipe to engine
74 Liquid oxygen tank rear pressure bulkhead
75 Fuel pipes to roll control reaction jets
76 Liquid hydrogen fuel tank for ramjet engine
77 Access panels
78 Starboard wing panel
79 Roll control reaction jets
80 Interchangeable starboard wing tip
81 Wing tip instrumentation
82 Fixed trailing edge section
83 Starboard landing flap
84 Aft attaching links to NB-52 launcher pylon
85 Anhydrous ammonia main fuel tank
86 Tank dividing bulkheads
87 A-frame wing mounting struts
88 Flap jack attachment
89 Ammonia filler point
90 Ammonia fuel feed pipe
91 Inconel-X welded tank skins
92 Ammonia tank rear pressure bulkhead
93 Welded external tank stiffeners
94 Liquid oxygen feed pipe
95 Access panels
96 Turbopump HTP fuel tank, 64 US gal (242 litres)

North American X-15 variants

X-15 (initial configuration): for initial flight trials the first two X-15s (56-6670 and 56-6671) were powered by two four-chamber XLR11 rocket engines, each producing 8,000-lb (3629-kg) thrust

X-15 (final configuration): identical to the earlier configuration but with the XLR11 engines replaced by a 57,000-lb (25855-kg) thrust XLR99 engine; the first two X-15s were retrofitted with this engine while the third (56-6672, c/n 240-3) was originally fitted with the XLR99; for most of the later flights the ventral fin was removed to improve lateral stability during high angle-of-attack re-entry

X-15A-2: designation given to the second X-15 after it had been modified in 1963 to investigate higher speeds; two external propellant tanks were attached beneath the fuselage and the windshield design was improved; to withstand the higher temperatures caused by aerodynamically-induced friction, the X-15A-2 could be finished with M25S ablative coating

X-15 (with delta wing): proposed modification of the third X-15, which was to have had its straight trapezoidal wing replaced by a slender delta wing and scramjet engine mounted on its fin; this project was abandoned following the loss of the aircraft before modification

X-15 (satellite launcher): the use of the X-15 to launch a Scout satellite was considered briefly but rejected as being more expensive than conventional launch methods

Booster-launched X-15: North American proposed an **'X-15B'** as an alternative for the Project Mercury manned space programmel the 'X-15B' was to have used a Navaho missile booster for launch; the company later proposed the use of the X-15 as an expendable spacecraft to be launched into space by four Martin Titan rockets; neither project was realized

had already retained the services of A. Scott Crossfield, an experienced NACA test pilot who had flown the X-1, D-558-1, and D-558-2, and who on 20 November 1953 had made the world's first Mach 2+ flight. With Scott Crossfield strapped in the cockpit, the first X-15 was mated to the NB-52A launch aircraft for its initial unpowered flight on 8 June 1959. Control oversensitivity, noted during this flight, forced a postponement of powered flights until appropriate modifications had been made.

Powered flight trials began on 17 September 1959 when Scott Crossfield reached Mach 2.11 at an altitude of 52,341 ft

(15954 m) in the XLR11-powered second X-15 (56-6671, c/n 240-2). A near repeat flight was made one month later without problems, but the fourth flight on 5 November was marred by an engine fire and an emergency landing at Rosamund Dry Lake, during which fuselage structural failure occurred. Fortunately, Crossfield was not injured and 55-6671 was repaired to fly again on 11 February 1960 (the programme's sixth flight). NACA having been reorganized into the National Aeronautics & Space Administration during 1958, it was for NASA that Joe Walker made the X-15's ninth flight on 25 March 1960 to become the first government pilot to fly the type. Walker also became the first pilot to fly the X-15 at more than Mach 3.0 when he reached Mach 3.19 with the XLR11-powered first prototype on 12 May. Other agencies soon joined the flight trials: on 13 April 1960 Captain Robert White made the first USAF flight, and on 23 September 1960 Commander Forrest Peterson first flew the X-15 for the US Navy. Flown by the contractor's pilot and by government pilots, the X-15 made a total of 29 flights with the XLR11 engines, reaching a top speed of Mach 3.50 (2,275

97 Vertical stabilizer fixed stub section
98 Starboard all-moving tailplane
99 Instrumented leading wedge
100 Vertical stabilizer upper rudder section
101 Rudder spar pivot
102 Rudder jack
103 Communications aerial
104 Wedge section rudder
105 Helium tank to pressurize liquid nitrogen
106 Airbrake
107 Airbrake jack mechanism
108 Rocket chamber nozzle
109 Liquid oxygen jettison pipe
110 Turbopump lubrication tank
111 Engine mounting struts
112 Thiokol XLR99 rocket engine
113 Rear fuselage frames
114 Rocket engine turbopumps
115 Tailplane spar pivot
116 Tailplane jack
117 Port all-moving tailplane
118 Inconel-X tailplane construction
119 Port main landing skid
120 Skid lowering hydraulic jack strut
121 Position of wedge section ventral rudder, jettisonable for landing
122 Port landing flap
123 Square section trailing edge
124 Fixed trailing edge section
125 Inconel-X multi-spar wing construction
126 Roll control reaction jets
127 Leading edge construction
128 Inconel-X leading edge heat sink strip
129 Thermal expansion slots in leading edge
130 Port external fuel tank, liquid oxygen, 7,494 lb (3399 kg)
131 Mylar-type wrapped insulated tank skins
132 Auxiliary ramjet engine (replaces ventral rudder)
133 Ground handling wheeled dolly

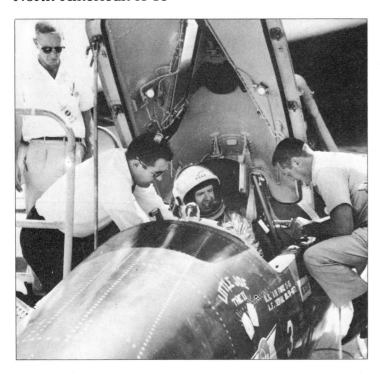

Joseph A. Walker, the test pilot for NASA in the X-15 programme, prepares for another flight during 1964. One of the original test pilot team, Walker made the government's first X-15 flight on 25 March 1960; and on 22 August 1963 flew X-15A-2 to 345,200 ft (107960 m) – a winged aircraft altitude record.

mph/3661 km/h) on 7 February 1961 when Captain White made the last XLR11-powered flight.

By then the second X-15 had already been re-engined with the XLR99 and had been flown thrice by Scott Crossfield. On its first flight in the hands of a government pilot, this aircraft reached Mach 4.43 on 7 March 1961. Maximum Mach was then progressively increased until 9 September 1961 when, piloted by Captain White, the X-15 flew at Mach 6.04 to achieve its original design speed. This performance was exceeded only once when on 5 December 1963 Major Robert Rushworth took the first X-15 (now fitted with its XLR99) to Mach 6.06 (4,018 mph/6466 km/h). Flying the same aircraft at a slightly lower Mach (Mach 5.92), but under conditions favouring true air speed, Joe Walker set an unofficial speed record of 4,104 mph (6605 km/h) on 27 June 1962. Maximum altitude flights took the X-15 above the 200,000-ft (60960-m) mark on 11 October 1961, to a record of 354,200 ft (107960 m) on 22 August 1963.

On 9 November 1962, following an engine malfunction, 56-6671 made an emergency landing without flaps at Mud Lake and rebounded; the left skid then collapsed and the aircraft ended on its back. The NASA pilot, John McKay, was hospitalized for surgery to crushed vertebrae and the X-15 was returned to the factory. Rather than rebuilding the aircraft to its original configuration, it was decided to take advantage of the forced programme delay to incorporate several modifications which would enable the X-15 to reach even greater speeds. On the basis of earlier tests, it was known that this was achievable relatively inexpensively and without undue risks by increasing the amount of propellant carried and thus increasing the rocket engine's burning time from 86 to 145 seconds, by modifying the windshield to eliminate the critical point of high thermal conditions, and by making use of an ablative coating to withstand higher aerodynamic heating problems (temperatures were expected to reach locally over 3,000°F/1649°C). The first goal was obtained by adding two large external tanks (the left tank containing liquid oxygen, and the right one anhydrous

ammonia), while the second necessitated the substitution of three-pane elliptical windshields in place of the two-pane rectangular units used initially. The resin and glass bead powder M-25S ablative coating was sprayed before very-high-speed missions and replaced after each flight.

Now designated X-15A-2, 56-6671 began new trials on 25 June 1964, without ablative coating or external tanks. The first test of the empty tanks was successfully conducted on 3 November 1965; but on 1 July 1966 the first mission with filled tanks had to be cut short. After careful planning, the X-15A-2 finally made the world's fastest flight on 3 October 1967 when Captain Knight flew at Mach 6.70 (4,520 mph/7274 km/h) with the use of the ablative coating and external tanks. During that flight, a dummy ramjet engine was attached beneath the aircraft's ventral stub fin. However, when aerodynamic heating burned through the ramjet pylon and created an emergency, Knight was forced to make an immediate landing at a weight exceeding design limits. The X-15A-2 was damaged beyond economical repair and was donated to the Air Force Museum.

Disintegration in flight

The third X-15 was less fortunate and its pilot, Major Michael Adams, lost his life on 15 November 1967 when the aircraft disintegrated in flight due to a combination of errors and mechanical failures. During 1968, the remaining aircraft (56-6670) made eight more flights, the last taking place on 24 October. Five additional flights were attempted with this aircraft but weather forced their cancellation, thus depriving the manufacturer, the sponsors and the pilots of the satisfaction of obtaining the type's 200th flight. The X-15 programme was then terminated and 56-6670 went to the Smithsonian Institution's National Air and Space Museum.

Altogether, the first X-15 made one unpowered flight, 20 flights with the XLR11 rocket motor and 60 with the XLR99; the second aircraft had flown nine times with the XLR11, 22 times with the XLR99, and 22 times in the X-15A-2 configuration; and the third aircraft made 65 flights with the XLR99. Fourteen of these flights were by North American's test pilot A. Scott Crossfield, five were by Commander Forrest S. Peterson for the US Navy, 89 by five US Air Force pilots (Majors Michael J. Adams and Robert A. Rushworth, and Captains Joseph H. Engle, William J. Knight, and Robert M. White), and 91 flights by five NASA pilots (Neil A. Armstrong, William H. Dana, John B. McKay, Milton O. Thompson, and Joseph A. Walker). Major Rushworth, USAF, made 29 flights to become the most experienced X-15 pilot.

The X-15A-2 is about to be launched from the NB-52B for its last and eventful flight on 3 October 1967. Noteworthy are the ablative coating, the two large jettisonable propellant tanks, and (albeit barely visible) the dummy ramjet beneath the ventral fin. Before making an emergency landing at the end of this flight, the X-15A-2 became the world's fastest aircraft when it took William Knight to a remarkable 4,520 mph (7274 km/h), or Mach 6.70.

Lockheed SR-71 'Blackbird'

The SR-71 began life on the drawing board almost a quarter of a century ago. Maintained in service at incredible effort and expense, and with no replacement in sight, Strategic Air Command's few SR-71s are still so secret that many details of the aircraft's performance and history have never been revealed.

The story of Lockheed's Blackbird series of high-speed, high-altitude reconnaissance planes goes back to 1958. Ostensibly, the CIA declared that it could no longer rely on the Lockheed U-2 for its overflights of the Soviet Union because despite its cruising altitude of around 70,000 ft (21,500 m) it was no longer safe from fighters and ground-to-air missiles.

Whether or not this story is true may never be revealed, but the CIA could well have originated such studies of a U-2 replacement. In the event, Gary Powers' U-2 was shot down near Sverdlovsk by an SA-2 on 1 May 1960, and it may well have been only on Powers' release that it was discovered that he had fallen asleep during his final mission, and had allowed the aircraft to descend to 47,000 ft (14325 m), where it came within the reach of ground defences. Hence higher reconnaissance may have been in demand from 1960 onward.

However, Clarence ('Kelly') Johnson, at that time head of Lockheed's Advanced Development Projects group, known less formally as 'The Skunk Works', said in subsequent lectures that the project began as a long-range interceptor. Sources within the USAF have been quoted as saying that the original requirement called for an altitude capability of at least 106,000 ft (32310 m). It is also known that the development contract was awarded to Lockheed in August 1959, following competitive bidding by Boeing, General Dynamics and North American.

Whatever the original basis for the programme (and it is quite possible that the USAF and CIA collaborated in funding an aircraft that would form the basis for both an interceptor and a high-altitude reconnaissance penetrator), the problems facing Lockheed were probably the most difficult that have ever been posed to an aircraft manufacturer. To put the required technological advance into perspective, consider the fact that the highly advanced Lockheed F-104A, which could reach 60,000 ft (18290 m) and touch Mach 2.0 for a few minutes, had just begun to be delivered to the USAF in 1958. Now the company had to design something that could cruise at Mach 3.0 for sustained periods, at much higher altitudes. High Mach numbers had certainly been attained by experimental aircraft, using the brute force of rocket engines in the thin air of the upper atmosphere, but this new design would need much more refined aerodynamics, together with materials to enable the structure, windscreen and radomes to withstand high temperatures over long periods, and engines and aircraft systems to match. If ever an aircraft was designed completely from scratch, this was the one.

Long range

Aerodynamically speaking, instead of designing a fighter, Lockheed produced a small supersonic airliner in order to achieve the high values of lift/drag ratio and fuel fraction that were required to attain long range. This was a completely different approach to that adopted in the Soviet Union with the Mikoyan-Gurevich MiG-25 'Foxbat', which is believed to have first flown in 1963, can attain similar speeds and is much more manoeuvrable, but has far less range.

In order to achieve long range, Lockheed had to emphasize low drag in the cruise condition at the expense of other performance aspects such as turn rate and airfield require-

One of the first photographs released for publication, this side-view of a YF-12A revealed nothing whatever of the aircraft's revolutionary wing planform. The full serial was 60–6934, and it may be distinguished as a YF-12A by the cut-back chine at the nose and the three underfins, the centre one folded to the side.

Three of the Lockheed A-11 batch were built to a modified standard to serve as prototypes for a Mach 3 interceptor that would have been capable of providing air defence against supersonic Russian bombers. The resulting YF-12A had cut-back chines, three underfins, a radar nose and four Hughes XAIM-47 missiles in the chines.

Many of the Lockheed SR-71 Blackbird's technical details are still strictly secret. With its maximum speed of more than three times the speed of sound, and a cruising height of about 82,000 ft (25,000 m), it is still the fastest and highest-flying aircraft in the world. (*Photo: Lockheed*)

ments. Low drag at Mach 3 implied a highly swept delta wing. Since the engines and the long fuselage (needed to house a vast amount of fuel and to bring the centre of gravity forward) projected ahead of the wing, they were given 'chines' to make them act as lifting surfaces and to improve directional stability. The fuselage was canted up relative to the thrust line, to make it act as a fixed lifting canard.

One of the disadvantages of the delta wing is that the vertical tail tends to be ineffective at high angles of attack (AOA). Lockheed therefore replaced the conventional single fin over the rear fuselage with two vertical tails on the engine nacelles. The customary wind tunnel tests were run to measure drag and predict handling characteristics, but in some respects the latter objective proved difficult to attain, since the fuselage flexes appreciably under inertia and aerodynamic loads, and since it is distorted by the cooling effect of the fuel in contact with the undersurface.

Fortunately, the very high temperatures created by kinetic heating from the surrounding air were predicable with accuracy. These structural temperatures range at cruise speed from 800°F (425°C, hotter than a soldering iron) – around the leading edges and intakes to 450–500°F (230–260°C, hotter than the maximum temperature in a household oven) for most of the wings and fuselage. The outside skin temperatures around the rear of the engine nacelles reach 900–1,100°F (480–595°C). The jetpipes glow white hot, even with the minimum afterburner setting required in cruise, so bright that they can be used as a reference in night-time formation flying.

High temperature problems

To cope with these extremely high temperatures for lengthy periods, approximately 93 per cent of the structure was designed in titanium alloy, although this involved extremely high costs and required the development of new fabrication techniques. Likewise, conventional fuels could not be used. These aircraft use JP-7, which has a very low vapour pressure and is fully compatible with high temperature operation, although it is contained in integral tanks with no insulation between the fuel and the aircraft skin. Conventional lubricants (oils and greases) are likewise unusable in such aircraft: the specially developed oil used in the Pratt & Whitney J58 engines has to be preheated to 86°F (30°C) before each flight. Hydraulic fluid and seals, electrical connectors, windscreen transparencies, radomes and wiring were other problem areas resulting from the high temperatures encountered in flight.

Lockheed SR-71A serial 64–17955 shortly after touchdown, with braking parachute deployed. Note the parachute housing on top of the rear fuselage, the upward angle on the elevons, the unique three-abreast mainwheel arrangement (unusually for an American aircraft, the doors are left open), and the forebody chine.

In order to reduce the problems of structural expansion caused by the heat, chordwise corrugations were incorporated in the wing skin. To minimize the heat problems of the main landing gear, the wheels are retracted into the fuselage, where they can be cooled more easily than in the wing. The wing fuel is used first (during the climb) because of the heating problem caused by the disproportionately large surface area of these thin, flat tanks. The whole aircraft is painted in a special high-emissivity dark blue paint (visually indistinguishable from black), which emits heat at 2103 times the rate of unpainted titanium, and gives a surface temperature reduction of 25–50°F (14–28°C) during cruise.

The J58 engine (manufacturer's designation JT11D-20B) is a single-spool afterburning turbojet with a high titanium content. In order to minimize the probability of surging at high speeds, air is bled continuously from the fourth compressor stage and ducted to the afterburner, where it reduces operating temperatures and improves thrust augmentation. As stated above, the JP-7 fuel has little tendency to vaporize at normal temperatures, and it has been reported that a lighted match can safely be dropped into a pool of JP-7 without the fuel catching fire! Because of this characteristic, engine and afterburner ignition have to be achieved chemically, rather than electrically: triethyl borane (TEB) is injected, producing instant combustion on coming into contact with the JP-7. For inflight-refuelling, the JP-7 is carried in special tanker aircraft, designated KC-135Qs.

The engine is fed with air through a conical multi-shock intake with a translating spike, which is automatically angled to compensate for AOA and sideslip. It exhausts via an ejector nozzle with blow-in doors. According to Lockheed, the hardest design problem was to make the engine inlet and exhaust work correctly. The inlet cone translates through a distance of almost 3 ft (91.4 cm) to keep the shock wave pattern in the optimum position, the force required from the hydraulic actuator being almost equal to the maximum static thrust of the engine.

To revert to the history of the 'Blackbird' series, the first A-11 had its maiden flight in great secrecy on 26 April 1962, some 32 months from signature of contract, an incredibly short gestation period for such an advanced aircraft. The

Lockheed SR-71

Specification

Lockheed SR-71A 'Blackbird'

Type: tandem-seat strategic reconnaissance aircraft

Powerplant: two afterburning Pratt & Whitney J58 turbojets, each of 29,750-lb (13494-kg) static thrust (Mks B, C. Pratt & Whitney J 58-1 (JT) 11D-20B continuous bleed after burning turbojets of 32,500 lb (14.742 kg))

Performance: maximum speed 2,189 mph (3523 km/h); operational ceiling approximately 85,000 ft (25908 m); range at least 3,300 miles (5311 km) without flight refuelling

Weights: (estimated) empty 60,000 lb (27215 kg); maximum take-off weight 145,000 lb (65770 kg) (later 170,000 lb (77.112 kg))

Dimensions: span 55 ft 7 in (16.95 m); length 107 ft 5 in (32.74 m); height 18 ft 6 in (5.64 m); wing area 1,800 sq ft (167.3 m²)

All the external design features of the Lockhead SR-71A are to be seen in this illustration which also shows the fact that the 'Blackbird' is really painted a very dark blue. The wing planform is basically a delta, although there is considerable taper on the trailing edge, rounded tips, and cut-outs for the engine exhausts. Despite the long inboard chords, the wing is relatively thin, as shown by the head-on view. This also brings out the wing-body blending and the camber of the outboard leading edge, which in some photographs makes the wing appear to be kinked. Immediately aft of the two-seat cockpit is a window for the Northrop astro-inertial navigation system, and the flight refuelling receptacle.

Lockheed 'Blackbird' variants

A–11: initial model including original prototype; 18 aircraft built, of which three were converted to YF–12As; some A–11s were used operationally in the reconnaissance role.

YF–12A: three aircraft converted from A–11 to evaluate potential as an interceptor armed with four AAMs

YF–12C: YF–12A with longer fuselage and second cockpit, used as prototype for SR–71

SR–71A: standard reconnaissance version; 31 believed built, of which two were converted to SR–71Bs in the course of construction; approximately nine still in operation, but others held in reserve

SR–71B: pilot-training version with raised rear cockpit and two small underfins added below the nacelles to offset the effect of the cockpit on directional stability; two built, one written off

SR–71C: pilot-training version externally identical to SR–71B, but possibly different equipment standard; one built flight took place at a location often referred to simply as 'The Ranch', and more formally known as Watertown Strip at Groom Dry Lake, Nevada. How the aircraft came to be designated A-11 has never been explained; the preceding Lockheed F-104 began life as the Model 83. However, the company appears to refer to the latest of its more secret designs merely as 'The Article', hence it is possible that the design that went ahead in 1959 was simply the 11th drawing in that series of 'Articles'.

The number of A-11s built has never been declared officially, but some sources put the number as high as 18, with serials running from 60–6924 to 60–6941. Of these, three (60–6934, 60–6935 and 60–6936) were built to a modified standard to become interceptor prototypes under the USAF designation YF-12A (possibly also designated A-12). One aircraft (66–6937) was built with a longer fuselage providing for a second cockpit and extra fuel, and increasing overall length from 101 ft (30.78 m) to 107 ft 5in (32.74m). It was designated YF-12C, and served as the prototype for the SR-71 reconnaissance aircraft. In the original A-11 and the SR-71 the fuselage chines were extended right to the nose of the aircraft. In the case of the YF-12A the chines were cut back to clear the nose radome, and this (combined with the fatter nose) reduced directional stability, so a folding centre-line underfin was added, together with two fixed stub-fins under the nacelles.

Announcement of project

The large tracts of land owned by the US Department of Defense made possible flight tests in complete secrecy (they are being used today to test 'Stealth' prototypes), and it was only on 29 February 1964 that the existence of the basic A-11 was disclosed, when President Lyndon B. Johnson made a brief statement on the project. At that time the only photographs released were side-views of the aircraft (60–6934, buzz number FX-934) on the ground, giving no clue to its wing planform. However, on 24 July 1964 the existence of the SR-71 project was revealed by President Johnson, and on 30 September a YF-12A was shown to the public at Edwards AFB, and its wing planform and chine configuration were finally unveiled.

The original role of the SR-71 is still something of a mystery, since its designation does not fit into any established series. The most widely accepted explanation is that the aircraft was really designated RS-71, following the North American RS-70 Mach 3 strike aircraft project (which sparked off development of the MiG 25), and that the President simply mixed up the two letters. Rather than admit his mistake, his staff then explained the 'SR' designation as meaning strategic reconnaissance.

This aircraft (serial 64–17956) was originally built as a standard SR-71A, but was later converted (along with 64–17951) to a SR-71B trainer. After one of these aircraft crashed, a further SR-71A (64–17981) was converted for pilot training and designated SR-71C, although the distinction from the SR-71B is not clear.

On the other hand, if the SR-71 began life as a strike aircraft with a secondary reconnaissance capability, how was it to deliver its warload? The YF-12A had had four relatively small Hughes XAIM-47 air-to-air missiles buried in the front fuselage chines (to be guided by a Hughes ASG-18 radar), but this method of stowage was not suitable for a multi-megaton warhead. Perhaps the obvious solution was to house the warhead in an external pod, as was done in the case of the Convair B-58A Hustler, which first flew in 1956.

Lockheed SR–71 'Blackbird' cutaway drawing key

1 Pitot tube
2 Nose mission equipment bay
3 Detachable nose cone joint frame
4 Cockpit front pressure bulkhead
5 Rudder pedals
6 Control column
7 Instrument panel
8 Instrument panel shroud
9 Knife edged windscreen panels
10 Engine throttle levers
11 Oxygen cylinder
12 Pilot's ejection seat
13 Upward hinged cockpit canopy cover
14 SR–71B dual control trainer variant
15 Raised instructor's rear cockpit
16 Reconnaissance systems officer's (RSO) canopy cover
17 RSO's zero-zero ejection seat
18 Side console panel
19 Cockpit environmental system equipment bay
20 Rear pressure bulkhead
21 Canopy hinge joint
22 Astro-navigation star tracker
23 Navigation and communications systems electronics
24 Nosewheel bay
25 Landing and taxiing lamps
26 Twin nosewheels
27 Torque scissor links
28 Nosewheel steering control jack
29 Nose undercarriage pivot fixing
30 Palletized reconnaissance equipment packages, interchangeable

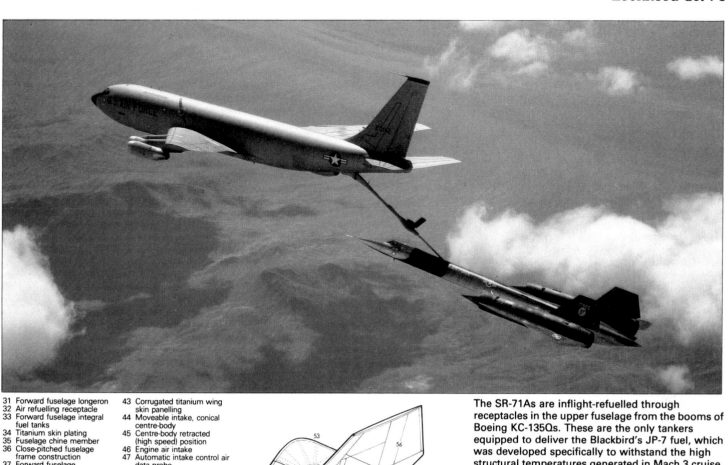

The SR-71As are inflight-refuelled through receptacles in the upper fuselage from the booms of Boeing KC-135Qs. These are the only tankers equipped to deliver the Blackbird's JP-7 fuel, which was developed specifically to withstand the high structural temperatures generated in Mach 3 cruise.

31 Forward fuselage longeron
32 Air refuelling receptacle
33 Forward fuselage integral fuel tanks
34 Titanium skin plating
35 Fuselage chine member
36 Close-pitched fuselage frame construction
37 Forward fuselage production joint
38 Blended wing/fuselage main integral fuel tanks (JP-7 fuel)
39 Main undercarriage wheel bay
40 Three-wheel main undercarriage bogie
41 Hydraulic retraction jack
42 Starboard main undercarriage, stowed position

43 Corrugated titanium wing skin panelling
44 Moveable intake, conical centre-body
45 Centre-body retracted (high speed) position
46 Engine air intake
47 Automatic intake control air data probe
48 Intake suction relief doors
49 Variable suction relief doors
50 Hinged engine cowling panel

51 By-pass duct blow-in doors
52 Starboard outer wing panel
53 Outboard, roll control, elevon
54 Engine bay, tertiary air flaps
55 Tailfin fixed root section
56 All-moving starboard fin
57 Exhaust nozzle ejector flaps
58 Inboard, pitch control, elevon

59 Aft, fuselage integral fuel tanks
60 Brake parachute doors
61 Ribbon parachute stowage
62 Rear fuselage longeron
63 Wing root rib
64 Inboard wing panel integral fuel tank
65 Close-pitched wing/fuselage frame construction
66 Elevon mixer unit

67 Tailcone
68 Fuel jettison
69 Port all-moving tailfin
70 Fin pivot fixing
71 All-moving fin hydraulic jack
72 Port engine exhaust nozzle
73 Ejection flaps
74 Ejector mixer duct
75 Port outer elevon titanium rib construction
76 Outer leading-edge rib

77 Under-cambered leading edge
78 Outer wing panel construction
79 Exhaust duct tertiary doors
80 Afterburner nozzle
81 Variable-area afterburner nozzle control jacks
82 Afterburner duct
83 Compressor bleed air by-pass ducts
84 Outer wing panel/engine cowling hinge axis
85 Pratt & Whitney JT11D–20B (J58) single spool turbo-ramjet engine
86 Engine accessory equipment bay
87 Outer wing panel/nacelle chine
88 Port main undercarriage three-wheel
89 Main undercarriage leg door
90 Intake duct secondary by-pass annular louvres

91 Centre-body bleed air louvres
92 Diffuser chamber
93 By-pass duct suction relief louvres
94 Intake annular by-pass duct
95 Centre-body boundary layer bleed air holes
96 Port engine intake
97 Intake moveable centre-body

What is known for sure is that at least two of the A-11s had a dorsal pylon to carry a small D-21 drone aircraft, powered by a Marquardt ramjet. The drone is sometimes referred to as the GTD-21, and is believed to have been codenamed 'Oxcart'. It is 40 ft (12.19 m) long, has a span of 17 ft (5.18 m), and is essentially similar to the engine pod of the parent aircraft, but fitted with its own delta wing and chines. At least 38 are said to have been built in the period 1964–9, and it might be conjectured that the drone could carry either a nuclear weapon or reconnaissance sensors.

Reports suggest that two A-11s were fitted with the pylon, and were each given a second cockpit in place of a camera bay, so that a man would be carried to check the functioning of the drone's equipment and to launch it. Launching was achieved by ejecting the drone forcibly upward. It is believed that this was attempted only once, on 5 January 1967, when the drone separated but came down and struck the launch aircraft. Both crashed. The drone was then equipped with a rocket booster to permit launches from much slower aircraft, and was fitted under the wing of a small number of B-52s for reconnaissance tests codenamed 'Tagboard' over South East Asia. Some 19 D-21s were returned to Davis-Monthan AFB, and 17 are still there. Several A-11s were lost in accidents, and it is said that the remainder were held in reserve for possible use in the reconnaissance role from 1968 to October 1976, when they were finally retired.

The YF-12A established nine performance records in the course of a single day, 1 May 1965. These included a sustained altitude of 80,275 ft (24462 m), a speed of 2,070 mph (3331 km/h) and a speed over a closed circuit of 1,689 mph (2718 km/h). The type was evaluated in 1969 by the USAF under the Improved Manned Interceptor programme, but no production order resulted, probably because of the high cost of operating these hand-made aircraft and the dwindling threat of the manned supersonic bomber. Two YF-12As (60–6935 and 60–6936) were used in a joint USAF/NASA high-Mach, high-altitude Advanced Supersonic Technology research programme from 1970 to 1974. The remaining A-11s and YF-12As (a total of at least nine) are now stored under guard at the Lockheed facility at Palmdale, California.

The first SR-71A had its maiden flight at Palmdale on 22 December 1964. The number built is still classified, but it is generally believed that there were three batches, totalling 31 aircraft, with serials running from 64–17950 to 64–17980, all delivered in the period 1966–9. Two (64–17951 and 64–17956) were converted to SR-71B trainers, with raised rear cockpits and the YF-12A's two fixed underfins restored to improve weathercock stability. Following the loss of one trainer, a further aircraft (64–17981) was built and given the designation SR-71C, although the difference from SR-71B has not been revealed.

Deliveries to SAC's Beale AFB in northern California began in January 1966, to the 9th Strategic Reconnaissance Wing, part of the 14th Air Division of the 15th Air Force. It is believed that nine SR-71s were operated by the 1st SRS, although the two training aircraft may now be flown by the 5th SRTS. Detachments of SR-71s fly routinely from Mildenhall in England and Kadena in Okinawa. The aircraft has been used operationally over the Middle East on several occasions, over South East Asia, and over North Korea.

The SR-71s of the 9th SRW have established numerous records. On 26 April 1971 an aircraft piloted by Lieutenant Colonel Estes covered 15,000 miles (24140 km) in approximately 10 hours 30 minutes, cruising at Mach 3 when not refuelling. For this flight the crew were awarded the USAF Mackay Trophy. On 1 September 1974 an SR-71 (64–1792) flew the 3,490 miles (5616 km) from New York to London in 1 hour 56 minutes, piloted by Major Sullivan, and on 8 September the aircraft established a new record from London to Los Angeles, a distance of 5,645 miles (9084 km) covered in 3 hours 47 minutes, arriving (in terms of local time) roughly four hours before take-off!

In July 1976 a number of records were established, including two which were still world records in 1982. On 27th July, an SR-71A flown by Major Adolphus Bledsoe Jr flew a 621-mile (1,000-km) circular course at an average speed of 2,092.33 mph (3367.13 km/h). On the following day, an SR-71A flown by Captain Robert Holt flew a horizontal endurance flight at 85,073 ft (25929 m). On the very same day, an SR-71A flown by Captain Eldon Joersz flew a straight 9.3–15.5 mile (15/25 km) straight course at an average speed of 2,193.21 mph (3529.47 km/h). Depending on the air temperature at the time, this could have been equivalent to Mach 3.3. Whether we still need such a costly aircraft in the age of the spy satellite is very much open to question.

Small wonder, therefore, that when General David Jones, USAF, was Chairman of the Joint Chiefs of Staff, he described the SR-71 as 'the most survivable US platform for manned overflights of heavily defended areas'.

Boeing 727

What makes a winner in the cut-and-thrust of commercial aviation design? The answer is much hard work, adequate research funding, and a keen eye on the demands of a difficult market. Boeing gambled much on its neat Model 727, and were rewarded when sales exceeded the most sanguine hopes.

Long before the introduction of the successful 707 and 720 series, Boeing's headquarters in Seattle was carrying out a preliminary study for a medium-capacity airliner of short-to-medium range to supply the demand for domestic flights in the USA. A high-performance jet aircraft suitable for short runways and with a low landing speed was required, to take a place in the market which was not being filled by the long-haul Douglas DC-8, Convair 880 and Boeing 707/720, which were rather too large, and the shorter-range Sud-Aviation S210 Caravelle and Douglas DC-9 which were still at an early stage of development. There was no doubt that there was a market for such an aircraft. But as always, Boeing needed buyers for the plane before they could start producing it. This meant that, apart from the USA, there had to be good prospects of selling high-performance medium-range airliners abroad as well. Boeing was also afraid that the new British de Havilland D.H. 121 Trident, with its unique three-jet configuration, would be a strong rival which might be hard to overtake. At the end of the 1950s, the outlook for the commercial aircraft industry was a very bright one. There was a pressing need for larger passenger capacity on the busy US and European routes. The old Douglas DC-3, Douglas DC-6 and Lockheed L-749, which were piston-engined, and the relatively new Lockheed L-188 Electra turboprop were cheap to run, but too slow, and the new Caravelle had too small a capacity.

The design of the Boeing Model 727, as the new type was named, started in February 1956, and the parameters laid before Boeing's preliminary design group were exacting. Whereas other companies, notably de Havilland (later merged with the Hawker Siddeley group), were vying for high cruise Mach numbers to reduce seat-air mile costs, Boeing wanted this factor on its Model 727, but combined with field operating characteristics that, in such a large aircraft, at first seemed impossible to attain. Put basically, this meant a high power/weight ratio for sprightly acceleration and take-off and, of course, a highly adaptable and efficient wing. The wing design of the Model 727 broached new horizons, and its unique system of lift-augmentation flaps and slats allied with spoilers was to become the format in the mighty Model 747. By the time that design work had been finalized, on 18 September 1959, the wing structure had developed into a low-wing format of 3° dihedral, a thickness chord-ratio of between 8 and 9 per cent, with 2° incidence and special Boeing aerofoil sections: sweepback at quarter-chord was 32° and was less than that of the Model 707. But if the basic wing was of routine design, then the high-lift and lift-dump devices most certainly were not: on the trailing edge of the wing massive triple-slotted flaps, totalling 388 sq ft (36.04 m²) with 40° setting, were combined with four leading-edge slats on the outer two-thirds of the wing, and three Krueger leading-edge flaps on the inner one-third portion. These were joined by seven spoilers on each upper wing surface (0–40°) which doubled as airbrakes and/

This Boeing 727-256, construction no. 20595, first flew on 23 October 1972 and was delivered to Iberia on 11 May the following year. Named *Vascongadas*, it is currently in service with a further 36 of the same type on Iberia's European and North African services.

Boeing 727-277 (construction no. 22641) of Ansett Airlines, Australia, in the new livery adopted in 1981. The aircraft was first flown as N8278V and was the 1753rd example of 1832 built. It entered service with Ansett on 20 June 1981 and is one of 16 Boeing 727-277s currently operated.

A Boeing 727-200 of Alaska Airlines, which uses the type largely for services within Alaska and to Seattle. The company has four such aircraft, plus four of the shorter-fuselage Model 727-100s.

This Boeing 727-81 was the 124th to be built and was delivered to All Nippon Airways on 18 March 1965. Alaska Airlines subsequently leased it, on 22 June 1972, and bought it on 14 December 1974 as N124AS. The aircraft was written off in a landing accident at Ketchikan on 5 April 1976.

Boeing 727-113C of Ariana Afghan Airlines. The aircraft first flew on 30 December 1969 and was delivered to Ariana on 15 January 1970, enabling the airline to commence jet services to London and Moscow. Ariana operates two Boeing 727s.

or roll augmentation spoilers. This beautiful wing was the key behind what was to be the phenomenal success story of the Boeing 727: it gave the aircraft immense utility. Clean, the aircraft was as fast and efficient as the best; dump the flaps and the Kruegers and even at maximum landing weight the pilot could land on any small municipal or rural field in the United States.

Taking shape

Allied with the excellent field performance, the new Model 727 had lively performance and good fuel economy with the adoption of the 14,000-lb (6350-kg) thrust Pratt & Whitney JT8D-1 turbofan in August 1960. The fuselage upper portion was identical to that of the Model 707/720 series: this saved some $3 million in jig and tool costing, standardized the flight deck layouts and gave the aircraft intercontinental six-abreast cabin accommodation for the passengers. In addition much stress was laid upon independence of operation: the Model 727 needed nothing on the ground if a stop-go transit was required, having a Garrett Ai Research GTC 85 auxiliary

Thirty-seven Boeing 727-256 aircraft provide the mainstay of Iberia's short/medium-haul operations. Each aircraft is able to carry up to 189 passengers over a range of 2,465 miles (3965 km).

power unit for electrics, pneumatic-starting and cabin conditioning, an airstar on Door 1 Left and a ventral staircase to the rear. With a very high maximum landing weight, as a result of wing stressing and landing gear strength, the Model 727 could take on fuel at the originating station, fly several transits, and gain quick turn-arounds. All these facets were built in during the course of very thorough research and design, entailing 150 studies of which 68 underwent some 1,500 hours of tunnel-testing. Construction go-ahead was given in August 1960, with Boeing acting on the good faith of Eastern Air Lines and United Air Lines. Actually, it was not until 5 December 1960 that these operators placed their orders: 20 for United with another 20 on option, and 40 for Eastern. By February 1963 four Model 727s were on the lines at Renton.

At 11.33 on 9 February 1963 the first flight was made from Renton when Lew Wallick, Boeing's senior experimental test pilot, lifted N7001U off after a run of 3,000 ft (914 m); the co-pilot was Dick Loesch and the engineer M. K. Shulenberger. N7001U weighed in at 130,000 lb (58968 kg), carried 5,500 US gal (20200 litres) of fuel and 16,000 lb (7258 kg) of test equipment, and flew for 2 hours 1 minute before Wallick put her down in 2,000 ft (610 m) on Paine Field's limited concrete. To the assembled Press, Wallick said that 'She

Boeing 727

AIR PORTUGAL

CS-TBW

CS-TBW is the 13th Boeing 727 supplied to TAP, Transportes Aereos Portugueses, the national airline of Portugal. TAP's early 727s were short-bodied 082s, or convertible 727-172C aircraft, but the latest are of the current standard model, the precise series being 727-282. Altogether these advanced 727s are fast, capable and extremely trouble-free aircraft, their most serious faults being relatively old engines which result in noise and fuel consumption that compares unfavourably with today's aircraft, such as the Boeing 757 or Airbus Industrie A310. The dark grills on all three engines are the outlets for the thrust-reversers. On the trailing edge of the 32°-swept wing are inboard high-speed ailerons (between the inboard and outboard sections of triple-slotted flap) and outboard ailerons used at low speeds only, all operating in conjunction with the spoilers seen on the upper surface. Just visible in the side view under the no. 1 engine nozzle is the hydraulically operated aft stairway; many airlines sealed this stairway shut after a hijacker with over a million US dollars parachuted through it!

Specification

Boeing 727-200

Type: medium-range passenger or mixed-traffic airliner

Powerplant: three Pratt & Whitney JT8D-9A (14,500 lb/6577 kg thrust), JT8D-15 (15,500 lb/7031 kg) or JT8D-17 (17,400 lb/7893 kg) turbofans

Performance: maximum cruising speed 599 mph (964 km/h); range at long-range cruise speed of 542 mph (872 km/h) with maximum fuel 2,729 miles (4392 km)

Weights: empty equipped 102,000 lb (46675 kg); maximum take-off 209,500 lb (95027 kg)

Dimensions: span 108 ft 0 in (32.92 m); length 153 ft 2 in (46.69m); height 34 ft 0 in (10.36 m); wing area 1,700 sq ft (157.9 m²)

Accommodation: flight crew of three, variable cabin crew for up to 189 passengers, typical mixed-class seating, 14 first and 131 tourist

---

Boeing Model 727 variants

Model 727-100: first production model, there being no prototypes; fuselage length 133 ft 2 in (40.59 m); standard transport for up to 131 passengers with three Pratt & Whitney JT8D-1 or D-7 turbofans, with later models having JT8D-9s; maximum take-off weight of 160,000 lb (72576 kg), with later variants certified to 169,000 lb (76668 kg)

Model 727-100C: convertible passenger cargo model with freight door, strengthened floor and floor beams, but otherwise identical to Model 727-100; optional payloads of 94 mixed-class passengers, or of 52 passengers and baggage plus 22,700 lb (10297 kg) of cargo on four pallets, or of 38,000 lb (17237 kg) on eight pallets

Model 727-100QC: installation of roller-bearing floors for palletized galley and seating and/or palletized freight; conversion from cargo to all-passenger achievable within 30 minutes; freighter conversion with increased ramp weight to 170,000 lb (77112 kg), maximum take-off weight of 169,000 lb (76658 kg), and maximum landing weight of 142,000 lb (64411 kg)

Model 727-100 Business Jet: optional fittings for luxury or business travel; extra fuel tanks in lower cargo compartments to provide a range with 10,700 US gal (40504 litres) of about 4,150 miles (6680 km) with a 4,000-lb (1814-kg) payload; option for dual Carousel IV or Litton LTN501 INS and long-range weather radar

Model 727-200: stretched version with fuselage length of 136 ft 2 in (41.50 m), andk basic accommodation for 163 passengers and a maximum capacity of 189; structurally strengthened; revised centre engine air inlet; three JT9D-9 turbofans, each rated at 14,500-lb (6577-kg) thrust to 84°F, standard with JT8D-11s or JT8D-15s

Advanced Model 727-200: increased ramp weight to 191,000 lb (86638 kg) and fitted with sound-suppression; improved avionics with options for INS. Flight Management, dual FD-108 flight directors or Collins FD-110, or Sperry Z-15 flight directors, and Sperry SP-150 Model 5 auto-pilot

Advanced Model 727-200F: pure freighter model with JT8D-17A turbofans; no windows, and up to 11 pallets can be loaded through a port-side hatch; the first customer was Federal Express

Mike Badrocke /83

Supplementing the Lockheed C-130 Hercules in the long-range transport role, the Royal New Zealand Air Force operates three ex-United Air Lines Boeing 727-100Cs, one of which is being cannibalized for spares.

Air Charter International of France operates two Boeing 727-2X3 aircraft powered by three Pratt & Whitney JTD-15 turbofans. The airline leases additional aircraft from Air France, Air Inter and EAS when required.

behaved as expected, even better than expected in many respects.' And indeed few problems cropped up during subsequent testing. The second Model 727 (N72700) flew on 12 March, and by the end of the month four Model 727s were undergoing thorough flight trials from Paine, Seattle, Edwards AFB, Denver and Albuquerque. By mid-May N7001U had completed 430 hours on flutter and structural damping tests up to Mach 0.9; 320 hours had been completed by N72700 on systems and braking; 180 hours on Model 727 no. 3, including handling high-g pull-ups, side-slipping and even barrel-rolls; while 313 hours had been completed in furnishing and air-conditioning on Model 727 no. 4. The order book was filling: 25 to American Air Lines, 40 to United, 10 to TWA, 12 to Lufthansa, and four to the Australian TAA and Ansett-ANA.

FAA certification for the production Model 727-100 was signed on 20 December 1963. Analyses of performance showed that the Model 727-100's parameters were 10 per cent in excess of Boeing's original guarantees: it was faster with better specific fuel consumption offered by the JT8D-1s, slower on the approach, and used reduced field lengths, being quite capable of operations from 5,000-ft (1525-m) runways at maximum weights. In the 1,100 hours of tests since 9 February 1963, dives in excess of Mach 0.95, take-offs at 160,000 lb (72576 kg), take-offs on two engines, and maximum-energy stops in less than 900 ft (274 m) had been made. Significantly, it was at this juncture that the Model 727's arch rival was being readied; on 19 December 1963 the Trident 1 (G-ARPF) completed crew training to be scheduled for its first service with BEA in April.

Already a battle royal was in progress between Boeing with its Model 727 and Hawker Siddeley with the Trident 1C and 1E for the lucrative foreign export markets. In November 1963 Boeing 727 N7003U completed its world tour started on 17 September of that year: out-bound from Montreal it plied the route to Tokyo via the Azores, Rome, Beirut, Karachi (where an uneasy meeting with Trident 1 G-ARPE took place), Calcutta, Bangkok and Manila. Thence the route went via Manila to Australia, followed by visits to Johannesburg and Nairobi, and back via Europe to the States. At home Eastern Air Lines signed up its first Model 727-100 on 22 October 1963 with the intention of starting scheduled services between Miami and New York (La Guardia) in January. The airline flew its first service with the Model 727-100 on 1 February 1964 from Miami to Philadelphia with a Washington (National) transit. Five days later United Air Lines started its schedules: daily Denver/San Francisco shuttles were started, with the line commencing operations on the high-intensity New York-Los Angeles-San Francisco-Seattle routes. In the meantime the salesmen were busy.

Boeing Advanced 727-200 cutaway drawing key

1 Radome
2 Radar dish
3 Radar scanner mounting
4 Pressure bulkhead
5 Windscreen panels
6 Instrument panel shroud
7 Back of instrument panel
8 Rudder pedals
9 Radar transmitter and receiver
10 Pitot tube
11 Cockpit floor control ducting
12 Control column
13 Pilot's seat
14 Cockpit eyebrow windows
15 Co-pilot's seat
16 Engineer's control panel
17 Flight engineer's seat
18 Cockpit door
19 Observer's seat
20 Nosewheel bay
21 Nosewheel doors
22 Twin nosewheels
23 Retractable airstairs (optional)
24 Handrail
25 Escape chute pack
26 Front entry door
27 Front toilet
28 Galley
29 Starboard galley service door
30 Cabin bulkhead
31 Closet
32 Window frame panel
33 Radio and electronics bay
34 First class passenger cabin, 18 seats in mixed layout
35 Cabin roof construction
36 Seat rails
37 Cabin floor beams
38 Cargo door
39 Anti-collision light
40 Air conditioning supply ducting
41 Forward cargo hold
42 Cargo hold floor
43 Baggage pallet container
44 Tourist class passenger cabin, 119 seats in mixed layout

45 Communications antenna
46 Fuselage frame and stringer construction
47 Cabin window frame panels
48 Air conditioning system intake
49 Air conditioning plant
50 Overhead air ducting
51 Main fuselage frames
52 Escape hatches, port and starboard
53 Wing centre section no. 2 fuel tank
54 Centre section stringer construction
55 Cabin floor construction
56 Starboard wing no 3 fuel tank
57 Inboard Krueger flaps
58 Krueger flap hydraulic jack
59 Leading edge fence
60 Outboard leading edge slat segments
61 Slat hydraulic jacks
62 Fuel vent surge tank
63 Navigation lights
64 Starboard wing tip
65 Fuel jettison pipe
66 Static dischargers
67 Outboard, low speed, aileron
68 Aileron balance tab
69 Outboard spoilers
70 Outboard slotted flap
71 Flap screw jack mechanism
72 Inboard, high speed, aileron
73 Trim tab
74 Inboard spoilers
75 Inboard slotted flap
76 Fuselage centre section construction
77 Pressurized floor over starboard main undercarriage bay

78 Auxiliary power unit (APU)
79 Port main undercarriage bay
80 Tourist class, six-abreast, passenger seating
81 Overhead hand baggage stowage bins
82 Cabin trim panels
83 Rear cargo door
84 Aft cargo compartment floor
85 Passenger overhead service panels
86 Starboard service door/rear emergency exit
87 Aft galleys
88 Closet
89 Toilets, port and starboard
90 Cabin rear entry door
91 Starboard engine cowling
92 Centre engine intake
93 Noise attenuating intake lining
94 Intake S-duct
95 Duct de-icing
96 Fin root fairing construction
97 Fin construction
98 VOR aerial
99 Elevator control cables

Above Boeing 727-212 of Singapore Airlines, which received the aircraft on 30 August 1977. It was then sold to International Lease Finance on 6 June 1980 and subsequently leased to VASP as PP-SRK, until it was written off in an accident on 8 June 1982. In 1986 Singapore Airlines had two Boeing 727-212s.

Above This Boeing 727-243 of Alitalia was rolled out on 10 September 1976. Named *Città di Siena*, it and 17 more of the same type were currently operated throughout Europe and North Africa and to Tel Aviv. The entire fleet was replaced by McDonnell Douglas MD-80s, and the 727s were sold to People Express via McDonnell Douglas in late 1983/early 1984.

100 Tailplane trim jack
101 Starboard tailplane
102 Elevator horn balance
103 Static dischargers
104 Starboard elevator
105 Elevator tab
106 Fin bullet fairing
107 VHF aerial boom
108 Elevator control jack
109 Port elevator
110 Tailplane construction
111 Port tailplane
112 Rudder upper section
113 Rudder control jacks
114 Rudder lower section
115 Lower section trim jack
116 Centre engine mounting pylon
117 Centre engine exhaust pipe
118 Thrust reverser
119 Centre engine

120 Rear fuselage construction
121 Side engine thrust reverser
122 Engine pylon fairing
123 Rear pressure bulkhead
124 Bleed air system pipes
125 Pratt & Whitney JT8D-9A turbofan engine
126 Detachable cowlings
127 Rear entry ventral airstairs
128 Engine air intake
129 Port rear service door/emergency exit
130 Lower lobe fuselage frame construction
131 Trailing edge fillet

132 Inboard flap
133 Flap track fairings
134 Flap track mechanism
135 Inboard spoilers
136 Main undercarriage leg pivot
137 Retraction mechanism
138 Rear spar
139 Wing rib construction
140 Front spar
141 Leading edge construction
142 Landing and taxiing lamp
143 De-icing air duct
144 Inboard Krueger flap segments
145 Landing lamp
146 Main undercarriage leg
147 Twin mainwheels
148 Wing stringer construction
149 Inboard, high speed, aileron
150 Aileron trim tab
151 Flaps down position
152 Outboard spoilers
153 No. 1 wing integral fuel tank, total capacity 8,186 US gal (30984 litres)
154 Refuelling connectors
155 Leading edge fence
156 Leading edge slat segments
157 Slat hydraulic jacks
158 Slat track mechanism
159 Outboard slotted trailing edge flap
160 Flap track fairings
161 Outboard flap track mechanism
162 Aileron balance tab
163 Outboard, low speed, aileron
164 Aileron control jack
165 Fuel vent surge tank
166 Port navigation lights
167 Static dischargers
168 Fuel jettison pipe

Originally intended for Continental Airlines, this Boeing 727-224 was delivered to Libyan Arab Airlines on 28 December 1970. It was shot down by an Israeli Air Force F-4 in the Sinai desert on 21 February 1973, killing all 110 on board.

Boeing 727-2B6 of Royal Air Maroc, who took delivery of this 1236th example on 9 December 1970. Eight further Boeing727-2B6s were used by the airline from its base at Anfa Airport, Casablanca, to points in North Africa and Europe.

Lufthansa's first Model 727-100 (D-ABIB) was rolled out in January 1964, the first of 12 for crew training and the start of the Europa-Jet schedules intended for a start in April (first operation on 16 April 1964); on 10 May the German operator flew its first Frankfurt-Heathrow service, and by July 1964 six of its Model 727-100s were serving the European and Middle Eastern network.

The announcement of the decision taken by Japan Air Lines and All Nippon to choose the Model 727-100 instead of the Trident came as a bitter blow to Hawker Siddeley. Both airlines looked upon the Trident 1C and 1E with favour, but wanted the stretched Trident 1F. But the latter was not due for certification until the spring of 1966, and JAL and All Nippon's intention was to start internal services by April of that year: the Model 727-100 was for them the obvious choice with deliveries promised for October 1965. All Nippon was swung by the decision of its big brother, and no doubt by the poor showing of the Trident from Osaka's 6,200-ft (1890-m) runway in hot weather: in July and August when seasonal temperatures approached 40°C the Trident's poor field operating characteristics would have precluded break-even loads. On 15 May 1964 JAL signed a purchase and loan agreement for six Model 727-100s, the deal being worth $37.5 million with spares. The basic price of the aircraft was $4.5 million, with Boeing promising the first in August 1965.

As if to underline the Model 727-100's first-rate field operating abilities, Boeing's Jack Waddell took one into Bolivia's La Paz airport (field elevation 13,358 ft/4072 m) on 23 May 1964: the first jet commercial transport ever to land at La Paz took off within 7,400 ft (2256 m) in 44°F at a weight of 129,000 lb (58514 kg). And as if to bring it home, Waddell demonstrated an engine failure on take-off. Standard Boeing 727-100s were by now certified for up to 131 passengers, with maximum take-off weights of either 160,000 lb (72576 kg), or up to 169,000 lb (76658 kg); 14,000-lb (6530-kg) thrust Pratt & Whitney JT8D-7s were standard, with the option of the 14,500-lb (6577-kg) thrust JT8D-9s.

A diversity of options

Despite the sales success of the Model 727, the deliveries and options of some 200 were still about 100 short of the break-even figure. On 22 July 1964 Boeing announced its promotion of the Model 727-100C convertible cargo/passenger model: brochures gave operation from a 5,000-ft (1525-m) runway with carriage of 30,000-lb (13608-kg) payloads over a distance of 1,900 miles (3058 km), or the carriage of eight pallets (36,750 lb/16670 kg) over 1,500 miles (2414 km). The St Paul-Minneapolis-based Northwest Orient signed for three as the first customer. Identical to the Model 727-100 except for heavier flooring and floor beams and the cargo-door of the Model 707-320C, the Model 727-100C gave operators the option of flying passengers by day and freight by night, thus enhancing utilization: galleys and seats

were quickly removable, hatracks could be stowed, and the aircraft could be changed to passenger/cargo or all-cargo configuration within two hours.

By April 1967 the Model 727 was the most widely used commercial jet airliner in service: in that month Sabena took delivery of the 400th aircraft while a total of 586 was on order, in comparison with 564 Model 707s. In June 1967 Pan American placed an order for the milestone 600th, and the aircraft was on option or in service with 32 carriers. On 27 July 1967 Wallick took the first Model 727-200 (N7270C) off Renton's runway and, after a flight of 2 hours 10 minutes, landed at Paine Field for FAA inspection. Certification followed on 30 November 1967 after 457 hours of test flying. Announced on 5 August 1965, the Model 727-200 was the stretched version offering 163 seats, up to a maximum of 189: the fuselage was lengthened by 10 ft (3.05 m) both forward and aft of the main landing gear wheel-well, with localized structural strengthening. Three JT8D-9s powered the Model 727-200, with options for 15,000-lb (6804-kg) thrust JT8D-11s, or 15,500-lb (7031-kg) thrust Pratt & Whitney JT8D-15s. In the meantime Boeing had given the market the Model 727-100QC with palletized passenger seats and galleys, and advanced cargo-loading techniques; ramp weight was increased to 170,000 lb (77,112 kg). Luxurious furnishings and advanced communications were also available on the Model 727-100 Business Jet, the first being ordered by International Telephone and Telegraph on 13 November 1970. The Advanced Boeing 727-200 was announced on 12 May 1971, with a ramp weight of 209,000 lb (86638 kg), and deliveries started in June of the next year. With increased fuel capacity and JT8D-15s, the aircraft offered a range 800 miles (1287 km) greater than that of earlier models.

The Boeing 727 has long been the most successful commercial jet airliner with a production run of more than 1,500. The number of aircraft sold exceeded the wildest dreams of Boeing's builders and managers. Finally, after 1,832 machines had been built, production ceased in 1984.

Lufthansa was one of the first airlines to buy the 727, and later exchanged it for the more modern 727-200. The picture shows a 727-230 Adv., of which Lufthansa still owned 34 in 1986.

Mikoyan-Gurevich MiG-23 & MiG 27

Since World War 2 the military world has welcomed half a dozen classic fighter aircraft which were built in thousands. One of them is still being built and developed after 20 years of production – the Mikoyan-Gurevich swing-wing fighter family known to NATO as 'Flogger'.

Work on the Mikoyan-Gurevich 'Flogger' began in the early 1960s after a large number of MiG-21s and Sukhoi Su-7s had been supplied to Soviet front-line air forces and tactical air defence units. At the time these types compared very favourably with Western aircraft in terms of speed and manoeuvrability, but so far as weaponry, range, and navigation and combat equipment they left a great deal to be desired from the very outset. As there was little prospect of correcting these shortcomings, it was no surprise that when they issued specifications for the next generation of fighter-bombers to come into use in 1970, Frontal Aviation, the Soviet tactical air defence/strike force, placed great emphasis on firepower, range and sophistication.

The requirement was issued before April 1965, when the first engagement between USAF and North Vietnamese fighters heralded a new era in air warfare. The requirement did not call for greatly improved agility in air combat; the standards set by the MiG-21 would be quite adequate. Instead, the new fighter was to have greater endurance, a heavier armament and a much more powerful radar than its predecessor, and the air-to-ground strike mission was at least as important as air combat. Field performance was to be comparable with that of the smaller and lighter MiG-21.

The MiG bureau produced two prototype aircraft to the FA's specification, apparently sharing some common design features. One of these resembled an enlarged MiG-21, with the same mid-set delta wing and conventional tail, but to reduce the field length within reasonable bounds it was fitted with two lift-jet engines in the centre-section. The other, designated Ye-231, was a straightforward application of the then-fashionable variable-sweep, or variable-geometry (VG) formula. It is probable that both prototypes made their first flights in late 1966 or early 1967; by the time they appeared at the air show held at Domodedovo, near Moscow, in July 1967, the weight penalties and control complications inherent in the lift-jet design had led to its abandonment in favour of the swing-wing Ye-231. Following the show, the delta received the NATO codename 'Faithless' and the Ye-231 was labelled 'Flogger'.

These MiG-23BNs, here shown flying in formation, belong to the Indian Air Force. The model is something of a hybrid, with the nose, the pylons and main engines of the MiG-27 and the air intakes, thrust nozzles and cannons of the MiG-23.

A Libyan MiG-23 'Flogger-E', armed with K-13A missiles. In its first major action in the Middle East, in 1982, the MiG-23 proved no match for the IAI Kfir or General Dynamics F-16, though this was largely because of great disparity in pilot tactics and skill. Israeli pilots consider the 'Flogger'

inferior to the MiG-21 as a dogfighter, while the export version shown here has a similar radar and weapons.

Mikoyan-Gurevich MiG-23

Specification

Mikoyan MiG-23MF 'Flogger-G'
Type: single-seat tactical fighter and interceptor
Powerplant: one Tumansky R-29B turbojet of 17,637-lb (8000-kg)
dry thrust and 25,353-lb (11500-kg) augmented thrust
Performance: maximum speed 1,553 mph (2500 km/h) or Mach
2.35 at altitude; maximum speed 839 mph (1350 km/h) or Mach 1.1
at sea level; combat radius with four AAMs and external fuel 578
miles (930 km)
Weights: empty about 24,912 lb (11300 kg); normal take-off 38,029
lb (17250 kg); maximum take-off 40,785 lb (18500 kg)
Dimensions: span (spread) 46 ft 9 in (14.25 m) and (swept) 27 ft 2¾
in (8.30 m); length including probe 59 ft 10½ in (18.25 m); height
14 ft 3¼in (4.35 m); wing area 400.43 sq ft (37.20 m²)
Armament: one twin-barrel GSh-23 23-mm cannon in lower
fuselage; two medium-range AA-7 'Apex' AAMs on glove pylons;
four short-range AA-8 'Aphid' AAMs on two twin launchers under
inlet ducts or 8,820 lb (4000 kg) bombload

Western intelligence continued to track the development of the Ye-231, including the construction and deployment of a small pilot batch of 'Flogger-A' aircraft closely resembling the prototype. It was not until early 1973, though, that the US Department of Defense could publicly confirm that the type was entering service in quantity and that its service designation was MiG-23; this designation has previously been attributed to the MiG-25 'Foxbat'. Later in that year, the true production MiG-23 entered service with Soviet units in East Germany, and photographs were leaked to Western magazines, revealing the design philosophy.

Variable geometry
The MiG-23 falls squarely into the group of VG aircraft conceived in the 1960s. All of them followed NASA's discovery that the fundamental problem of VG (the wings move aft as they are swept, creating a massive trim imbalance) could be solved without physically sliding the wing root through the fuselage as had been done on earlier VG designs. By moving the pivots outboard, twisting and tapering the outer wing panels and fitting a large and powerful all-moving tailplane, the trim problem could be kept under control without sacrificing the many advantages of VG. Maximum sweep could be sharper than was practical with a fixed wing, allowing high speeds at low level and good transonic acceleration, while the spread configuration was efficient in subsonic cruise and provided good field performance at high weights.

VG made a particularly good match for the newly developed augmented turbofan engine. The turbofan's excellent thrust/weight ratio in reheat could drive a VG aircraft well above Mach 2. Without reheat, its miserly fuel consumption put previously unattainable range performance within reach of the fighter aircraft. All the VG aircraft designed in the early 1960s had augmented turbofan powerplants, including the MiG-23; designated R-27, its engine was designed by the Tumansky bureau, which had powered the MiG-19, the MiG-21 and most of Mikoyan's prototypes.

The basic Ye-231 was a typically clean, straightforward design. The nose inlet featured on earlier MiGs gave way to side inlets, to make room for a useful search radar; the inlets were very like those of the F-4, with vertical moving ramps and wide boundary-layer ducts, and were efficient over a wide speed range without excessive weight or complexity. Thanks to the elimination of the full-length nose inlet ducts, the lean fuselage could hold a respectable amount of internal fuel in addition to the pilot, gun and avionics.

Early MiG-23 'Flogger-B' of a Soviet Frontal Aviation unit. Noteworthy points include the chin housing for an infra-red detection system or, possibly, a laser-ranging device – eliminated from later aircraft – and armament of four K-13A (AA-2 'Atoll') infra-red-homing missiles.

MiG-23 'Flogger' variants
Ye-231 'Flogger-A': bureau designation for prototype aircraft, flown in 1966–7
MiG-23 'Flogger-A': small batch of service-test aircraft, similar to prototype, produced in 1969–70
MiG-23MF 'Flogger-B': much modified standard fighter variant, in service since 1973: steadily improved with R-29B engine, provision for external fuel and other modifications
MiG-23U 'Flogger-C': two-seat conversion/proficiency trainer based on MiG-23MF
MiG-27 'Flogger-D': dedicated ground-attack aircraft based on MiG-23MF airframe with new forward fuselage, relocated pylons, six-barrel cannon and other changes
MiG-23 'Flogger-E': export fighter development of MiG-23MF with R-27 engine, 'Jay Bird' radar and AA-2 'Atoll' missiles
MiG-23BN 'Flogger-F': export ground-attack type with MiG-27 forward fuselage and MiG-23-type inlets and nozzle
MiG-23MF 'Flogger-G': further improved fighter with shorter dorsal fin extension and new nose landing gear; recent versions have six-missile armament
MiG-23BN 'Flogger-H': similar to 'Flogger-F', but with additional antennae
MiG-27 'Flogger-J': recent MiG-27 variant with modified nose and wing leading-edge root extensions; has been seen with underwing gun pods as primary armament

Mikoyan MiG-23MF 'Flogger-G' cutaway drawing key

1 Pitot tube
2 Radome
3 'High Lark' radar scanner dish
4 Radar dish tracking mechanism
5 ILS antenna
6 Avionics cooling air scoop
7 Radar and avionics equipment bay
8 Ventral doppler antenna
9 Yaw vane
10 Air data probe
11 SRO-2 'Odd-Rods' IFF antenna
12 Armoured windscreen panel
13 Head-up display
14 Instrument panel shroud
15 Radar 'head-down' display
16 Instrument panel
17 Rudder pedals
18 Angle of attack transmitter
19 Laser rangefinder housing
20 Nosewheel steering unit
21 Torque scissor links
22 Pivoted axle beam
23 Twin aft-retracting nosewheels
24 Nosewheel spray/debris guard
25 Shock absorber strut
26 Nosewheel doors
27 Hydraulic retraction jack
28 Control column
29 Ejection seat firing handles
30 Wing sweep control lever
31 Engine throttle control lever
32 Pilot's ejection seat
33 Electrically heated rear view mirror
34 Ejection seat headrest
35 Upward hingeing cockpit canopy cover
36 Canopy jack
37 Starboard air intake
38 Canopy hinge point
39 Boundary layer splitter plate
40 Boundary layer bleed air holes
41 Port engine air intake
42 Intake internal flow fences
43 Retractable landing/taxiing lamp, port and starboard
44 Temperature probe
45 Variable area intake ramp doors
46 Boundary layer bleed air ejector
47 Avionics equipment bay
48 ADF sense aerial
49 Boundary layer air duct
50 Forward fuselage fuel tank
51 Ventral cannon ammunition magazines
52 Ground power connections
53 Intake suction relief doors
54 Weapons system electronic control units
55 SO-69 Sirena 3 radar warning antennae
56 Fuselage flank fuel tanks
57 Wing glove fairing
58 Starboard Sirena 3 radar warning antennae
59 176-gal (800-litre) jettisonable fuel tank
60 Nose section of MiG-23U 'Flogger-C' two-seat tandem trainer variant
61 Student pilot's cockpit
62 Folding blind-flying hood
63 Rear seat periscope, extended
64 Instructor's cockpit
65 MiG-23BN 'Flogger-F' dedicated ground attack variant
66 Ventral radar ranging antenna
67 Laser ranger nose fairing
68 Raised cockpit section
69 Armoured fuselage side panels
70 Wing leading edge flap, lowered
71 Starboard navigation light
72 Wing fully forward (16-deg sweep) position
73 Port wing integral fuel tank, total internal fuel capacity 1,265 gal (5750 litres)
74 Full span plain flap, lowered
75 Starboard wing intermediate (45-deg sweep) position
76 Starboard wing full (72-deg sweep) position
77 Two-segment spoilers/lift dumpers
78 Non-swivelling, jettisonable wing pylon

'Flogger-C' is a trainer with limited combat capability, because of its small radar and reduced fuel capacity. The instructor's basically poor view is partly improved by the use of a periscope. This example was delivered to Libya in 1975.

Selected to fulfil the Indian Air Force's Tactical Air Support Aircraft (TASA) requirement, the MiG-23BN equips Nos 10, 220 and 221 Sqns and replaced the Sukhoi Su-7, HAL HF-24 and Hawker Hunter. This version retained the GSh centreline cannon and six underwing and wing-glove hardpoints.

(wings restricted to forward swept position)
79 Wing glove sealing plate
80 Wing pivot bearing
81 Wing pivot box carry-through unit, welded construction
82 VHF aerial
83 Wing sweep control screw jacks
84 Fin root fillet
85 Rear fuselage fuel tank

86 Tumansky R-29B afterburning turbojet engine
87 Afterburner duct cooling air scoop
88 Cut-back fin root fillet (some 'Flogger-G' aircraft)
89 Tailplane control and hydraulic equipment bay
90 Starboard all-moving tailplane
91 Tailfin

92 Short wave ground control communications aerial
93 UHF aerial
94 ILS aerial
95 Sirena 3 tail warning radar
96 ECM aerials
97 Tail navigation light
98 Static discharger
99 Rudder
100 Rudder hydraulic actuators, port and starboard
101 Brake parachute housing
102 Split conic fairing parachute door
103 Variable area afterburner nozzle
104 Fixed tailplane tab
105 Static discharger
106 Port all-moving tailplane

107 Afterburner nozzle control jacks (six)
108 Tailplane pivot bearing
109 Tailplane hydraulic jack
110 Airbrakes (four), upper and lower surfaces
111 Airbrake hydraulic jack
112 Afterburner duct
113 Ventral fin, folded (undercarriage down) position
114 Ventral fin control jack
115 Lower UHF aerial
116 Ventral fin down position
117 Engine accessory equipment bay
118 Wing root seal
119 Port spoilers/lift dumpers
120 Flap guide rails
121 Port plain flap

122 Fixed spoiler strips
123 Static discharger
124 Port navigation light
125 Leading edge flap, lowered
126 Port wing integral fuel tank
127 Wing pylon mounting rib
128 Extended chord sawtooth leading edge
129 Port mainwheel
130 Mainwheel door/debris guard

131 Shock absorber strut
132 Hinged axle beam
133 Articulated mainwheel leg strut
134 Hydraulic retraction jack
135 Fuselage stores pylon
136 Twin missile launcher
137 AA-8 'Aphid' short-range air-to-air missile
138 GSh-23L twin-barrel 23-mm ventral cannon pack

139 Gun gas venting air scoop
140 AA-2 'Atoll' air-to-air missile
141 Fuselage centreline pylon
142 176-gal (800-litre) ventral fuel tank
143 Wing glove pylon
144 Missile launch rail
145 AA-7 'Apex' long range air-to-air missile

Something of an oddity, this 'export model' Flogger-E is marked as a PVO (national air defence) interceptor. It has been suggested that such aircraft have been supplied to Soviet forces because production of the advanced systems fitted to the 'Flogger-G' cannot match the output of airframes.

The outer wings were hydraulically driven from 16° to 72° sweep (an intermediate 45° position could be selected, but full-range, automatic control was not provided) and were attached to the ends of a heavy structural box passing through the upper fuselage above the inlet ducts. The swing-wing geometry of the original Ye-231 was not unlike that of the General Dynamics F-111, with outboard pivots, sizable fixed gloves and the tailerons (tailplane halves capable of collective and differential movement) located close behind the wings at the same high position. In the interests of simplicity, there were no swivelling wing pylons, and the wing high-lift devices were confined to full-span three-section plain flaps and drooped outboard leading edges. Overwing spoilers and the large tailerons were used for roll control.

One of the problems of a VG aircraft is the landing gear, banished from its usual place in the wings. The MiG team arrived at a unique main gear design: the mainwheels were suspended from two rigid beams, L-shaped in front view, which were pivoted at the fuselage keel and swung upwards into the fuselage sides. This gave the aircraft a wide track, but a pronounced nose-up sit which left no room for conventional ventral fins. Instead, a single large ventral fin was fitted, and this folded right and upwards as the main gear was extended. Four separate airbrakes were grouped around the tail; this provided ample deceleration with minimal trim change.

Design problems

Flight tests of the Ye-231 soon revealed serious stability and control problems in high-speed manoeuvring flight, and full production was postponed while some drastic modifications were made to the basic design. The tailerons and dorsal fin were moved some 3 ft 3.37 in (1.0 m) rearwards, and the wings were redesigned: the new outer wings featured large leading-edge extensions, terminating in dogteeth at the junction with the fixed glove. The new wings were more sharply tapered, shifting the aerodynamic centre forwards, while the claws served the same purpose as dog-teeth or fences, shedding a vortex across the upper wing and inhibiting the spanwise-and-rearwards flow which causes tip-stalling The effect of the modifications was to reduce pitch-up in high-speed turns, reduce the shift of the aerodynamic centre with increasing sweep, and increase the effectiveness of the tail surfaces at all speeds.

The modifications were incorporated in the first major production version, the MiG-23MF 'Flogger-B', which entered service in 1973.

The MiG-23MF was also designed to carry the new weapons and avionics which had been developed for the type. Glove pylons carried a pair of large air-to-air R-32R missiles, codenamed AA-7 'Apex' by NATO, while belly pylons were fitted for two very small, highly manoeuvrable R-60 AA-8 'Aphid' missiles. (Up to 1976, however, MiG-23MFs were often seen with launch rails for the older K-13A AA-2 'Atoll' and AA-2-2 Advanced Atoll). In the lower fuselage, between the intakes, the MiG-23MF carried the newly developed GSh-23 cannon, a remarkable weapon with two ultra-short barrels and an effective range of about 1,000 yards (915 m), firing at a rate of 3,000 rounds per minute. A large nose radome housed the Soviet Union's first pulse-Doppler fire-control radar, named 'High Lark' by NATO, and a laser rangefinder, probably for use in air-to-air gunnery, was mounted under the nose. More antennae, housed in the tip of the fin, the ends of the claws and the forward fuselage, betrayed the presence of comprehensive electronic countermeasures and surveillance equipment.

As the MiG-23 entered service, another new version of the type was completing its trials. While the MiG-23MF was designed to replace the MiG-21 in the tactical air-defence role, the new version was intended to supersede the Su-7 ground-attack fighter, and was extensively modified for the strike role. Designated MiG-27, the new version appeared in East Germany in 1975, and was code-named 'Flogger-D'.

The MiG-27 used the basic airframe of the MiG-23, but had a completely new forward fuselage. Shorter than the fighter's nose, it sloped more steeply ahead of the cockpit and offered a better downward view. Its sides were armoured, and it housed a laser rangefinder, a small ranging radar and Doppler navigation equipment. The variable-area inlets and nozzle of the MiG-23 were replaced by lighter fixed inlets and a simpler exhaust, reducing speed at high altitude but saving weight. The glove pylons were retained, but the ventral pylons were moved out to the inlet ducts to make room for larger stores. Another pair of smaller pylons was provided on the sides of the rear fuselage, possibly for counter-measures equipment or rocket-assisted take-off gear.

The MiG-27 is armed with a range of guided air-to-surface missiles (ASMs). Very little is known about these missiles (it appears that they are seldom carried outside secure areas of the Soviet Union, and certainly not in East Germany) but the US Department of Defense has stated that the Soviet Union has developed seven new tactical ASMs since the mid-

Both the MiG-27 and MiG-23BN appear to be in Soviet service in some numbers; this is an example of the latter. The location of the pylons under the belly rather than the inlet ducts reduces the external load, and the aircraft carries a less powerful gun than the MiG-27.

The cut-back dorsal fin of the 'Flogger-G' is a ready identification mark; other changes include the redesigned nosewheel leg and bulged doors. The centreline drop tank is almost invariably carried. The finish is a standard Frontal Aviation/Warsaw Pact scheme.

Algeria was an early export recipient of the MiG-23BN 'Flogger-F' strike fighter. Three squadrons of the type, totalling some 40 aircraft, were reported to be in service in early 1984. Most were delivered in 1975-6; they have not been used in action.

1970s. They included the radio-commanded AS-7 'Kerry', the long-range anti-radar AS-9 (although this weapon is more usually associated with the larger Su-24), the laser-guided AS-10 and guided glide bombs.

Other improvements applied to the MiG-27 were also incorporated on the MiG-23 in the course of production. These included the more powerful Tumansky R-29B engine and provision for fuel tanks under the outer wings. These were carried on fixed pylons, and were designed to be jettisoned before the wings were swept back.

With these two versions established in production, the Soviet Union's output of 'Floggers' reached a peak rate of nearly 500 aircraft per year in the mid-1970s. By the end of 1982, it was estimated that some 3,500 of the type had been built. The result has been that Soviet and allied air forces have been able to re-equip very fully and quickly with the MiG-23 family, and it would be fair to say that the MiG fighter was the main element in a rapid improvement in Warsaw Pact airpower in the late 1970s.

All the other members of the 'Flogger' family stem from the MiG-27. The first of these to appear was the MiG-23U 'Flogger-C', a two-seat trainer version of the MiG-23MF with a slightly raised rear cockpit and a smaller radar. The MiG-23U is used as the trainer for the MiG-27 and other attack variants as well as for the MiG-23 fighters, and some sources have suggested that similar two-seat aircraft may be used in the ECM and defence-suppression roles.

Middle Eastern allies of the Soviet Union were the first export customers for the MiG-23; Egypt, Libya and Syria took delivery of their first batches in the course of 1975. All of them, however, received deliberately downgraded export models of the type. The first of these was the 'Flogger-E' fighter, which differed from the MiG-23MF in having a much smaller radar (probably related to the 'Jay Bird' system fitted to later MiG-21s) and in being armed with AA-2 'Atoll' missiles. More recently, however, export customers appear to have received the more potent MiG-23MF.

A hybrid version of the family, combining MiG-23 and MiG-27 features, was first seen in 1975 and was at first thought to be a MiG-27 development aircraft. It soon became apparent, however, that it was an attack aircraft for non-Soviet forces, and it is designated MiG-23BN. It has the nose of the MiG-27, and the same duct-mounted pylons and enlarged mainwheels. However, it has the inlets, exhaust and gun of the MiG-23. The initial version was code-named 'Flogger-F' by NATO; the version supplied to Eastern European air forces, with additional antennae, is identified as 'Flogger-H'. This version is also being built under licence in India, alongside the 'Flogger-C' trainer.

The first-line fighter version of the MiG-23 has been continuously refined. NATO applies the designation 'Flogger-G' to MiG-23s produced since 1978; these are distinguished by a shorter dorsal fin and a modified nose landing gear housed under bulged doors. Recent improve-

Late-model 'Flogger-G' in landing configuration. Note the slender external tank, designed to be retained at supersonic speeds. The type is more festooned with antennae than any other fighter aircraft, indicating the type's comprehensive electronics suite.

Standard MiG-23U 'Flogger-C' trainers of Soviet Frontal Aviation. MiG-23 pilots are trained according to a precise manual of tactics, designed to suit their fast but unmanoeuvrable aircraft. As in the West, two-seaters are attached to each unit for refresher training and check-outs.

ments are reported to include improved head-up displays; new MiG-23s, like modern Western fighters, dispense with a full-time radar scope in the cockpit. Since 1982, 'Flogger-G' has also been seen in a six-missile configuration, with duct-mounted twin pylons for four AA-8 missiles. The 'High Lark'/AA-7 combination has also been improved; the MiG-23MF is believed to have 'some ability to engage low-flying targets' according to the Department of Defense, and the type is now used alongside the Su-15 by Soviet PVO air-defence units as well as by Frontal Aviation.

The latest MiG-27 version is known as 'Flogger-J', and is distinguished by changes to the nose and small leading-edge root extensions (LERXs). These seem too small to have any great aerodynamic effect, and may house antennae for an improved ECM suite. The type has also been seen with a pair of gun pods under the wing gloves, with barrels which can be depressed for attacking ground targets. The MiG-27 is still used mainly by the Soviet air forces.

MiG-23s have seen action in the war between Iraq and Iran, and between Syria and Israel. Syria's 'Flogger-Es' suffered heavy losses in action against the Israeli IAI Kfirs and General Dynamics F-16s in June 1982, but this was ascribed to tactics rather more than technology. Generally, the MiG-23 is regarded as a well equipped and capable aircraft, much less agile than the F-16 but somewhat faster and,

currently, carrying a heavier, longer-range armament; this imbalance exists largely because the USAF has elected to wait for the new AIM-120 instead of integrating the earlier Sparrow missile with the F-16. So far, the MiG-23 and MiG-27 have been available in greater numbers than the F-16.

An unexpected operator of the MiG-23 is the US Air Force, which is known to maintain one or two of the type at a base in Nevada. Obtained from Egypt after its rift with the Soviet Union, they are used for the development of air combat tactics. In late 1983, Atlanta-based aviation services company Flight International proposed to acquire and support more ex-Egyptian MiG-23s for the US Navy.

It seems that production of the MiG-23/27 has been slowed down during recent years and the Soviet Union is now concentrating more on the MiG-29 'Fulcrum', the MiG-31 'Foxhound' and other very sophisticated types. It is possible that the MiG-29 is intended to replace the MiG-23. The US Defense Ministry regards the 'Fulcrum' as a proper multi-purpose fighter aircraft like the American McDonnell Douglas F-18 or F-16: an aircraft which can be used both as a fighter and an attack aircraft without any modifications being needed. The MiG-23 will doubtless go on being built and used for another few years before being replaced by the new types. The success of the 'Flogger' lies mainly in its well-balanced specifications, flexible and advanced design and unique serial production. The result is an aircraft which stands up well under any kind of use.

By 1986, sources in the West estimated that some 450 'Flogger B/G' interceptors were operational with the Soviet strategic air defence arm, with about 3,000 marks in other offensive/defense roles.

A rare view of MiG-23BN 'Flogger-H' strike fighters in service with the Indian Air Force. The type is being produced under licence by Hindustan Aeronautics Limited (HAL) and it is expected that some 200 domestically built aircraft will join the current force of 90 MiG-23BNs. The IAF also has the 'Flogger-G.'

Boeing 747 'Jumbo Jet'

While Douglas merely stretched the DC-8, Boeing went back to a clean sheet of paper to create a civil airliner much larger than any previously built. Immediately dubbed 'The Jumbo Jet', it revolutionized today's air-transport world in which two great advances, the wide-body airliner and the high bypass ratio fan engine, move more traffic with less noise and at much lower unit cost.

Ever since it came into being, the Boeing Company (formerly Boeing Airplane Company) has repeatedly made daring decisions to develop new transport or bomber aircraft which have shown to be in the forefront of technology. This has often been despite the fact that they have had no advance orders for an aircraft when they have begun planning it, and often also despite putting the company's entire assets on the line to develop the aircraft. The greatest risk Boeing ever took was the Boeing 747, even though it had one order from PanAm. In fact, this was probably the greatest risk any manufacturing company has ever taken. But it paid off, and once again Boeing established a milestone in the history of aviation.

This single type of aircraft, even today the most powerful, the heaviest and most capable ever constructed (not forgetting the old airships and giant flying boats of the past), transformed air transport by more than doubling the load of passengers or cargo that could be carried, by more than quadrupling the available payload volume, and not least by introducing a wholly new form of propulsion giving jet speed but with much reduced fuel consumption and less than one-tenth as much noise.

New generation jetliners

Boeing Commercial Airplane Company, the subsidiary responsible for civil transport aircraft, began to study a new-generation jetliner in the early 1960s for long-range high-traffic routes. Rival Douglas was in the throes of eking out DC-8 production by a dramatic process of stretching in the Super Sixty series. Boeing eventually chose not to reply with a super-stretched 707 but to build a totally new and much larger aircraft with a wider fuselage; it was to usher in a new era of so-called wide-body transports. Such an aircraft was possible because, at the same time, General Electric and Pratt & Whitney were developing completely new large turbofan engines for the US Air Force CX-HLS competition for a giant military freighter (won by Lockheed with its C-5A).

With aircraft of this size, new configurations of fuselage became possible. Boeing engineers exhaustively studied double-bubble schemes with two pressurized tubes full of passengers, either side-by-side or superimposed, as well as a single giant tube with two decks inside. In the event the decision was taken to use a single tube but with only one enormous passenger floor, extending right to the nose. Underneath there was room for the capacious bays for electronics, electrics, air-conditioning and hydraulics, as well as cargo holds of unprecedented size. If necessary, galleys and other passenger-service items could be at the lower level. The flight deck was placed above the ceiling of

Named *City of Esch-sur-Alzette* (written in English), this 747-200F is one of a pair operated on intensive all-cargo services, mainly to the USA, by Cargolux Airlines International of Luxembourg. This windowless front-loading variant is far more capable than any other airline freighter, carrying 254,640 lb (115500 kg).

Probably the most costly production aircraft in history, the E-4 AABNCP (Advanced Airborne National Command Post) would in time of crisis become the seat of government of the United States. This drawing shows the first E-4A as built with JT9D engines. Later it was fitted with F103 engines and became an E-4B.

the passenger deck, forming a slight blister above the nose and extended to the rear in an upper deck for typically 32 passengers. The main deck could seat up to 500 passengers in high-density 10-abreast seating (3 + 4 + 3), but 350 was judged a more likely number with an ultra-luxurious first-class section (seating passengers in pairs along the sides of the nose) extending right up to the radar filling the tip of the nose.

Boeing went for a high cruising speed with the model 747, adopting an advanced design of wing with the exceptional sweep-back angle of $37\frac{1}{2}°$ at 25 per cent chord (one-quarter of the way back from the leading edge). The leading edge was given a typically ambitious high-lift system, with three sections of Krueger flap hinged down from the under surface of the wing inboard of the inner engines, five sections of novel variable-camber flap between the engines, and five more sections between the outer engines and the tip on each side. The variable-camber flaps resembled traditional slats but comprised flexible skins carried on pivoted links in such a way that as they were hydraulically extended ahead of and below the leading edge they arched into a curve to give maximum control of the airflow at high angles. On the trailing edge were placed enormous triple-slotted flaps, with each section running on steel tracks with prominent fairings projecting behind the trailing edge. Above the wing on each side were added six sections of aluminium honeycomb spoiler, four outboard for control in flight (augmenting the roll power of the conventional trailing-edge low-speed ailerons) and two ground spoilers inboard to destroy lift after landing and thus increase braking power. High-speed ailerons were added at the trailing edge behind the inboard engines where the flaps could not be used.

Though the engine installation looked conventional, being arranged on four widely separated wing pylons as in the model 707 of 15 years earlier, they were on a scale never before seen except on the military C-5A. In fact Boeing picked the loser in the C-5A engine competition. Pratt &

Left Up to the end of 1985, more than 670 Boeing 747s of all versions had been ordered. In the Everett hangars, aircraft are being completed for Air France and Alitalia, as well as a shortened SP version for the Australian airline, Qantas.

N7470 was the very first Jumbo, seen here on its maiden flight (on which the landing gear was not retracted) on 9 February 1969. Even at that time there was a very healthy customer-list, as shown by the 28 airline symbols on the forward fuselage. Retained by Boeing, and later fitted with a tanker boom, this 747 is now N1352B.

Whitney, whose JT9D was offered as a robust and reliable turbofan of the new high-bypass-ratio type with a thrust of 41,000 lb (18598 kg). Extremely difficult engineering problems had to be solved in hanging the engines, in arranging a fan-duct reverse and hot-stream spoiler, and in reducing drag. Another tough engineering problem was the landing gear, eventually solved by using four main gear four-wheel bogies, two of them on tall inwards-retracting legs pivoted to the wings and the other pair on forward-retracting units pivoted to the fuselage, the four retracted bogies lying together in a large bay amidships under the floor. All flight controls are hydraulically powered, the rudder and elevators being divided into equal-size halves, no tabs being used anywhere. The APU (auxiliary power unit) for ground air conditioning and electric power was placed in the extreme tail of the fuselage.

Not only did Boeing have to build the 747: the company also had to build a new factory to make it, and the new plant at Everett, swiftly created in a 780-acre clearing in a forest, is the largest building (in cubic capacity) in the world. Together with many other programmes Boeing's commitments were awesome, and employment in 1968 peaked at 105,000, compared with 60,000 at the peak in World War 2. The risk on the model 747 easily topped one billion dollars, but thankfully orders kept rolling in, and when the first aircraft off the production line (Ship RA001) emerged from the new plant on 30 September 1968 a total of 158 orders had been gained from 26 airlines.

Engine snags

With so new and complex an aircraft it would have been surprising if there had been no snags, but in fact the difficulties, mainly centred on the engines, were prolonged. In crosswinds the engines were difficult to start and ran roughly, and distortion (so-called ovalization) of the casings caused blades to rub in a way that had not been apparent in more than two years of ground testing and flight development using a B-52. Pratt & Whitney had to devise a Y-shaped frame to hang the engine differently, and eventually produced a new version of JT9D that avoided the problem. But the first flight was delayed until 9 February 1969. This aircraft was retained by Boeing for many development purposes. The first to be delivered was handed to Pan American on 12 December 1969, and that airline – after an unprecedented amount of engineering and training effort and investment in new ground facilities – finally got the model 747 into service on the New York–London service on 22 January 1970.

Popularly called the 'Jumbo Jet', the model 747 hit the headlines as well as the pockets of its customers and the world's airport authorities. For a while it appeared almost to be premature, because traffic did not grow as expected and load factor (proportion of seats filled) was often low. With great courage, Boeing continued production at maximum rate, and both the orders and the variants continued to grow. From the outset Boeing had organized a vast manufacturing programme with major sections of airframe made by subcontractors: Northrop make the main fuselage sections, for example; and Fairchild Republic build the flaps, ailerons, slats and spoilers. With such large structures, exceptional

Boeing 747-127

Few aircraft have ever worked harder than *Big Orange*, a 747-127 which since 1978 has flown the gruelling round trip from Dallas to London Gatwick every 24 hours. Today Braniff has five 747-200s and three SPs, one of the latter (N603BN) having been painted the same colour. Braniff chooses a body/tail hue for each aircraft.

BRANIFF INTERNATIONAL

Specification

Type: long-range commercial transport
Powerplant: four 45,000-lb (20412-kg) Pratt & Whitney JT9D-3A turbofans; later models JT9D, CF6-50, -45 or -80, or RB.211 turbofans each of 56,000-lb (25400-kg) thrust
Performance: maximum speed at maximum weight 601 mph (969 km/h): maximum cruising speed 583 mph (939 km/h); maximum payload 163,200 lb (74030 kg) for range of 4,014 miles (6460 km), later versions up to 154,300 lb (69990 kg) for 6,239 miles (10040 km) or 254,640 lb (115500 kg) of cargo
Weights: empty 363,300 lb (167300 kg); maximum take-off 710,000 lb (322100 kg), (later versions 833,000 lb/377840 kg)
Dimensions: span 195 ft 8 in (59.64 m); length 231 ft 10 in (70.66 m); height 65 ft 5 in (19.94 m); wing area 5,500 sq ft (510.95 m²)

In 1974 the Imperial Iranian air force, then a large and expanding body, studied the C-5A but decided instead to buy 747s secondhand and convert them for military use in cargo, air-refuelling tanker and command-post roles. Three 747-124Fs were bought from Continental and nine 747-131Fs from TWA, as well as four new 747-2J9Fs.

precision is needed if there are not to be problems when the parts all come together at Everett. One unusual technique used in assembly is to mount completed aircraft on air-cushion pads so that they can be easily moved in any direction across a smooth concrete floor.

The initial version was designated model 747-100, and 167 of this model were sold. In the course of production not only did Pratt & Whitney introduce a succession of improved variants of the JT9D engine, offering power increased in stages from 41,000 (18598 kg) to 53,000 lb (24040 kg) thrust, but other engines became available. General Electric offered the lighter and equally powerful CF6-50 series, chosen by several airlines, while Rolls-Royce's RB.211-524 series gradually came from behind and in recent years has won several important model 747 orders because of its unequalled low fuel consumption – a matter of special importance to long-haul aircraft. The Rolls-Royce engine is distinctively shorter and neater than the installed US engines, and is claimed also to offer lower drag, though it is heavy.

On 11 October 1970 Boeing flew the first model 747-200, with greater fuel capacity and gross weight increased from 738,000 lb (334751 kg) to an initial 775,000 lb (351535 kg), subsequently increased to 820,000 lb (371945 kg) and now to 833,000 lb (377840 kg). Many tests have been made at weights up to more than 850,000 lb (385560 kg), almost 100,000 lb (45360 kg) heavier than any other aircraft. The basic passenger version is the model 747-200B, while the model 747-200F is a dedicated cargo version with no windows, a hinged nose for straight-in loading of pallets and containers (up to 29 standard 10-ft/3.05-m ISO containers, plus 30 lower-lobe containers for up to 249,000 lb/112946 kg of cargo) with a computerized, powered loading system which enables two loaders to load or unload the aircraft in less than 30 minutes. The model 747-200B Combi is a mixed-traffic aircraft with a movable (or removable) bulkhead separating the passenger sections from any desired length of cargo area. The Model 747-200C Convertible can be converted from all-passenger to all-cargo use, and vice versa.

Produced specifically for very long-range routes, the Boeing 747SP was introduced in 1975. The fuselage is shortened, reducing passenger capacity to a maximum of 316, but reduced weights combined with standard tankage effects a range of 6,736 miles (10841 km) with up to 321 passengers.

Boeing 747-200 cutaway drawing key

1. Radome
2. Radar dish
3. Pressure bulkhead
4. Radar scanner mounting
5. First class cabin, typically 32 seats
6. Windscreen
7. Instrument panel shroud
8. Rudder pedals
9. Control column
10. Flight-deck floor construction
11. First-class bar unit
12. Window panel
13. Nose undercarriage bay
14. Nosewheel door
15. Steering mechanism
16. Twin nosewheels
17. Radio and electronics racks
18. Captain's seat
19. Co-pilot's seat
20. Flight engineer's panel
21. Observer's seat
22. Upper deck door, port and starboard
23. Circular staircase between decks
24. Cockpit air conditioning duct
25. First-class galley
26. First-class toilets
27. Plug-type forward cabin door, No. 1.
28. First-class seats
29. Cabin dividing bulkhead
30. Anti-collision light
31. Cabin roof construction
32. Upper deck toilet
33. Upper deck seating, up to 32 passengers
34. Window panel
35. Air conditioning supply ducts
36. Forward fuselage construction
37. Baggage pallet containers
38. Forward under-floor freight compartment
39. Communications aerial
40. Upper deck galley
41. Meal trolley elevator
42. Lower deck forward galley
43. No. 2 passenger door, port and starboard
44. Air conditioning system intake
45. Wing-root fairing
46. Air conditioning plant
47. Wing spar bulkhead
48. Fresh water tanks
49. Forward economy-class cabin, typically 141 seats
50. Wing centre section fuel tank, capacity 17,000 US gal (64345 litres)
51. Centre section stringer construction
52. Cabin floor construction
53. Fuselage frame and stringer construction
54. Main fuselage frame
55. Air distribution duct
56. Air condition cross-feed ducts
57. Risers to distribution ducts
58. Machine main frame
59. Satellite navigation aerial
60. Starboard wing inboard fuel tank, capacity 12,300 US gal (36555 litres)
61. Fuel pumps
62. Engine bleed-air supply
63. Krueger flap operating jacks
64. Inboard Krueger flap
65. Starboard inner engine
66. Starboard inner engine pylon
67. Leading edge Krueger flap segments
68. Krueger flap drive mechanism
69. Krueger flap motors
70. Re-fuelling panel
71. Starboard wing outboard fuel tank, capacity 4,420 US gal (16730 litres)
72. Starboard outer engine
73. Starboard outer engine pylon
74. Outboard Krueger flap segments
75. Krueger flap drive mechanism
76. Extended range fuel tank, capacity 800 US gal (3028 litres) each wing
77. Surge tank
78. Starboard wing tip
79. Navigation light
80. VHF aerial boom
81. Fuel vent
82. Static dischargers
83. Outboard, low-speed, aileron
84. Outboard spoilers

Avianca (Aerovias Nacionales de Colombia) is, next to KLM, the world's longest-established airline. This aircraft is its 747-124 passenger aircraft used on routes from Bogota to many cities in North America and Europe. Avianca also operates a 747-200B with a 120 × 134-in (3.05 × 3.4-m) cargo door for mixed use.

Announced on 3 September 1973, the 747SP (Special Performance) is a highly specialized ultra-long-range aircraft with many major airframe changes. Like the 747 it was sponsored by PanAm, but for a while it appeared doubtful there would be many other customers. Today 11 others have signed, one being Taiwan's China Airlines.

85 Outboard slotted flaps
86 Flap drive mechanism
87 Inboard, high-speed, aileron
88 Trailing, edge beam
89 Inboard spoilers
90 Inboard slotted flap
91 Flap drive mechanism
92 Centre fuselage construction
93 Starboard undercarriage bay housing
94 No. 3 passenger door
95 Wing-mounted main undercarriage bay
96 Flap driver motors
97 Undercarriage beam
98 Fuselage-mounted main undercarriage bay
99 Main undercarriage jack
100 Floor panels
101 Spat rails
102 Cabin window trim panels
103 Centre cabin economy-class seating, typically 82 passengers
104 Nine-abreast seating
105 Air distribution ducts
106 No. 4 passenger door, port and starboard
107 Centre cabin galley
108 Overhead baggage racks (with doors)
109 Main air supply duct
110 Rear cabin galley
111 Rear cabin seating, typically 114 passengers
112 Economy-class seating
113 Oversea baggage racks
114 Cabin roof panels
115 Control cable runs

116 Rear fuselage construction
117 Rear cabin seats
118 Rear cabin toilets
119 Wardrobes
120 Rear pressure dome bulkhead
121 Fin root fairing
122 Starboard tailplane
123 Static dischargers
124 Starboard elevator
125 Fin leading edge construction
126 Fin spar construction
127 Fin-tip fairing
128 VOR aerial
129 Static dischargers
130 Upper rudder segment
131 Lower rudder segment
132 Rudder jacks
133 Tailcone fairing
134 APU exhaust
135 Auxiliary power unit (APU)
136 Port elevator inner segment
137 Port elevator outer segment
138 Static dischargers
139 Tailplane construction
140 Elevator jacks
141 Tailplane sealing plate
142 Aft fuselage frames
143 Fin attachment
144 Tailplane centre section
145 Moving tailplane jack
146 APU air duct

147 No. 5 passenger door, port and starboard
148 Rear fuselage window panel
149 Rear under-floor freight hold
150 Freight and baggage pallet container
151 Fuselage frame and stringer construction
152 Trailing edge fillet
153 Fuselage-mounted undercarriage pivot
154 Trailing edge beam
155 Port inboard slotted flap
156 Flap tracks
157 Flap track fairings
158 Inboard spoilers
159 Flap drive shaft
160 Flap down position
161 Fuselage-mounted main undercarriage bogie
162 Wing spar and rib construction
163 Wing root attachment plate
164 Front spar

165 Engine bleed air supply pipe
166 Leading edge ribs
167 Landing lamps
168 Inboard Krueger flap

169 Krueger flap motor and drive
170 Wing-mounted main undercarriage leg
171 Four-wheel main undercarriage bogie
172 Main undercarriage side brace
173 Wing-mounted undercarriage jack
174 Wing skins
175 Wing stringer construction
176 Inboard engine mounting beam
177 Pylon attachment strut
178 Port inner pylon construction
179 Heat exchanger
180 Engine intake
181 Rolls-Royce RB.211–524B engine

182 Engine driven gearbox
183 Outer fan ducting
184 Core engine exhaust
185 Integral fuel tankage
186 Inboard, high-speed aileron
187 Aileron jack
188 Outboard slotted flap
189 Flap track fairing
190 Flap down position
191 Outboard spoilers
192 Flap tracks
193 Flap track mounting beams
194 Wing spar and rib construction
195 Leading edge construction
196 Krueger flap segments
197 Krueger flap mechanism
198 Outboard engine mounting beam
199 Port outer engine pylon
200 Heat exchanger air duct
201 Port outer engine cowlings

202 Thrust reverser cascades
203 Thrust reverser cowling door, open
204 Door operating jacks
205 Outer Krueger flap segments
206 Krueger flap mechanism
207 Outer wing construction
208 Aileron jacks
209 Outboard, low-speed, aileron
210 Static dischargers
211 Fuel vent
212 Wing-tip fairing
213 Navigation light
214 VHF aerial boom

A unique 747 is NASA's 747-123, an old ex-American Airlines aircraft acquired in 1977 and largely rebuilt to carry the first Space Shuttle Orbiter on captive and later free-flight tests. Originally a 738,000-lb (334755-kg) aircraft, it emerged with endplate fins, dorsal mountings, release systems and a revised gross weight.

Further variants

In 1978 Boeing introduced the model 747-100B as an updated replacement for the model 747-100 with strengthened structure and more powerful and efficient engines. The model 747SR (short-range) is a variant of the model 747-100B with structure further reinforced for frequent take-offs and landings and higher performance because of its lighter weight, despite a payload of up to 516 passengers.

From the model 747-100B Boeing took another bold decision in September 1973 in going ahead with the model 747SP (Special Performance). Though 90 per cent of the parts were unchanged, the other 10 per cent represented very substantial engineering effort and investment, and the model 747SP came out looking strikingly different from its predecessors. Intended for ultra-long routes, the model 747SP has a fuselage 47 ft 1 in (14.35 m) shorter, which in turn demanded a vertical tail 5 ft (1.52 m) taller, with double-hinged rudders, and a tailplane increased in span by 10 ft (3.05 m). The flaps were changed to the single-slotted variable-pivot type, without the prominent fairings, and there are many smaller changes. Despite having gross weight lower than other versions, the model 747SP has extremely long range, demonstrated by a delivery flight by South African Airways which, with 50 passengers and a heavy load of spare parts, flew nonstop 10,290 miles (16560 km) to Cape Town and arrived with 2½ hours of fuel remaining. Captain Walter H. Millikin of Pan American has flown round the world in a model 747SP in 1 day 22 hours 50 seconds (average 503 mph/809 km/h) as well as round the globe.

Last of the announced commercial 747 types in late 1981,

The 747 SUD (Stretched Upper Deck), later called the 747-300, under construction. By this means the upper passenger accommodation was increased from 32 to 64. Also added was a new emergency exit and extra windows. The FAA certificate was announced on 7 March 1983.

the model 747SUD (Stretched Upper Deck) is the opposite of the SP in providing increased passenger capacity. Since before the first flight Boeing had been studying double-deck versions, and eventually the market appeared right for a modest move in this direction with an order by Swissair in the summer of 1980 for the model 747SUD with the upper deck extended behind the flight deck a further 23 ft (7.01 m). This increases the upper-deck seating from 32 to 69 in standard economy configuration (3 + 3). A new straight stairway is added at the rear (other 747s have a spiral staircase forward, and if this is removed the model 747SUD can seat a further seven passengers) and a new emergency exit is added, as well as extra windows. The SUD is now available on all models except the 747SP. By late 1981 total Boeing 747 orders exceeded 575, and over 5½ million passengers were being carried, mostly over very long distances, each month.

July 1985 saw the go-ahead of the 747-400 advanced long-range version of the 747-300. Finished models were anticipated in early 1988. British Airways has ordered 16 of these aircraft and expects delivery before 1990.

Military customers

Several 747s have been sold to military customers, a fleet which at one time numbered 11 having been supplied to the former Imperial (now Islamic) Iranian air force for air-tanker, electronic-warfare and other strategic roles. Saudi Arabia took delivery of a very special Rolls-engined Boeing 747SP with extremely comprehensive navigation and communications equipment fitted out mainly by E-Systems. The same Texas-based company teamed with another Boeing subsidiary, Boeing Aerospace Company, to provide the US Air Force with the very costly E-4.

Known as the AABNCP (Advanced Airborne National Command Post), the E-4 is basically a Boeing 747-200B carrying extremely comprehensive communications (command/control) and other equipment in order to serve as the HQ of the US National Military Command System and the operational HQ of SAC (Strategic Air Command) in time of crisis. The E-4s replace various types of EC-135. Originally two E-4A aircraft were delivered, in 1974–5. These had JT9D engines (later replaced by General Electric F103-100s, military versions of the CF6-50) and carried equipment taken mainly from the earlier Boeing EC-135s.

Eventually, most 747s were fitted with EC-135s. In April 1975 the first true E-4B left the test stand, and a fully-equipped E-4B was delivered in 1978. All four machines now fly under this designation and have SHF antennae located in a large dome on top of the fuselage, 1200 kW on-board electrical power, advanced environmental control systems, nuclear and thermal insulation, low frequency systems with (LF/VLF) trailing aerials several miles/kilometres in length, inflight refuelling facilities and a range (without inflight refuelling) of 73 hours. The inside of the aircraft is divided into various functional areas: the main deck contains a command post, conference and presentation rooms, a workroom for more than 60 crew, communications control rooms and rest areas. These aircraft are stationed at the US Air Force base at Offutt, Nebraska.

Boeing 747 variants

Boeing 747-100: original production version with JT9D-1 or -3 engines, 738,000-lb (334751-kg) maximum weight
Boeing 747-100B: advanced derivative of model 747-100 with strengthened structure and weight up to 753,000-lb (341555-kg), 46,950-lb (21297-kg) JT9D-7A engines, or various other JT9D versions, or CF6-45 or -50, or RB.211-524
Boeing 747-200B: long-range model with weights up to 833,000-lb (377840-kg) and increased fuel capacity, JT9D-7AW, -7FW, -7J or -7Q engines, or General Electric CF6-50E series; or RB.211-524B, C or D units rated at up to 53,110-lb (2409)1-kg) thrust
Boeing 747-200B Combi: convertible passenger/cargo model with cargo side door aft of wing, all-passenger or up to 12 pallets/containers

Boeing 747-200C Convertible: equipped with basic freight floor and loading system for conversion from all-cargo to all-passenger, or a mix. Weight up to 833,000 lb (377845 kg), same powerplant options as model 747-200B
Boeing 747-200F: dedicated cargo aircraft with upwards hinged nose, normally windowless, capable of delivering 200,000-lb (90720-kg) of palletized or containerized cargo over a range of 4,720 miles (7600 km)
Boeing 747SR: high-capacity short-range aircraft with structural changes, gross weight 603,000 lb (273520 kg) or 735,000 lb (333396 kg)
Boeing 747SP: special-performance long-range model with short body, enlarged tail and weights 603,000 lb (273520 kg) to 702,000 lb (318420 kg), various engines, 289-440 passengers
Boeing 747SUD: stretched upper deck for 37-44 extra passengers

Concorde

One of the greatest challenges in the history of aviation, Concorde is also among the very greatest technical triumphs. Yet, though its purpose was to bring people closer together, it generated a giant organized lobby of opposition, and the soaring price of fuel has made its operating economics marginal.

A British Airways Concorde bears menacingly down the runway displaying its protective visor, drooped to give vision to the pilot who otherwise, in flight, sees nothing of the outside airspace. The engineering of the visor streamlines the nose and protects the windscreen in flight.

Speed is an important factor which can make or break a decision whether or not to buy an aircraft. As long as other factors, such as running costs, were kept within reasonable limits, there was never any serious doubt that the building of increasingly fast airliners was only a question of time and technical progress. Since World War 2 it has been Britain, first and foremost, that has striven to turn this concept into reality. It was here that the development of the de Havilland D.H.106 Comet began, which almost became the first of the new generation of jet airliners on the world market. When the Comet project ran aground in the mid-1950s due to

previously unknown metallurgical problems with fatigue, the British aviation authorities sat round the table with members of the aircraft industry to discuss the building of a supersonic airliner. This resulted in the founding of the Supersonic Transport Aircraft Committee, or STAC, which met for the first time in 1956.

The four Rolls-Royce/SNECMA Olympus 593 engines allow the Concorde to travel at twice the speed of sound. Because of the aircraft's steep take-off and landing angles, the nose tilts downwards slightly to give a better view from the cockpit.

The STAC embraced not only government technologists, top men from engine and airframe companies and numerous officials, but also nominees from civil airlines. Nobody then could possibly foresee that opposition to such a project would assume the proportions of a national crusade, or that for political reasons the USA and many other countries would delay for years admitting such an aircraft to its airports or even permit it to fly overhead, and certainly the price of fuel was not expected to be multiplied tenfold. All that could be seen clearly was that the technical problems were of an order of magnitude greater than those of other aircraft. Just one immutable problem was that, for any given amount of wing lift, the drag is more than doubled as the vehicle accelerates from Mach 0.9 to beyond Mach 1.

Three options

It was obvious that a supersonic airliner would need a novel configuration, with a wing of very low aspect ratio and an extremely long body of minimal cross-section. The STAC studied three main answers. One was an area-ruled aircraft with a curious M-wing, initially swept forward and then back to the tips, cruising at Mach 1.2 (800 mph/1285 km/h) for 1,500 miles (2414 km). Second was a slender delta, very much like the eventual Concorde, but cruising at Mach 1.8 (1,200 mph/1930 km/h) for 3,500 miles (5635 km). Third was a steel/titanium monster cruising at Mach 3 (2,000 mph/3220 km/h) for 3,500 miles (5635 km). The third idea was deemed technically too difficult and costly, though for a further 14 years it consumed over $2,000 million in the USA. In March 1959 the STAC recommended Mach 1.2 short-range or Mach 1.8 transAtlantic, and the Ministry of Aviation awarded contracts for detailed studies of the latter aircraft. By late 1960 it was clear not only that the slender delta, with an ogival (curved) leading edge, was the best shape but also that its aerodynamic efficiency improved up to about Mach 2.2. This not only reduced journey time but improved propulsion efficiency, because the latter depends on the ram pressure generated in the engine inlet and this rises rapidly with increasing Mach number.

By 1960 Bristol Aircraft, then in the process of merging into the British Aircraft Corporation (BAC), had schemed the Type 198, a 130-passenger transAtlantic SST looking much like today's Concorde but powered by six Bristol Siddeley Olympus engines.

In the summer of 1961 the aviation ministry decided a 380,000-lb (172368-kg) six-engine aircraft was too ambitious, and asked for a 100-seater weighing 250,000 lb (113400 kg) with four engines. By this time Sud-Aviation in France, likewise in the throes of becoming part of a giant group (SNIAS or Aérospatiale), had studied Mach 2 SSTs and decided on a very similar configuration but aimed at short ranges as a 70/80-seat successor to the company's Caravelle. At the Paris Air Show in June 1961 Sud displayed a model of its idea, named Super Caravelle. Some months previously BAC had, on government insistence, put out feelers to possible foreign partners, and Sud-Aviation was the only positive response. The first formal meetings were held during the Paris Air Show, and a month later at Weybridge.

British Airways' third Concorde sits on the tarmac at Melbourne, Australia. The airline and manufacturers spent much time and trouble proving the route to Australia, but met with much opposition from overflown countries and residents local to destination airports. Concorde was banned from landing at the airport at Sydney.

Concorde

The similarity between the British and French proposals was amazing, almost the only difference apart from size, weight and range being that Sud thought it could get away without using a hinged 'droop snoot' nose, while BAC considered such a feature essential for adequate forward view during the nose-high landing. After many further talks, an inter-government agreement of 29 November 1962 formally launched the project, with government funding on a 50/50 basis and the main effort shared between BAC and Aérospatiale on the airframe and Bristol Siddeley (from 1966 Rolls-Royce) and SNECMA on propulsion, using as a basis an enlarged Olympus called the Olympus 593. The British partner was charged with developing a transAtlantic version, while the French adhered to a short-haul model with a ventral stairway instead of fuel in the rear fuselage. A Committee of Directors was appointed to run the airframe, and another to manage the engine, and there were separate British and French government contracts to each national industrial group.

Suffice to say that such an arrangement will never be repeated, but it was made to work by the goodwill and towering stature of the main engineers involved. Sir George Edwards, who when head of Vickers-Armstrongs (Aircraft) in 1958 had predicted the entire future course of events with extreme accuracy, was the architect of the whole project. Top designers at Bristol were Sir Archibald Russell and Dr Bill Strang, while leaders at Aérospatiale were Pierre Satre and Lucien Servanty. Collaboration extended down through the main airframe and engine teams to the hundreds of major suppliers of systems and equipment.

Gradually the French accepted the idea of a transAtlantic SST, especially after a large meeting of possible airline customers had shown in 1963 that the feeling of the market was that the proposal was not bold enough. A powerful body of opinion held that the Anglo-French SST would be outmoded by the promised later American SST to carry some 250 passengers at Mach 3. It needed steady nerves to stick to the belief that 100 passengers at about Mach 2 was right.

Specification

Type: supersonic commercial transport
Powerplant: four Rolls Royce/SNECMA Olympus 593 Mk 610 turbojet engines, each rated at 38,050-lb (17259-kg) thrust with 17 per cent afterburning
Performance: cruising speed for optimum range Mach 2.04 at 51,300 ft (15635 m), equivalent to 1,354 mph (2179 km/h); service ceiling 60,000 ft (18290 m); range with maximum fuel 4,090 miles (6582 km) with FAR fuel reserves and payload of 19,500 lb (8845 kg); range with maximum payload at Mach 2.02 cruise 3,870 miles (6228 km) with FAR fuel reserves

Weights: operating empty 173,500 lb (78698 kg); maximum take-off 408,000 lb (185066 kg)
Dimensions: span 83 ft 10 in (25.55 m); length 203 ft 9 in (62.10 m); height 37 ft 5 in (11.40 m); wing area 3,856 sq ft (358.22 m²)

Aérospatiale/British Aerospace Concorde

The sixth production Concorde, which first flew on 5 November 1975 and entered service with British Airways on 21 January 1976 when it flew a service from London to Bahrain. The elegantly simple lines of the Concorde, optimized for an economical cruising speed of just over Mach 2, tend to disguise the extreme complexity, in both aerodynamics and systems, of this pioneering SST. Some indication of the sophisticated aerodynamic factors is indeed given by the modified ogival wing planform with its cambered leading edges, but the intricacies of the powerplant/fuel and electronics systems are not even suggested. The latter are the key to the effective operation of the aircraft, controlling the trim of the machine and the performance of the engines to suit exactly the relevant flight conditions. Though the nose is shown in the raised position, the visor is not extended.

Concorde

Named Concorde in 1963, the Anglo-French machine grew from 262,000 lb to 286,000 lb (118843 kg to 129730 kg), increasing the seating for the full range from 90 to 100, but the engine team then redesigned the Olympus, as the Mk 593B, to give much greater power, and this allowed the Concorde to follow the pressures of the market and grow to 326,000 lb (147874 kg) with 118 seats. In early 1965 design was brought to a halt, and construction of prototypes 001 and 002 began. In parallel a colossal research programme was funded, including a complete airframe thermal rig at Farnborough and the Handley Page H.P.115 and BAC.221 research aircraft were put to use flight-testing many of the new systems.

Though part of the agreement was that there should be an assembly line in both countries, producing odd-numbered aircraft at Toulouse St Martin and even-numbered at Filton (Bristol), there was no duplication in actual manufacture. Thus BAC was assigned the nose, tail and engine installations, and Aérospatiale the wings, centre fuselage and landing gears. France actually had about 60 per cent of the airframe because the UK had most of the engine, while systems were shared more or less evenly and included a number of items from the USA.

Aerodynamically the design is a tailless ogival delta. The wing has continuous subtle curvatures, with strong conical camber giving pronounced leading-edge droop outboard, but the basic thickness is extremely low, only 3 per cent inboard and 2.15 per cent outboard of the engines. Wing sections were made at Bouguenais, Toulouse, St Nazaire and Marignane, and the section outboard of the engines was made by Dassault at Bourges. Flight control is by six elevons, two of them inboard of the engines, each driven by a Dowty Boulton Paul tandem jack in the 4,000-lb/sq in (281.2-kg/cm²) hydraulic system. One of the drawbacks is that at take-off and landing these surfaces cannot be used to increase wing camber and thus lift and drag, but the problem of trimming out the change in centre of pressure (the point through which the resultant lift force acts) was solved very neatly without causing any drag. Most of the 26,330 Imp gal (119695 litres) of fuel is housed in integral tanks in the thin wing and under the passenger floor, but by using extra tanks at the extreme front of the wing and in the tail of the fuselage it was found possible to shift the centre of gravity of the aircraft to match the shift in the centre of pressure. During transonic acceleration the contents of the forward tanks are pumped into the rear trim tank and main tankage. At the end

Aérospatiale/BAe Concorde cutaway drawing key

1 Variable geometry drooping nose
2 Weather radar
3 Spring pot
4 Visor jack
5 'A'-frame
6 Visor uplock
7 Visor guide rails and carriage
8 Droop nose jacks
9 Droop nose guide rails
10 Droop nose hinge
11 Rudder pedals
12 Captain's seat
13 Instrument panel shroud
14 Forward pressure bulkhead
15 Retracting visor
16 Multi-layer windscreen
17 Windscreen fluid rain clearance and wipers
18 Second pilot's seat
19 Roof panel
20 Flight-deck air duct
21 3rd crew member's seat
22 Control relay jacks
23 1st supernumerary's seat
24 2nd supernumerary's folding seat (optional)
25 Radio and electronics racks (Channel 2)
26 Radio and electronics racks (Channel 1)
27 Plug-type forward passenger door
28 Slide/life-raft pack stowage
29 Cabin staff tip-up seat
30 Forward galley units (port and starboard)
31 Toilets (2)
32 Coats (crew and passengers)
33 Twelve 26-man life-rafts
34 VHF 1 antenna
35 Overhead baggage racks (with doors)
36 Cabin furnishing (heat and sound insulated)
37 4-abreast one-class passenger accommodation
38 Seat rails
39 Metal-faced floor panels
40 Nosewheel well
41 Nosewheel main doors
42 Nosewheel leg
43 Shock absorber
44 Twin nosewheels
45 Torque links

46 Steering mechanism
47 Telescopic strut
48 Lateral bracing struts
49 Nosewheel actuating jacks
50 Underfloor air-conditioning ducts
51 Nosewheel door actuator
52 Nosewheel secondary (aft) doors
53 Fuselage frame (single flange)
54 Machined window panel
55 Underfloor forward baggage compartment (237 cu ft/6.72 m³)
56 Fuel lines
57 Lattice ribs
58 No. 9 (port forward) trim tank
59 Single-web spar
60 No. 10 (port forward) trim tank
61 Middle passenger doors (port and starboard)
62 Cabin staff tip-up seat
63 Toilets
64 Emergency radio stowage
65 Provision for VHF3
66 Overhead baggage racks (with doors)
67 Cabin aft section
68 Fuselage frame
69 Tank vent gallery
70 No. 1 forward collector tank
71 Lattice ribs
72 Engine-feed pumps
73 Accumulator
74 No. 5 fuel tank
75 Trim transfer gallery
76 Leading-edge machined ribs
77 Removable leading-edge sections with:
78 Expansion joints between sections
79 Contents unit
80 Inlet control valve
81 Transfer pumps
82 Flight-deck air duct
83 No. 8 fuselage tank

84 Vapour seal above tank
85 Pressure-floor curved membranes
86 Pre-stretched integrally machined wing skin panels
87 No. 8 wing tank
88 No. 4 forward collector tank
89 No. 10 starboard forward trim tank
90 No. 9 starboard forward trim tank
91 Quick-lock removable inspection panels
92 Spraymat leading-edge de-icing panels
93 Leading-edge anti-icing strip
94 Spar-box machined girder side pieces
95 No. 7 fuel tank
96 No. 7a fuel tank
97 Static dischargers
98 Elevon
99 Inter-elevon flexible joint nozzles/reverser buckets
100 Combined secondary nozzles/reverser buckets
101 Nozzle-mounting spigots
102 Cabin air delivery/distribution
103 Inspection panels
104 Cold-air unit
105 Fuel-cooled heat exchanger
106 Fuel/hydraulic oil heat exchanger
107 Fire-suppression bottles
108 Main spar frame
109 Accumulator
110 No. 3 aft collector tank
111 Control linkage
112 'Z'-section spot-welded stringers

113 Riser to distribution duct
114 Anti-surge bulkheads
115 No. 6 (underfloor) fuel tank
116 Machined pressurised keel box
117 Fuselage frame
118 Double-flange frame/floor join
119 Machined pressure-floor support beams
120 Port undercarriage well
121 Mainwheel door
122 Fuselage/wing attachments
123 Main spar frame
124 Mainwheel retraction link
125 Mainwheel actuating jack
126 Cross beam
127 Forked link
128 Drag strut
129 Mainwheel leg
130 Shock absorber
131 Pitch dampers
132 Four-wheel main undercarriage
133 Bogie beam
134 Torque links
135 Intake boundary layer splitter
136 Honeycomb intake nose section
137 Spraymat intake lip de-icing
138 Ramp motor and gearbox
139 Forward ramp
140 Aft ramp
141 Inlet flap

142 Spill door actuator
143 Intake duct
144 Tank vent gallery
145 Engine front support links
146 Engine-mounting transverse equalizers
147 Oil tank
148 Primary heat exchanger
149 Secondary heat exchanger
150 Heat-exchanger exhaust air
151 Rolls-Royce/SNECMA Olympus 593 Mk 610 turbojet
152 Outer wing fixing (340 high-tensile steel bolts)
153 Engine main mounting
154 Power control unit mounting
155 No. 5a fuel tank
156 Tank vent
157 Transfer pump
158 Port outer elevon control unit fairing
159 Static dischargers
160 Honeycomb elevon structure
161 Flexible joint

162 Port middle elevon control hinge/fairing
163 Power control unit twin output
164 Control rod linkage
165 Nacelle aft support link
166 Reverse-bucket actuating screw jack
167 Retractable silencer lobes ('spades')
168 Primary (inner) variable nozzle
169 Pneumatic nozzle actuators
170 Nozzle-mounting spigots
171 Port inner elevon control hinge/fairing
172 Control rod linkage
173 Location of ram-air turbine (RAT) in production aircraft
174 Accumulator
175 Vent and pressurisation system

Singapore Airlines were an enthusiastic potential partner on the British Airways far eastern route, and for a time some Concordes were painted in Singapore colours on one side of the fuselage. But, once again, overflying rights became a drag on the costs and benefits of the operation and Singapore was forced to withdraw.

of supersonic cruise the contents of the rear trim tank are pumped forward into the front trim and main tanks.

Ruling structural material is an aluminium alloy developed in the UK as RR.58 and produced in France under the designation AU2GN. The engines, however, are almost entirely of ferrous alloys, titanium alloys, Waspaloy or high-nickel alloys, and they are fed by extremely large ducts leading from fully variable sharp-edged inlets with electric anti-icing, and with front and rear variable upper wall ramps and controllable doors in the underside through which air can be admitted or expelled. In the course of development the engine was further increased in power, given a new jetpipe combining afterburner, variable nozzle and reverser, and also vaporizing combustors which eliminated visible

176 Forged wing/fuselage main frames
177 Ground-supply air-conditioning connection
178 Control mixing unit
179 Control rod (elevon) linkage
180 Aft galley unit
181 Rear emergency doors (port and starboard)
182 Wingroot fillet

183 Air-conditioning manual discharge valve
184 Automatic discharge/relief valve
185 First-aid oxygen cylinders
186 Rear baggage compartment (door to starboard)
187 Rear pressure bulkhead
188 Fin support frames

189 No. 11 aft trim tank
190 Machined centre posts
191 Shock absorber
192 Retractable tail bumper
193 Tail bumper door
194 Tank overflow and pressure relief lines
195 Tail cone bulkhead

196 Fuel jettison
197 Monergol-powered emergency power unit (pre-production aircraft only)
198 Tail cone
199 Rear navigation light
200 Rudder lower section
201 Servo control unit fairing (manual stand-by)
202 Fixed rubber stub
203 Multi-bolt fin-spar attachment
204 Fin construction
205 Fin spar
206 Air-conditioning ducting
207 HF antennae
208 Finroot fairing
209 Leading-edge structure
210 Servo unit threshold bellcrank
211 Servo control unit fairing
212 VOR antenna
213 Rudder upper section
214 Static dischargers

smoke. The four-wheel main gears fold inward and have Dunlop carbon/carbon brakes, the first service application of such brakes in the world and indicative of the unprecedented severity of the rejected take-off of the fully loaded aircraft. There is no braking parachute or airbrake, and leading edges are fixed. Systems, however, are advanced and complex, though the hydraulic pressure had been used on the Bristol Britannia. The system marking the biggest jump in complexity was undoubtedly the engine inlets, followed by environmental control, with the high cabin pressure-differential of 10.7 lb/sq in (0.75 kg/cm²) and the fuel used as a heat-sink.

By 1966 major pieces of structure were on thermal/fatigue test, the engine was running with its variable exhaust system and the main flight simulator was in use. Prototype 001 was rolled out at Toulouse on 11 December 1967, but it was the following August before it taxied and the first flight was delayed until 2 March 1969, the pilot being André Turcat. No. 002 flew in command of Brian Trubshaw from Filton a month later. Airline pilots first flew the prototypes in November 1969, and from the first there were no major problems connected with the aircraft. The problems stemmed from protesters, who considered SST a menace to the environment (apparently on the grounds mainly of noise), and from soaring increase in development cost, half of which was the result of the childishly low initial estimate, which made no allowance for the progressive increases in size and capability of the aircraft, and half of inflation, for which no allowance at all had been made.

Contracts signed

By 1971 the prototypes were making long overseas trips, and in December that year the first pre-production aircraft, with visibly different vizor, longer forward fuselage and extended tail, made its first flight from Filton to the UK test base at Fairford. On 28 July 1972 British Airways signed with BAC for five aircraft and Air France signed with Aérospatiale for four. There had previously been options by PanAm and purchase agreements by China, but these were never taken up. Prototype 001 was retired to a museum at Le Bourget in October 1973, two months before the first flight by the first production aircraft. By 1975 there was hardly a major city that had not been visited by at least one Concorde, and very intensive route proving was showing a remarkable reliability even at this early date. Scheduled services began on 21 January 1976, British Airways flying London–Bahrain with aircraft 206 and Air France flying Paris–Dakar–Rio with 205. Services to Washington were begun by both airlines on 24 May 1976. Prototype 002 was retired to Yeovilton on 4 March 1976 and 01 to Duxford on 20 August 1977. Category III autoland was cleared in passenger operation on 1 September 1978.

Though passenger operations could not have been more successful, both in terms of passenger appeal and reliability

(to the extent that in 1981 Concorde was several times the most punctual type in British Airways service according to the monthly report to the airline board, averaging 94 per cent), political troubles and rising fuel costs crippled the global plans for using the aircraft properly and had by late 1982 reduced utilization to an extremely low figure. A joint British Airways/Braniff service from Washington on to Dallas was suspended in June 1980, and the British Airways service to Singapore followed five months later. In April 1982 Air France discontinued services to Caracas and Rio, and by summer 1982 the only scheduled services were (British Airways) twice daily to New York and thrice weekly to Washington, and (Air France) 11 a week to New York, to which two continue to Washington and two to Mexico City. A small amount of additional flying is made up by charters to business companies and enthusiast groups.

Certainly the main traffic routes are transAtlantic, and so far they have brought British Airways some 495,000 passengers and Air France about 360,000, out of a total of just over a million. The aircraft has sustained reliability in excess of 93 per cent on sectors up to 4,000 miles (6440 km) in length, total service flight time being over 67,000 hours on more than 20,000 scheduled departures. Small changes, for example to the inlet lips and rudder trailing edge, have had a significant good effect on operating economics, but profitability remains marginal. Both airlines have announced they believe they are entering an era of Concorde profitability. Indeed British Airways has been looking at ways to increase Concorde operations, including running a cargo service in partnership with Federal Express, opening passenger service to Miami and a nonstop route to Lagos, Nigeria.

At government level, a great deal has been done to minimize the costs of research projects, which are only really necessary if a new generation of Concordes is envisaged. In May 1982 the then British Trade and Industry Minister, Norman Lamont, held formal talks with the French Transport Minister, Charles Fitermann, to carry out a detailed review of the whole project. But even before this, it was established that giving up the project would cost more money than it would save. The discussions centred around the question whether it would be possible to spread the remaining costs more equitably. Although both British Aerospace and Aérospatiale envisage a new generation with an improved lift/drag ratio of 10 compared with the present Concorde's 7, as well as further improving the engines, there is little chance that these proposals will ever come to fruition. In the current environment, there is no long-term future for supersonic airliners.

Air France's routes to South America looked promising with little but the Sahara desert and the Atlantic Ocean to overfly. But crippling fuel costs ruined the route despite the exceptional appeal and reliability of the service. Air France now flies Concorde only to New York, Washington and Mexico City.

McDonnell Douglas F-15 Eagle

Spawned by the long-range air combat requirements of the Vietnam War, and proved by the Israelis in dogfights and strike escort missions, the McDonnell Douglas F-15 is without doubt the world's finest all-weather day/night air superiority fighter.

Although everyone hopes it will never happen, if there were military conflict between the two superpowers, the Soviet side would outnumber the Americans both on the ground and in the air. To win a conventional war, as demonstrated in the final stages of World War 2 against Germany and Japan, and in Korea at the beginning of the 1950s, the Americans would need air superiority. As today's fighting forces have to operate in almost every conceivable situation, this air superiority would have to apply to night-time flying and to every possible type of weather. In the Western world there is only one aircraft type that is superior to the best of the Soviet Union's military aircraft, even when outnumbered by the other side. This is the McDonnell Douglas F-15 Eagle.

It is an essential part of USAF doctrine that the first and highest priority of tactical air forces is to achieve air superiority, denying the opposing force the effective use of air space, while simultaneously accomplishing their own missions. In Korea, air superiority was evidenced by a kill ratio of better than 10:1 in favour of the North American F-86 Sabre, which shot down 810 enemy aircraft for 78 F-86s lost in the air. A crucial factor in this success was that the F-86 had bases reasonably close to the combat area: Suwon was only 270 miles (430 km) from where the MiGs patrolled, and Kimpo was even closer. At one stage (January 1951) the F-86s were forced to withdraw to Johnson AFB in Japan, which took them out of reach of the Korean action.

An F-15A of the 49th Tactical Fighter Wing, based at Holloman AFB, New Mexico. Note the massive dorsal airbrake, which has given rise to some criticism regarding its effect on rear view in combat. This photograph also illustrates the excellent all-round view that the canopy provides, and the wide spacing of the fins.

An F-15A of the 1st Tactical Fighter Wing (based at Langley AFB, Virginia) flying over the base, which is also the headquarters of Tactical Air Command, whose badge is painted on the fin. The 1st TFW is now part of the United States Rapid Deployment Joint Task Force, which would deploy to the Middle East in emergency.

No substitute for piston engines

Jet fighters were thus not true replacements for the long-range piston-engined fighters of World War 2, such as the North American P-51 Mustang, Republic P-47 Thunderbolt and Lockheed P-38 Lightning. This point was driven home in the 1960s, when the USAF attempted to win control of the air over North Vietnam. Some degree of control was eventually won, but at times the monthly kill ratio favoured the enemy's Mikoyan-Gurevich MiG-17s and MiG-21s, and the USAF prevailed only by the extensive use of inflight refuelling for its fighters.

It appears to be common practice after a war for air forces to decide that aerial dogfights are a thing of the past. Fighter speeds progress, and the air staffs judge that close combat is no longer possible: the opposing aircraft will be moving too fast to see one another or to manoeuvre to maintain contact, and (in any case) the pilots will be subjected to crushing g-loads. Whether for these or other reasons, the idea of an air superiority fighter was largely abandoned by the USAF after Korea. The service took little interest in the Lockheed F-104 Starfighter, funding instead nuclear strike aircraft such as the Republic F-105 and General Dynamics F-111, and all-weather interceptors such as the Convair F-102 and F-106.

The commitment of USAF aircraft to the Vietnam war in 1962 thus found the service with only a handful of F-104Cs

McDonnell Douglas F-15C Eagle cutaway drawing key

1 Tailplane honeycomb construction
2 Boron fibre skin panel
3 Tailplane spars
4 All-moving tailplane pivot fixing
5 Leading edge dog-tooth
6 Low-voltage formation lighting strip
7 Fin root attachment frames
8 Rudder hydraulic rotary actuator
9 Rudder honeycomb construction
10 Fin spar construction
11 Boron fibre skin panel
12 Anti-collision light
13 Electronic counter-measures aerials (ECM)
14 Variable area afterburner exhaust nozzles
15 Nozzle sealing flaps
16 Fueldraulic nozzle actuators
17 Afterburner duct
18 Engine bay titanium ring frames
19 Rear engine mounting frame
20 Engine bay titanium frame and stringer construction
21 Titanium skin panelling
22 Port tailplane hydraulic actuator
23 Tailplane hinge arm
24 Port rudder
25 Tailboom fairing
26 ECM aerial
27 Port tailplane
28 Tail navigation light
29 ECM aerial
30 Radar warning aerials
31 Boron fibre skin panelling
32 Fin leading edge
33 Port air system equipment bay
34 Forward engine mounting
35 Engine mounting frame
36 Bleed air system ducting
37 Engine support link
38 Engine bay fireproof bulkhead
39 Pratt & Whitney F100-PW-100 afterburning turbofan engine
40 Starboard air system equipment bay
41 Engine bleed air primary heat exchanger
42 Heat exchanger ventral exhaust duct
43 Retractable runway arrester hook
44 Wing trailing edge fuel tank
45 Flap hydraulic jack
46 Starboard plain flap
47 Flap and aileron honeycomb panel construction
48 Starboard aileron
49 Aileron hydraulic actuator
50 Fuel jettison pipe
51 Aluminium honeycomb wing tip fairing
52 Low-voltage formation lighting
53 Starboard navigation light
54 ECM aerial
55 Westinghouse ECM equipment pod

The first prototype of the F-15A Eagle was rolled out at St Louis in June 1972, and made its first flight on 27 July, being joined in the flight test programme by the first two-seat F-15B on 7 July 1973. Note the nose boom for test instrumentation (including yaw and angle of attack vanes), which was deleted on the production aircraft.

This F-15B or -15D lacks any national insignia, and appears to have been used for tests of a new camouflage scheme, reminiscent of the schemes that were applied to battleships during World War 1. This type of camouflage clearly breaks up the basic shape of the aircraft, and may be effective on the ground.

56 Outboard wing stores pylon
57 Pylon attachment spigot
58 Cambered leading edge ribs
59 Front spar
60 Machined wing skin/stringer panels
61 Outboard pylon fixing
62 HF flush aerial
63 Leading edge fuel tank
64 Inboard pylon fixing
65 Wing rib construction
66 Starboard wing integral fuel tank, total internal fuel load, 13,455-lb (6103-kg)
67 Wing root rib support struts
68 Titanium wing spars
69 Wing spar/fuselage attachment pin joints
70 Machined fuselage main bulkheads

71 Wing/fuselage fuel tank interconnections
72 Airframe mounted engine accessory gearbox
73 Standby hydraulic generator
74 Jet fuel starter (JFS)/auxiliary power unit (APU)
75 Engine intake compressor face
76 Cooling system intake bleed air spill duct
77 Port wing trailing edge fuel tank
78 Port plain flap
79 Flap hydraulic jack
80 Aileron control rod
81 Aileron hydraulic actuator
82 Port aileron

83 Fuel jettison pipe
84 Wing tip fairing
85 Low-voltage formation lighting
86 Port navigation light
87 ECM aerial
88 Cambered leading edge
89 Outboard pylon fixing
90 Port wing internal fuel tank
91 Fuel system piping
92 Inboard pylon fixing
93 Leading edge fuel tank
94 Anti-collision light
95 Boom-type air refuelling receptacle
96 Bleed air duct to air conditioning plant
97 Control rod runs

98 Dorsal airbrake, open
99 Airbrake glass-fibre honeycomb construction
100 Airbrake hydraulic jack
101 Centre fuselage fuel tanks
102 Intake ducting
103 Ammunition feed chute
104 M61A-1 Vulcan 20-mm cannon
105 Hydraulic rotary cannon drive unit
106 Starboard anti-collision light
107 Ventral main undercarriage wheel bay
108 Main undercarriage leg strut
109 Starboard mainwheel
110 Inboard stores pylon
111 Air-to-air missile adaptor
112 Bomb rack
113 Mk 82 low drag 500-lb (227-kg) HE bombs
114 Bomb triple ejector rack
115 Missile launch rail
116 AIM-9L Sidewinder air-to-air missile
117 AIM-7F Sparrow air-to-air missile

118 Sparrow missile launcher unit
119 Cannon muzzle aperture
120 Cannon barrels
121 Central ammunition drum 940-rounds
122 Airbrake hinges
123 Forward fuselage fuel tanks
124 UHF aerial
125 Intake duct bleed air louvres
126 Intake by-pass air spill duct
127 Variable area intake ramp hydraulic actuator
128 Air conditioning system cooling air exhaust duct
129 Canopy hinge point
130 Air conditioning plant
131 Intake incidence control jack
132 Intake duct variable area ramp doors
133 Intake pivot fixing
134 Starboard engine air intake
135 Nosewheel leg door
136 Nose undercarriage leg strut
137 Nosewheel
138 Landing/taxiing lamps
139 Nosewheel retraction strut

140 Rear underfloor equipment bay
141 Tactical electronic warfare system (TEWS) racks
142 Cockpit coaming
143 Rear pressure bulkhead
144 Canopy jack
145 Cockpit pressurization valves
146 Structural space provision for second crew member (F-15D)
147 Cockpit aft decking
148 Canopy arch
149 Port intake external compression lip
150 Fuel and sensor tactical (FAST) pack, conformal fuel pallet, capacity 5,000-lb (2268-kg)
151 600-US gal (2270-litre) external fuel tank
152 Cockpit canopy cover
153 Ejection seat headrest
154 Seat safety handle/arming lever
155 Canopy emergency jettison linkage
156 Ejection seat launch rails
157 Safety harness
158 McDonnell-Douglas ACES II 'zero-zero' ejection seat
159 Cockpit sloping bulkhead
160 Pilot's side console panel
161 Air conditioning ducting
162 Forward underfloor equipment bay, built-in test equipment (BITE) and liquid oxygen converter

163 Low-voltage formation lighting strip
164 Port side retractable boarding ladder
165 TACAN aerial
166 Angle of attack probe
167 Rudder pedals
168 Control column
169 Pilot's head-up display (HUD)
170 Instrument panel shroud
171 Frameless windscreen panel
172 ADF sense aerial
173 Radio and electronics equipment bay, port and starboard
174 Cockpit front pressure bulkhead

175 Pitot tube
176 UHF aerial
177 Radar mounting bulkhead
178 Radome hinge mounting
179 ILS aerial
180 Radar scanner mounting and tracking mechanism
181 Huges APG-63 pulse doppler radar scanner
182 Scanner mounted IFF aerial array
183 Glass-fibre radome

McDonnell Douglas
F-15A Eagle

HOLLOMAN'S EAGLE

Specification

Type: single-seat air-superiority fighter

Powerplant: two Pratt & Whitney F100-PW-100 afterburning turbofans, each of about 25,000-lb (11340-kg) static thrust

Dimensions: span 42 ft 9½ in (13.04 m); length 63 ft 9½ in (19.44 m); height 18 ft 6 in (5.64 m); wing area 608 sq ft (56.48 m²)

Armament: one 20-mm M61A1 cannon with 940 rounds, four AIM-7F Sparrow and four AIM-9L Sidewinder air-to-air missiles and five external locations for a maximum of 16,000 lb (7258 kg)

Performance: maximum speed (time limited) 1,650 mph (2655 km/h) or Mach 2.5 at altitude, or 936 mph (1506 km/h) or Mach 1.23 at sea level; service ceiling 63,000 ft (19200 m); radius of action about 600 miles (966 km)

Weights: empty 27,000 lb (12247 kg); normal take-off, clean, with four AIM-7 Sparrow missiles 41,500 lb (18824 kg); maximum take-off 56,000 lb (25402 kg)

Probably an aircraft used by the 49th Tactical Fighter Wing at Holloman AFB, New Mexico, for air displays, 'Holloman's Eagle' (full serial 760049) is a standard F-15A painted in air superiority pale grey. It is shown here armed with four AIM-7 Sparrow medium-range missiles and four AIM-9 Sidewinders for close combat.

McDonnell Douglas F-15 Eagle

An F-15 being refuelled by a KC-135, the simple vee-form of the boom controls indicating that the tanker is not the more advanced KC-10. The refuelling receptacle of the F-15 is set in the port intake fairing, opposite the M61 cannon on the starboard side. It will be seen from the shadow that contact has not yet been made.

in the air-superiority category. This was initially of no great consequence, since it was a counter-insurgency war with no opposing aircraft, but when bombing missions were scheduled against North Vietnam late in 1964, the gap in the inventory gave rise to serious problems.

Following unsuccessful trials with various types of fighter (including the F-102 and F-104) in the air-superiority role, the USAF was forced to adopt the US Navy's McDonnell F-4 Phantom all-weather interceptor. This was first (F-4D) fitted with an external gunpod (the F-4's missile armament having limited value in a dogfight, especially in terms of g-capability and combat persistence), and later was given a nose cannon and leading-edge manoeuvring flaps. The resulting F-4E entered service in October 1967, and proved invaluable both for MiGCAP (MiG combat air patrol) duties and as a bomb-carrier.

However, the radius of action needed in Vietnam was far greater than that required in Korea, and the problem was compounded by the new fighter generation's fuel-guzzling afterburning engines. Missions to Hanoi and Haiphong had to be flown from remote, secure bases in South Vietnam and Thailand, over a radius of 400 miles (640 km) or more. Although the Phantom was designed for relatively long range and endurance, the only way that adequate combat time could be achieved at such distances was by inflight refuelling, which was generally used both into and out of the target.

Lavish use of aerial tankers (Boeing KC-135s) allowed the F-4E to protect USAF strike aircraft and go hunting for MiGs, but it was blindingly clear that in a 'hotter' scenario the tankers would not enjoy such a permissive operating environment, and that many more of them would be needed to support the strategic bombers, rather than tactical fighters. What was required was a new class of fighter that could beat anything the Russians put in the air, yet would have sufficient range and combat persistence significantly to reduce demands on tanker support.

In 1965 the USAF requested funding for feasibility studies of a new air-superiority fighter, designated F-X, and in due course an RFP (Request For Proposals) was issued in September 1968. The finalists in the competition were Fairchild-Republic, North American Rockwell, and the McDonnell Aircraft (McAir) division of the McDonnell Douglas Corporation (MDC). In December 1969 McAir was selected to proceed with the development of the F-15 under

the direction of Air Force Systems Command, with formal authorization in January 1970. This was the first completely new fighter developed specifically for the USAF since the F-101 Voodoo, also a McAir product, which first flew on 29 September 1954.

The initial contract covered the manufacture of 20 pre-series aircraft: 18 single-seat F-15As and two TF-15A (later redesignated F-15B) tandem-seat trainers. The F-X requirement had called for a single-seat, twin-engined aircraft to perform the fighter sweep, escort and CAP missions. Preliminary details suggested that the F-15 would be twice as good as the F-4E in rate of climb and acceleration.

To achieve this breakthorough in performance, the F-15 was given a relatively low wing loading and a thrust/weight ratio in excess of unity, the first time so much power had been installed in a non-V/STOL fighter. In broad terms, it would have a clean weight of 40,000 lb (18144 kg), and a total thrust of 50,000 lb (22680 kg). In terms of level flight speed, this thrust would give a sea-level capability of about Mach 1.2, a sustained level speed of Mach 2.2 at altitude, and a dash speed in excess of Mach 2.5.

The installation of so much thrust was possible by virtue of a new generation of engines, with a thrust/weight ratio of around 8:1, giving so light a powerplant weight that there was still plenty of scope for internal fuel. The engine chosen was the Pratt & Whitney F100 afterburning turbofan, selected in February 1970. A few months later the Hughes APG-63 radar was chosen, giving an all-aspect, look-down, shoot-down capability in combination with AIM-7F Sparrow and AIM-9L Sidewinder missiles.

First flight

The F-15 was also to have had the Philco-Ford GAU-7A 25-mm Gatling gun with caseless ammunition. In this concept the projectile is bonded to a solid block of propellant, to eliminate the weight of the normal case and the time needed to extract it after firing.

The Strike Eagle (serial 71291) in ground attack configuration, with clusters of Mk 82 bombs on wing pylons and on the conformal fuel tanks mounted on the sides of the fuselage, and Sidewinders on the sides of the wing pylons. Strike Eagle is a private venture by McDonnell Douglas.

An F-15A in USAF air superiority grey, the LA on the fin designating that it belongs to the 58th Tactical Fighter Training Wing at Luke AFB, Arizona. The badge on the fin is that of Tactical Air Command, and that on the side of the air intake is that of the unit. The F-15A is externally identical to the F-15C.

An F-15A of the Israeli air force. Both single- and two-seat Eagles were supplied to Israel from 1976 under the Peace Fox programme. The number exported were 51 and the F-15s fly with No. 133 Sqn. Saudi Arabia took 62 F-15Cs and 15 F-15Ds.

Unfortunately, development problems with the gun and its revolutionary ammunition led to its cancellation, and the F-15 reverted to the well-proven General Electric M61 Vulcan gun that arms most American fighters.

The first F-15A was formally rolled out in June 1972, and had its maiden flight on 27 July, being followed by the first two-seater on 7 July 1973. Funding for the first 30 production aircraft was released late in 1973, and for a further 77 aircraft (to complete the first wing) a year later. The first of 729 production F-15s then planned (one in seven being a two-seater) left the ground on 25 November 1974. Initial operational capability was declared in July 1975, following delivery of the 24th aircraft. The first wing was fully equipped by the end of 1976.

Having got the F-15 into service, this may be a convenient point to describe the aircraft that McAir had produced. In several respects the F-15 bears a strong family resemblance to the preceding F-4, despite being a completely new design. The highly tapered, moderately swept wing is broadly in line with F-4 practice, although it is set high on the fuselage and avoids the need for the steep outboard dihedral of its predecessor. A better clue to the F-15's ancestry comes from the semi-recessed Sparrow missiles and the way the jetpipes are cut short, with the tail mounted well aft. In the case of the F-4, there is a single fin mounted on what is effectively a vestigial fuselage or tail boom. for the F-15, the use of Vigilante-style intakes necessitated the use of twin vertical tails to avoid the destabilizing airflow from the flat upper surface of the cowlings, so the aircraft has been given twin tail-booms on either side of the afterburners, with half the vertical tail and half the tailplane mounted on each.

One of the most important considerations in the design of the F-15 was operation at high angles of attack (AOA). This led to the choice of horizontal-ramp two-dimensional intakes, rather than the vertical ramps used on the F-4. A feature unique to the F-15 is that the intakes are hinged about the lower lip, and rotated downward as AOA increases, which minimizes spillage drag and its adverse effect on the vertical tails. Another important consideration was all-round view: the F-15 provided the best rear view of any fighter since the F-86, with the pilot seated high in a bubble canopy. Combat effectiveness also benefits from the use of an advanced head-up display (HUD) and the fact that most of the control functions needed in combat can be carried out without the pilot removing his hands from the control column and throttles. This HOTAS (hands-on-throttle-and-stick) system has controls for radar and missiles, gun, airbrake, microphone button and weapons release.

The F-15 airframe is relatively conventional in construction, but the rear fuselage is largely built of titanium, which makes up 26.5 per cent of structure weight. Graphite composites are used in the airbrake and the tail surfaces, but represent only 1.0 per cent of the structure. Dash speeds of more than Mach 2.5 are permitted, as are indicated airspeeds of 936 mph (1506 km/h), and load factors of +9g and −3g. The aircraft has been flown to an AOA of +120° and −60°. In air-superiority configuration, the F-15 takes off in 900 ft (275 m) and lands in 2,500 ft (760 m).

Perhaps the most dramatic demonstration of the aircraft's performance was the USAF 'Strike Eagle' project of early 1975, in which an F-15 set new record times to eight altitudes, beating figures previously set by the F-4 for the lower five and the Soviet Union's E-266 (MiG-25 'Foxbat') for the upper three heights. The new times were: 27.57 sec to 9,845 ft (3000 m) 39.33 sec to 19,685 ft (6000 m), 48.86 sec to 29,530 ft (9000 m), 59.38 sec to 39,370 ft (12000 m), 77.04 sec to 49,215 ft (15000 m), 122.94 sec to 65,615 ft (20000 m), 161.02 sec to 82,020 ft (25000 m) and 207.8 sec to 98,425 ft (30000 m).

The F-15 thus made its mark even before the first unit was fully equipped. In 1986 the USAF had nine F-15 squadrons in the continental USA, four in Europe, and three in the Pacific. Aside from the 57th Tactical Training Wing (tail code WA) at Nellis AFB, Nevada and the 58th TTW at Luke AFB, Arizona (code LA), the F-15 equips the 1st Tactical Fighter Wing (code FF) at Langley AFB, Virginia, the 36th TFW (code BT) at Bitburg AB in Germany, the 49th TFW (code HO) at Holloman AFB, New Mexico, the 33rd TFW (code ED) at Eglin AFB, Florida, the 32nd Tactical Fighter Squadron (code CR) at Camp New Amsterdam in the Netherlands, and the 18th TFW at Kadena AB, Okinawa (code ZZ).

The USAF also had plans to buy a total of 240 additional F-15s to replace the F-106 in the air defence of the continental USA (CONUS). In July 1981 deliveries began to the 48th Fighter Interceptor Squadron at Langley.

Export customers

The F-15A and F-15B have also been sold to Israel under the 'Peace Fox' programme, which involved 51 aircraft, of which deliveries began in 1976. The F-15s are flown by No. 133 Sqn, apparently as escorts to strike and reconnaissance aircraft. They have been involved in several dogfights with Syrian MiG-21s and MiG-23s over Lebanon (with very satisfactory results), and escorted the F-16s making the strike against Iraq's Osirak nuclear powerplant on 7 June 1981, covering a radius of 600 miles (960 km).

On 26 February 1979 the first of the new F-15Cs took to the air, and deliveries began in the middle of 1980. This second single-seat model has its internal fuel increased from 11,635 lb (5278 kg) to 13,455 lb (6103 kg) under the PEP-2000 programme. The F-15C also has provision for FAST (Fuel And Sensor Tactical) packs on each side of the fuselage, each giving an additional 5,000 lb (2268 kg) of fuel. With FAST packs in place and three 600-US gal (2271-litre) tanks on pylons, the F-15C's gross weight is increased to 66,700 lb (30255 kg). This gives an endurance of over five hours, and an unrefuelled ferry range of 3,080 miles (4957 km). The F-15C and the corresponding F-15D two-seater also have a programmable radar signal processor, giving a fourfold increase in computer capacity, and the ability to continue tracking one target while searching for others at the same time.

The Japanese Air Self-Defense Force (JASDF) acquired 88 F-15s to replace four squadrons of F-104Js and operate alongside six squadrons of F-4EJs, the latter apparently being tasked with the less difficult targets. Deliveries began in July 1980. This 'Peace Eagle' programme includes 12 F-15DJ two-seaters, which, like the first two F-15J single-seaters, will be built at St Louis by McAir. The remaining 86 F-15Js will be constructed by Mitsubishi Heavy Industries. The first F-15J, which is identical to the F-15C aside from some avionics changes, was handed over in July 1981, and the first operational squadron was activated at Nyutabaru AB in late 1982 or early 1983.

The third export customer for the F-15 is Saudi Arabia, which took 62 F-15Cs and 15 F-15Ds delivered between early 1982 and late 1984, with two further F-15Cs as attrition reserves. These aircraft replaced three BAe (BAC) Lightning squadrons based at Dharan, Taif and Khamis Mushayt. Their primary role is be air defence, but the Royal Saudi air force has also requested FAST packs, inflight refuelling provisions, multiple ejection racks (MERs), glide bombs and cluster bomb units (CBUs).

Eagle modifications
At the Farnborough Air Show in 1980 McAir displayed a modified F-15 termed Strike Eagle, a two-seater with FAST packs, provision for up to 12,000 lb (5443 kg) of external stores, and with its Hughes APG-63 modified to function

An F-15A of the 58th Tactical Fighter Training Wing, based at Luke AFB, Arizona. The 58th TFTW is the equivalent of an operational conversion unit in British terminology, and is composed of the 461st, 550th, and 551st Tactical Fighter Training Squadrons. Weapons training is performed by the 57th Tactical Training Wing.

as a synthetic aperture radar (SAR), giving extremely high resolution against ground targets, without loss of the normal air-to-air modes. It has been reported that with this modification the radar can distinguish between two points less than 10 ft (3 m) apart, from a range of 11 miles (18.5 km).

Deriving from the Strike Eagle demonstrations, the USAF is now to buy approximately 400 F-15E two-seaters for the all-weather ground-attack role. It is not known whether or not this new variant will have SAR, but it is expected to have some avionics changes, provisions for new types of weapon, and possibly a forward-looking infra-red (FLIR) sensor.

Other possible uses for the F-15 in the future are photo reconnaissance (with the RF-15 being used as a replacement for the FR-4E), and 'Wild Weasel', or defense suppression using non-heat-sensitive AGM-88A high-speed rockets (HARM) built by Texas Instruments. The F-15 is also currently being tested as a launch platform for Anti-Satellite Rockets (ASAT).

McDonnell Douglas F-15 Eagle variants

F-15A: Initial single-seat production version for USAF and Israeli Air Force, with internal fuel limited to 11,635 lb (5278 kg)

F-15B: Initial two-seat trainer version of F-15A, weighing approximately 800 lb (363 kg) more empty; overall dimensions unchanged but canopy shape revised to allow for second pilot

F-15C: Improved single-seater with 13,455 lb (6103 kg) of internal fuel, provision for FAST packs, and a programmable radar signal processor; ordered by USAF and Royal Saudi air force, and forms the basis for the F-15J

F-15D: two-seat equivalent of F-15C

F-15DJ: two-seater for Japan, based on F-15D

F-15E: two-seat operational aircraft for USAF with increased emphasis on ground attack; has larger HUD, higher capacity computer, improved equipment cooling, forward-looking infra-red (FLIR) and provision for Maverick and AMRAAM

F-15J: single-seater for Japan, based on F-15C, but with locally-developed electronic warfare equipment and GCI data-link; most of these aircraft to be built by Mitsubishi under licence

TF-15: original designation for F-15B; abandoned on 1 December 1977

Strike Eagle: McAir private-venture two-seater with all-weather ground attack capability based on synthetic aperture radar (modified APG-63)

Ascendant Airbus

The first wide-body twin-engined commercial aircraft to enter service, bringing new standards of quietness and fuel economy to regional routes around the world, the A300/310 family is outstanding proof of Europe's technological, industrial and financial capabilities, making Airbus Industrie the principal competitor to Boeing.

Since the first A300 made its maiden flight on 28 October 1972, Airbus Industrie has experienced a meteoric rise as one of the major manufacturers of large-capacity airliners, and has proved to be Boeing's most dangerous rival. This new form of joint venture, described in French law as a 'Groupement d'Interêt Economique', has attained its current share of the market by developing a totally new type of airliner used on a dense network of short and medium distance routes and combining financial benefits with reliability and safety.

What follows is the story of how a number of European companies combined their technological and industrial capabilities successfully to challenge the virtual monopoly of commercial transports enjoyed by US manufacturers throughout most of the post-war years.

Studies of wide-body airliners began on both sides of the Atlantic in the 1960s, with American manufacturers concentrating on larger, longer-range aircraft such as the four-engine Boeing 747, which flew in 1969, and the three-engine DC-10 and TriStar, which both flew in 1970. European manufacturers were meanwhile projecting smaller, short-range aircraft, and in 1965 French and West German manufacturers combined to establish a study group (Studiengruppe

Airbus). At that stage British European Airways was in the market for a 200-seater to replace the Vickers Vanguard and, in view of the impact of rising fuel prices on traffic growth in the 1970s, this would have been a very practical size of aircraft. However, the other major European airlines felt at that stage that a capacity of 250–300 seats would be more economical in terms of seat-mile costs, and was essential if aircraft movements at the main airports were to be controlled.

Competitive mix

An element of competition was introduced by the industrial groupings that developed. Sud-Aviation worked with Dassault on the Galion, while Hawker Siddeley Aviation combined efforts with Breguet and Nord-Aviation on the HBN-100, the latter eventually forming basis for the A300. The principal contractors for the three countries were to have been HSA, Sud-Aviation and Arbeitsgemeinschaft

Line-up of A300s at the flight test building at Toulouse. Garuda Indonesian Airways has ordered nine A300B4-200s, of which six have been delivered. Eastern Air Lines has two A300B2-200s and has received 23 of 32 A300B4s on order. Iberia has all six of its A300B4-100s, which, like Garuda's B4s, are Pratt & Whitney-powered.

Airbus Industrie A300

Specification

Airbus Industrie A300B4-101
Type: medium-haul wide-body commercial transport aircraft
Crew: three flight crew and eight-ten cabin staff
Passenger accommodation: 24 first class and 223 economy class
Powerplant: two General Electric CF6-50C turbofans, each rated 51,000-lb (23134-kg) static thrust

Performance: economical cruising speed 530 mph (853 km/h); typical range with 269 passengers and baggage 2,994 miles (4818 km); maximum range 3,445 miles (5544 km) with 29,325-lb (13300-kg) payload (most customers have chosen the A300B4-200, weighing 363,760 lb/165000 kg) which carries a full passenger payload (3,565 miles/5740 km)
Weights: operating empty 196,210 lb (89000 kg); maximum payload 81,130 lb (36800 kg); maximum take-off 337,365 lb (153000 kg)
Dimensions: span 147 ft 1½ in (44.84 m); length 175 ft 11 in (53.62 m); height 54 ft 2 in (16.53 m); wing area 2,799 sq ft (260 m²)

This A300B4 of Lufthansa German Airlines (Deutsche Lufthansa AG) is named *Lindau/Bodensee*, and was delivered on 23 March 1979. The airline has purchased a total of 11 A300s, six short-range B2-100 series and five of the A300B4-100 series, all powered by the General Electric CF6-50C engine. Deliveries began on 2 February 1976 with D-AIAA *Garmisch-Partenkirchen* and were completed with D-AIBF *Kronberg/Taunus* on 21 April 1979. Nine of these aircraft are now in operation on internal routes and between European capitals, but also as far afield as Las Palmas and Tehran, making use of the B4-100 series' range of up to 3,445 miles (5500 km). Two of Lufthansa's A300B4s have been leased to Air Algerie. The remaining aircraft are reported to average 5.97 flying hours per day.

Airbus A300

D-AIBC

The purchase of five A300B4-200s by Trans-Australia Airlines signalled a change in the country's two-airline policy of identical equipment for TAA and Ansett, the latter choosing the Boeing 767. TAA's A300s, the only wide-bodied airliners on Australia's domestic routes, link Brisbane, Sydney, Melbourne and Perth.

Airbus, which last in 1967 became Deutsche Airbus GmbH. The two engines were to have been Rolls-Royce RB.178-51s, later superseded by RB.207s. However, at that time the TriStar appeared to be moving ahead much more quickly and to have an assured future, so Rolls-Royce dropped development of the RB.207 to concentrate on the RB.211 for the Lockheed aircraft. (The engine was later found to require so much financial investment that Rolls-Royce had to be taken over by the British government.)

The UK role in what was to prove the most successsful European collaborative air transport venture of all time then suffered a further blow when the British government declined to join in funding development of the A300 because of lack of orders. Nevertheless, in May 1969 the French and German governments decided to go ahead, and construction of the first prototype A300B1 began in October of that year. The UK's only major part in the programme was that HSA acted as a subcontractor to Airbus Industrie, designing, developing and manufacturing the wings (although the leading and trailing edges were built by VFW-Fokker, later Fokker BV). This arrangement subsequently provided a great deal of 'tin-bashing' work for the UK, but the country's failure to seize the lead in the Airbus programme gave to France key areas such as the front fuselage, which was of far greater significance to equipment suppliers. The Airbus thus began on the basis of French and German funding, with Fokker-VFW of the Netherlands and CASA of Spain joining the industrial grouping, in December 1970/1971.

The aircraft that emerged was somewhat smaller than the 300-seater envisaged when the designation A300 had been chosen, hence the name A300 for the (approximate) 250-passenger redesign. The reason for this reduction in size was partly that potential customers had begun saying that the original concept would have had excessively high plane-mile costs, and partly that the high thrust of the RB.207 was no longer available. The A300B was designed so that in principle it could accept the General Electric CF6, or the Pratt & Whitney JT9D, or the RB.211, although all the initial aircraft used the CF6 in a standard McDonnell Douglas wingpod. Some later A300s have the JT9D, but in 1986 the RB.211 had not yet found an A300 launch customer.

Further co-operation

Airbus Industrie was formally constituted in December 1970 with Sud-Aviation and Deutsche Airbus as the principal industrial partners. As further countries joined in the programme, the work-split became more complex. Sud-Aviation (later part of Aérospatiale) was allocated the all-important nose fuselage, lower centre fuselage and engine

Airbus Industrie A310 cutaway drawing key

1 Radome
2 Weather radar scanner
3 Radar scanner mounting
4 VOR localizer aerial
5 Front pressure bulkhead
6 Windscreen panels
7 Windscreen wipers
8 Instrument panel shroud
9 Control column
10 Rudder pedals
11 Cockpit floor level
12 ILS aerial
13 Pitot tubes
14 Access ladder to lower deck
15 Captain's seat
16 Centre control pedestal
17 Opening side window panels
18 First Officer's seat
19 Overhead systems control panel
20 Maintenance side panel
21 Observer's seat
22 Folding fourth seat
23 Cockpit bulkhead
24 Air conditioning ducting
25 Crew wardrobe/locker
26 Nose undercarriage wheel bay
27 Hydraulic retraction jack
28 Taxiing lamp
29 Steering jacks
30 Nosewheel doors
31 Forward toilet
32 Wash hand basin
33 Galley
34 Starboard entry/service door
35 Door mounted escape chute
36 Cabin attendant's folding seat
37 Hand baggage locker/wardrobe
38 Port main entry door
39 Door latch
40 Door surround structure
41 Radio and electronics racks
42 Runway turn-off lights
43 Fuselage frame and stringer construction
44 Floor beam construction
45 Forward freight hold
46 Freight hold door
47 Cabin wall trim panels
48 VHF communications aerial
49 Overhead stowage bins
50 Curtained cabin divider
51 First-class passenger compartment, 18 seats
52 Air system ducting
53 Cabin window panels
54 Overhead baggage lockers
55 Galley unit
56 Air system circulation fan
57 Tourist-class seating, 193 seats
58 Air conditioning supply ducting
59 Water tank

One of eight A300B4-100s operated by Olympic Airways. Now entirely owned by the Greek government, Olympic was originally founded in 1957 by Aristotle Onassis, who bought TAE Greek National Airlines and thus gained a monopoly of internal routes and national designation for overseas services.

Airbus Industrie A300 and A310 variants

(Note: the following list deals only with the principal variants; the model number (A300) is followed by a function letter, B indicating basic passenger version, C convertible, and F freighter; the airframe designation number as set out below has its last two digits modified to show the type of powerplant, numbers 01 to 19 for General Electric engines, 20 to 39 for Pratt & Whitney engines, and 40 to 59 reserved for Rolls-Royce; it is followed by two digits indicating variations in design weights)

A300B1: designation allocated to the two prototype aircraft, of which only one is now flying (a/c SN2)
A300B2-100: initial production short-haul version with 'simple' wing leading edge, as used by Air France to introduce the series into regular service in May 1974
A300B2-200: similar to A300B2-100 series, but with wing-root leading-edge Krueger flaps (as developed for the A300B4 series) and with the A300B4's wheels and brakes, to give the aircraft the capability to operate from hot/high airfields (e.g. by South African Airways); examples of this series include the **A300B2-201** with CF6-50C and the **A300B2-220** with JT9D-59A engines
A300B2-300: similar to A300B2-200, but with increased zero-fuel and landing weights for improved payload and multi-stop flexibility; first operator was SAS
A300B2-600: based on A300B2-200, but stretched to provide two extra seat rows and space for two extra LD3 containers; it also has slightly uprated engines, the rear fuselage and tailplane of the A310, more composite materials, and slightly more range

A300B4-100: basic medium-haul version, with additional fuel tank in the centre wing box, slightly stronger structure, uprated wheels and brakes, and Krueger flaps at the wing leading-edge root, first operator was Germanair; this series includes the **A300B4-101** with CF6-50C and the **A300B4-120** with JT9D-59A engines
A300B4-200: similar to A300B4-100, but with increased take-off weight by virtue of strengthened wings, fuselage and landing gear, allowing a higher payload or a range up to 3,600 miles (5795 km) for transcontinental operations
A300B4-600: stretched version derived from A300B4-200, with modifications as for A300B2-600; first ordered by Saudi Arabian Airlines
A300C4: convertible freighter version with large upper-deck cargo door on port side of aircraft, a reinforced cabin floor, smoke detection system in the main cabin, and interior trim adaptable to the freighter role; first operated by Hapag-Lloyd
A300F4: all-freighter version similiar to A300C4, but with all passenger provisions removed and cabin windows blanked over
A310-200: short-fuselage derivative of A300, typically seating 237; has new, smaller and aerodynamically advanced wing, smaller tailplane, redesigned rear fuselage, two-man cockpit, and higher proportion of composite materials; sub-series include **A310-202** with CF6-80A, **A310-221** with JT9D-7R4D1, and A310-241 with **RB.211-524D4** engines
A310-300: extended-range version with increased fuel capacity and higher take-off weight, and with fuel transfer between the main tanks and a tailplane tank to reduce trim drag
A310C: convertible freighter version

60 LD3 baggage container (eight in forward hold)
61 Slat drive shaft gearbox
62 Wing spar centre section carry-through
63 Ventral air conditioning packs (two)
64 Port overwing emergency exit door
65 Wing centre-box fuel tank, capacity 4,234 Imp gal (19250 litres)
66 Centre section floor beams
67 Wing spar attachment main frame
68 Fuselage centre section construction
69 Starboard overwing emergency exit door
70 Starboard wing inboard fuel tank, capacity 3,066 Imp gal (13937 litres)
71 Nacelle pylon
72 Starboard Pratt & Whitney JT9D engine nacelle
73 Alternative General Electric CF6-80A1 turbofan engine
74 Common nacelle pylon beam
75 Pylon attachment points
76 Pylon tail fairing
77 Pressure refuelling connections
78 Slat screw jacks
79 Screw jack drive shaft
80 Leading edge slat segments
81 Fuel tank divider rib
82 Fuel pumps
83 Outboard fuel tank, capacity 866 Imp gal (3938 litres)
84 Fuel system piping
85 Vent surge tank
86 Starboard navigation lights
87 Wing tip fairing
88 Tail navigation and strobe lights
89 Static discharge wicks
90 Fixed portion of trailing edge
91 Outboard spoilers
92 Spoiler hydraulic jacks
93 Flap screw jacks
94 Flap carriage mechanism
95 Outboard single-slotted Fowler-type flap
96 Fuel jettison pipe
97 Centre spoilers/airbrakes
98 Flap drive shaft
99 Aileron triplex hydraulic jacks
100 Starboard all-speed aileron
101 Inboard spoilers/lift dumpers
102 Inboard double slotted flap
103 Wing rear spar/fuselage main frame
104 Centre cabin air circulation fan
105 Pressure floor above wheel bay
106 Starboard main undercarriage, retracted position
107 Undercarriage door jack
108 Equipment bay walkway
109 Undercarriage bay pressure bulkhead
110 Flap drive motor
111 Eight-abreast tourist class seating
112 Fuselage frame and stringer construction
113 Rear freight hold door
114 LD3 baggage container (six in rear hold)
115 Freight hold bulkhead
116 Cabin floor panels
117 Seat attachments rails
118 Rear cabin air circulation fan
119 ADF aerials
120 Fuselage skin plating
121 Central overhead stowage bins
122 Ceiling lighting panels
123 Starboard rear entry door
124 Galley units
125 Fin root fairing
126 Fin attachment bolted joints
127 Fin spars
128 Starboard tailplane
129 Starboard elevator
130 Tailfin construction
131 Glass-fibre reinforced leading edge
132 Fin tip fairing
133 Static discharge wicks
134 Carbon fibre rudder skin panels
135 Honeycomb rudder construction
136 Rudder triplex hydraulic jacks
137 APU equipment bay
138 Garrett GTCP 331–250 auxiliary power unit
139 Tailcone fairing
140 APU exhaust duct
141 Port elevator construction
142 Elevator triplex hydraulic jacks
143 Static discharge wicks
144 Port tailplane construction
145 Leading edge nose ribs
146 Tailplane pivot fixing
147 Moving tailplane sealing plate
148 Tailplane centre section
149 Tailplane trim screw jack
150 Fin support structure
151 Rear pressure bulkhead
152 Rear toilet compartment
153 Cabin attendant's folding seat
154 Rear entry door
155 Cabin window panel
156 Eight-abreast rear cabin seating
157 Cabin side wall frames
158 Bulk cargo hold
159 Freight hold skin panelling
160 Wing trailing edge fillet
161 Port inboard double slotted flap
162 Spoiler/lift dumpers
163 Undercarriage side struts
164 Main undercarriage pivot fixing
165 Inboard flap track mechanism
166 Aileron triplex hydraulic jacks
167 Port all-speed aileron construction
168 Port spoiler/airbrakes
169 Flap down position
170 Flap guide rails
171 Fuel jettison pipe
172 Flap track fairings
173 Fixed portion of trailing edge
174 Static dischargers
175 Tail navigation and strobe lights
176 Wing tip fairing
177 Port navigation lights
178 Wing rear spar
179 Front spar
180 Port leading edge-slats
181 Slat screw jacks
182 Slat guide rails
183 Leading edge de-icing air piping
184 Telescopic de-icing air duct
185 Wing skin joint strap
186 Wing stringer construction
187 Port wing integral fuel tank bays
188 Wing rib construction
189 Main undercarriage leg strut
190 Hydraulic retraction jack
191 Port main undercarriage four-wheel bogie
192 Nacelle pylon attachment joint
193 Engine mounting pylon
194 Hot stream exhaust nozzle
195 Fan air exhaust duct
196 Reverser cascade, closed
197 Bleed air ducting
198 Pratt & Whitney JT9D-7R4D turbofan engine
199 Engine fan blades
200 Intake ducting
201 Detachable engine cowlings
202 Bleed air system pre-cooler
203 Inboard leading edge slat
204 Bleed air delivery ducting
205 Inner wing integral fuel tank
206 Leading edge wing root fairing
207 Wing root Krueger flap

In 1986 only one of the three General Electric-powered A300B4-200s for Air Afrique had been delivered. Constituted in 1961 by agreement between 11 independent African states that were formerly French colonies, Air Afrique operates services linking 22 African countries to France, Italy, Switzerland and the USA.

One of three A300B4-100s currently operated by Philippine Airlines (PAL), which has two additional aircraft of the same type yet to be delivered. One of the older airlines in the Far East, PAL was formed in 1941, but soon had to terminate operations due to the war. The airline resumed its operations in February 1946.

pylons. Messerschmitt-Bölkow-Blohm (MBB) was given the rear fuselage, vertical tail, and upper centre fuselage, plus the flap guides. VFW-Fokker (more recently a subsidiary of MBB) builds the cylindrical fuselage section ahead of the wing. Fokker (as mentioned earlier) makes the wing leading and trailing edges, while HSA (now British Aerospace) was given responsibility for the main torsion box. CASA makes the horizontal tail and front fuselage door. Messier of France produces the landing gear. Both SNECMA in France and MTU in Germany make parts for the CF6 engine, which for the Airbus series is assembled by SNECMA. Major components of the A300 are flown between factories in Airbus Industrie's Super Guppies for assembly.

Behind the three-crew flight deck, the fuselage of 18 ft 6 in (5.64 m) diameter provides for six-abreast seating in first class, seven in business, eight in economy, or nine in charter, while the underfloor hold accommodates up to 20 LD3 containers in pairs abreast. All current models of the A300B take 220–345 seats, depending on cabin configuration, although 269 is typical of all-tourist (eight abreast) seating, and have a two-crew flight deck.

The wing is moderately swept, with a very advanced aerofoil section that permits a high cruise speed without significant compressibility effects, i.e. drag rise due to shock-induced separations. It is fitted with leading-edge flaps and two-slot Fowler trailing-edge flaps. Each wing has two ailerons, the inboard one functioning at all speeds and drooping in sympathy with the flaps, and the outboard one working only at low speeds. Four spoilers on each side act as airbrakes, and three as lift-dumpers. The flying controls are powered by triple hydraulic systems, with manual reversion. The landing gear has twin-wheel nose unit and four-wheel bogies on each main leg.

Reverting to the development history of the A300B, the first of two B1s (F-WUAB, later F-OCAZ) had its maiden flight on 28 October 1972, followed by the second (F-WUAC, now OO-TEF) on 5 February 1973. The first of the initial production series (F-WUAD the first A300B2 short-haul version) took to the air on 28 June 1973 and second A300B2 (F-WUAA) on 20 November 1973. The A300B2 was awarded Franco-German certification on 15 March 1973, and FAA certification on 30 May 1974. The A300B2 entered service with Air France on the Paris–London run on 23 May 1974.

Thus ended the first phase of the struggle to develop a major European commercial transport aircraft that could be sold successfully all over the world. However, some of the most difficult days for Airbus Industrie were yet to come. The critics who had claimed that the aircraft would be a technical flop now changed their argument to say that it would never be sold in economical numbers. In the mid-1970s sales were certainly slow to materialize (only one aircraft was sold in 1976). One of the keys to the success of Airbus was the launching of the A300B4 for medium-haul routes, a heavier version which offered a range of 3,000 miles (4825 km) and later 3,600-miles (5800 km) in comparison with the 1,845-mile (2970-km) range of the A300B2, all these figures relating to 269 passenger loads. Four of the A300B4s were taken by Eastern Air Lines on a six-month lease, beginning late in 1977. The following April, delighted with the results obtained with the A300B4s, Eastern bought them and ordered 25 more with options on a further nine. The acceptance of the aircraft by a major US operator was a turning point in sales of the A300B series and, although Airbus never succeeded in winning over other American airlines, orders started pouring in from the rest of the world, including certain areas (such as the Far East) that were enjoying a substantial growth in traffic. In 1978 Airbus (with 23 per cent of the market) was second only to Boeing in wide-body sales, and within three years had pushed Boeing out of the lead.

Efficiency, reliability and sales

As sales boomed, development continued on variants of the A300B theme. The A300C4 was produced as a convertible freighter version, which entered service with Hapag-Lloyd of Germany in 1980. An A300B equipped with Pratt & Whitney JT9D engines flew in May 1979, and in the following January the A300B2 with JT9D-59As entered service with Scandinavian Airlines. Garuda Indonesian Airways and Iberia also use the Airbus with JT9Ds. It may be added that Garuda was the first airline to take delivery of the A300 equipped with the two-crew 'forward-facing crew cockpit' (FFCC), as developed for the later A310, the delivery taking place in January 1982. Two months later, on 4 March, the A300B celebrated its millionth accident-free flying hour, a remarkable achievement by any standard. Since its introduction into service, the A300B has averaged a technical dispatch reliability of 98.5 per cent, higher than that of any other wide-body. Airbus Industrie is also rightly proud of the fact that US Civil Aeronautics Board figures show that the A300B's direct maintenance costs in the USA are the lowest for all wide-bodies currently in service.

Although chronologically out of step, since it comes after the short-fuselage A310, it is convenient to complete the current story of A300B development with mention of the A300-600, which Airbus decided to fund in December 1980.

Egyptair has ordered eight A300B4-200s, of which five have been delivered, and are operated alongside one B4-100 leased from Hapag Lloyd. Formed in 1932 as Misr Airwork (later Misrair), the airline became United Arab Airlines in 1960, and in 1971 was renamed Egyptair. The fleet includes seven Boeing 707-320Cs and seven Boeing 737s.

Toa Domestic Airlines has ordered nine A300B2-200s, of which six are so far in operation. This airline was formed in 1971 by the merger of Japan Domestic Airlines and Toa Airways. Services are provided over an extensive network of scheduled domestic routes, serving 35 Japanese cities.

The 'Dash-600' is a slightly stretched version, with two extra seat rows, typically seating 285 in all-tourist class, and providing space for two extra LD3 containers under the floor. It has uprated CF6-80C or JT9D-7R4H engines, the more sharply tapered rear fuselage and smaller horizontal tail developed for the A310, considerably more components made of composite materials, and slightly more range. The Dash-600 made its first flight around mid-1983, and entered service in the spring of 1984, following certification with Pratt & Whitney engines in the first half of that year.

In the longer term Airbus Industrie can only secure a major share of the overall commercial transport market (the aim appears to be around one-third) by developing aircraft across a broad spectrum, rather than exploiting one narrow slot. Market surveys have shown some demand for variants of the A300B offering longer range and for others offering higher seating capacity over short/medium stages, but these potential markets appear to be comparatively small and a

long way in the future. There were, however, strong indications of a much larger demand for a wide-body aircraft seating around 225, i.e. a short-fuselage A300. It was on this basis that development of the A310 was given the go-ahead in July 1978, leading to first flight of the aircraft (F-WZLH) on 3 April 1982, painted in Lufthansa colours on the port side, and Swissair to starboard. The A310 entered service in 1983, followed by the longer-range A310-300 in 1986.

The A310 fuselage is shortened by 11 frames in comparison with that of the A300, i.e. by 22 ft 10 in (6.96 m), to give a capacity of 211–289 seats. A typical mixed-class configuration would seat 237, with which payload the A310 has range of 3,530 miles (5680 km). The A310-300 will use a fuel

Formed in 1972 to succeed MSA (Malaysia-Singapore Airlines), Singapore Airlines (SIA) has ordered 12 A300B4-200s, of which five were in service in late 1982. Airbus Industrie has been extremely successful in its sales to the Far East.

In March 1983 the first three Airbus A310s were delivered to Lufthansa, which had ordered 25 in April 1979 as successors to the Boeing 727. The type A300 differs from the shorter A310 in having transsonic wings and the 'Forward Facing Crew Concept', with only two pilots and new computer screen and keyboard technology.

transfer system between the main tanks and a tank in the tailplane to reduce trim drag, extending this range to 4,055 miles (6525 km).

The A310 also has a new, smaller, and aerodynamically advanced wing, JT9D-7R4D-E1 or CF6-80A1 or Dash-80A3 engines, and (as mentioned above) a smaller and lighter horizontal tail, a redesigned rear fuselage, a two-man cockpit, and a higher percentage of composite materials. The British wing is so successful that no vortex generators or fences are required (making the A310 the only new-generation airliner with a completely 'clean' wing), yet optimum cruise Mach number has been increased from 0.78 to 0.805. In addition, buffet-limited coefficient has been increased by 10 per cent, with the result that the A310 can fly 2,000 ft (610 m) higher at the same weight, or can carry 11 tons (11.177 tonnes) more payload at a given height.

In the course of a remarkable route-proving programme through the Middle and Far East, the second A310 (F-WZLI), carrying a load equivalent to 210 passengers and their baggage, and flying in the face of headwinds averaging 52 mph (83.5 km/h), flew nonstop from Kuwait to Singapore, a distance of 4,625 miles (7445 km). Flying from Kuala Lumpur to Bangkok, the A310 reached 43,000 ft (13105 m), a remarkable altitude for an aircraft of its class. More significantly, it was found that at Mach 0.80 the aircraft burns 6.5 per cent less fuel than predicted – a remarkable saving.

In order primarily to share in the A310 programme, British Aerospace became a full partner in Airbus Industrie in January 1979. In the combined A300/310 programme, Aérospatiale (France) has a 37.9 per cent share, as does Deutsche Airbus (representing MBB of Germany), while British Aerospace has 20 per cent, and CASA (Spain) has 4.2 per cent. Fokker of the Netherlands and Belairbus of Belgium are both Airbus Industrie associates, the latter participating only in the A310.

In early 1984 it was decided that the small Airbus A320 would be built: a short- and medium-range aircraft for around 150 passengers and a narrow fuselage cross-section. This was the first subsonic airliner with full fly-by-wire steering and sidesticks instead of control rods. This type had received more than 250 orders and options by the beginning of 1986, and is planned to come into use in 1989. Around 400 Airbuses of other types had been ordered by that time. Airbus Industrie is also planning two totally new versions, the four-engined very long-range A340 and the twin-engined medium-range A330, carrying more than 300 passengers. A start to the programme was made in 1987.

This photograph of the A310 assembly line includes two aircraft approaching completion for Swissair.

Panavia Tornado Euro-defender

The first warplane to be designed to meet the needs of three nations — the UK, West Germany and Italy — the Panavia Tornado is now in production both as an attack aircraft and as an all-weather interceptor. Possessing capabilities much greater than those of any previous aircraft of its size, it can carry every weapon in the NATO tactical armoury.

The Panavia Tornado was born out of an international design programme shared by three companies who had been on opposite sides in World War 2: Messerschmitt, of Germany, Supermarine, of England, and Fiat of Italy. It is now one of the most powerful defence systems in the whole arsenal of the West, not least because it combines weaponry from all three countries and thus constitutes a real deterrent against potential attack.

The multi-national Tornado programme can be traced back to 1967, when many NATO countries were planning a new combat aircraft, and looking for partners to share development costs. The original leaders in this enterprise were West Germany and Canada, with Belgium, Italy and the Netherlands all showing interest in taking up smaller shares of the design and production workload. In that same year France withdrew from a proposed co-operation programme with the UK on a variable-sweep fighter, in order to concentrate on her own Dassault Mirage series. This left the UK to find other means to obtain what was primarily an English Electric Canberra bomber replacement.

Multi-nationalism under way

In the talks that followed, Canada and the four Continental nations placed emphasis on air superiority (their basic need was for a Lockheed F-104G Starfighter replacement), while the UK's interest centred on low-level strike. This diversity of roles made a variable-geometry aircraft virtually essential, and the would-be partners agreed that it should be a two-seat, twin-engined design. At that stage the project was designated MRCA-75 (Multi-Role Combat Aircraft for 1975), although in the event its development was to take rather longer than was envisaged in the late 1960s.

What might have become a six-nation transAtlantic programme then experienced a series of set-backs, when Canada's new Trudeau government pulled out, followed by the Belgians and the Dutch, all acting from a combination of political and economic motives. However, there remained the two most powerful nations, West Germany and the UK, who where ready to proceed as equal partners, and Italy as a relatively minor yet still important member of the team.

By pooling the requirements of the German air force (Luftwaffe) and navy (Marineflieger), the Royal Air Force, and the Italian air force (Aeronautica Militare Italiana), the new aircraft's basic roles were defined as: close air support for ground forces in the battle area; interdiction/strike against ground installations, airfields, supply depots, communications, etc; naval strike against shipping and coastal targets; air superiority above the battlefield; air defence/interception; tactical and long-range reconnaissance at both high and low levels; and aircrew training, while remaining operational.

To manage the development and production of the Tornado weapon system (including the powerplant and the special

The 16th and last of the Tornado prototypes is seen here in Marineflieger colours, with serial 9803 on the front fuselage, and the badge of MFG 1 (based at Schleswig) on the fin. It is carrying four MBB Kormoran anti-shipping missiles. The Tornado is replacing the F-104G Starfighter in German navy missions over the Baltic.

Panavia Tornado

Tornado 9805 is shown here in the paint scheme and markings of the Bundesmarine, having formerly flown with the test serial D9592. It is carrying four MBB Kormoran anti-shipping missiles. This aircraft was destroyed in an accident on 17 April 1980 while its crew were practising for the Hanover Air Show.

cannon), Panavia Aircraft was formed in Munich in 1969 by the three airframe participants, now designated Messerschmitt-Bölkow-Blohm (MBB), British Aerospace (BAe) and Aeritalia (AIT). In the same year Turbo-Union was formed in London by Rolls Royce, MTU and Fiat, to develop and manufacture the new RB.199 turbo-fan engine. Panavia now has as its principal subcontractors MBB, BAe, AIT, Turbo-Union, IWKA-Mauser (for the cannon) and Elliott's EASAMS division for avionics system integration. The Tornado project was given the formal go-ahead in 1970 by the tri-national government agency NAMMA, with costs to be split on a 42.5/42.5/15.0 per cent basis between the three countries.

Once the needs of the four services had been translated into practical terms, the Tornado had to possess five basic capabilities: to take off and land in very short distances, in order to continue operations from bomb-damaged runways; to fly at high speeds at low level for long distances, without excessive crew fatigue; to make low-level penetrations by day or night, regardless of weather conditions; to strike accurately with a heavy warload in a single-pass attack; and to fly at high supersonic speeds at altitude.

To achieve these capabilities, one of the main features of the aircraft was to be a variable-sweep wing. In the 'unswept' configuration this could generate high lift coefficients for take-off and landing, giving slow unstick and touchdown speeds. In the fully swept position, it would provide minimum gust response and hence a smooth ride during low-level penetrations, and low wave drag for supersonic flight at altitude.

In addition, the Tornado had to have engines of unusually low specific fuel consumption (SFC), yet with a high afterburning thrust to blast it off the runway in a short distance even with a heavy bombload, and to enable it to perform effectively in the air-to-air role. The engines also had to have thrust reversers, to stop the aircraft in a short distance when landing between bomb craters.

All-weather low-level penetration implied fully automatic terrain following, something never before achieved. First-pass attacks demanded highly accurate navigation, so that the crew could deliver their weapons without seeing the target, if necessary. Altogether, the Tornado was clearly going to be a large, complex aircraft, much more expensive than a single-role fighter, but infinitely more useful in stopping a Russian attack at night, or in the very limited visibility that is characteristic of European operations.

Design and development of the 'swing-wing' undoubtedly benefited from earlier experience at Warton (the BAe division concerned with Tornado). This dates back to wind-tunnel tests in 1964 on the P.45 project, and continued with work on the ill-fated Anglo-French VG fighter. The key to the design of this category of wing is the central carry-through structure box, which in this case is of electron-beam-welded construction (that of the earlier General Dynamics F-111 was of bolted steel), with Teflon-coated pivots.

The Tornado wing sweep varies from 25° in the fully forward position to 68° fully aft. On the interdiction/strike Tornado the wing is positioned manually, but in the air-

248

Panavia Tornado F Mk 2 cutaway drawing key

1 Starboard taileron construction
2 Honeycomb trailing edge panels
3 Compound sweep taileron leading edge
4 Taileron pivot fixing
5 Afterburner ducting
6 Thrust reverser bucket door actuator
7 Afterburner nozzle jack
8 Starboard fully variable engine exhaust nozzle
9 Thrust reverser bucket doors, open
10 Dorsal spine end fairing
11 Honeycomb rudder construction
12 Fuel jettison pipes
13 Tail navigation light
14 Aft passive ECM housing
15 Tail radar warning antenna
16 Dielectric fin tip antenna housing
17 VHF aerial
18 Electronic tuning coils
19 VOR aerials
20 Forward passive ECM housing
21 Underneath view showing semi-recessed missile positions
22 Extra fuselage bay
23 Extended radar equipment bay
24 Radome
25 Secondary heat exchanger intake
26 Wing pylon-mounted missile rails
27 Port taileron
28 Fin leading edge
29 Railfin construction
30 Vortex generators
31 Heat shield
32 Rudder actuator (Fairey Hydraulics)
33 Engine bay centre firewall
34 Starboard airbrake, open
35 Airbrake jack
36 Taileron actuator (Fairey Hydraulics)
37 Fly-by-wire taileron control unit
38 Turbo-Union RB.199-34R-4 Mk 101 (Improved) three-spool afterburning turbofan enginer
39 Engine bay bulkhead
40 Bleed air duct
41 Fin attachment joint
42 Heat exchanger exhaust duct
43 Primary heat exchanger
44 Ram air intake
45 HF aerial fairing

Panavia Tornado

A Luftwaffe Tornado two-seat trainer, based at the Tri-national Tornado Training Establishment at RAF Cottesmore. Those Tornadoes with dual flying controls are indistinguishable externally from the standard strike aircraft, aside from the TTTE fin number, those below 50 indicating that the aircraft is a trainer.

An RAF Tornado GR.Mk 1, based at TTTE, Cottesmore. Note the arrowhead unit fin flash and the B-50 fleet number, indicating that the aircraft is British and is the first strike aircraft at Cottesmore. This is the second production strike Tornado for the RAF (construction number BS002, serial ZA322).

46 Engine compressor faces
47 Rear fuselage bag-type fuel tank
48 Intake trunking
49 Wing root pneumatic seal
50 KHD/Microtecnical/Lucas T312 APU
51 Hydraulic system accumulator
52 Engine driven auxiliary gearbox
53 Starboard full-span, double-slotted flaps, extended
54 Spoiler housing
55 Starboard wing fully swept position
56 Flap screw jacks
57 Wing tip antenna
58 Starboard navigation light
59 Structural provision for outboard pylon mounting
60 Full-span leading-edge slats, extended
61 Starboard external fuel tank, capacity 330 Imp gal (1500 litres)
62 Swivelling wing pylon
63 Missile launching rail
64 AIM-9L Sidewinder air-to-air missile
65 Leading edge slat screw jacks
66 Slat rails
67 Wing torsion box
68 Swivelling pylon mounting
69 Starboard wing integral fuel tank
70 Main undercarriage leg strut
71 Starboard mainwheel
72 Mainwheel door
73 Undercarriage breaker strut
74 Wing pivot sealing fairing
75 Sweep actuator attachment horn
76 Starboard wing pivot bearing
77 Flexible wing seats
78 Wing pivot carry through (electron beam welded titanium box construction)
79 Wing pivot box integral fuel tank
80 Pitch and roll control non-linear gearing mechanism
81 Air conditioning supply ducting
82 Dorsal spine fairing
83 Anti-collision light
84 UHF aerials
85 Port wing pivot bearing
86 Flexible trailing edge seals
87 Spoiler actuators
88 Port spoilers
89 Port wing fully swept position
90 Full span double-slotted flaps, extended
91 Wing tip antenna
92 Port navigation light
93 Full span leading-edge slats, extended
94 Port wing integral fuel tank
95 Pylon swivelling linkage
96 Port wing sweep actuator
97 Wing flap and leading edge slat drive motors
98 Starboard wing sweep actuator (Microtechnical)
99 Hydraulic drive motor and gearbox
100 Extended wing root glove fairing
101 Supplementary 'blow-in' intake doors
102 Landing/taxiing lamp
103 Starboard fully variable engine air intake
104 Formation light
105 Variable intake ramps
106 Ramp hydraulic jacks
107 Bleed air exit louvres
108 Automatic intake control system (Nord-Micro)
109 Enlarged forward fuselage bag-type fuel tank (Uniroyal)
110 Cockpit canopy pivot
111 Air conditioning plant (Normalair-Garrett)
112 Port intake bleed air outlet fairing
113 AIM-9L Sidewinder air-to-air missile
114 Port external fuel tank, capacity 330 Imp gal (1500 litres)
115 Intake lip
116 Navigator's cockpit enclosure
117 Navigator's ejection seat (Martin-Baker Mk 10A 'zero-zero' seats)
118 Canopy jack strut
119 Cockpit rear pressure bulkhead
120 Engine air intake-curved inboard sidewall
121 Missile system electronics
122 BAe Sky Flash air-to-air missile
123 Ventral, semi-recessed missile housing
124 Cannon ammunition box
125 Navigator's side console panel
126 Canopy arch
127 Navigator's instrumental panel
128 One-piece cockpit canopy cover (Kopperschmidt)
129 Pilot's ejection seat
130 Side console panel
131 Ammunition feed chute
132 Mauser 27-mm cannon
133 Instrument pressure sensor
134 Cannon barrel
135 Radome open position
136 Nosewheel leg strut
137 Twin nosewheels
138 Nosewheel doors
139 Cannon muzzle blast tube
140 Control and Stability Augmentation System (CSAS) equipment bay
141 Control column
142 Instrument panel shroud
143 Pilot's head-up display (Smiths)
144 Windscreen panels (Lucas Aerospace)
145 Windscreen rain dispersal duct
146 Cockpit front pressure bulkhead
147 Avionics bay, communications and navigation equipment
148 Angle of attack probe
149 IFF aerial
150 In-flight refuelling probe, extended
151 Marconi-Elliot Foxhunter airborne interception radar
152 Scanner tracking mechanism
153 Cassegrain radar antenna
154 Radar unit hinged to starboard for access to Line Replaceable Units (LRUs)
155 Extended radome
156 Pitot tube

Three-view of an RAF Tornado GR.Mk 1 as it is expected to appear in production form with laser ranger and marked-target seeker under the front fuselage. It is shown armed with eight 1,000-lb (454-kg) bombs, and fitted with two 330 Imp gal (1500 litre) tanks and two ECM jamming pods. This is a typical configuration for long-range low-level strike.

Panavia Tornado

Specification

Type: two-seat multi-role combat aircraft

Powerplant: two Turbo-Union RB.199-34R afterburning turbofans, each of approximately 16,000-lb (7256-kg) static thrust

Performance: maximum speed (clean) 921 mph (1482 km/h) at sea level, and over Mach 2.0 at altitude; time to height less than 2 minutes from brake release to 30,000 ft (9146 m); ADV can remain on station for over 2 hours at 400 miles (640 km) radius; IDS hi-lo-hi strike radius 830 miles (1335 km); ferry range 2,420 miles (3890 km)

Weights: basic empty IDS 30,000 lb (13600 kg), ADV 31,000 lb (14060 kg); maximum take-off 60,000 lb (27210 kg); typical ADV take-off with two 330-Imp gal (1500-litre) tanks, four Sky Flash, two Sidewinders 52,000 lb (23583 kg)

Dimensions: span, swept 28 ft 2.5 in (8.60 m), unswept 45 ft 7.2 in (13.9 m); length IDS 54 ft 9.5 in (16.7 m), ADV 59 ft 3 in (18.06 m); height 19 ft (5.79 m); wing area 322.9 sq ft (30 m²)

Armament: (IDS) two or (ADV) one Mauser 27-mm cannon; plus seven (IDS) or eight (ADV) external store locations providing for warloads totalling up to 20,000 lb (9070 kg); ADV is normally armed with four BAe Sky Flash missiles semi-recessed under fuselage and two Sidewinder missiles on variable-sweep inboard wing pylons

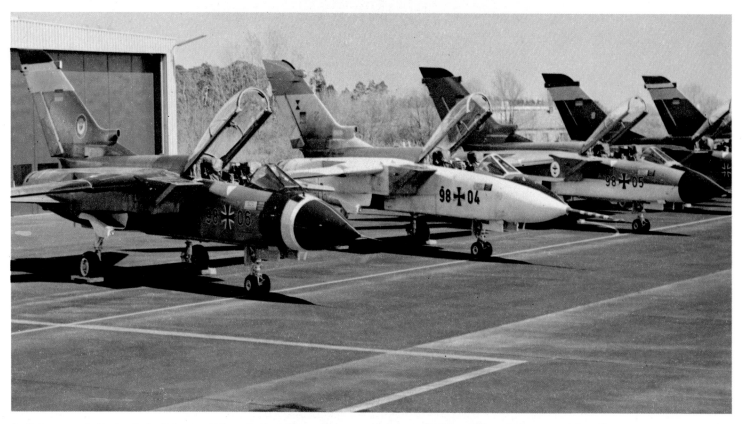

At Cottesmore in England, the Trinational Tornado Training Establishment converts pilots to a type which is new to them. In the foreground are Tornadoes in the colours of the Luftwaffe (left) and the Marineflieger with its white and grey colouring, as well as a mock-up in the 'house colours' of MBB.

defence variant (ADV) wing sweep is controlled automatically. The wing halves are moved by two separate hydraulic actuators, but if a discrepancy in wing sweep of 0.5° arises, the wings are automatically locked in place. If for any reason the wings should lock in the fully aft position (in which case the flaps cannot be used), the Tornado can still be landed safely, although the distance required is then similar to that for a conventional high performance aircraft, rather than a STOL design.

Most of the wing trailing edge is taken up with double-slotted flaps, while the leading edge is fitted with slats, with a Krueger flap on the inboard 'glove'. The slats and trailing-edge flaps can be used with the wing in the mid-swept position to enhance manoeuvrability. There are no ailerons, roll control being provided by differential tailplane movements (hence the name 'tailerons'), augmented by differential wing spoiler action at sweep angles below 45°. These spoilers also act as lift dumpers in the landing run, increasing the weight on the undercarriage and thus the aircraft's braking ability.

Fly-by-wire controls

All the flying controls are moved in response to electrical signals (i.e. 'fly-by-wire'), in which pilot demands from the control column and rudder bar are modulated by a CSAS (command stability augmentation system). However, in emergency the aircraft can be flown without the CSAS, and if the electrical signalling fails the Tornado can be flown by means of direct mechanical links to the tailerons.

The Turbo-Union RB.199 turbofan that was developed specifically to meet the Tornado's needs is noteworthy for its three-spool configuration, remarkably small size, short after-burner, and very low SFC. A three-spool layout was chosen to permit the highest possible pressure ratio (and hence the

lowest SFC) with minimum risk of engine surges. The RB.199 is only 34 in (86.4 cm) in maximum diameter and a mere 126 in (3.2 m) long. It weighs only 1,800 lb (816 kg).

To achieve the shortest possible landing run, the pilot can preselect thrust reverses before touchdown, and the buckets will then be deployed within one second of ground impact by microswitches on the undercarriage legs. To enhance directional stability while using thrust reversers, yaw damping is automatic via the nosewheel steering circuit.

Turning to the subject of the aircraft's avionics, Tornado has no fewer than five navigation modes. The principal mode employs a mix of data from the Ferranti inertial system and the Decca Doppler radar, giving less than half the position error of a pure inertial system. It also has a twin-gyro platform providing heading and altitude data, which can be used either with Doppler or air-data velocity inputs. Alternatively, the aircraft can be navigated in a pure inertial mode, and can combine inertial heading information with air data velocity.

Navigation data is supplied to the pilot in the form of Ferranti's optically projected moving map display, while the navigator has the same display combined with the returns from the ground mapping radar (GMR). In addition to the GMR antenna, the Tornado's nose houses that of the terrain-following radar (TFR), both of these radars being Texas Instruments products. The TFR enables the aircraft to be flown automatically via the CSAS at up to Mach 1.2 and at a pre-set clearance height above the ground, which the pilot can vary between 200 ft (60 m) and 1,500 ft (460 m). The TFR returns are also displayed to the pilot, so that he can monitor the functioning of the automatic system. He can also select the amount of g that the TF system can apply to the aircraft, thus controlling the roughness of ride. In the event of failure of the TFR, low level flight can be continued in a terrain-avoidance mode (i.e. making lateral manoeuvres, rather than in a vertical plane), using the contour mapping of the GMR.

In addition to the items of equipment listed above, the Tornado has an advanced Smiths head-up display (HUD), a radar altimeter, and a retractable laser ranger and marked-target seeker, developed by Ferranti.

The ninth prototype Tornado (and the second to be assembled in Italy) is seen here in the early paint scheme applied by all three countries. Its Italian air force serial is MM589, and it was based at Decimomannu in Sardinia for weapon trials, including external stores and tests of the autopilot.

The 11th prototype Tornado (9801) in Luftwaffe colour scheme and markings. This is possibly a minor variation on the standard colours, which consist of two shades of green and a somewhat darker grey than shown here. This aircraft was with Erprobungsstelle 61 at Manching, testing flying qualities.

Diversity of offensive armament

The Tornado will carry a wide range of external stores, including nuclear weapons, the 'Paveway' laser-guided bomb, Maverick air-to-ground missiles, the GBU-15 TV-guided glide bomb, Kormoran and P3T Sea Eagle anti-shipping missiles, the British BL755 cluster bomb, and JP233 airfield denial weapon, and West Germany's MW-1 (Mehrzweckwaffe, or multi-purpose weapon) bomblet dispenser, which will be used against tanks, aircraft hangars, runways, and aircraft parked in the open. The interdiction/strike (IDS) Tornado is also fitted with two Mauser 27-mm revolver cannon and 360 rounds of ammunition. Two rates of fire are available.

The IDS Tornado and the externally identical training aircraft represent the two initial production series. As described above, the IDS aircraft has an air-to-air capability, but UK requirements have now developed to place greater emphasis on long-endurance combat air patrol at considerable distance from any airfield. The RAF needed this capability to replace the McDonnell Douglas F-4 Phantom in providing air cover for convoys and Royal Navy units between the Arctic Circle and the English Channel, and in

The first prototype of the air defence variant of Tornado is seen here in standard configuration, with four BAe Sky Flash medium-range air-to-air missiles semi-recessed under the fuselage, two auxiliary fuel tanks on the wing pylons, and two AIM-9 Sidewinders mounted on the sides of the tank pylons.

Panavia Tornado

One of seven Italian air force Tornadoes at Cottesmore, this is the first Italian-built trainer (IT001), which first flew on 25 September 1981. It is shown here bearing the TTTE fleet number I-40 and the Italian AF serial RS-01, presumably allocated by the Reparto Sperimentale for tests at Practica di Mare, near Rome.

Tornado F.Mk 2, as it is being operated by the RAF in the combat air patrol role over the waters surrounding the UK. Note the absence of a cannon on the port side, and the deletion of the laser unit under the front fuselage. The dark area at the fin tip is dielectric material, and those at the base of the fin are titanium panels to avoid scorching by hot air.

patrolling the Iceland-Faroes gap against incoming Soviet bombers and reconnaissance aircraft. These demands led to a major new derivative of the IDS Tornado, the air defence variant (ADV).

The ADV retains 80 per cent commonality with the IDS Tornado, but differs in various respects: the fuselage is extended by 53 in (1.34 m) to provide for ventral carriage of missiles, and more fuel and equipment space; the IDS radars are replaced by the Marconi-Elliott Foxhunter air intercept radar in a new nose shape; provision is made for four semi-recessed BAe Sky Flash radar-guided missiles under the fuselage. These are normally augmented by two Sidewinder IR-homing dogfight missiles on the sides of the inboard wing pylons; the left-hand Mauser cannon is removed to provide equipment space; the wing glove leading edge is swept 68°, rather than 60°; the avionics fit is revised to suit the new role; and visual target identification is assisted by a low-light TV camera mounted behind the windscreen, giving the pilot an enlarged and brightened view of the other aircraft. In daylight this TV facility will give positive identification in good time for a front-hemisphere firing of Sky Flash. In starlight conditions, it provides for shadowing and missile release.

The Foxhunter radar is a major advance, providing target acquisition at approximately 115 miles (185 km). It will be able to detect low-flying aircraft, and operate against multiple targets in a track-while-scan mode. The Sky Flash missiles will be effective against both aircraft and the larger cruise missiles, providing a firing range of over 28 miles (45 km), and the capability to destroy targets flying at less than 300 ft (90 m) above the ground.

Nine prototype and six pre-series IDS aircraft and three ADV prototypes have been built, and these are to be followed by 805 production aircraft, which will be augmented by four of the pre-series IDS Tornadoes being converted to full production standard. Of the 809 operational aircraft, 212 will serve with the German air force, 112 with the German navy, 385 with the RAF, and 100 with the Italian air force.

Tornado in service

It is envisaged that 165 of the RAF Tornadoes will be ADVs, but this number may be increased by at least 20 in the light of recent changes in UK defence plans. Three production contracts have so far been signed for 40, 110, and 164 aircraft, and manufacture of the fourth batch of 162 has now been authorized. Aircraft construction is split between the three countries (Germany making the centre fuselage, the UK the front and rear fuselage, and Italy the wings), but each country assembles aircraft for its own services. By mid-1981 over 60 Tornadoes had flown, and plans called for production to peak at 12 units monthly. To put these figures into perspective, the first prototype had flown in August 1974, and the first production aircraft only in July 1979, while the first ADV prototype made its maiden flight in October 1979.

Initial production deliveries took place in July 1980 to the Trinational Tornado Training Establishment at RAF Cottesmore. The first formal course began in January 1981, and at its peak Tornadoes will be used to produce up to 160 operational crews per year. From there, RAF crews will progress to the Weapons Conversion Units (WCU) at Honington, while German crews go to Jever for weapons training. The first RAF unit to receive the Tornado GR Mk 1 for operational use was No. 617 ('Dambusters') Sqn at Scampton, where it replaced the Vulcan B.2. The type also replaced the overland BAe (Blackburn) Buccaneers in No. 1 Group and RAF Germany, as well as reconnaissance Canberras and some SEPECAT Jaguars in RAF Germany. The first German unit was MFG1 at Schleswig, and the first Italian unit was the 6th Stormo at Ghedi.

The Royal Air Force has ordered 220 Tornado GR.Mk 1s, including trainer versions. The first delivery was to No. 9 Squadron in January 1982. A total of seven Strike/Attack Squadrons of the RAF are stationed in West Germany with their Tornadoes, which can also be equipped with tactical nuclear weapons, and there is also one squadron with reconnaissance planes. The RAF has a total of 165 Tornado F.Mk 2s defending its airspace.

In February 1986, eight F-3s were exported to Oman and 24 to the Saudi Arabian air force.

Panavia Tornado variants

GR MK 1: RAF designation for the IDS (interdiction/strike) aircraft that is standard in the four Tornado-user services (526 planned)

GR Mk 1 (T): RAF designation for the trainer version of the IDS aircraft, which is externally identical to the GR Mk 1 (118 planned) for four services

F Mk 2: RAF air defence variant (ADV) with longer fuselage, more fuel, revised avionics, a single cannon, increased sweep on the wing glove, and provision for four ventral Sky Flash missiles (165 planned)

Index